Wood & Ingram

•

A Huntingdonshire Nursery
1742–1950

John Drake

ISBN No. 978-0-9538542-1-9
Copyright ©John Drake 2008
Typeset by Axis Design, Over, Cambridgeshire CB24 5PW
Printed by King Printers of Over, Cambridgeshire CB24 5NB

All rights reserved. No part of this publication may be reproduced, stored in a retrieval system or transmitted in any form or means, electronic, mechanical, photocopying, recording or otherwise, without prior permission of the publishers.

The right of John Drake to be identified as author of this work has been asserted in accordance with the Copyright, Designs & Patents Act 1998.

Sponsored by
The Dovehouse Trust
The Goodliff Fund of the Huntingdonshire Local History Society
The Stanley Smith (UK) Horticultural Trust

CAMBRIDGESHIRE GARDENS TRUST
Registered Charity no. 1064795

Published by Cambridgeshire Gardens Trust, The Grange, Easton, Huntingdon PE18 0TU
www.cambsgardens.org.uk
2008

Today we live in a 'throw away' society whether it be automotive parts or e-mails. Therefore for us, it is remarkable that an almost complete history covering two hundred years should still exist for a firm which ceased to trade in 1950. Due credit must be paid to the members of The Cambridgeshire Gardens Trust who unearthed and assembled all the records and ledgers and particular credit to John Drake for his industrious enthusiasm in producing a book, which will provide fascinating reading for anyone interested in garden history and in particular the nursery trade.

The Lord Fairhaven
President, Cambridgeshire Gardens Trust

FOREWORD

The last thirty or so years have seen an explosion of interest in matters horticultural and particularly in the history of gardens and gardening. The detailed research into the story of the development of parks and gardens, the origins of plants and their discovery in remote corners of the world, as well as their breeding and cultivation, has resulted in books by the score as well as dozens of academic papers in learned journals. The lives of gardeners too have been subjected to detailed examination, as have their social backgrounds and their creations. It is perhaps surprising that far less has been written on the immediate source for many of the plants that have given gardens and parks their great diversity since the seventeenth century, the commercial nurseries and nurserymen. The principal reason for this has been the lack of detailed documentation about nurserymen, few of whom ensured that their usually copious records survived. Even the day-to-day running of the internationally famous and long-lived Veitch nurseries is virtually unknown as most of the firm's papers have not been kept.

Now, partly as a result of an accident of survival, but also of the fine detective work by members of the Cambridgeshire Gardens Trust, the history of a remarkable but perhaps typical firm of nurserymen from the mid eighteenth to the mid twentieth century has been unearthed and presented to us in this book. It is difficult to overemphasise the value for garden historians of the information contained in it. Details of sales of almost everything from forest trees to roses are there, as well as the evidence for understanding how a large complex nursery was actually run in times of both peace and war. And what exactly was purchased by its customers, whether owners of great estates, national institutions, farmers or small householders, is all listed, thus allowing insights into what was fashionable, sought after or required in gardening and agriculture.

At the same time, the book also includes information that will be of value to non-garden historians. Aspects of the enclosure movement, employment and transportation, the history of estate management and even meteorology are covered. Not all of the details are immediately obvious. Some reveal almost completely forgotten aspects of events taking place far beyond the confines of Huntingdonshire. Thus the demands on the nursery for trees in 1917 was the result of a national fear of a future shortage of the enormous quantities of timber that were required for trench warfare. This is a book for gardeners and non-gardeners alike. It is full of interest, and packed with information about commercial horticulture over two centuries.

Christopher Taylor

CONTENTS

vi	List of illustrations
viii	Acknowledgements
x	Introduction
1	*Chapter 1* James Wood – Nurseryman
19	*Chapter 2* Landed and Landscape Clients
50	*Chapter 3* John Wood Continues His Father's Nursery
58	*Chapter 4* John Ingram's Diary 1857–75
81	*Chapter 5* John Wood Ingram Continues the Diary 1875–77
96	*Chapter 6* The Nursery Expands 1880–1903
107	*Chapter 7* Wood & Ingram Under New Ownership
116	*Chapter 8* Open For Business During the First World War
145	*Chapter 9* The Nursery Recovers After The First World War
168	*Chapter 10* Roses at the Nursery During the 20th Century
188	*Chapter 11* The Years 1930–39
201	*Chapter 12* The Final Years
225	Family Tree
226	*Appendix 1:* The List of 740 Roses in Wood & Ingram's Stock List of 1890
232	*Appendix 2:* Rose Breeders Contacted by Wood & Ingram prior to 1900
234	*Appendix 3:* Rose Breeders Contacted by Wood & Ingram after 1904
237	Select Bibliography
239	Index

LIST OF ILLUSTRATIONS

Front Cover: *Dodecathon media*, The American Cowslip

Back Cover: Collection of 20th Century 'Wood & Ingram' ledgers. *Private Collection*

1 Map of the principal estate owners in Huntingdonshire made for the Duke of Manchester by Bowen c1750. *Cambridgeshire County Council*

2 List of James Wood's expenses 1742 in his Account Ledger. *Huntingdon Archives ref Acc 5016*

3 List of visitors to James Wood's Nursery in his Account Ledger. *Huntingdon Archives ref Acc 5016*

4 Two pages from James Wood's Account Ledger. *Huntingdon Archives ref Acc 5016*

5 The Earl of Hardwicke's order for trees at Wimpole. *Huntingdon Archives ref Acc 5016*

6 Anonymous 'Before' and 'After' plans for the North Park at Wimpole 1767. *Wimpole Hall The Bambridge Collection (The National Trust)*

7 Lancelot 'Capability' Brown's order in James Wood's Account Ledger. *Huntingdon Archives ref Acc 5016*

8a First page of John Ingram's Diary, Monday 6th July 1857.

8b John Wood Ingram records the death of his father in the Diary. *Photocopy of a Diary Huntingdon Archives Acc 2268/2*

9 Late 19th century grafting shed at Wood & Ingram's Nursery in Brampton.

10 Wood & Ingram order to William Bonsall, The Nurseries, Harrogate, Yorks, dated 11th November 1918. *Private Collection*

11 Wood & Ingram order to The Cambridgeshire Tuberculosis Colony, Papworth Hall, Cambridgeshire, dated 19th December 1918. *Private Collection*

12 Wood & Ingram part order to The Duke of Rutland, Belvoir Castle, Grantham, dated 15th January 1919. *Private Collection*

13 Wood & Ingram part order to Buckingham Palace, London, dated 16th March 1931. *Private Collection*

14 Wood & Ingram order to Mrs Lucy Boston, The Manor, Hemingford Grey, Cambridgeshire, dated 1st December 1941. *Private Collection*

15 Wood & Ingram's residence at their St Germain Street Nursery, Huntingdon. *Sale Particulars 1950, Huntingdon Archives, Acc 1082*

16 Aerial photograph of Huntingdon, showing the St Germain Street Nursery. *Private Collection*

All photographs taken by Howard Rice

ACKNOWLEDGEMENTS

I wish to acknowledge the initial research that Audrey Osborne carried out into the history of Wood & Ingram's Nursery.

Undertaking further research to complete this history of Wood & Ingram has been most rewarding and I would particularly like to record my thanks to the following:

To Group Captain S. J. Perkins (grandson of Mr John Perkins) for his reminiscences on the family and for the loan of his family's photographs.

To the late Lord Pym for kindly giving me a copy of his book 'Sentimental Journey' recording the history of Hazells Hall, Bedfordshire, and to the Countess of Erroll for information about Everton Hall, also in Bedfordshire. To Lord Fairhaven and my cousin Michael Drake for their knowledge of Newmarket horse trainers. To Lord De Ramsey for his comments on Abbots Ripton Hall and the Huntingdon Elm. To Christopher Vane Percy for his help regarding the history of Island Hall and to Professor Echinique for the history of Farm Hall, both in Godmanchester. To the late Dame Miriam Rothschild for her comments on her family's rose orders and to the late Lady Scott (Valerie Finnis) for her comments on alpines. To Peter Inskip for information relating to Bedfordshire families.

To Peter Beales whose knowledge of roses is second to none in this country, and without whose help the chapter dealing with roses that Wood & Ingram grew could never have been attempted. To Graham Damant, Georges Potirakis and Philip Whaites at Wimpole Hall, now owned by The National Trust for allowing me to inspect Capability Brown's plans for his scheme at Wimpole Hall and to David Adshead, Head Curator and Architectural Historian, The National Trust for his suggestions for further research.

To Peter Bruus of the River Lane Nursery, Brampton and his sister Margaret Mitchell for showing me their copies of Wood & Ingram's Stock Books. To Grenville Sewell for showing me the nursery buildings which still remain to the north of the Thrapston Road rose fields at Brampton. To Mr Leverton of Buckden and Mr Wady of West Perry, who were both employees of Wood & Ingram's nursery, for describing their employment at the nursery. To Herbie Cohen goes my thanks for showing me the advertisement for the first Nursery and Seed Trade Association Ltd and his first hand knowledge of working in a local nursery maintaining a large range of glasshouse plants. To Alice Whitney for presenting me with an early copy of Wood & Ingram's colour catalogue.

To Brent Elliott, Librarian of The Royal Horticultural Society's Lindley Library, London; to Sue Palmer, the Librarian, and the Chairman of the Trustees of The Sir John Soane Museum, London; to the staff at the University Library, Cambridge; to the staff at the Huntingdon Record Office and in particular Mr and Mrs Akeroyd; to the staff of the Library in Huntingdon and to the staff of the Hertfordshire Record Office in Hertford. To the Archivist of the Chatsworth Estates, Chatsworth, Derbyshire for help with correspondence regarding orchids and head gardeners at Chatsworth.

To Brian Halliwell and Dr. Tim Upson for help with early plant introductions. To Philip Hellier for information regarding Clematis breeders. To Rosemary Gardiner for unravelling the names of French roses in the earliest Stock Book. To Howard Rice for photographing maps and plant lists which now form part of the Cambridgeshire Gardens Trust archive of Wood & Ingram. I would like to thank Dr. Alan Leslie for his help with botanical nomenclature and his knowledge of rhododendrons. To Victor Rogers-Phillips for advice on American plants and John Bartram.

To members of the Northamptonshire Gardens Trust for helping trace the home of the Perkins family. To members of Suffolk Gardens Trust for their recollections of the garden designer Major Daniels.

I am exceedingly grateful to the following members of The Cambridgeshire Gardens Trust:– To Daphne Astor for her encouragement. To Christopher Taylor and Charles Malyon for their valuable suggestions for structuring the amount of information contained in this history; and also to Charles Malyon for correcting my manuscript. To Alan Brown and Beth Davis for their help with further research. To Lady Cynthia Postan for identifying aristocratic and academic plantsmen. To Margaret Helme for her local knowledge and support. To Beth Davis for commenting on the early 20th century Wood & Ingram Ledgers and correcting my manuscript and to her husband Dr. Brian Davis for reading the manuscript. To David Cozens for his continued interest and support. To Hugh Stewart of Great Staughton for putting me in touch with Mr Wady. To Jane Brown for suggesting I examine American plant introductions, for lending me her copy of R. Harkness & Co's 1912 Rose Catalogue, for information about John Codrington and for her advice after reading the first draft of my manuscript. To Dr. Jill Cremer (whose Great Great Great Great Grandfather met John Bartram when he was entertained by the Governor of North Carolina) who has lent me various publications related to the Aristocracy, and who has patiently read and corrected my text and prodded me to complete this history after my recent illness.

To others, too many to record, who have indicated possible avenues of further research; and who kindly donated catalogues, information and invoices relating to the nursery my grateful thanks.

Finally I would like to record my very great appreciation to Bob and Julie Bickerdike who have permitted me to study in depth the hundred 20th century Wood & Ingram ledgers they saved since the nursery closed in 1950, without which this history would not have been complete.

John Drake

INTRODUCTION

This history of Wood and Ingram, a Huntingdonshire Nursery, covers over 200 years from 1742 to 1948. Without the extensive range of source material available today this history could not have been attempted. The range of original material is unique and includes Wood and Ingram ledgers, diaries, correspondence, catalogues, local newspaper reports, and reminiscences of a member of the family and past employees. Some documents are deposited in the Huntingdon Record Office and others have been made available to the Cambridgeshire Gardens Trust by local private individuals.

The sources are of remarkable value both to garden and landscape historians, social historians and local historians alike. Not only have some owners of great estates destroyed their garden records but numerous nurseries have also destroyed records of their trading activities. During recent research by members of the Cambridgeshire Gardens Trust and local appeals more ledgers of the nursery have come to light. The earliest is the original 18th century ledger, which was given to the Huntingdon Record Office following its discovery in the attic of a shop in Ramsey when restoration of the shop was in progress. This ledger lists the Duke of Manchester and the Earl of Sandwich of the time when they were improving their grounds in Huntingdonshire, and other landowners of the surrounding counties of Bedfordshire, Northamptonshire and Cambridgeshire. Two such landowners have links with the famous 18th century landscaper Lancelot 'Capability' Brown, who towards the end of his life was Lord of the Manor in Fenstanton, Cambridgeshire. Other landowners include the Church and Cambridge University who were also customers during this period. This ledger also contains an early list of plants from America and Russia. Where possible 18th century names of plants have been identified as listed in John Harvey's 'Early Gardening Catalogues' published by Phillimore & Co. Ltd, 1972.

Huntingdonshire has often been overlooked by garden historians travelling north from London on the Great North Road to richer pastures. The evidence in Wood and Ingram's ledgers and documents reveals that there was extensive planting by local landowners and much still survives today. Local patronage together with representation in Parliament in the 18th century was very evident in the county and the Earl of Sandwich's judgement in choosing Wood and Ingram's nursery was widely copied. Many local families followed the Earl of Sandwich's choice and continued, like his family, to obtain trees and shrubs from the nursery over the next 200 years. The new Enclosure Acts provided the nursery with another source of income, and the local Enclosure

Surveyor, Mr Dumbleton, is recorded as buying 60,000 quicks from the nursery for planting locally. Obtaining trees and shrubs from other nurseries is recorded, located as far afield as Oakham in Rutland, Northamptonshire and London.

Also in the Huntingdon Record Office is a copy of John Ingram's 19th century diary 1857–1876, which gives a day-by-day detailed account of the weather, tasks undertaken and those employed by the nursery. It also lists the range of plants which the nursery offered for sale during this period. Many of these were recent introductions from warmer climates and required heated glasshouses to be built on the nursery site for propagation. Displays of plants at local shows are recorded in the diary; and the visit to the Crystal Palace to admire the great fountains and the display of French roses indicates John Ingram venturing forth to inspect national exhibitions.

His son John Wood Ingram continued the diary from 1877 for only two months. He recounts the preparations for the visit by H.R.H. The Prince of Wales to Huntingdon on his way to Hinchingbrook and Kimbolton Castle, which were also reported in the local Cambridge Chronicle and Huntingdon Gazette. His visits to other nurseries in the country as far away as Sheffield were recorded and his business relationships with other nursery owners led to his joining the committee of the newly formed Nursery and Seed Trade Association.

The earliest surviving printed catalogues of Wood & Ingram are to be found in the Royal Horticultural Society's Lindley Library and date from 1887. These indicate the importance of forest trees for large estates and the extensive lists of fruit trees and roses reveal the importance of both orchards and rose gardens in horticulture of the time. The nursery was then moving from strength to strength but in 1903 it surprisingly changed hands. John E. Perkins became the new owner and the nursery continued to grow in importance through difficult times.

The continued rise in importance of the nursery is illustrated in the contents of the many 20th century ledgers that still survive today, discovered recently in outdoor sheds of one of the former nursery sites. The Cambridgeshire Gardens Trust has been very grateful to have been given access to these ledgers by the owner, who has kindly given permission for research into the contents of these 100 ledgers, many of which comprise 1,000 orders. 20th century sources are as important for horticultural research as 18th century sources. The information contained in these order ledgers and correspondence ledgers gives a unique insight into the workings of this nursery. Here the exact spelling and names of plants in customers' orders have been copied as in the original.

The correspondence ledgers indicate that the nursery did not close in the First World War and customers continued to buy plants from nurseries during this period. The administrative problems associated with running this nursery during that war are tackled with a firm controlling hand. The ledgers record that the nursery became famous as the leading grower of roses at a time when the country was experiencing the impact of depression after the war.

Turning the 1,000 pages of a typical Wood and Ingram ledger one discovers that the nursery had established close connections with all the famous French rose breeders until 1914 and that after the First World War the nursery was forced to establish similar connections with North American rose breeders. All orders were dispatched by the efficient rail system in this country and then, if required, were shipped overseas. The nursery was surprisingly generous during these times to local charities and societies. Wood & Ingram was the first nursery to send a gift to devastated Northern France towards the end of the First World War consisting of 1,000 fruit trees to be planted to re-establish annihilated orchards. Veitch's nursery considered a similar donation at a later date. Between 1918 and 1950 the Nursery provided trees, shrubs and roses for Buckingham Palace, 10 Downing Street, London Parks, and the Duke of York's Royal Military School in Dover, all maintained by His Majesty's Office of Works.

Local employees still have fond memories and recount with pride the annual display of flowering roses which became popular for visitors. It is the re-discovery of the extensive information about this nursery, which has remained hidden for so long, that has encouraged the following history to be recounted.

CHAPTER 1

JAMES WOOD – NURSERYMAN

James Wood's accounts' ledger commenced in 1742 and contains amongst many orders a surprising list of plants. It would be easy to ignore this short list as the whole ledger is filled to capacity with various orders for the Nobility and Gentry, the Church, Cambridge University Physic Garden and local clients. What is recorded is patronage of the nursery by successive Earls of Sandwich whose family seat was Hinchingbrooke, a large estate lying between Huntingdon and Brampton. Lord Sandwich's name appears in the ledger. His close Montagu relative was the Duke of Manchester of Kimbolton Castle some miles to the west of Huntingdon. It is possible that James Wood had been gardener to one or other of these influential peers. Upon further inspection, this list of plants, mainly from America and Siberia, indicates the importance of James Wood as a nurseryman and as an accomplished propagator of recently introduced plants. Certain events indicate the route plants from abroad came into England by 1742 and then were distributed to leading gardeners of the period.

In 1721 Lord Mandeville, 2nd Duke of Manchester (1700–1739) of Kimbolton Castle, was accompanying Charles Lennox, 2nd Duke of Richmond (1701–1750) of Goodwood in Sussex on the Grand Tour. Both had a love of architecture and met their architect Alessandro Galilei whilst in Italy. At that time Galilei was completing Kimbolton Castle for Lord Mandeville and he was also designing a new house for the 2nd Duke of Richmond at Goodwood in Sussex. Surprisingly, both these gentlemen shared another interest, that of obtaining American plants from a Mr Peter Collinson (1694–1768), an English Quaker and plant collector who introduced many North American plants into English gardens. Collinson's garden in Peckham, south of London, soon became famous and was visited by plant collectors. By 1760 Collinson had introduced over 200 plants for the first time into this country, the majority from America and a few from Siberia.

Collinson was a successful London merchant with reliable connections with the North American colonies particularly Pennsylvania. He knew of Joseph Breintnall, an enterprising merchant trading in Philadelphia, who proved to be a reliable person through whom letters and goods could be brought across the Atlantic to and from the port of London. A Dr. Samuel Chew in 1720 had introduced Collinson to John Bartram (1699–1777) also a Quaker and, although they never actually met, they kept up a correspondence and an exchange of plants till Collinson's death.

Bartram was born in the village of Darby, a small town 7 miles south-west from

Philadelphia. He became a skilled amateur doctor and in 1728 he bought 5 acres of land on the banks of the Schuylkill river in Philadelphia and there he planted a garden, which is the oldest surviving Botanic Garden in North America today. According to Linnaeus, Bartram was 'the greatest natural botanist in the world'. Bartram sent a sketch of his garden to Collinson entitled *'A Draught of John Bartram's House and Garden as It Appears from The River'* dated 1758, showing a fenced 'common' flower garden, a 'new' flower garden and his 'Seed House'. Trees and shrubs were grouped in a 250 acre arboretum. One of Bartram's close friends was the merchant Joseph Breintnall, who continued for many years to be responsible for the safe delivery of Bartram's boxes of plants and seeds to Collinson in London. Collinson recorded that:

> *"John Bartram was recommended as a very proper person for gathering seed and sending over plants. The profits Bartram gathered from sending seeds would enable him to support his numerous family. At first it was not thought that sending over would prove a trade but with the demand the price was fixed at £5 5s 0d a box. Besides myself the next person that gave John Bartram encouragement was Lord Petre at Thorndon, Essex, who continued to employ him from 1736–1740 when orders of the Dukes of Richmond, Norfolk and Bedford began".*

Collinson later wrote:

> *"I employed John Bartram to collect specimens, 100 specimens in a box at 5 guineas each, from the year 1735 to 1760, about 20 boxes a year one with another, which I have, to oblige the curious in planting, distributing among the nobility and gentry".*

Many of Bartram's plants sent to Collinson were first introductions into this country. Often a box was kept in his garden for two years so that rare plants might be well established before being distributed.

The Siberian plants which Collinson obtained resulted from his correspondence with Dr. Ammann (*Senecio singularis*), Professor Gmelin (*Cytisus capitatus*), Professor Sigesbeck (*Rheum palmatum*) of St Petersburg, and Mr Demidorff of Moscow who sent seeds of a particularly good black form of *Lilium martagon sibericum* which flowered for the first time on May 24th 1756. These seeds would have arrived in England by way of the diplomatic bag from the British Embassy. Many of the plants Collinson had received from abroad were grown in his garden in Peckham and later when he moved they were transferred to the new garden around his villa in Mill Hill in 1749.

Included in Collinson's list of plant subscribers were Lord Petre and the Dukes of Richmond, Bedford and Manchester. All, together with the Duke of Sandwich were Fellows of The Royal Society (as was Collinson) and Fellows of The Society of Arts. In that small world of politics and gardeners, newly introduced plants moved quickly to Huntingdonshire and who better to propagate them for further sale than James Wood, a local reliable and first rate nurseryman.

Mr Philip Miller (1691–1771), who was curator of The Apothecaries' Garden in Chelsea, London, became a Fellow of The Royal Society in 1730. He published The Gardeners' Dictionary in 1731 which ran into eight updated editions to 1768. Meeting Lord Petre and the Duke of Bedford enabled Miller to establish a base in the capital where 'American' plants could be raised and later distributed. Miller's second son Charles was appointed director of the new Physic Garden in Cambridge and was greatly helped by his father and Messrs Grey, Williamson and Gordon, nurserymen at 25 Fen Church Street in the City of London. James Gordon, who had been head gardener to Lord Petre, was forced to set up a nursery, following the early death of his employer.

On the inside page of the back cover of his earliest ledger, James Wood records the following list which includes native plants recently introduced into England from America and Siberia:–

```
May 22 1748
A catalogue of ye plants
– Abutilon Dodonei ....................................................... £  0s  6d
– a curious foxglove from virginey with yellow flower .....  1   0
– ....................odorata ...............................................  0   6
– ........eminal siberian flax with a large purple flower.....  1   0
– Malva Arborata ..........................................................  0   6
– American foxglove with purple flower or non stamen
    Doctor Matchel ........................................................
– Barbar Ivies Hispan Muller ........................................  1   0
– large American convolvulus with red flowers ..............  0   6
– do with scarlett flowers .............................................  0   6
– new white scented peas ............................................  1   0
– fine double dwarf popy .............................................  0   6
– Virginey Pistachia nut ................................................  5   0
– caragtoy ham ............................................................  0   4
– A plant of ye gum cistus ............................................  2   6
– caragtoy sun sim .......................................................  0   6
```

The following comments may help in the identification of the plants in this unusual list.

Abutilon Dodonei – John Gerard mentions an Abutilon in his Garden List of 1596 which was revised and enlarged by Thomas Johnson in 1633 and called *The Herbal or General*

History of Plants. In Chapter 354 *Of the Yellow Lillie* which he calls *Althea lutea* the Yellow Mallow, Gerard, when discussing the plant's name, states 'Some think this to be Abutilon, and recorded by Theophrastrus in his ninth book of the History of Plants'. *Abutilon theophrastrus* is the species longest known in cultivation. This was an annual plant which may explain its long cultivation. Introduced into this country from either Spain or Italy, the plant flowers in September. This may be the same plant renamed or it may refer to the mainly tropical genus of shrubs of which one is named, perhaps, after Philip Miller as *Abutilon x milleri (A. megapotamicum x A. pictum)* which has mottled leaves and bell-shaped orange flowers. But most Abutilons which are grown today arrived in this country after 1836 from either Chile or Brazil.

A curious foxglove from virginey with yellow flower – Collinson lists *Gerardia flava* as "Jan. 30, 1756, received from J. Bartram, one sod of great yellow Perennial Digitalis" but he did not list it in his catalogue. Perhaps Wood had realised its rarity and therefore priced it as an expensive foxglove.

..........odorata – possibly a form of the above foxglove with a strong scent. (The blanks occur where a piece of the ledger has been torn away.)

...........eminal siberian flax with a large purple flower – Collinson lists *Linum sibiricum*, now named *L. perenne* as "*Linum sibiricum majus flore caeruleo*". Flax was often grown in the middle of the 17th century as an improvement to the land and appeared in lists of seeds with clover, lucerne and sanfoin. Until this purple flowered form arrived in England most linums were all European and hence Wood priced his plant accordingly. *Linum perenne* is now thought to be only short lived.

Malva Arborata – the tree mallow was first included in Fuller's catalogue of 1688. He was the principal seedsman patronised by William Russell (1616–1700) 1st Duke of Bedford. Fuller's shop was located in Covent Garden, London.

American foxglove with purple flower or non stamen. Doctor Gronovius mentions it in *"Flora Virginica"* as belonging to Collinson, who recorded on March 10, 1757, "that he received from J. Bartram, two sods of Perennial Digitalis". Collinson did not list it in his catalogue.

Barbar Ivies Hispan Muller – the Barberries are a group of thorny shrubs grown in shrubberies for their various coloured berries. This is the earliest record of this plant being in this country, and pre-dates surviving nursery catalogues some 27 years later by John and George Telford of York and by John Mackie, who founded the Lakenham nursery in Norfolk. Both these later catalogues include a few Barberries. *Berberis hispanica* has blue-black berries which follow the orange-yellow flowers, but this plant is not described by Telford, suggesting this is an early introduction from Southern Spain or North Africa. Later Berberis introductions came mainly from America or the Far East. Wood may have obtained his Berberis from Phillip Miller, who was the head gardener at the Chelsea Physic Garden in London from 1722–1771, and priced it accordingly.

large American convolvulus with red flowers – this is possibly a species of Ipomea commonly known today as Morning Glory and may be *Ipomea coccinea*.

large American convolvulus with scarlett flowers – is possibly *Ipomea hederifolia*.

Virginey Pistachia Nut – recorded in John Clayton's *Flora Virginiana* of 1762 as *Pistachia virginiana sylvestris trifolia, Staphylea trifolia* is a deciduous shrub growing between 10 and 15ft high. A native of the eastern United States, but seldom grown in England as considered not ornamental enough. It is easily recognised from other species by its very downy leaves.

Caragtoy ham – *Caragana arborescens* – the yellow Siberian garagana or the 'Siberian pea tree' was available in this country by 1742 and this record in James Wood's Ledger of 1742 is the earliest this plant is mentioned in the nursery trade. Some 27 years later the Telfords of York were charging 1s 6d for this tree in their catalogue. There are two caraganas listed in his introductions: "Caragana Chamlagu – Pere Heberstein sent me from China, what he calls the bastard Acacia; they make fine yellow of the buttons of flowers" may be the tree Wood referred to in his ledger.

A plant of ye gum cistus – *Cistus ladanifer*, grown for its white petals each with a brown blotch, was introduced into this country in 1629 and was also illustrated in *Catalogus Plantarum* published in 1730. Although hardy in the capital it does not stand up to severe frosts.

Caragatoy sun sim – this may be the second caragana that Collinson introduced and named *Caragana altagana (C. microphylla)*. He recorded that it was "Found in great plenty about the city of Tomskoi in Siberia. The girls string the seeds and make necklaces of them for their necks and hand; the seeds are eaten, boiled in three or four waters to take off their bitterness".

James Wood's reliability for propagating rare plants stood him in good stead with his famous patrons, but his nursery did not rely solely on grand patrons. Not every gardener's plot was as large as the Duke of Manchester's park at Kimbolton or that of the Earl of Hardwicke at Wimpole Hall in Cambridgeshire. The majority of the population in Huntingdon and nearby villages had tiny gardens by comparison. Local tradesmen and professionals owned reasonable sized houses and gardens and were sometimes able to employ a gardener. Starting a nursery required expert knowledge gained from earlier training under a head gardener or nurseryman, a suitable site for raising the plants, a nearby source of water, basic business acumen and green fingers. Being the son of a respected local family with property near an established centre of population and with good communications also helped. A Plan of Hospital Lands lying in and about the Town of Huntingdon, dated 1752, shows a nursery (no 25) adjoining Mr Watson's House, Garden and Orchard (no 24), south of Priory Lane to the east of the High Street. A far larger nursery is indicated immediately to the south of this smaller plot surrounded by enclosed pasture. It was at these sites that James Wood set up his nursery.

It had long been the tradition in England that head gardeners collected seeds from the gardens they worked in. Any surplus seeds would be exchanged with seeds from other gardens, and even plants were exchanged if they could not be grown from seed. James Wood's earlier training would have easily enabled him to set up as a nurseryman in Huntingdon, concentrating on offering a wide range of seeds for sale and roots of asparagus, the vegetable in great demand at that time. From 1750 – 1760 his income relied largely on the sale of such salad, vegetable and flower seeds and plants for local customers, as well as charging some customers for their garden maintenance.

Although James Wood's ledger records many priced orders commencing in 1742, there is no indication in the ledger that his nursery started at that particular date. On page 2 of his ledger is a fascinating list of visitors to the nursery, starting in December 1748 when they each paid a small sum of money for a choice plant. During this time it was customary for genteel people of reasonable means to take an afternoon walk and visit their local nursery. They would be met by the owner and shown plants of interest during a tour of the nursery and perhaps a plant would be bought to be given in exchange for a plant grown by a friend. Such were two clergyman's daughters who exchanged letters during the 1740s, one sister still at home near Norwich, the other married to a clergyman whose parish was near King's Lynn. These two sisters exchanged plants, mostly pinks, lily of the valley and hyacinths explaining in their correspondence: "put them in Dutch glasses and watch them grow".

James Wood records the following visitors and the money they paid:–

December 1748

	31st	Mr Hodson	1s	0d
Jan	15th	Mr Metchel		6
	16th	Mess Natelton of wesle		6
	31st	Mr Thong	1	0
	28th	Mr Oukle	1	0
Feb	25th	Mr Lucas		6
April	6th	a Capton wth Mr Willams	1	0
	18th	Mess Williams	1	0
	19th	Mess Natelton of Wesle & her company	2	0
	19th	Mr Thomas	1	0
	22nd	Mr Blin		6
	27th	Mrs Blin company		6
		for tow young women		6
May	1st	Mr Blin		6
	9th	Mr Picks company	1	0
	13th	Mr 7166452	1	0
	14th	Mr Gick	1	0
	15th	Dr. Walker	2	0
		Mr Barnes company	1	0

The visitors continued through June and July, but no visitors came to the nursery during the next three months. Visitors were welcomed back during the autumn:–

Oct	16th	Mr Williams	1s	0d
	18th	Mr Lines	2	6
		Mr Hatchet	2	6
	20th	Mr Banrum	1	0
		Mr Beale	2	0
	28th	Lady Barnet	2	6

James Wood totals the amounts and enters £4 3s 6d into his ledger.

It is recorded that James Wood was one of a large family of five children. He had two younger brothers, John and Samuel, and two sisters – one whose name is not recorded and his youngest sister Anne. There is no record of his parents running a nursery firm, or how their children spent their childhood. James, their eldest son, kept a ledger recording the monies paid out and received by his nursery. His book keeping is irregular, the orders are written in different hands until the final entry in 1784. Early transactions give detailed evidence of vegetable seed and fruit tree orders. Within ten years his range of plants increased to include trees, shrubs, hedging, roses and flowers. Such was his reliability that, with the extensive list of plants which he grew for sale, his fame spread and orders were delivered to other nurserymen and customers who lived outside the county of Huntingdonshire.

Listed in the ledger are records of the price of personal effects and food, events and personal loans. He recorded the cost in 1742 of *"burrying my old wife 3s 3d"*, and also listed the cost of his own clothing:–

For a new coat making	4s 6d
A new pair of boots	5s 0d
Mending Boots	2s 0d
Breeches	£1 1s 0d

The cost of burying his 'old' wife would indicate that he had been married before his recorded marriage to Elizabeth Greensmith. Elizabeth was born in Clapham in Surrey. To meet her, James would either have worked as a head gardener's apprentice on a large country estate or for a nurseryman. Such establishments were where employees from afar were able to meet and be trained. James may have been an apprentice at James Maddock's nursery at Clapham Rise, London, which had been established in 1715, and have met Elizabeth whilst working in the capital. They married in 1762.

James Wood's ledger lists in detail his transactions as a nurseryman from 1748 until 1784. Apart from the priced list of plants for sale on the end cover of his ledger, there is no record of an 18th century printed catalogue surviving, which might state the range and prices of the plants his nursery offered. What is recorded in his ledger gives more detailed information concerning the scope of his nursery, than would be found from a catalogue of that period. A series of orders for local residents shows the importance of vegetable seeds and also the daily rate charged for supplying a gardener. One such customer was a Mrs Vinter who lived in Huntingdon and obviously required garden help. Her order in James Wood's ledger records (on page 7):–

Feb	13th 1752	myself 1 Day	£0	1s 6d
		A man 3 Dayes		3 0
		4 lb spinage		9
		19th a man 4 dayes		4 0
		2lb Carrot		1 0
		2lb onion		1 0
		2lb Readish		1 0
		2lb pearseley		4
		1oz Lettuce		4
		2lb cress & Muster		5
Mr	9th	sallere & Greens		6
	12th	a man 1 day		1 0
	14th	Couls sallere		6
	21st	a man 4 days		4 0
	28th	a man 6 days		6 0
		1 pk Turnep		3

			£	s	d
		2oz Sallere 2oz Carrots		0	4
		2 Score Curly flower		2	0
		5 Score Cabbage pl		1	0
Ap	3rd	6 Dayes a man		6	0
		2 pk Beanes			10
		2 Qr pease		1	0
		a man 6 days		6	0
		2 oz onion			6
		1 oz Carrot			4
		parsle Seed			2
		1 Score Culeflower		1	0
		2 Score Cabbage pla			6
Ap	21st	a man 2 days		2	0
		2 oz Creass 2 oz mus			3
	23rd	100 asparagrass		2	0
		Carrots			2
	24th	100 asparagrass		2	2
	25th	6 oz Cress & mus			4
		a man 3 Days		3	0
Ap	30th	a man 3 Days		3	0
		1 Quart kidno beanes			6
		100 asparagrass		1	0

This order continued with similar purchases and wages until August the same year.

James Wood charged more for his day's work than a nursery employee to garden for Mrs Vinter. It is obvious that he visited her garden at the start of the arrangement, advised her how to grow vegetables and proposed that one of his staff should attend regularly to help her maintain her vegetable garden. Mrs Vinter may have been recently widowed and wanted to keep the garden going which her husband had established and her local nurseryman was able to oblige. No fruit trees were supplied which indicates that James Wood, like other nurserymen of that date, often concentrated on supplying vegetables and salad crops.

The cost of 100 asparagus varied during April 1752. Asparagus was one of the spoils of war prized by the Arabs in their North African and Spanish conquests. The plant found its way back into Europe via France in the 15th century and reached England in the 16th century. *Argenteuil*, a late French variety of superb flavour, came into England via France.

By 1760 James Wood had built up a stock of fruit trees. In 1762 his orders of vegetable seed included small numbers of fruit trees, including apricots and peaches. His nursery continued to expand and soon he had sufficient stocks of trees to offer to richer customers who owned larger gardens and estates. By 1764 a typical order for fruit trees is noted for Mr Reed Peacock (page 44):–

Dec 4th 1764	2 Mulberes	£ 10s	0d
	8 Cheres	6	0
	8 Standrd aples	6	0
	3 Standrd ploms	2	3
	2 Dwarf ploms	1	6
	3 Larg Wallnut tres	1	6
	3 French do Small	1	1
	3 Figs standrd	1	6
	3 pars	2	3
	10 Dwarf aples	7	6
	2 Standrd Duble peches	4	0
	2 Standrd Duble Cheres	2	0
	2 frut bearing almonds	4	0
	6 Gelder Roses	3	0
	5 Grapes	3	9
	2 Dwarfe plums	1	6
	2 Codlins	1	6
	8 Dwarf aples	6	0
	myself journey to Ramsey to plant the trees	5	0
	turnpike		6
	a man going to Ramsey	1	6

It is not recorded if this was the Mr Peacock who resided in Huntingdon and was the bespoke tailor who supplied members of the town council with their ceremonial robes. Mr Reed Peacock had property in the town of Ramsey to the north of Huntingdon. His order indicated his plan to establish either an orchard, or to plant an existing walled garden.

During this period apprentices were taken on to help in the expanding nursery and in 1762 the clothing required for an apprentice was recorded:–

1 pair of shoes	4s	0d
Paid for stuff for Frock and Waistcoat	14s	6d
Making	3s	6d
For Frock & Waistcoat and making	17s	6d
1 pair of shoes	5s	0d

John Turland, a poor boy of the parish of St John in the Borough of Huntingdon, joined as an apprentice in 1763 for 7 years. James Wood, in signing the Indenture, agreed to: *'teach and instruct or cause to be taught and instructed the best Way and manner that he can, finding and allowing to his said Apprentice sufficient Meat, Drink, Clothes, Washing, Lodging and all other Necessities during the said Term.'* In 1769 Abraham Stanford was taken on as another apprentice in the *'Art and Business of a Gardener and Nursery Man'* for a period of 8 years.

On page 153 of the ledger is a list of charges for hire of horses and carts in 1770–1771 to Mr Mosle:–

			£	s	d
1770	August	Hors to Ganes		1s	0d
		Hors to Storton		1	6
		Next Day		1	0
Aug	19th	Hors to Thrapston		2	6
	17th	Hors to Storton 2 days		2	6
Sept	5th	Hors to Storton 2 days		2	6
	7th	Hors to Shille		1	0
	11th	Hors & cart to Gravely		1	6
	12th	Hors to Gravely		1	0
	14th	Hors to Cambridge 2 days		3	6
	18th	Hors to Storton			
	19th	Hors to Bedford		3	6
	20th	Hors to Storton		1	6
1771					
April	24th	Hors & cart to Storton		1	6
May	2nd	Horse to Storton		1	6
	7th	Horse to Storton		1	6
	10th	Horse to Storton		1	6
April	10th	Horse & cart to Bronton		1	6

1760 to 1770 was obviously a period of great activity in the nursery. His two brothers, John and Samuel, were both helping in the nursery, as certain orders in the ledger refer to them taking orders when a customer visited the nursery. During this busy time James had married his second wife, Elizabeth, who gave birth to three children: a daughter Anne born in 1763 and two sons John (b.1765 d.1844) and James (b.1766 d.1786). The nursery was now proving successful and, with the birth of his two sons who could be trained to help him in the business, his thoughts turned to enlarging the nursery in the future. James Wood was successful in obtaining 4 acres, 2 rods and 30 poles in the nearby village of Brampton in 1772, which is confirmed later in the Enclosure Award by 1775. This site was larger than his nursery in Huntingdon and gave him more space to grow a wider range of trees and shrubs than he had been able to do before.

He was also granted the right of stocking Portholm, the large meadow bounded by the Great Ouse west of Godmanchester, with the number of cattle agreed. The family kept cows and pigs, which were required for both food and manure, and there are references in the ledger to the sale of 10 pigs for £4 5s 0d and a calf sold for £2 6s 0d.

ENCLOSURES IN HUNTINGDONSHIRE

The population greatly increased after the Industrial Revolution when more people flocked to the towns for employment. There was a need for more food to feed the growing population. In earlier periods landlords had spent little money on improving their lands, but in the 18th century the chief motive for enclosure was to improve the productivity of the land by expending capital on it. New Parliamentary Enclosure Acts were now required in the 18th century and affected all the land in a parish or manor. During George II's reign 226 Enclosure Acts were implemented, rising to 3,554 in George III's reign.

The greatest period of enclosure of the common fields was between 1761 and 1801. This brought new work for labourers such as planting 'quicks' (quickthorn – *Crataegus oxycantha*) for hedging, new drainage and road improvement. The cost for fencing was £3 an acre, half of which went into the labourer's pocket. Other costs were fees for commissioners, surveyors and solicitors, the latter usually coming off best.

Commissioners were appointed to act with impartiality and had to swear an oath for that purpose, but often they acted as surveyors themselves. Their first duties were to organise the laying out of roads. A public meeting was held to agree to the preparation of the procedure whereby the open fields or commons were to be enclosed by the Act. Although final decisions depended on the majority, one owner who possessed four-fifths of the land could easily override all others present though the commissioner's impartiality usually avoided such discrepancies.

Following the local public meeting the common fields and rights were valued. The soil was carefully examined and the herbage for its latent qualities, what seasons suited it best, how it was managed and due regard was paid to its situation. Then there followed a survey which recorded the measurements of every parcel of land which had been separately valued. The survey had to be completed and laid before the commissioners by the beginning of October in each year, the agreed time of the year when the crops had been gathered in, fallows had been made and the season best for sowing and planting. Enclosure was expected to improve the land. In the words of the Acts the commissioners were to 'divide the fields according to the respective interests of all the proprietors therein, without undue preference to any, but paying due regard to situation, quality, and convenience'.

James Wood's Ledger lists extensive orders from landowners and farmers for quicks (hawthorn) hedging, which was usually sold in multiples of 100 up to 60,000. He had been astute to see the need to supply hedging to enclose new field boundaries and he established a large quantity in order to become the sole supplier in the county.

The Ledger records many clients and the numbers of quicks they required:

Mrs Jenkins, Huntingdon	paid 6d for 100 quicks
Sir Giles Paine, Tempsford in Bedfordshire	paid 8s 0d for 2,000 quicks
Lord Sandwich, Hinchingbrook	paid £2 8s 0d for 12,000 quicks,
Mr Peet, Ellington	paid £5 12s 0d for 28,000 quicks

Lord Sandwich ordered 42,200 quicks from James Wood for the sum of £9 8s 6d between 1760 and 1783.

Mr Dumbleton was the surveyor/commissioner for the parish of Little Stukely and he was responsible for surveying and producing a map in 1783 of *A Plan of the Estate belonging to the Right Honourable John Earl of Sandwich situated in the Parish of Little Stukely in the County of Huntingdonshire*. Mr Dumbleton paid £12 0s 0d for 60,000 quicks on 12th February 1783.

Supplying hedging for enclosures in Huntingdonshire reached a peak between 1780–83 and during this period the nursery supplied over 525,000 quicks to various clients. In the month of February 1783 109,000 quicks were sold at the height of the planting season.

A typical list of clients and the quicks they required from James Wood's nursery appears on page 77:–

Date	Client	Quantity	Item	s	d
28th Oct 1782	Ted Lovit	1,000	quick	4s	6d
9th Nov	Mr Hewit	400	do	2	0
10th Nov	Mr Lovit	1,000	do	4	6
13th	Mr Tingue	2,500	do	11	3
	Mr Hewit	400	do	2	0
14th Dec	Sir Giles Paine	1,000	do	4	6
1st Jan 1783	Mr White Hilkam	500	do	2	6
4th	Mr Hewit	200	do	1	0
6th	Mr Rust	1,000	do	4	6
7th	Mr Hatfield	1,000	do	4	6
	Mr Parvin	150	do		9
8th	do	1,000	do	4	6
11th	do	200	do	1	0
	Mr Jenkins	2,000	do	9	0
	Sir Guils Payne	1,000	do	4	0
	Sir Guil Payne	200	do	1	0
14th	Sir Guil Payne	4,000	do	16	0
17th	Mr Jenkins	2,000	do	9	0
	Mr Martain	500	do	2	3
	Sir gilis Payne	4,000	do	16	0
18th	Mr Heding	500	do	2	0
	Richd Groun	4,000	do	18	0

	Mr Pamer Kimb	500	do............................2s	3d
27th	Ld Sandwich	3,000	do..........................13	6
	Mr Rust	500	do..........................2	3
28th	Ld Sandwick	3,000	do..........................13	6
29th	Sandw	1,000	do............................4	6
10th Feb	Mr Rust	1,000	do............................4	6
	do	100	do............................	6
	Mr Luds Wolly	4,000	do..........................18	0
13th	Mr Parvin	100	do............................	6
	Mr Arundel	1,000	do............................4	6

Upon closer examination of the above list, James Wood gave more favourable rates to some clients than to others, which might be when there was no need for carriage – Mr Heding could have lived closer to the nursery than other clients. Sir Giles Paine in Bedfordshire was not charged as much for 4,000 quicks as was Mr Wolly, the former having ordered on a more regular basis from the nursery. Lord Sandwich received no preferential treatment which might suggest James Wood would have judged him sufficiently rich to pay the going price.

On page 161 of the Ledger John Wood proudly recalls that '*A Memorandum of Brampton Enclosure – It was enclosed Feb and March in 1775 and at the same time the Oaks was planted in the Hedgerow, Elms at the same time and Firs was planted. Note the Oaks was only one year old when planted. Elms six and seven feet high when planted. John Wood*'. It is of interest that the month of planting hedgerows is recorded and that fir trees were included as suitable trees for hedgerows at this date. He then reveals the date of the parish of Stukely Enclosure:– '*Stukely Enclosure The trees was planted the same time Mr Wood*'

HEWITT'S NURSERY, LONDON

Towards the end of the ledger are lists of fruit trees to be obtained from Hewitt of London. Henry Hewitt (died 1771) and his brother Samuel (died 1793) established their nursery close to Brompton Park in London during the 1730s. The Hewitt brothers adopted the method of personal visits initiated by George London (1673–1714), who made visits to country estates twice a year and obtained large orders from various estates. Records of their orders of trees for the Duke of Manchester still survive. Some of Hewitt's ledgers survive and show that they also carried on a thriving trade with provincial nurserymen all over the country. James Wood's was one such nursery. Hewitt's concluded trading in 1833.

James Wood ordered mainly fruit trees with special comments from Hewitt and part of the lengthy order can be found on page 169 (no date or price were recorded towards the end of his ledger):–

Sent for to Mr Hewet
- 12 Gelder Roses
- 2 Standrd figs
- 12 arbutes let them be good
- 12 portugal Lorils
- 6 Duble Whit Roses
- 12 Moss Roses
- 10 Turke aprecock
- 2 Standrd Turke aprecock
- 6 Red Roman Nectrin
- 20 Duk cheres standrds
- 20 Comon Cheres stand and strong
- 6 Greengag Dwarfs
- 6 plums Dwarfs

This order typifies the solution that many nurseries used when unable to supply complete orders to their customers. Other nurseries were contacted and enquiries sent out to find who were able to supply plants to complete orders – a practice that still continues today. Here Hewitt was contacted to find out if he could supply the above plants to James Wood.

MR ORDOYNO'S NURSERY, OUNDLE, NORTHAMPTONSHIRE

The ledger refers to another contact: Mr Ordoyno, Oundel. James Wood, like Mr Hewitt of London, also supplied to other nurseries as long as they were some distance from Huntingdon. Oundle, situated 25 miles away in Northamptonshire, was not considered to be in competition with the nursery. The brothers Garrett Ordoyno (c.1723–1795) and Jacob Ordoyno (c.1735–1812) ran what was the Nobles' old nursery in Newark-upon-Trent. In 1776 Jacob subscribed to John Kennedy's *Treatise upon Planting*, and the firm appears in Bailey's Directory as nursery and seedsmen. Garrett's son, Garrett Ordoyno junior, was left his father's share in the nursery but seems to have sold it at once, as in 1796 the business was named as Ordoyno & Withers. The Ordoyno brothers later established a nursery in Oundle, Northamptonshire and were sent quantities of plants from James Wood to both Oundle and Newark.

In March 1769 James Wood sent the following plants to Mr Ordoyno, Oundle (page 115):–

10th March 1769
- 100 Holles .... £ 12s 0d
- A box of Mertels 10 0
- 1,000 Elms, to be delivered at mucklemus to

24th Feb 1770	mr ordno oundle at 30 shiling pr hundrd £15	0s	0d	
3rd April 1771	200 Par Stocks	4	0	
	6 Spanish Chesnuts	9	0	
	4 Mulbres	6	0	
	50 Spanish brooms	2	0	
	50 Spruse firs	16	8	
	50 Laburnums	2	0	
	50 Stripd holes 1	5	0	
	100 Carols	2	0	(Poplars)

In 1780 the ledger records (page 151) that Mr Ordino to have in October:–

Paid £1 to carriage ....£	13s	4d
Balance of Accounts 3	17	10
And Paid. Balanced Accounts 1	4	0

On 8th Nov 1781 a further order (page 152) is sent to Mr Ordino, Newark:–

	120 Lorestinuess (laurustinus) £1	0s	0d	
	50 Moss Roses 1	5	0	
	50 Evergreen Suckl	16	4	
	1 Matt	1	3	
	Lettuce		3½	
5th October 82	Balance ? & Payd 3	2	10½	
	To Balance 2	4	0	

In 1783 James Woods records on a later page (p162) in the Ledger that on the

11th August	Mr Ordino to bill £8	0s	0d	
	Paid to Balance 6	5	0	
	50 felarays (Phillyreas)	10	0	
	50 Moss Roses 1	5	0	(Rosa centifolia muscosa)
	50 or 100 Lorestrys (Laurustinus) 1	0	0	
	6 Brod leaf Elms	1	6	
	1 Weeping ash	1	0	
	6 Mulberys	6	0	

It is difficult to work out if the Ordoyno brothers ever paid their bill in full. James Wood often records the settlement of an account by a cross through the whole order of other customers. In the case of a fellow nurseryman this practice does not seem to be carried out when the final bill was partly paid.

PHYSIC GARDEN, CAMBRIDGE

There are two separate orders for Mr Salton (Keeper) of the Physic Garden, Cambridge dated 1782 and 1783. Charles Miller, the first superintendent, had resigned earlier in 1770. Loggan's Map of Cambridge dated 1688 is the earliest map of the city that shows the site of this garden along Downing Street. Two vegetable plots are depicted edged with fruit trees, separated by a central path. William Custance's map of 1798 shows alterations to the layout. Smaller beds for plants now replace the large vegetable plots and in the centre is a narrow pool with semicircular ends. The boundary of the garden is planted with trees. The earlier of the two orders, dated 1782, is recorded on page 12 in the ledger:–

1782 Mr Salter Phisic Garden Cambr

		£	s	d
31st Oct	2 Peaches trained		10s	0d
	2 Nectrons do		10	0
	1 Apricock trained		5	0
	1 pare		1	0
	bil in with Goods	1	6	0
Oct 30th (83)	Recd the Bill to	1	0	9
Nov 4th	To 1 Dwf Pare			9
	To 2 Dwf Plums		1	6
	1 Dwf Apple			9
	bill in with goods	1	3	9
Sept 10th(83)	bil payd			

His order continues:–

		£	s	d
Feb 27th 1783	5 Dwf Apples		5s	0d
	3 Dwf Cherrys		3	0
	2 Dwf Plums		2	0
	7 Dwf Peaches		10	6
	1 L Trained Peach		6	0
	2 Trained Nectarins		8	0
	2 Dwf Apricots		3	0
	2 Arborvitaes		3	0 (Thuja occidentalis)
	Bill wth Goods	2	0	6

Sept 10th (83) bil payed

A further order is to be found on page 13 (obviously using up blank spaces in the ledger). It has a more interesting range of plants for the Physic Garden:–

1783   Mr Salter Cambridge

		£	s	d
March 17th	6 Large Portugal Laul		9s	0d
	4 Large Common do		2	0

		£	s	d	
6 Moss Roses			6s	0d	
(Rosa centifolia muscosa)					
12 Honey suckles			3	0	
2 Trained Cherries			2	6	
2 Arbutus's			3	0	
6 Altheas Bt sorts			3	0	(Hibiscus Syraicus)
Sept 10th Payd					

The Physic Garden in Cambridge remained on its original site until it moved to its present site along the Trumpington Road in 1831 when it became the University of Cambridge Botanic Garden. The new garden was opened in 1846.

CHAPTER 2

LANDED AND LANDSCAPE CLIENTS

During the 18th century landed property/ country estates continued to be the foundation of English society and the basis of political influence. Land provided the nation with its sustenance, raw materials and the most extensive means of employment. Landowners derived from the soil both wealth and the right to govern. The building of great houses by the peers of the realm, the gentry and the church in a setting of gardens and parkland were the symbols of status and power. During the Younger Pitt's premiership the number of English peers in early years of the 19th century had only reached 170.

In Huntingdonshire and the neighbouring Northamptonshire the Montagu family was prominent among the peerage. In the 17th century Sir Edward Montagu of Barnwell and Hemington married Elizabeth Harrington. They resided at Boughton and their three sons each established families of great wealth and influence. Ralph, 1st Duke of Montagu laid out the great park at Boughton in 1670 in the grand Versailles manner, and established the Dukes of Buccleuch through the female line. Edward Montagu's fourth son Henry established the Montagu line of the Dukes of Manchester who lived at Kimbolton Castle. Sidney, his seventh son, established the Earls of Sandwich line that lived at Hinchingbrooke near Huntingdon.

The gentry were a far larger group, less exclusive and more diverse in origins. The wealthy gentry – baronets and knights – consisted of about 1,400 families and the lesser gentry – esquires and gentlemen – were 15,000 in number. Thus gentry formed a numerous and diverse middle class in landed society. During the reign of George III (1760 – 1820) the average income of the great landlords was about £10,000 a year, while lesser gentry could support a modest country residence on around £1,000 a year.

By the end of the 18th century, the relative importance of agriculture in the economy began to decline significantly. In 1800 commercial and industrial middle classes were more numerous than the landlords. Fortunes made in the colonial trade, the slave trade and by trade in Europe and the East helped to create an expanding body of commercial plutocrats. They married into landed families and frequently bought up estates of impoverished gentry.

The gardens and park of a country house at this time were almost equal in importance to the house itself. Much money and the labour of many years were lavished on producing an impressive approach and pleasing environment. New ideas of park-making encouraged landowners to continue the expansion of their private grounds, as no view was complete without a stream or lake, and large sums were spent in damming and changing the course of streams. Vistas were created to give the impression of rolling parkland stretching to the horizon. Many owners were prepared to spend hundreds of pounds in carrying out improvements proposed by a new group of landscapers like Lancelot 'Capability' Brown or one of his contemporaries.

It had become a popular excursion with local gentry and travellers to visit great houses and view their splendours. Observations about the grounds were often recorded in diaries. Prior permission was usually sought and strangers, if they were reasonably dressed, were seldom refused admission. So the latest park improvement could be observed and commented upon.

Lancelot Brown's schemes for his early patrons proved successful and word soon spread throughout the aristocracy. His designs for parks included moving villages out of sight, changing the contours of the land, damming streams to create serpentine lakes crossed by elegant bridges and planting groups or specimen trees in a new landscape. Many eyebrows must have been raised. In recognition of his achievements, his patrons sought to have him appreciated by the monarchy and in 1764 Brown was made Master Gardener to George III. Brown had already submitted two plans for the Queen's House garden, the site of Buckingham Palace garden today. Both proposals used the perimeter shelterbelt of trees and within it a drive and the later plan included a large oval lake on axis with the house. This scheme was not carried out because the King's architect Sir William Chambers (1723–96) did not like the design. Chambers promoted gardens which included his own interests, that of the Chinese style with pagodas and bridges all inspired by the Orient.

In Huntingdonshire the Duke of Manchester at Kimbolton Castle and his kinsman the Earl of Sandwich at Hinchingbrooke House had both spent time enlarging their parks. The Earl of Hardwicke, at Wimpole in Cambridgeshire, had plans to improve his park to the north of the house. The alterations to established parks must have seemed revolutionary to local landowners. None could have fully comprehended what a mature Brown design would look like a century later.

A map by Emanuel Bowen titled *'Accurate Map of the County of Huntingdonshire, 1760' is 'Divided into its Hundreds. Drawn from Surveys and Illustrated with various additional Improvements: Also Historical Extracts relating to its Trade, Manufactures, Natural History etc. is dedicated to the Most noble Robert Montagu Duke of Manchester, Lord Lieutenant and Custos Rotulorum of the County of Huntingdon and one of the Gentlemen of His Majesty's Bedchamber'*. It shows a rural scene of farm labourers cutting turf, loading it onto a horse-driven cart. In the distance is a stream meandering through a landscape with sheep and cattle grazing along its banks. Listed beneath the map are Lords of the Manors of Huntingdonshire:–

The Duke of Manchester –	Lord of the Manor of Catworth, Covington, Hollywell, Old Hurst, St Ives, Keyston, Kimbolton, Spaldwick and Stow.
The Duke of Montagu –	Lord of the Manor of Caldecote, Copingford and Winick.
The Earl of Sandwich –	Lord of the Manor of Brampton, Eynesbury, St Neots and Little Ravely.
The Duke of Devonshire –	Lord of the Manor of Sawtry.
The Duke of Bedford –	Lord of the Manor of Stebbington.
The Lord Bishop of Lincoln –	Lord of the Manor of Buckden.
The Dean and Chapter of Westminster –	Lords of the Manor of Offord Cluny.
Sir John Bernard Bart. –	Lord of the Manor of Houghton.
Esquire Thornhill –	Lord of the Manor at Diddington.
Esquire Astell –	Lord of the Manor of Everton.
Esquire Bonfoy –	Lord of the Manor of Wennington and Abbots Ripton.

Most of the county was under the control of just a few landowners, four of whom were absentee landlords not residing in the county. With the exception of the Dukes of Bedford, Devonshire, and Montagu, and the Dean and Chapter of Westminster, all the above landowners used a reliable local nurseryman to supply the trees for their new landscape schemes. James Wood of Huntingdon proved to be a popular choice with the landowners who ordered from a wide selection of trees and shrubs now available at his Nursery during the second half of the 18th century. James Wood's original nursery ledger (1748–1784) lists priced orders of plants and trees required by these patrons. There are also orders for patrons further afield in Bedfordshire, Cambridgeshire and Northamptonshire.

The Duke of Manchester had already obtained plants from Thomas Hewitt's London nursery, but ordered from James Wood's nursery once it was established. The Earls of Sandwich bought plants from the nursery from the 18th through to the 20th century. The Earl of Hardwicke found his visionary landscape advisor in Lancelot Brown and, by 1770, both James Wood and Brown had found local patrons of great wealth and influence and, in turn, contributed together towards important new schemes of landscaping and planting.

Listed below are some of the landowning patrons of James Wood; each order illustrates their individual planting schemes which were in progress between 1748–1784. No two schemes are identical, but there was much activity with extensive improvements with the planting of trees and flowering shrubs and the raising of vegetables and fruit for the table:–

THE DUKE OF MANCHESTER

From 1615 to 1950 Kimbolton Castle, its park and vast estate were owned by the Montagu family, later becoming the Dukes of Manchester. George Montagu, 4th Duke (1737–88) was the son of Robert, 3rd Duke of Manchester, who was Vice Chamberlain to Queen Caroline and Queen Charlotte. In 1761 the 4th Duke was elected as Member of Parliament for Huntingdonshire in the Whig interest. George succeeded to the dukedom on 10th May 1762 and was appointed Lord Lieutenant of Huntingdonshire and High Steward of Godmanchester, as well as collector of subsidies of tonnage in the Port of London. (Throughout the struggle with America he always sided with the colonials. He was appointed Lord Chamberlain in 1782 and became a Privy Councillor. His political career ended when he was named as Ambassador to France in 1783 and caught a chill while attending the trial of Warren Hastings. He was buried at Kimbolton, Huntingdonshire.)

Cosmo Wallace's plan of Kimbolton dated 1763 shows a large rectangular plot to the west of the Castle which is the site of the walled garden. (Wallace was possibly a local surveyor employed by the 4th Duke.) An unnamed visitor in 1727 mentioned "the gardens are 18 acres, with a canal in them. The park is 800 acre, with fine ridings". So by this date the parkland had already been planted. Robert Adam designed the gatehouse, and the estate wall and new kitchen gardens (now a housing estate) date from this time.

An order (page 57) in James Wood's ledger for the Duke of Manchester at Kimbolton Castle includes both vegetable and flower seeds for his new walled kitchen garden:–

	£ s d
Nov 23rd 1765	
9 Pkts of Garden Persnip at 1s pr pkt	£ 9s 0d
6 Scor Culyflowers pls	6 0
3 Scor Red Cabage pls	1 0
Jan 1st 1766	
1 Bushel onions	5 0
2 Bushel pottatoes / horsredish	3 0
233 holihocks	7 6
150 Sweet Williams	6 6
190 Canterberebels	3 0
April 25th 1766	
8 Bushel Pottato	1 2 0
Carriage	8 0
400 Cabage Plants 3d, long plant roots	2 0

Of interest is the supply of vegetable plants and only parsnip seeds, which indicates that James Wood had sufficient ground at the nursery not only to collect his own seed but also to have space to sow and grow vegetable plants for sale.

Parsnips have been eaten in England for more than two thousand years and may even be a British native plant. They need a depth of soil which many gardens lack. John Gerard the 16th century herbalist was not an addict of the plant. He reported that his friend Mr Plat had made a pleasant bread from parsnip roots but added 'which I have made no tryall of, nor meane to do'. A Swelling parsnep was available at 1s 6d for 1lb of seed in 1730. (John Aislabie accounts for vegetable seed at Studley Royal, Yorkshire.) One pound of seed is a large quantity to obtain and it could be that parsnips were thought highly of as a winter crop for the table. Wood's prices would have reflected this.

Cosmo Wallace also proposed a menagerie and orangery garden to the north east of the Castle in 1764 for the Duchess of Manchester. It was the equivalent of the 'horticultural enclosure' at William Chamber's Kew – a place of intensive horticulture, a place for exotic floras and faunas.

THE EARL OF SANDWICH

John Montagu, 4th Earl of Sandwich (1718–1792), a kinsman of the Duke of Manchester, was educated at Eton and Trinity College, Cambridge. Like many young men of this time he toured Europe and the East between 1737–39. He took his seat in the House of Commons in 1739 when he came of age and attached himself to the Duke of Bedford, a leading Whig. This was a period of electioneering organisation and intrigue, when the influence of the parliamentary candidate rather than the measures he advocated decided the elections. No matter how large or how small a constituency might be, the influence lay with the individual or some small group of individuals, so elections were seldom contested. Lord Sandwich threw himself heartily into the organisation of the Huntingdon constituencies, and it was during his lifetime that the Montagu influence reached its height in politics. He resided at Hinchingbrooke House in Brampton and owned a large acreage in the parish.

He was elected a Fellow of the Royal Society in 1744 and in the same year became Lord Commissioner of the Admiralty. His career in the Admiralty went from strength to strength and he was made First Lord of the Admiralty in 1748. He was a knowledgeable and committed naval administrator and remained at the Admiralty as one of Lord North's principal lieutenants throughout his premiership. However, when war broke out with France in 1778, the Navy was found inadequate and the naval storehouses empty. Later the Earl of Sandwich's systematic conferring of unsuitable voters to public offices under his patronage while he was at the Admiralty brought him into public discredit during the American War of Independence, from which he never recovered politically. Lord North made a strong defence of his colleague when Charles James Fox tried to censure Sandwich in 1782 'into the Causes of Want of Success of the British Navy', arguing that since Sandwich had come into office the state of the navy had much improved. Following his fall from grace, the Earl of Sandwich was appointed to the office of Ranger of Hyde and St James's Parks in London. He continued to manipulate elections and nominated Lancelot Brown (the son of Lancelot 'Capability' Brown of Fenstanton) who lived at Stirtloe House, Buckden, between 1784 until 1790 as a Tory member for the Borough of Huntingdon in 1784.

The Earl's interest in all things horticultural was shown through the writings of John Ellis and by his patronage of Sir Joseph Banks. John Ellis (1710–76), a Naturalist and Fellow of The Royal Society whose career in business was as a merchant in the City of London, published *A Description of the Mangostan and the Breadfruit* in 1775 with a dedication to the Earl of Sandwich, First Lord of the Admiralty. Through the Earl of Sandwich's influence, Sir Joseph Banks was given leave by the government to join Captain Cook's expedition to the South Seas in H.M.S. Endeavour between 1768 and 1771.

A large order in James Wood's ledger (p90) for Lord Sandwich lists a range of roses, fruit trees and vegetable seeds:–

```
1767   December 4th
       80 Goosberes & Currants (?) at 3d each ............... £1 0s 0d

1768   February 8th
       21 Elms at 4d each........................................  7 0
       March 2nd
       7 Moss Rooses...............................................  7 0    (Rosa centifolia muscosa)
       12 Dutch hundred lefd ................................. 12 0    (Rosa centifolia var.)
       12 Velvet Roses ............................................  6 0    (Rosa gallica var)
       2 Stripd monthle............................................  2 0    (Rosa damascena var)
       12 monthle Roses .........................................  6 0    (Rosa damascena var)
       12 Double Sweet Briars................................ 12 0    (Rosa eglanteria)
       12 provence Roses........................................  6 0    (Rosa centifolia muscosa)
       18 Jesemines .................................................  6 0    Jasmine
       2 Vines                                                  2 6
       6 Morelo Cheres ...........................................  6 0    Morello cherries
       12 Rockets ....................................................           Rocket
       2 Calcedonica................................................  2 0    (Laburnum alpinum)
       6 Doble Black Wall.......................................  2 0    Double Black Wallflowers

       March 23rd
       1 Bushel Onions ...........................................  4 0
```

3 Bushel Pottatos ....£	8s	0d
Oct 2nd		
400 Wall Nuts..	2	0
Nov 3rd		
6 Good White Dutch Currents		
5 Grapes	2	6
2 Standrd Apels..	2	0
Nov 10th		
2 Dozen Goosberes..	6	0
1 Doz Whit Dutch Cur	3	0
April 10th		
1 Bushel Pottatos for sets	1	0

Apart from the 21 elms, the majority of this order is for his walled gardens. The large numbers of roses required, together with the flowering jasmines, would have produced wafts of scents on summer evenings. Morello cherries would have been planted on the north side of walls where they would have benefited from the cool shade, as walled kitchen gardens get very hot during the summer with no cool air for circulation. The soft fruit chosen may not have been planted in the walled garden. Often it was found that the outer side of a west-facing wall gave better growing conditions.

There is correspondence between the Earl of Sandwich and Lancelot Brown which throws light on their relationship. There is evidence of The Earl of Sandwich bestowing naval commissions to his friends and giving advice regarding local political appointments.

He writes to Brown from his office[1]:–

Admiralty   Aug: 11, 1772

Dear Sir

The enclosed (which you will be so good as to return) will shew you that your son has long before this time got a firm commission, as the Savage has been sailed above these two months, and is of course long ago arrived at her destination. I am always happy when it is in my power to prove the truth & regard with which I am.

Your very sincere friend
& humble servant

Sandwich

---

[1] (*Packenham Corres 35*, Lindley Library, Royal Horticultural Society)

A further letter to Brown written from Huntingdon explains[2]:–

Hinchingbrook   Dec: 6, 1772

Dear Sir

The letter with which you have just favoured me requires a repetition of my acknowledgement. I have seen some of your Fenstanton friends, & have received from them a confirmation of the good efforts of your application.

No candidate is as yet declared against us, nor have our opponents acquired any additional strength; indeed I am in hope that the early declaration of yourself and others of my good friends, will make them see their error in time, & prevent our coming to a real contest.

I am with great truth and regard

Your much obliged
& most obedient servant

Sandwich

THE EARL OF EXETER

An order to James Wood from Brownlow Cecil, the 9th Earl of Exeter (1725–94) at Burghley is of interest not only because Lancelot Brown was advising the 9th Earl, but also as it includes phillyreas – the evergreen plant *par excellence* for topiary much recommended by John Evelyn during the 17th century. Today it is hardly ever used because of the difficulty of propagating the plant. 17th and 18th century nurserymen had much better success. Note that evergreens and firs were required for Burghley.

The order dated February 23rd 1770 (page 132) listed:–

	£ s d	
10 Silver Spruse Firs 7ft	15s 0d	(Picea abies)
20 Pheleras	6 8	(Phillyrea latifolia)
20 Lorel lynes	6 8	(Viburnum tinus)

A further order followed on April 4th for:–

20 Sweet Briers	5 0	

A small addition on April 11th for:–

4 Arbutes	8 0	(Arbutus unedo)
2 matts	2 0	

Brownlow Cecil contacted Lancelot Brown at the end of 1754 asking him to undertake an important commission at Burghley. He had succeeded to the earldom in November of that year and set about putting the estate in order. Brown was to work on the park

---

[2](*Packenham Corres*, Lindley Library, Royal Horticultural Society)

and house for a period spanning 26 years. Commencing in 1756 Brown swept away the vast formal garden of avenues and walks planted earlier by London and Wise, made a lake of 27 acres, sowed enormous sweeps of lawn and planted lime trees in his usual style but on a grander scale than ever before.

By 1770 Brown was living at Fenstanton and would have advised the 9th Earl of the plants he required for Burghley from James Wood's nursery, which would have been able to supply them promptly. The park at Burghley is the finest complete Brown commission surviving today because limes, not elms, were planted as the dominant tree in the park.

Brown received his first payment at Burghley in January 1769 from the Earl of Exeter by a Mr Hurst of £500. By June 1773 Brown had been paid £3,972.16s 3d. He received further payments from 1773–1779 totalling £3,650. 0s 0d[3].

THE EARL OF HARDWICKE

In James Wood's ledger is a large order for the Earl of Hardwicke at Wimpole dated 1769. Philip Yorke (1720–1790), who was to become the 2nd Earl of Hardwicke, married Jemima, Marchioness Grey (1722–1797) the daughter of the Earl of Breadalban and grand-daughter of Henry de Grey, Duke of Kent, on 22nd May 1740.

Jemima's grandfather died two weeks after her marriage and her inheritance consisted of Wrest House, Bedfordshire; the gardens and park and the estate. The gardens were the glory of Wrest Park. They were the lifelong interest of her grandfather and had been created by him over the last sixty years.

Jemima employed Lancelot Brown at Wrest Park during the early 1760s. He added the serpentine Broad water on the south and east sides of the grounds and designed the bath house (near the later Orangery) as a two-roomed ruin. According to Horace Walpole, Brown had carefully respected the existing formal gardens and the Great Canal. During the first years of their marriage the young couple were only occasionally at Wrest and, when not in London, spent every summer with the Yorke family at Wimpole Hall, Cambridgeshire. Having seen Brown's work at Wrest Park, the 2nd Earl of Hardwicke did not hesitate to employ him at Wimpole after the death of his father in 1764. The 1st Earl of Hardwicke had employed Bridgeman to lay out extensive formal gardens around his house. In 1767 Brown was called in to transform the grounds to the north of Wimpole Hall into a landscape view. Brown thinned the north avenue to open views across it, which can still be appreciated today.

---

[3] (*Brown's Account Book*, original in The British Museum, Dorothy Stroud's copy at The Sir John Soane Museum.)

The large plan by Brown at Wimpole Hall shows his proposals for this commission. It indicates clearly that only a few trees of the formal north avenue should be retained. He proposed dense perimeter plantations, and by damming a small stream created two lakes, with two bridges, out of a series of ponds. In the far distance a sham ruined castle had been proposed by Sanderson Miller. Brown arranged for the castle to be built. He received the following letter from his client[4]:–

> London   Decr 24th 1767
>
> Sir
>
> I hope you will have leisure in the Holy days to make out the Minute for our proceedings at Wimpole; specifying more particularly the Plan of operating for next Year with your Expenses therof; & making out dans le gros the works for the 2 succeeding Years, when (viz: in 1770) the Whole Plan to be completed. Perhaps it is absurd to look so far forward, but however the Sketch of the whole may be of use in every event.
>
> I am Sir
>
> Your most obedient
> Servant
>
> Hardwicke
>
> PS
> If it were not too old fashioned I wd make you the complimts. of the Season.

The order for this extensive boundary planting scheme is shown in James Wood's ledger (pages 120, 121) as follows-

Oct 18th 1769 The Earl of Hardwicke Wimpole

	250 Larg elms, 12 feet	£7	10s	0d
	50 Limes, 10 feet	2	0	0
	150 Small elms, 6 feet	2	5	0
	100 Larg chestnuts, 9 feet	3	0	0
	100 Larch, 6 feet	3	6	8
	50 Mountain ash, 8 feet	2	0	0
	100 planes, 8 feet	3	10	0
Nov 8	500 Larg Elms, 14 feet	15	0	0
	400 Small Elms, 6 feet	6	0	0
	50 Chestnuts, 8 feet	1	10	0
	50 planes Large, 12 feet	1	17	6
	50 Limes, 8 & 10 feet	2	6	8
	50 Whit poplars, 10–12 feet	1	10	0
Nov 11	660 Larg Elms, 10 & 12 feet	22	0	0

[4] (*Packenham correspondence No 57*, Lindley Library, Royal Horticultural Society.)

		£	s	d
	250 Small elms, 6 feet	4	3	4
	100 ashes large, 14 feet	3	0	0
	50 Chestnuts, 6 and 8 feet	1	10	0
	50 Mountan Ash, 8 and 10 feet	2	0	0
	50 Whit poplars, 10 and 12feet	1	5	0
	50 ashes, 10 and 12 feet	1	5	0
	100 Limes, 9 and 10 feet	3	0	0
	500 Large elms, 10 and 12 feet	19	6	8
	200 Small elms	3	6	8
	6 Larg mats		5	0
	3 Small mats		1	6
Nov 21	50 Chestnuts, 6 and 8 feet	1	0	0
	93 ashes, 10 and 12 feet	2	6	6
	550 Larg elms, 10 and 12 feet	16	10	0
	100 Small elms, 4 feet	1	10	0

On page 121 the order continues:–

		£	s	d
Dec 7	550 Larg Elms, 10 feet	15	0	0
	550 Small Elms, 6 feet	8	5	0
	100 Ashes, 10 and 12 feet	2	0	0
	100 Chestnuts, 8 and 10 feet	2	10	0
	200 Okes, 3 and 4 feet	1	0	0
	200 Beech, 3 and 4 feet	2	10	0
	3 Large mats		3	0

A total of 6,403 trees costing £175 13s 4d is the largest order for a single client that James Wood recorded in his ledger. Wood charged for the use of large and small mats in which nurserymen at that period wrapped bare rooted trees and shrubs to avoid damage by frost between lifting and planting on site. Because the order is so large Wood obviously decided to waive the cost of carriage, not wanting to cause offence to the Earl of Hardwicke by seeming to overcharge. Modern nursery catalogues often state that orders over a certain amount are sent free of charge. Wood needed a large acreage to grow so many large trees for planting during one season and, if he were tight for space on the nursery, the trees would have needed to be planted at close spaces. This would have required annual lifting and replanting to check root growth.

Lancelot Brown's account books[5] show his fees in relation to the staged landscape work he carried out at Wimpole:–

1767	In December Received of the Earl of Hardwick on account of the work at Wimpole	£300.00

---

[5](Lancelot Brown's Account Book, original in British Museum, Dorothy Stroud's copy at The Sir John Soane's Museum, London.)

Ap 1768	Recd:–	£300.00
	Sept the 23rd. 1768 Recd	300.00
1769:	Feb: The 10th Recd	200.00
	do : June Recd ..	200.00
Sep:	Recd	300.00
1770	in Feby Recd	200.00
	June 14 Recd	330.00
	Oct 13 Recd	200.00
	Nov: 29 Recd	200.00
	Received	£2530.00
	The First Contract	2400.00
		130.00
1771	In April Recd. Of his Lordship	250.00
	June the 21st Recd of his Lordship	300.00
	Sep: the 30th Recd	250.00
		930.00
July 1772	Recd. For Balance of all accts. Excepting what is doing at the Tower & what has been done there by Brisley Several Journeys since & nothing paid since last July 1772 by his Lordship.	

Although from Lancelot Brown's accounts his final fee was still unpaid, the Bank Book of the 2nd Earl shows a payment made to Brown for £306.00 on 23rd July 1772[6]. Seemingly the total sum paid amounted to £3,636.

Philip Yorke, 2nd Earl of Hardwicke, unlike his father never became absorbed in politics, preferring to spend time on his estate and indulging in his lifelong interest in collecting original documents. He was quiet and reserved but intelligent. He became a Fellow of the Royal Society in 1741 and of the Society of Antiquaries in 1744. Yorke was a newcomer to large-scale land ownership, and had not undertaken the Grand Tour himself. Although not a great builder, he soon acquired a good eye for a country house. To him tours in Britain were an essential part of his development. He made nine tours, often with his wife, and recorded these in his diary: 'The Travel Journeys of Philip Yorke, 1744–63'. What enthused him most was the convenience of a great house and its stabling, the quality of the pictures and above all the extent and disposition of its gardens, water and park.

In August 1744 he travelled north from Wrest, visiting the finest grand houses and estates, finally reaching Scarborough. He stayed at Stowe (Brown was employed at

[6](Herts Record Office D/E Cd F81)

Stowe from 1740–1751), Easton Neston, Althorp (Brown advised in 1780), Wollaton, Wentworth Castle, Bramham, Studley Royal, Fountains Abbey and Belvoir Castle (Brown visited in 1779).

On their way to Staffordshire in July 1748, the earl and his wife visited Trentham (Brown worked here in c1759), Hawkstone, Shugborough, Kenilworth Castle and Warwick Castle (Brown carried out extensive work to the castle and grounds c1749–51). Two years later in July they journeyed through East Anglia, staying at Cambridge, Bury St Edmunds, Culford, Euston Hall (Brown worked here in 1767–69), Yarmouth, Wolterton (Mr H. Walpole's), Blickling (Lord Buckingham's), Holkham Hall, Rainham Hall, and finally Houghton Hall. Employing the same landscape gardener, as many of the great estates did, obviously was a topic of much comparison and established firm relationships.

When at Euston, Norfolk, the home of the Duke of Grafton, Hardwicke recounted in much detail the landscape established by Brown's great predecessor, William Kent:

'The gardens contain about 80 acres, laid out chiefly by Mr Kent. In the lower part of them is an irregular piece of water which has been joined to a serpentine river, which rises some miles out of the park, winds though it, and surrounds nearly half the garden. The sides are planted with clumps of trees, and the windings of the banks very naturally contrived. You see from it some of the finest spots in the park, particularly the new rustic temple built by Mr Kent. The park is about 8 miles round, diversified with great inequalities of ground and variety of plantations, the old part of which are thrown into large woods, and the new ones spread over the lawns in small clumps in Mr Kent's manner. The Duke has much improved the face of the county by extensive plantations all round him'.

In his wife's diary, the Marchioness Grey recalls her somewhat cool enthusiasm for the new emerging landscape. She remarked:

'Mr Brown has been leading me such a fairy circle and his magic wand has raised such landscapes to the eye – not visionary for they were all there but his touch has brought them out with the same effect as a painter's pencil upon canvas – that after having hobbled over rough ground to points that I had never seen before, for two hours, I returned half-tired and foot sore . . .'[7]

Among the estate papers for Wimpole is an *Inventory of the Tools, Utensils and Implements of Gardening* belonging to the Right Honourable the Earl of Hardwicke at Wimpole to be kept in repair by the Gardener taken Dec 29th 1779 which included:–

---

[7] (Bedfordshire Record Office, L39/9a/6 p117.)

"883 Garden Pots in the Green-House of different sizes, 7 Orange Tubs with Trees, 45 Hand Glasses with Tin Frames at their Bottoms, 85 Fruiting Pine Plants in the large Hot House with their Pots, A Sett of Old Horse Boots to be renewed, 3 Three Light Cucumber Frames, 6 Dung Barrows, 2 Grass Barrows, 1 Iron Roller, 3 Stone Roller and 1 Wooden Roller, 1 Watering Engine and 1 Smoking Engine to be repaired."

Of the same date:–
An Estimate of the Expenses of Wimpole Gardens for One Year:–
To 6 Men 11 Months at £1: 6: 0 to each Man per Month
1 Month at £1:17: 4 and 1 Month at £2:16: 0 ....£113 16 0
To 6d per week extra to 1 man for attending the Gardens on
Sundays and making the fires to the Hot-House & Vine Walls 1   6 0
To 2 Women 6 Months at 14sh to each Woman per Month
1 month at £1: 1: 0 and 1 Month at £1: 8: 0 13   6 0
To Seeds, Matts & Wall Trees with a toleration of Saving Seeds
for my own use 6   0 0
To Tools and other necessareys...8   0 0
To Nails and Wires 1 15 0
To Garden Pots for Pine Plants 0 12 0
To Self for attendance 58 16 0
                                  ....£203 11 0
To Tons & Firing 39   3 4
                                  ....£242 14 4

The 2nd Earl of Hardwicke's brother, the Reverend James Yorke, was the Bishop of Ely and a record dated June 14th 1790 shows:– *Paid to a Man for carrying Fruit to Ely* . . . *£0: 5: 0.*

THE BISHOP OF LINCOLN'S PALACE AT BUCKDEN

Buckden Palace was one of the many residences of sixty successive Bishops of Lincoln from the 13th century until 1840. Many royal visitors stayed at Buckden, including Henry III, Edward I, Richard III, James I and the Prince Regent. Catherine of Aragon stayed for two years following the annulment of her marriage to Henry VIII. The diocese of Lincoln stretched from the Humber to the Thames and Buckden Palace, to the south of Huntingdon, was used as a resting place for Bishops on their journey to London. In 1654 Bishop John Williams restored the park around the Palace and constructed a raised perimeter walk, shaded by yews with a viewing mound to the north. This was destroyed during the civil war and restored in 1660.

John Green, Bishop of Lincoln (1706–1779), who ordered plants from James Wood, was made a Fellow of St John's College, Cambridge in 1730 and became Doctor of Divinity in 1749. He was vicar of Hinxton from 1731–47, Rector of Burrough Green in

1747 and Rector of Somersham from 1749-56. After a brief spell teaching as assistant master at Lichfield Grammar School, where he met Garrick and Johnson, he became Regius Professor of Divinity at Cambridge University from 1748–56, and Master of Corpus Christi College, Cambridge from 1750–63. Charles, Duke of Somerset, when Chancellor of the University appointed Green as his domestic chaplain, a position he continued under the Duke of Newcastle when he succeeded Somerset. He was appointed Dean of Lincoln and Vice Chancellor of Cambridge University in 1756, and greatly helped Lord Hardwicke in his contest for the Stewardship of Cambridge. He became Chaplain to the King from 1753–6 and was given a residentiary canonry at St Paul's Cathedral in 1771. He was appointed Bishop of Lincoln from 1761–79, supported by the Duke of Newcastle who became his constant patron.

The largest order for John Green, Bishop of Lincoln (1761–79) is dated December 1768 (page 108):–

	£ s d	
11 Standerd Cheres	11s 0d	
7 Morelo Cheres	5 3	
4 Plums	3 0	
3 Luckers Brums 4d	1 0	(Genista, Broom from Lucca)
2 Tamerins 9d	1 6	(Tamarix gallica)
1 Pursland tree	6	(Portulasaria afra)
1 Larg Pashon flower	2 0	(Passiflora coerulea)
2 Qrt Peas	1 0	
1 Fly Sucklings	6	(Lonicera xylosteum)
2 Cornela	1 6	(Cornus mas)
2 Whit Meserens	1 6	(Daphne mezereum alba)
1 Ceder of Libnes	2 0	(Cedrus libani)
1 Carolena tree	2 0	(Populus angulata)
1 Duck hundred leaved Rose	1 0	(Rosa gallica var)
1 verigated Elder	9	(Sambucus nigra)

Note the fruit trees for the orchard at Buckden Palace and the cedar tree (sadly no longer growing in the park) – the only cedar listed in the orders of James Wood's ledger. By 1777 William and John Perfect, Nurserymen of Pontefract, Yorkshire, listed passion flowers in their priced catalogue for 1s 0d. Passion flowers were introduced in 1699 – James Wood thought of them as exotic and priced the plant accordingly. *Populus angulata,* the Carolina Poplar, is a large open-headed tree and was introduced from North America in the early 18th century; it is rare in this country, liking a warmer climate and was originally grown in southern France for its timber.

LORD LUDLOW

Peter Ludlow was created Baron Ludlow in 1755 and Earl Ludlow (an Irish peerage) in 1760. He was recommended by the Duke of Manchester, to whom the nomination of the other member of parliament belonged, as one of the two contenders for the two Parliamentary seats for Huntingdonshire. In 1768 canvassing for the elections was in earnest and, after much confusion of the candidates, Lord Hinchingbrooke and Lord Ludlow were returned as Members of Parliament for the county. The other candidate, Sir Robert Bernard, was defeated in this election. Lord Hinchingbrooke retained his seat until the death of his father, the 4th Earl of Sandwich, in 1792, and Lord Ludlow continued until the dissolution of parliament in 1796. On the Duke of Manchester's advice Lord Ludlow, in order to make himself eligible as a candidate, had to buy a house and lands in the county. Although Lord Sandwich agreed to this arrangement, he fell out with Lord Ludlow over the question of the American War. Lord Ludlow in 1768 purchased one-fourth of the Crown Manor of Great Staughton to the east of Kimbolton, the estate of the Duke of Manchester.

In James Wood's ledger there is a very lengthy order for trees and plants for Lord Ludlow, dated November 22nd 1764 (page 41), which suggests that by this date Lord Ludlow had already purchased Great Staughton, with its park and large walled garden to the south west and was engaged in extensive plantings around his property, prior to the political manoeuvres of the 1768 parliamentary election.

Lord Ludlow's first order from James Wood:–

Nov 22nd 1764

	£ s d	
4 Arbutes 2s 6d	10s 0d	(Arbutus unedo)
14 portugal Lorel 10d	12 0	(Prunus lusitanica)
6 Green Lorel 4d	2 0	(Prunus laurocerasus)
2 Tulip Trees	6 0	(Liriodendron tulipifera)
4 Shrub Sage	2 0	(Phlomis fruticosa)
2 Duble Cheres	2 0	
6 moss province roses	9 0	(Rosa centifolia muscosa)
8 monthle roses	4 0	(Rosa damascena var)
3 Duch hundred roses	4 6	(Rosa gallica)
3 Velvet roses	3 0	(Rosa gallica var)
6 Mezarens	5 0	(Daphne mezereum)
6 Althes frutax 8d	4 0	(Hibiscus syraicus)
4 Stripd holles	6 0	
4 Duble flower bramble	2 0	(Rubus fruticosus fl pl)
4 Duble flower almond	6 0	
4 hyperacam frutex	2 0	(Spiraea hypericifolia)
4 pyrecanter	2 0	(Pyracantha coccinea)
6 Scorpion sens	2 0	(Coronilla emerus)

	£	s	d	
6 Ever Green Sucklings		6s	0d	(Lonicera x america)
3 Balsam trees		1	6	(Populus candicans)
4 Duble flowing peches		6	0	
4 persion Jesemes		2	0	(Syringa persica)
2 Scarlet Okes		2	0	(Quercus coccinea
4 Euonimus		3	0	(Euonymus latifolius)
1 Grunsel Tree		1	0	(Baccharis halimifolia)
2 Ramnoides		1	0	(Hippophae rhamnoides)
2 Caroline poplars		2	0	(Populus angulatus)
4 Sweedish Juniper		2	0	(J. communis suecica)
4 Ceanothes		4	0	(Ceanothus americanus)
8 Lucca Brom		2	8	
2 Oleaster		2	0	(Elaeagnus angustifolia)
2 Carolina Gelder Roses		1	0	(Viburnum trilobum)
2 Chere plum		2	0	
3 Virgine Ston crop Trees		1	0	(Atriplex halimus)
2 Scarlet Maples		2	0	(Acer rubrum)
6 Dwarf almonds		2	0	
2 Spanish Brom		1	0	
2 Venes Rag Wort		1	0	(Senecio cineraria)
2 True Pheleras		1	0	(Phillyrea latifolia)
2 Sweet Bays		2	6	(Laurus noblilis)
2 Larg mats		2	0	
3 Balm of Giled firs		4	6	(Abies balsamea)
300 Large Firs	10	0	0	
200 Small Firs at 50 shiling pr hundred	5	0	0	
3 Mats		3	0	

This order shows the extensive range of trees, shrubs roses etc, which were available from James Wood's nursery. Except for the firs, which were probably used for boundary shelter belts on his estate, Lord Ludlow was certainly not planting out a large park with specimen or groups of deciduous trees with this order. Instead he was concentrating on flowering shrubs, roses and decorative trees to plant around his newly acquired residence. Of interest are the *Viburnum trilobum* thought to have been introduced in 1812, *Ceanothus americanus* in 1713, the *Baccharis haliminfolia* in 1683, and the *Spiraea hypericifolia* in 1640. These were all rare shrubs from the North American continent of interest at that time, and the *Senecio cineraria,* thought to have arrived later from the Canary Isles in 1774, yet already available from James Wood's nursery in 1764. This again indicates the importance of this nursery in propagating and selling plants which recently had arrived in the country. Lord Ludlow was seeking to emulate the latest craze in horticulture of planting flowering shrubbery walks in his grounds. He could have seen the proposed layout of the Duchess of Manchester's scheme for her menagerie garden in1764, not far from his neighbouring estate at Great Staughton.

SIR ROBERT BERNARD

Sir Robert Bernard of Brampton Park was the son and heir of Sir John Bernard who died in 1766. He was born about 1740 and matriculated at Christ Church, Oxford. He succeeded to the Baronetcy in 1766 and became Member of Parliament for Huntingdonshire and subsequently for Westminster. He died unmarried on 2nd January 1789 when the Baronetcy became extinct. One of several orders from James Wood (p88):–

		£ s d	
Nov 1768	Sir Robert Barnet of James Wood		
	15 Large Silver Spruce Firs	£1 2s 6d	(Abies alba)
	9 Norway Spruce	13 6	(Picea abies)
	15 Scoch firs	15 0	(Pinus sylvestris)
	8 peches & Nectr	12 0	
	1 Chere	1 0	
	1 Large mat	1 0	
Feb 1769	2 Bushel potatoes	7 6	
	1 lb Onion	5 0	
	1 lb Spinag	1 6	
Mar 2nd	10 Silver Spruce Firs	15 0	
	10 Scoch do	10 0	(Pinus sylvestris)
	4 Acathus	6 0	(Robinia pseudacacia)
	2 Catalpes	3 0	(Catalpa bignonioides)
	2 Scarlet flower maple	3 0	(Acer rubrum)
	Ind Goa	1 6	(Indigo – Amorpha fruticosa)
	2 Veregated holey	3 0	
	2 Cypros	3 0	(Cypress sempervirens)
	2 Hyperecon frutax	1 0	(Spiraea hypericifolia)
	2 Althe frutax	1 6	(Hibiscus syriacus)
	2 Caralina Suckling	2 0	(Lonicera sempervirens)
	2 Ever Green do	2 0	(Lonicera x americana)
	4 Duble yeallow roses	4 0	(Rosa hemisphaerica)
	6 Moss provence do	6 0	(Rosa centifolia muscosa)
	2 Duck hundred leafed do	2 0	(Rosa gallica var.)
	60 Phelera large	1 8 0	(Phillyrea latifolia)

Again this order reveals the extensive range of plants James Wood held in his nursery. One particular plant *Amorpha fruticosa*, False Indigo, a sun-loving shrub with racemes of purplish-blue flowers in July, originally from the Southern States of America, was often planted in shrubberies and was first recorded by Philip Miller in the eighth edition of *The Gardeners Dictionary* (1768):

> *The seeds of this were sent to England from Carolina, by Mr Mark Catesby, F.R.S. in 1724, from which many plants were raised in the*

gardens near London; these were of quick growth, and many of the plants produced flowers in three years. At present it has become very common in all the gardens and nurseries, where it is propagated as a flowering shrub, for the ornament of the shrubbery. It is generally propagated from seeds which are annually sent to England from different parts of America.

Hillier's *Manual of Trees and Shrubs* (1974) states:

Lonicera x americana is a magnificent, free flowering, vigorous evergreen climber easily reaching 9m. It has long, fragrant, white flowers, soon passing to deep yellow, heavily tinged purple outside, appearing in whorls at the ends of the shoots and providing one of the most spectacular floral displays in June and July. Garden origin, before 1750.

Lancelot Brown was a great admirer of this plant. He included ten 'Evergreen Honeysuckles', *Lonicera x americana* for inclusion in the decorative planting along the Church Walk Wilderness at Syon House, Middlesex for the Duke of Northumberland in 1752.

COLONEL CLARKE

In 1696 Alured Clarke built Farm Hall along West Street, Godmanchester. His son Charles Clarke, the Recorder of Huntingdon and Baron of the Exchequer, altered the façades of the Hall during 1746 in keeping with the latest Georgian architectural fashion of the day, he also set out the 24 acres of parkland immediately to the south of the Hall and the landscape on the opposite side of West Street with pairs of gates and a Claire-voie, which revealed a canal with an outlet to the River Ouse.

There are several long plant orders addressed to Curnel (Colonel) Clark of Godmanchester. He was Alured's grandson and became Governor of Quebec. He died in 1799. Typical of several extensive orders is the order dated 1776 Dec 10 (page 74):–

	£ s d	
2 Lorels Green 6d	1s 0d	(Prunus laurocerasus)
4 White Swet Musk Roses & Duble at 10d	6 0	(Rosa moschata plena)
2 Stripd Monthl Roses	1 0	(Rosa damascena)
4 Stripd munde Roses	2 0	(Rosa gallica versicolor)
4 Large flder Roses	3 0	
4 Siringes 4d	1 4	(Philadelphus coronarius)
4 Lorel lynes 4 d	1 4	(Viburnum tinus)
4 White Damask Roses	2 0	(Rosa damascena var)
4 Ever Green Sucklings	4 0	(Lonicera x americana)
2 Hyperican frutax 4d	8	(Spiraea hypericifolia)

	£ s d	
2 Balsam trees	1s 0d	(Populus candicans)
3 White Lalicks large	1 6	(Syringa vulgaris alba)
3 Blue Lalicks	1 6	(Syringa vulgaris)
4 Blue Soringers	1 4	(Syringa vulgaris)
4 Laburnnems 4d	1 4	(Laburnum anagyroides)
3 Scorpin Seenes 4d	1 0	(Coronilla emerus)
6 Spanish Brums 6d	3 0	(Spartium germanica)
6 pursland trees 6d	3 0	(Portulacaria afra)
4 Stripd holes	6 0	(Ilex aquifolium vars)
2 three thornd acates	2 0	(Gleditschia triancanthos)
2 Stripd Sacamars 18d	3 0	(Acer pseudoplatanus albo-var.)
2 Dwarf Chere	2 0	
2 Carolina bird Chere	2 0	(Prunus caroliana)
2 Whit Spire frutax	1 0	(Hibiscus syriacus)
2 Althea frutax	1 4	(Hibiscus syriacus)
2 Vyburnums	8	(Viburnun lantana)
4 Blader Seenas 4d	1 4	(Colutia arborescens)
planted on the Bouling Green		
30 Sucklings	7 6	(Lonicera preiclymenum)
4 Lorels	2 0	(Prunus lauraceracus)
1 Lalock	6	(Syringa vulgaris)
1 Barbre	9	(Berberis vulgaris)
1 acah thorn	1 0	(Acacia pseudoacacia)
1 Green hole	6	(Ilex aquilfolium)
4 Laburnens	1 4	(Laburnun anagyroides)
2 pursland trees	1 0	(Portulacaria afra)
2 Spanish Brums	1 0	(Spartium germanica)
2 Soringas	8	(Philadelphus coronarius)
4 Blader Senes	1 4	(Coronilla arborescens)
1 Hyperican frutax	6	(Spiraea hypericifolia)
3 firs	1 6	

This order lists plants for a particular area of the garden at Farm Hall. Had the family grown tired of the formality of their bowling green? The time had now arrived to revitalise the area with scented climbers and flowering shrubs, so James Wood was asked to supply berberis, lilacs, honeysuckles and soringas (philadelphus) to create a more flowery atmosphere. Was the fashion for flowering shrubberies proposed by the Duchess of Manchester now being copied by other garden owners throughout the county?

ESQUIRE PYM

William Pym of The Hazells, near Sandy, Bedfordshire was born in November 1723, the eldest son of William and Catherine Pym. He married Elizabeth Kingsley in 1748, the daughter and heiress of Heylock Kingsley, who had purchased The Hazells from Baron Britten in 1721. In 1720 Baron Britten proposed selling all his Sandy property, including Hazells, to William Astell (see later) of Everton House, nearby for £4,200. This deal fell through, and he sold the Hazells estate to Heylock Kingsley.[8] Kingsley immediately enlarged the Hazells, adding two wings to the house and enclosed a number of fields around the house. William inherited The Hazells in 1760 as a widower with a young family.

Both Heylock and William between them saw the possibilities of the landscape and created the structure of the gardens which still exist today. William enlarged the park in 1765–6 and again in 1770. In 1766 Nathaniel Richmond, a landscape gardener and contemporary of Lancelot Brown, was paid £17 6s 6d for eleven days' attendance at The Hazells. Richmond may have advised on the work which was in progress, an extensive terrace with pavilions which remains to this day, and the three walled gardens. William Pym's orders include a range of fruit trees and soft fruit for the walled gardens (pages 25, 134 and 141):–

Date	Description	s	d
16th November 1763	Esq Pym		
	2 Trand peches........................£	8s	0d
1770	Pym Esq of Hasel hale		
	apels and pars........................	6	0
	goosberys...............................		3
	plums.....................................		6
	aples and cucumber..............		5½
	aples carots, frute..................		6½
	Tatose.....................................		3
30th November 1772	Esq Pym		
	3 Dozen small pots Garden..	3	0
22nd February	8 plums, apels & pars...........	8	0
20th February 1773	13 apels, pars Stand..............	13	0
27th March	3 pars stand...........................	2	0
	2 large mats...........................	2	0

William Pym was High Sheriff for Bedfordshire in 1764. He reckoned up his expenses at £144 12s 2d., which included dinners and suppers during Bedford Assizes, fees to the judges' officers and the provision of livery.[9] He died in July 1788, and was buried in

---
[8](Bedfordshire Record Office ref 130 Sandy). [9](Bedfordshire Record Office: DD PM 2380)

Sandy church and was succeeded by his eldest son Francis (1756–1833) who remodelled his father's house.

By 1790 when the alterations were completed, Francis turned his attention to the gardens and grounds, asking Humphry Repton for advice; this is shown in one of his Red Books, dated 1791. Nathaniel Richmond's Terrace overlooking the town of Sandy was much admired by Repton and left undisturbed. The enlargement of the park to the east with a new road between Everton and Sandy was successfully carried out and today the whole park is as Repton recommended.

ESQUIRE ASTELL

William Astell (1672–1741) of Everton, Huntingdonshire (now Bedfordshire) owned considerable property in both counties. He had purchased the estate at Everton in 1713 and immediately had a local builder erect Everton House on ground to the east of the village church (the ground was formerly owned by Clare College, Cambridge). His son, Richard Astell (1717–1777), married twice but was childless. In 1777 the Everton estate passed by entail to Richard Astell's nephew William Thornton, who took the name Astell. After a period of neglect and the expiration of the lease, Everton House was demolished in 1945. Nothing remains today of the house and its garden; a new home, Woodbury Hall, was built in the park to the north of the church. On the external south chancel wall of the church is a memorial to the Astell family's gardener:–

> In memory of the worth and faithful service
> Of an honest man and good Christian
> William Kingston
> Bailif and Gardener who lived 50 years
> In the family of Richard Astell Esq.,
> Died the 28th Nov 1784. Aged 69 years and
> Lies buried near this place.

There are four short orders in James Wood's ledger for Esq Asdale (Astell) of Everton, which their gardener William Kingston would have been in charge of planting (pages 14, 25, 89, 100):–

Date	Item	£	s	d	Notes
Dec 25th 1762	7 plums		7s	0d	
	3 pars		3	0	
	4 Calkcedonen tres		2	0	(Laburnum alpinum)
	8 Chestnuts		12	0	
Dec 24th	2oz Goss Lettuce		1	6	
	1lb Radsh Seed		1	0	
Mar 16th	1 Pk peas		3	6	
Nov 16th 1763	20 firs 4 feet hy 1s	1	0	0	

	1 pashon flower	£ 1s	6d	
	1 moss Rose	1	6	
	1 oz Goss Letuce	1	6	
	2 oz Duck Lettuce		8	
Jan 29th	3 pars Standards	3	6	
Oct 10th 1765	1 Apricock	1	6	
	6 moss provence Roses	9	0	(Rosa centifolia muscosa)
	1 Nectarine	1	6	
	1 Plum	1	0	
1776	2 peches	3	0	
	26 Elms 9d each	19s	6d	
	1 Scock Roose		6	(Rosa spinosissima)
	1 musk Roose	1	6	(Rosa moschata)
	2 Larg Rockets	2	0	
	2 Veregated holes	2	0	(Ilex aquifolium var)
	1 Romonorad		6	(Hipphophae rhamnoides)
	1 tee pursland		6	(Portulacaria afra)
1768 Nov 2nd	33 Larg lims		–	
	30 Larg Elms		–	
	1 Cocksagre	1	0	
	1 Indgo	1	0	(Amorpha fruticosa)
	1 pyrecanter		6	
	2 Larg Roots Rocket	2	0	
	1 Caroliana Bird Chere		6	(Prunus caroliniana)

ESQUIRE THORNHILL

George Thornhill (1681–1754) acquired Diddington, a small estate situated south of Buckden on the Great North Road, from the Bishops of Lincoln for £34 8s 6d in 1719. His father lived at Fixby in Yorkshire. At the same time he also acquired Cross Hall, a property with 140 acres to the north-west of St Neots, beside the Great North Road. He employed Mr Brazier from 1720-26 to 'keep the garden clear and pick up the rooks in the woods' and '20 oak trees were cut down for my own use' for the construction of Diddington Hall. By 1760 the family owned large estates in Islington, north London, stretching from Kings Cross to Highbury Fields. George Thornhill's third son, also named George (1738–1827), placed 10 orders for trees at Diddington and Cross Hall from James Wood between 1760 and 1780. Some are only for supplying quicks. Typical of the orders for trees and shrubs in the park at Diddington Hall is one dated February 1767 (page 76) and includes James Wood's rates for planting:–

4th February 1767 Esq Thornel Didington
  4 men 1 day each making holes at Cross Hall
  at 18d pr day ....£ 6s 0d

14th	3 Men making holes at Didington, 5 days each at 18d pr day...£1		2s	6d
17th	3 Men making holes at Didington 2 Days each...		9	0
20th	4 Men 3 days each planting at Diddington...........		18	0
	1 Man, 1 day – – – – –		1	6
	My Self 3 days		7	6
	For Carag at 2 load 3s Each time		6	0
	315 Elms at 6d 7		11	6
	40 Small elms 4d..		13	4
	1 Gilder Rose		0	6
	1 White Lalock			6
	1 Blu Lalock...			6
	1 Sweet brier..			4
	1 Lorel...			6
	1 pyrecanter...		1	4
	1 phelera			4
	1 Suckling..			4

A further order includes quantities of quicks:–

Esq Thornel

1st December 1767	200 English Elms at fifty shillings pr..................£5		0s	0d
27th February 1768	3,000 Quicks		15	0
12th March	1,000 Quicks		5	0
	Carag..		1	0
	Carag the trees to mak good the trees		1	0
	3 trees over		1	6
	1100 asparagrus 1		2	6

George Thornhill still required further elms, firs and quicks for his park and farm at Diddington:–

2nd March 1769	400 Elms at 6d £10		0s	0d
	122 Firs at 6d...3		1	0
	1,200 Quick		6	0
	Carag for part of the elms and firs.......................		5	0
	A man helping to plant the trees at 1s 6d ye day		10	6
	For hazarding[10] the hole at 1d per tree		6	0

Comparing the Earl of Hardwicke's order, for which no carriage was charged, Esq Thornhill paid for two deliveries to transport 715 elms to his park only a few miles south of the nursery. The Earl's order would have required the hire of horses and large carts for several journeys to transport over 6,000 large trees to Wimpole in Cambridgeshire.

---

[10]Hazarding = watering

ESQUIRE BONFOYS

Esquire Bonfoys was Lord of the Manor of Wennington and Abbots Ripton. After 1662 Abbots Ripton passed in separate moieties to Nicholas and Thomas Bonfoys, Hugh Ardley's grandnephews and heirs. By 1794 a large portion of the manor of Abbots Ripton had been acquired by William Henry Fellowes. Other parts of the estate were passed to descendants of Hugh Bonfoys. His son and grandson were both called Nicholas, the last becoming Serjeant of Arms to The House of Commons in 1775.

Most of the orders in James Wood's ledger for Esq. Bonfies are for vegetable seeds and plants for a kitchen garden. A typical order illustrates the more limited scope of his nursery before he began to sell fruit trees (page 14):

	1762 Esqr Bonfys		£	s	d
Feb	20th	2lb Readish		0	9
Mar	9th	2lb Carrot		1	6
		4th 4 Pasnep			6
		4lb onion			9
		2oz White Coss (lettuce)			6
		2pk marrow peas		1	6
		1oz Cabbage seed			6
		2oz Culy flower sed		1	6
Mar	13th	2oz pearsle			2
		Sweet mangram			3
Mar	21st	2 Score Cabbage plan		1	0
		2lb Strasburg onion		1	6
	27th	2 Score Culy flowrs		2	0
		2 Score Cabbag plan			8
April	27th Mr Bonfies Esqr				
		2 pk Beanes			6
		2 pk kidne beane			8
May	5th	2 Quarts peas		1	0
		2oz Lettuce			6
May	20th	200 Cabbag plan		3	9
		4 pk potatos		2	0
		2 Duzon pots			6
		2 Duzon pots		1	0
		3 Scor Culy flowers		3	0
		1 pint kidne bens			6
June	13th	4 pk peas		1	0
	17th	12oz Cres & Mustard		1	0
	26th	2oz Lettuce			6
		1oz peas			6

JOHN JACKSON OF GODMANCHESTER

John Jackson (1729–1790) was the only son of Original Jackson and Sarah Dowsing. Original Jackson, son of George Jackson of Woodwalton, a village to the north of Huntingdon, was elected to serve as one of the two bailiffs of Godmanchester five times between 1730 and 1752, in accordance with the Royal Charter of 1604 granted by King James I.

Originally completed by 1749, the building of 'The New Capital Messuage' (Island Hall) in Godmanchester was for his son John (described at that date as a merchant) just prior to his marriage to Elizabeth Cole of Pidley-cum-Fenton on 22nd October 1750. The wedding coincided with John Jackson's coming of age. Jackson's estate included numerous cottages and some 600 acres scattered around the Parish of Godmanchester. The new house looked east over parkland (now the site of the Primary School) to Bull Close and to the west with views over Portholme across the island pleasure ground with its later fashionable 'Chinese Chippendale' bridge of the 1770s. With its two identical facades Island Hall was built to impress and to emulate the grander houses of the day.

John Jackson, as his father before him, was elected as one of the Bailiffs of Godmanchester during 1749, 1753, 1758. In 1750, Lord Sandwich, after completing his negotiations at the Treaty of Aix-la-Chapelle and ambassadorial duties to The Hague, was elected as Recorder for Godmanchester and was presented with the freedom of the town. In 1763 Original and John Jackson were appointed Joint Receivers of the Land Tax for Huntingdonshire by Lord Sandwich. However, the Duke of Manchester as Lord Lieutenant of the County, regarded the annual appointment as his prerogative. Although he was vastly more wealthy than his cousin Lord Sandwich, it was Sandwich's political manoeuvring that won the day. After a promising start, John Jackson's affairs as Receiver General came to grief by 1775. He failed to pay the Exchequer and was summoned in 1780 to appear before the House of Commons. The Duke of Manchester challenged his suitability, but was over-ruled by Lord North (Prime Minister), again illustrating Lord North's support of Sandwich. In 1783 Jackson was still looking to Lord Sandwich for support and 1786 saw him serve as a bailiff for the last time.

After John's death, his only surviving son John became a Captain in the Navy. In 1776 under Sandwich, he was appointed to the Adjutancy of Plymouth Marine Barracks. Despite his attempts to pay off his own (gambling?) and his father's debts, his mortgages foreclosed and the family was forced to sell the house and parkland at an auction in April 1804. The Cambridge Chronicle announced on 31st March 1804 that:

> 'A *Mansion at Godmanchester, in Huntingdonshire was to be sold by Auction at the Fountain Inn in Huntingdon, on Monday the second day*

of April 1804 between the hours of five and six in the afternoon. With immediate possession:

That elegant double fronted modern built MANSION of red brick, ornamented with Freestone, the residence of the late Mrs Jackson; with a double Coach-house, ample Stabling and out offices, Kitchen and Flower Gardens adjoining, encompassed by lofty walls; a delightful Island of Pleasure Ground, of about two acres, surrounded by the navigable River Ouse, communicating with the Flower Garden by a Chinese bridge, and beautifully interspersed with Grovage, Fish Ponds, Walks, Shrubs, and Fruit Trees, commanding the most perfect view of Portholm Race Ground on the opposite shore, allowedly the first meadow in the kingdom, the town of Huntingdon, Hinchingbrook, &c. together with a Paddock and other contiguous Pasture of about Three Acres and 6 Common rights &c. &c. . . .

These premises have long been universally admired for their taste and elegance, and for the beauty and variety of the adjacent scenery'.

Esquire Jackson of Godmanchester ordered plants and seed from James Wood for his garden (page 100):–

27th October 1767	6 Nectrons 18d each	£	9s	0d
	2 Nectrons		3	0
	2 Larg Lorels		–	
	100 Cabag Plants		–	
	1 Larg Lorel		–	
7th February 1768	6 Choise Roses fr Pots		6	0
	6 ashes		3	0 (Fraxinus excelsior)
	2 Doz Coss Lettuce		1	0
	Radish Seed			4
20th November 1768	10 Spruce firs		10	0 (Picea abies)
	10 poplars		3	4
	1 Pashon flower		1	0 (Passiflora coerulea)
8th March 1769	5 Elms		–	
	60 Elms at 4d	1	0	0
	6 Broad leaved Elms at 6d each		3	0

On a separate sheet in the ledger:–

29th November 1769	1 Bushel Pottatos & Sets	£	2s	0d
22nd December	2 Pear Dwarfs		2	0
16th April 1770	7 Doz Cos Lettuce		3	6
17th April	4lb Parsley	1	0	4
9th November 1770	6 Nectrones		9	0
	8 Chestnuts at 4d each		2	8

2 Chestnuts at 6d each		1	0
1 Larg poplar			5
2 Packets of parsley		4	0
1 Pear – Swans Egg[11]		1	6

An order for Mr Jackson's Gardener (page 139):–

			£ s d	
14th October 1771	4 Moss Roses		4s 0d	
	4 Duck hundrd leaved		4 0	(Rosa centifolia var)
	4 Crimson Do		2 0	
	4 Monthle roses		2 0	(Rosa damascena var.)
	2 Duble Sweat Briars		2 0	(Rosa eleganteria)
	2 Duble yealo roses		2 0	(Rosa hemisphaerica)
	6 Lorel lynes		1 6	(Viburnum tinus)
	6 Sucklings		1 6	(Lonicera periclymenum)
	6 Duble Cachflyes		1 6	(Silene armeria)
	6 Campanela		1 6	
8th November	4 Pars		4 0	
	2 lbs pottatos		1 0	
	2 Pars		2 0	

At the end of the same year, John Jackson ordered more fruit trees and seed for his vegetable garden (page 139):–

		£ s d
4th December 1771	200 Onions	6s 0d
	2lb Radish Seed	2 6
23rd March 1772	1 Bure Pear	1 0
12th April	2 Pars	2 0
	2lb Duck Turnip	1 0

LANCELOT 'CAPABILITY' BROWN

Lancelot Brown (1716–1783) started his employment with Lord Cobham at Stowe in Buckinghamshire working in the kitchen garden. He soon progressed to the pleasure garden and once there became head gardener. During this period Lord Cobham was employing William Kent, having become dissatisfied with Charles Bridgeman's work. Kent made several architectural additions to the grounds and he gave Bridgeman's formal layouts a more relaxed look. These started in 1740 and by 1750 they were hardly

---

[11] The Swans Egg Pear was grown by John Evelyn at Sayes Court, Deptford, Kent in 1684 and is one of twenty-one pears planted around a new bowling green in his garden. (*John Evelyn's new garden at Sayes Court*, Prudence Leith-Ross, Journal of the Garden History Society Spring 2004 p 29) and described in Thomas Hogg's Fruit Manual of 1884 – '*Fruit, medium sized. Skin, smooth, yellowish green on the shaded side, and clear brownish red next the sun, and covered with pale brown russet. Flesh, tender, very juicy, with a sweet and piquant flavour and musky aroma. A fine old variety; ripe in October. The tree is very hardy, and an excellent bearer*'. It is available today from a specialist nursery.

finished. Helping William Kent execute this work was his pupil and practical assistant Lancelot Brown. Kent died in 1748 and his proposals were modified by Brown.

Lord Cobham was pleased with Brown's work and he raised no objections to his head gardener undertaking work for other landowners. As a result of his praise and his recommendations he actually obtained commissions for the young man. Brown's first major commission came from the Duke of Grafton, whose Wakefield Hunting Lodge was near Potterspury, Northamptonshire. Here Brown completed Kent's work on the grounds c.1748, while still at Stowe. "It was the good taste which Brown evinced, while employed by the Duke of Grafton, to whom he was recommended by Lord Cobham, that laid the foundation to his future fame and fortune".

While working for Thomas Barret, 17th Baron Dacre at Belhouse, Avely in Essex during 1753, Brown received a letter from the Earl of Exeter asking him to undertake an important commission at Cecil's house at Burghley. Brown had been unsuccessful in obtaining one of the Royal Appointments open to gardeners or to people who were called gardeners in 1757. With the accession of George III new Royal appointments were made and Brown was made Surveyor to His Majesty's Gardens and Waters at Hampton Court. He had privately hoped to be appointed as Royal Gardener at Kensington Palace. He was paid two thousand pounds a year, and with the job came an agreeable house with a garden inside the palace grounds. A later commission to improve Castle Ashby in Northamptonshire was to bring him the house he wanted.

Brown's client at Castle Ashby was the 7th Earl of Northampton and his commission was to replace a 17th century garden with a picturesque landscape. The Earl put the work in hand and immediately went abroad, and by 1766 a great deal of work to the landscape had been completed. Brown heard that the Earl of Northampton was thinking of selling one of his properties, the Manor of Fenstanton near Huntingdon, to the banker Mr Drummond. Brown immediately wrote to the earl asking that, if Mr Drummond did not buy the place, it might be offered to him.[12] During 1767, the Earl of Northampton had spent a great deal buying votes for his candidates in the parliamentary elections; he found he was unable to pay for the work carried out by Brown and his contractors so was forced to find ways of raising money. He now offered Fenstanton to Brown, who went to look at it in September and without hesitation agreed to buy it for £13,000.

In 1770 Brown was made High Sheriff of Huntingdonshire. He must have been delighted with this honour – three names of local landowners in the county were put forward to the King and George III chose his friend Brown when his name appeared on

---

[12] Castle Ashby Archives

the list that year. Brown was often away from Fenstanton and may have found the duties associated with High Sheriff rather irksome, but this office was, as it is today, only for one year. During his lifetime as a landscaper Brown made only a few orders on behalf of his clients. It was the client's responsibility to obtain and plant the trees himself. Today the position has changed and landscape architects are often engaged by clients to specify numbers and species of trees required and to manage the contract.

Brown's own account books seldom record his obtaining trees for his clients. Most clients ordered directly from their local tree nursery. For the Earl of Shelburne, Brown in 1763 obtained 100 elms @ 9d a tree for £3 17s 0d from Mr Ash's nursery at Twickenham and from Mr Scott of Wycombe Abbey he ordered 100 larches and 40 plane trees for £9 10s 0d for his commission. Brown charged his client also for 12,000 quicks @ 6d per hundred £3 2s 0d. At Ashridge in Hertfordshire, trees were also ordered from Mr Scott's nursery in 1773. For Corsham a number of trees were supplied from Kennedy and Lee of Hammersmith.

On February 12th 1770 Brown was sent trees from James Wood, for his own plantings to enhance the green at Hilton (a nearby village included in his manorial rights, south of Fenstanton). The entry in the ledger (page 131) states:–

Feb 12th 1770	Lanslot Brown Esq of James Wood Lord at fene Stanton		
	160 Elms at 6d each	£4	0s 0d
April 7th	Mr Robesun for Mr Brown to plant On Mrs Browns plot		
	3 Damsens	2	3
	1 Quince	1	0
	4 Cheres	3	0
	2 plums	1	6
	19 apels & pars at 9d	14	0
	4 peches & Nectron	4	0
	1 aprecock	1	0

On the same page a further entry:–

Feb 12th	Mr Robesun fene Stanton	
	4 peaches	–
	1 aprecock	–

These orders of fruit trees for Mrs Brown's plot indicate the domestic scale of their enclosed garden at Fenstanton. The Brown family was then resident at The Manor House, Chequers Street, Fenstanton. Brown's account ledger also records his fee for work at Hilton:–

	Lord Pigot	
	To a General plan for the place & Journeys	£52 10s 0d
1	Pigot Esq. Near Hilton	
	A general plan for the alterations of his place there	
	Two journeys there	£42 0s 0d

The first of these orders fills a further gap in our knowledge of the career of Lancelot Brown. Dorothy Stroud correctly suggested that the Hilton referred to in the above account is the nearby village south of Fenstanton in Cambridgeshire, and 'a General Plan' referred to a commission to landscape the extensive village green at Hilton with fine trees, where in 1660 a Mr William Sparrow had laid out a turf maze, which still exists today.

Lancelot Brown died on February 6th, 1783 at Hampton Court, aged 67. In addition to his landed estate of Fenstanton he left £100 guineas to Samuel Lapidge to complete his remaining contracts. To his wife he left an annuity of four hundred pounds a year and a sum of £1,000. His son Lancelot was left four thousand pounds. His daughter Bridget was left one thousand pounds and a dowry on her marriage to the architect Henry Holland. His second son John (see the Earl of Sandwich's letter 1772) was given two thousand five hundred pounds.

He is buried in Fenstanton churchyard, and inside the church is a memorial to him with the following inscription:–.

Lancelot Brown Esq. Died Feb 6, 1783, aged 67 years
Ye sons of elegance, who truly taste
The simple charms that genuine art supplies
Come from the sylvan scene his genius grac'd
And offer here your tributary sighs
But know that more than genius slumbers here.
Virtues were his, which arts best powers transcend
Come, ye superior train, who these revere
And weep the Christian, Husband, Father, Friend.

CHAPTER 3

JOHN WOOD CONTINUES HIS FATHER'S NURSERY

James Wood's ledger is filled with orders, every space is used and lists of clients are repeated on the last few pages. The final orders are dated 1784. In the same year both James and Anne Wood died leaving three children Anne, John and James. John was now only 19 years old and continued to run the nursery with the help of his uncle John. There is no record of the family keeping a further ledger. His brother James died two years after the death of his parents aged twenty, which left John and his sister Anne to manage the nursery.

In 1791 John Wood, son of the founder of the nursery, married Mary Blake. His sister Anne married Cawthorne Blake. The Blakes were a farming family who resided in Hartford, a riverside village close to the north-east of Huntingdon. So two local families became closely linked, the Woods, respectable nurserymen and the Blakes, established landowners and farmers. When Cawthorne died in 1805 he left all his land and tenements to his wife Anne. Through her, a portion of land north-east of the town became the Nursery's third site, known later as the Hartford Lane Nursery. The 1826 Map of Huntingdon indicates that plot 24 along Mill Lane (opposite the present junction with California Road) in Hartford was leased to James Wood.

Of several children born to John and Mary Wood, only two survived early childhood: James (b. 1792 d. 1830) and Mary Ann (b. 1793). Mary died bearing their last child in 1799, leaving John to bring up James and Mary Ann on his own. John must have realised that, if the business were to continue and flourish, he must take steps to ensure that his only son James received a good education to enable him to take over the family nursery. John Wood sent James to Kimbolton and to Biggleswade Grammar Schools. He was probably a boarder at both schools as the distances from Huntingdon made daily attendance unrealistic. James was a good student and when he left school he started to work for his father, helping to run the nursery as superintendent. A long-term working relationship of father and son was established in the early years of the 19th century, and the business became known as Messrs John Wood & Son, nurserymen of Huntingdon.

The Industrial Revolution was in full spate by the late 1780s and continued to gather momentum for the next twenty years. The banking system was expanding to keep pace and exporters were finding new markets, especially in the Americas. The population of the country rose by 8 per cent every decade from 1760 –1800 and many labourers moved to the industrial centres with their new large-scale factories. The interest in the country as a whole changed from the countryside to the town. Urban landscapes were important for the first time and the professional classes became increasingly powerful both economically and politically.

As a result of Britain's expanding export network, new lands were opened up for exploration, not only for traders but also for botanists. The natural landscape, designed earlier in the 18th century around a country house, was no longer the vogue. New plant introductions from abroad would have looked out of place in a Brownian landscape. Nurserymen propagated large numbers of new introductions to satisfy eager gardeners' demands. During George III's reign 6,056 new plants were introduced. Garden layouts were now laid out to be seen from the house for the pleasure of the occupant. Conservatories for exotics were often attached to the house and walled gardens for vegetables, fruit and flowers were sited closer

Those who moved to the towns for better employment had small gardens but, with limited space, managed to collect their favourite plants, mostly from friends, and grow them to perfection. In East Anglia early florist society meetings were recorded in local newspapers and the craze for growing plants like carnations, pinks, auriculas, tulips, hyacinths and polyanthus spread across the country. Florist Societies were formed in all major towns and cities. In towns in the north of England Florist Societies held on to their traditions well into the 19th century and the Wakefield and North of England Tulip Society still continues today.

The Horticultural Society of London was formed in 1804, (later becoming the Royal Horticultural Society in 1861). From this date provincial horticultural societies were formed in response to the new needs and outlook of the gardening world. On the 14th August 1821 the Huntingdon Horticultural Society was established by a group of practical and amateur gardeners and James Wood became the society's secretary in 1824. Good progress was made and soon the society was able to award prizes for fruits and flowers; by 1854 membership had reached 150, and the society's patrons included the Earl of Sandwich, the Earl Fitzwilliam, and the Earl de la Warr. The President was Edward Fellowes, Esq., and 21 vice-presidents included J. Bonfoy Rooper Esq. and George Thornhill Esq. Most of these families had ordered extensively from the nursery in the 18th century.

A Cambridge Florists' Society was established in 1826. The society's records mention that a Mr (James?) Wood was awarded prizes in their Dahlia Show at the Hoop Hotel on Tuesday, 20th September 1836. Several years later records state that at their Picotee Show on Monday July 24th of 1843 *"We must not omit to notice a very beautiful Seedling Picotee exhibited by Mr Wood of Huntingdon, and named Wood's Princess*

Alice; this flower obtained the first Seedling prize, and took first prize in its class beating all other varieties".

A Mr Wood (possibly the same Mr James Wood) was awarded further prizes by the Cambridge Florists for his Crimson Bizarres, Scarlet Flakes, Purple Flakes, Rose Flakes, in the Carnation Classes; and for his Red (heavy edged), Red (light edged), Purple (heavy edged), Purple (light edged), and Yellow all in the Picotee Classes.

By 1826 John Wood & Son printed invoices which advertised they were *Nurserymen, Seedsmen and Florists*. They were also able to recommend experienced gardeners for employment and were able to *supply Agricultural Seeds, and Tools of every description*. Here is an early example of a nursery expanding its business to include a range of services not undertaken today. Finding employment for gardeners involved much diplomacy and local knowledge, which was continued by the nursery well into the 20th century.

On the 21st June 1827 James Wood, grandson of the founder, now 35 years old, married Sarah Fletcher of the parish of St Benedict's in Huntingdon.

The Nursery was asked by the Corporation of Huntingdon to supply Lime trees for along the edge of the Common to the west of the town, known as The Walks:–

H Sweeting Esq.,
1820 Bt of John Wood & Son

	£	s	d
Jan 29 47 large Limes	4	14	0
For the Walkes			

Recd 1820 Novr 10 of H Sweeting Esq
Four Pounds fourteen shillings
For trees as per Bill
£4 – 14 – 0 John Wood[1]

Some years later a further order from the Corporation by order of D Creasey Esq., requires more limes and on January 31st 1826 John Wood & Son invoiced the Corporation for the supply of:

£   s   d

---

[1] (HB Box 10, Bundle 28, 29.)

56 Limes, 16 to 18ft	5	12	0
57 Holes digging at 4d each		19	0
3 Men 1 Day Planting		7	6
	6	18	6

Settled this 19 October 1826

James Wood[2]

The following year was obviously one of minimum rainfall and the nursery was required to water the trees. A further invoice to the Corporation was dated July 21st 1827 for:–

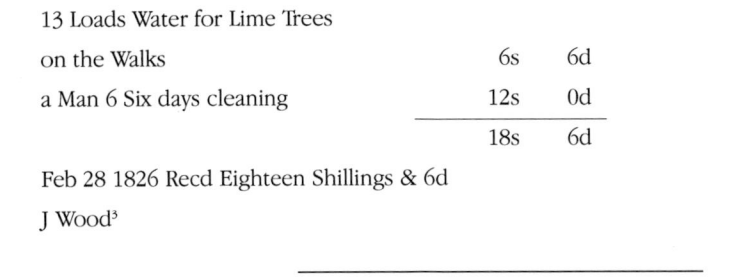

13 Loads Water for Lime Trees on the Walks	6s	6d
a Man 6 Six days cleaning	12s	0d
	18s	6d

Feb 28 1826 Recd Eighteen Shillings & 6d

J Wood[3]

Further work to the trees was carried out later during the year for £3 14s 6d and the final account of £4 13s 0d was settled by the Corporation on 28th February 1828. James Wood died suddenly, only 3 years after his marriage, on 18th November 1830 leaving no children. His obituary in the Gardener's Magazine reads:–

> 'Died, on the 18th of November, suddenly, at his residence in Huntingdon, Mr James Wood, aged 38, nurseryman and florist, who had been for some months afflicted with dyspepsia, accompanied by great depression of spirits. He was highly respected in his own neighbourhood, and well known to a large circle of horticulturists and florists; having for nearly twenty years had the superintendence of the business established by his father at Huntingdon, which was carried on under the names of "Messrs J. Wood and Son".
>
> He received the usual education of a tradesman's son at the grammar schools of Kimbolton and Biggleswade, and having early manifested great love of plants, with a singular precocity in acquiring a knowledge of their names, peculiarities, and habits, he became, when very young, a valuable acquisition to the rapidly increasing business of his father.

---

[2](HB Box10 Bundle 55.) [3](HB Box 10 Bundle 62.)

> *By unremitting assiduity, punctuality in his engagements, and obliging manners, and animated with an ardent desire for self-improvement, together with great zeal in the general advancement of horticulture, he became not only advantageously connected with the trade, but conspicuous in the floral world, and mainly contributed to the foundation and prosperity of that now flourishing establishment, the "Huntingdonshire Horticultural Society".*
>
> *In that and similar institutions at Baldock, Biggleswade, Bedford, Cambridge, and Whittlesea, he was one of the most successful competitors, particularly in the auricula and carnation tribes; though producing of late years at those Societies principally his own seedlings.*
>
> *We are indebted to him for those magnificent flowers, the Delphinium grandiflora majus, Dodecathon Media gigantean, and the Dodecathon Media elegans: the latter two raised from seeds. His sudden death is deeply lamented by his family and friends, and may justly be regretted by the profession, in which he was an ornament. F.*

These attractive plants were recognised by Robert Sweet as being associated with the nursery. In his book *The Ornamental Flower Garden Vol III, 1854, Dodecathon media var. elegans* was described and accompanied by a coloured illustration by Weddell:–

> "A beautiful herbaceous perennial, stemless producing several leaves from the base The elegant and superb variety of American Cowslip was raised by Messrs Wood and Son, Nurserymen, of Huntingdon, from seeds of the common D. media, and at the same time raises another variety, named gigantea; which produces under high cultivation a flower-stem three feet high, furnished with innumerable lilac-coloured flowers. The present is one of the finest of hardy herbaceous plants for the border, and should be grown in every garden. It thrives well in a rich light soil, and is readily increased by offsets from the root".

Although James had been more interested in raising new introductions for the nursery, his father was the partner responsible for maintaining the stock of trees and shrubs the nursery had become famous for over the last 80 years. One such tree, the Huntingdon Elm, was associated with John Wood. J. C. Loudon included it in his *'Arboretum et Fruticetum Britannicum'* or *'The Trees and Shrubs of Britain'* published in 1838. In volume 3 on page 1404 under Timber Trees, Loudon wrote:–

Ulmus vegata. U. montana vegeta in the Horticultural Society's garden: U. Americana Masters

The Huntingdon Elm, the Chichester Elm, the American Elm in some places, and perhaps, the Scampston Elm:–

This is by far the most vigorous-growing kind of elm propagated in British Nurseries, often making shoots from 6ft to 10ft in length in one season; and the tree attaining the height upwards of 30ft in 10 years from the graft. Having written to Hunt., Chichester, York, Newcastle and various other places, respecting this elm, we have received the following information from Mr John Wood, Nurseryman, near Huntingdon dated November 1836 – "The Huntingdon Elm" he says "was raised here about 80 or 90 years ago, by an uncle of mine, from seed collected in this neighbourhood. I have sent many plants of it all over the country: and it has been given out from Norwich, Bristol, and other places, under the name of the Chichester elm; but you may rely on my word that the Chichester elm and the Huntingdon Elm are one and the same thing.

The tree is the fastest grower and produces the best timber, of all elms. I have lately cut down some trees planted about 40 years ago, and have used the planks in various ways in house-building"

The young shoots of this elm sent to us by Mr Wood were 9ft long, and those sent to us by Mr Masters, under the name of the American Elm, which he considers as a synonym to the Huntingdon Elm, were about the same height.

We also observed that the shoots of Ulmus campestris alba masters and those of Ulmus campestris acutifolia Masters, strongly resembles those of the Huntingdon Elm. The tree marked as the Huntingdon Elm in the Horticultural Society's garden was in 1834, 35ft high, after being 10 years planted.

Plants of the Huntingdon Elm, in the London Nurseries, from 4ft to 5ft high (that is, one year grafted), are 25s per hundred: from 7ft to 9ft high (that is, 2 years from graft), 250s per hundred.

John Wood, now 65 years old, was faced with a dilemma. Having done everything to ensure that his son would take over the nursery, he found himself without a male heir to fulfil that role. The census for 1841 reveals that the following were living at the nursery in St Germain Street, Huntingdon: Mr John Wood, Mrs Susan Wood, Mrs Elisabeth Ingram and John Ingram. By 1841 John Wood had married for the second time. His wife Susan was a lady from Little Stukely. Also residing at the same address were a Mrs Elisabeth Ingram and a young man John Ingram, nurseryman who was 18 years old and her son. Is it too much to expect that Susan Wood and Elisabeth Ingram were sisters residing at the same address? If they were indeed sisters, then Mr John Wood was uncle to John Ingram.

John Wood died on the 22nd September 1844 aged 79 years, having outlived his son by 14 years. The Nursery continued to be run by his nephew John Ingram. In 1846 he married Mary Guarnerio of Little Stukely, Huntingdonshire. In the 1851 census they are shown living in Priory Lane, Huntingdon and the nursery's name had been changed to Wood & Ingram. Twenty men and boys were now employed by the Nursery.

A further Nursery site of one acre was acquired at this time by Wood & Ingram at Nos. 16 and 18 Cambridge Road, St Neots, which included a Residence, a Florist's Sale Shop and Glasshouses.

James Hatfield's publication *'History, Gazetteer & Directory of Huntingdonshire'* of 1854 recorded:–

> *"Among the many attractions of this little town, we must not omit to mention the well kept nursery grounds of Messrs Wood & Ingram established by one of the same family of 'Woods' nearly a century and a quarter since, a striking instance of the tenacity with which some families cling to the same associations and 'old familiar spots'. Here may be found all that the most enthusiastic votary of flora or romance can desire; or perhaps we should rather say here and at the extensive nurseries belonging to the same firm at Brampton, a small and picturesque village some two miles west from hence, where, in addition to the splendid and unique collection of fruit trees, an endless variety of evergreens and other ornamental trees and shrubs may be seen growing in the happiest luxuriance.*
>
> *At this period of the year, the latter end of June, when we were politely conducted over his nurseries, by the intelligent proprietor, with thousands of roses in full bloom, and impregnating the atmosphere with their delicious fragrance, the symmetrical ranunculus whose gorgeous colours "nature's own sweet and cunning hand laid on, "the lovely pink exhaling its particularly refreshing aromatic fragrance, indeed with "flowers of all hues" now in their meridian splendour. A visit to these grounds would amply repay every admirer of earth's most beautiful productions.*

> *We had almost forgotten, in our predilection for the hardy denizens of the garden, the choice collection of exotics, carrying one's mind irresistibly to the glorious vegetation of the tropics. These, combined with what we have before attempted to describe, will, we are convinced, fully satisfy every visitor to this storehouse of horticultural attractions".*

This publication also mentioned that their nurseries had been extended to over 30 acres and contained almost every variety of soil, and the nursery was able to recommend *"intelligent and practical gardeners of various capabilities"*, thus continuing a service established 28 years ago. John Ingram was very much a product of the Victorian era. He was methodical in his approach to the running of this well known established business, but was also an entrepreneur. He soon realised that the nursery had to change in order to keep abreast with the new gardening fashions.

Gardening had become a pleasant occupation taken up by all classes of society. John Loudon (1783–1843), the Scottish garden author and designer, wrote 'gardening was a source of agreeable domestic recreation'. His book *The Suburban Gardener and Villa Companion* (1838) coincided with the start of Queen Victoria's reign and devoted many pages to small and medium-sized gardens. Other intellectuals even recommended gardening to the poor 'as beneficial to physical, mental and spiritual well being'. Many more people had small gardens in which they cultivated vegetables and brightly coloured annual plants from seed. Only experienced nurserymen were able to propagate newly obtained plants from foreign plant hunting expeditions. New garden journals and periodicals were now available for this new gardening public to consult. The most widely influential were The Gardeners' Chronicle, first published in 1841, The Journal of Horticulture in 1848 and The Garden in 1871; all satisfied an ever-increasing desire for gardening knowledge.

CHAPTER 4

JOHN INGRAM'S DIARY 1857–75

John Ingram commenced a Diary in July 1857[1] noting the daily workings at his various nurseries. It recorded in detail his staff, the propagation they carried out of his extensive stock of plants in the nursery, weather conditions – the weather and its implications, thunderstorms and heat waves regularly noted – visits to garden shows and the standard of maintenance and cleanliness in his nursery. Although entries in the diary were of a repetitive nature, many indicated the quantity of plants that were tended and the attention to detail that the nursery gave to the extensive range of plants for inclusion in their catalogues. John Ingram kept his diary for 18 years until 22nd July 1875, a year before he died on 10th December 1876, aged 54 years. Although there are lapses recording daily tasks, his interest in all matters horticultural is noted throughout. The regular mentioning in the diary of the upkeep of the glasshouses and the paths indicates that the Nursery had customers from the highest social classes who came to inspect the plants they wanted to buy, so the nursery had to be kept in a very good condition. A clean site also indicated that the owners could keep pests under control. Many wholesale nurseries just tended to build new glasshouses, gave them one coat of paint and let them fall down, then replaced them if they were still in business.

6th July 57

Home Nursery:–

E Papworth putting in pinks, T Clark and Knight glazing, Lowton and Co repotting and preparing for Ely Show, Rowe's man altering manger in Nag's stable. Nag's eye pronounced by Bull to be better.

Hartford Lane:–

Searle tying up grapes, Carter hand weeding, Beale burning rubbish, Charles gone to Mr E Maules.

Brampton not visited today must go tomorrow, Carnations and Picotees[2] looking good.

---

[1] Huntingdon Record Office, 2268/2

[2] Carnations and Picotees were popular with Florist Society members and were grown in small town gardens for their silvery spreading tufts and fragrant big crimson flowers in July. They required annual propagation by layering their shoots in July.

7th July 57

>Home Nursery:–

>E Papworth tying up and thinning Dahlias[3] (to obtain fewer but larger flowers), other men preparing for Ely Show.

>Brampton: – collecting Swede seed – poor, never let anything stand without transplanting, 2 men training[4], Warren trimming Crab stock, others clipping hedges.

>Hartford Lane:– C Papworth gone to Mr Herberts, Beale and others clearing.

8th July 57

>Commenced Rose budding at Hartford Lane, started myself to Royston and slept at Buntingford.

9th July 57

>Returned after seeing Mr Price at small show at Buntingford, afraid shall loose Dillistone.

10th July 57

>Home Nursery:– Lowton and staff potting hardwood plants, Ted and staff amongst Anemone roots and other bulbs clearing them.

>Hartford Lane:– Charles and Searle budding Roses, Beale and Carter watering Cucumbers[5] and cleaning nursery.

>Went to Hemingford. Giddins has splendid Raspberries, no care whatever, strangely with all our care they don't survive.

>Brampton not visited, Carnations and Picotees opening fast.

---

[3] Dahlias first reached Kew in 1798 previously having been imported by the Spanish from Central and South America. By the early 1800s nurserymen were exploiting to the full the plant's highly variable progeny. Throughout Europe the passion for dahlias in the 1840s matched the tulip mania of the 17th century both in intensity and in the prices realised by the new plants. By 1881 The British National Dahlia Society had been formed and encouraged hybridisation and exhibitions of this plant.

Dahlias were usually hardened off and planted out at the end of May, then dispatched in June. The site prepared by thorough digging and putting a layer of manure in the bottom of the hole, but not to come in contact with its roots.

[4] "2 men training" possibly refers to fruit and soft fruit to produce cordons and fans. Warren was preparing crab stock ready for budding.

[5] Throughout his Diary, John Ingram mentions difficulties in growing cucumbers. Originally grown in Egypt, cucumbers were grown by the nobility after the dissolution of the monasteries. In the 19th century it was generally known that these plants required special conditions to grow well in England. The need for warmth and watering if the weather became too hot as did the temperature of the water, which had to be the same temperature as that in the greenhouse, required special attention by nurserymen. Mildew always attacked the plants when the air was humid and if the soil was dry, slugs and aphids devoured the leaves, and mosaic virus was brought by greenfly and infected plants had to be destroyed. Cucumbers were grown at the nursery for sale as few people had glasshouses to grow them. The plants would have been watered from a tank inside the cucumber house.

11th July 57

Home Nursery:– E Papworth tying Carnations and carding[6] flowers, hoeing etc., Lowton and men potting hardwood plants and tying them, J Clarke and Knight still painting and glazing.

Hartford Lane:– C Papworth Rose budding, others clearing.

Brampton:– Bell ground – harrowing after Turnip seed, others training Peaches, cleaning nursery.

12th July 57

Home Nursery:– Lowton potting seedling Cyclamens, Smith tying young Heaths, Papworth carding Carnations and Picotees which are very fine, Musk and Dixon cleaning nursery, Clark and J Papworth cleaning and resetting alpines.

Brampton:– Warren nailing Peaches against fence, 2 cleaning bell grounds[7], 2 training in the quarters and others cleaning, gathering Polyanthus and Welsh Onion seed.

Greenhouses had become very important not only for growing exotic plants from abroad but as a social statement of wealth. By 1850 most middle-class families had a gardener or two to look after a hot house and perhaps a peach house and to lend a hand in the conservatory. Country gentlemen were expected to have several gardeners and a range of hot houses for flowers, fruit and plants. Only rich landowners grew fruit in glasshouses; those who could not afford glasshouses for growing fruit relied on orchards for their fruit crops, which were often spoilt by late frosts. 'One wonders how a Duke could live without peaches and grapes, not to say pine-apples, forced strawberries, and kidney beans'. (*Gardener's Magazine Volume XII* 1836, p293.) It becomes obvious in his diary that John Ingram had a particular passion for introducing cool greenhouse and stove house plants for sale at his nursery.

During the following year the entries become longer and, although now written on a weekly basis, give in greater detail the extent of plants on the nursery, the importance of keeping glasshouses clean, plant problems, plant lists and reports on prevailing weather conditions:–

---

[6]'Carding' was the term used by nurserymen to display blooms of carnations to show them. 'A large circular card was supplied and the stem of the flower was thrust through a hole sufficiently large not to press the calyx, and under this a smaller card having 3½ inch cuts through its centre is pressed tightly underneath it, the cut portions fitting tightly and holding it in position. Then with a pair of ivory tweezers arrange the outer rows of petals on the upper card, being careful not to overdo size, a second row follows, and so on until the centre is reached, three or four neatly arranged petals finishing off the bloom' (*The Book of the Carnation*, R. P. Robertson 1903).

[7]"Cleaning Bell grounds" refers to bell like cloches which would have had pegs for ventilating

3rd March 58

Wednesday

Frost set in today after last writing and has continued ever since, at times the thermometer registering 12 degrees. Heavy falling of snow on Monday afternoon and mighty wind in the NE and very strong, making the cold intense, indeed Monday last I think was the coldest day we have had but it still continues very severe.

Brampton:– Cutting hay 1 day, and trimming stakes, Mangle seed sent home, seems a fairish lot, but Marne Radishes turned out very badly only 12 bushel an acre I believe to produce it.

Lowton and staff still potting and arranging bedding plants this morning rearranging stove.

Ted and staff cutting flower sticks.

Hartford Lane:– all cutting flower sticks and hooks, commenced plant list yesterday, but seem some what lazy over it.

13th March 58

Frost broke up last night, I sincerely hope for good. This morning beautifully mild and somewhat rainy, commenced business in good earnest after more than 3 weeks cessation, sadly fear it must spoil the spring trade. During the last 3 weeks our men busy with bedding stuff. Resetting plants in stove greenhouse.

Ted and staff cutting labels, flower sticks, putting in Dahlias[9], cutting etc,etc.

At Brampton yesterday men planting seedlings in such places as caught the sun and the land really seemed to work very nicely. Acacia longiflora magnifica[10] beautifully in bloom in greenhouse as also several Azalea, Roses etc in stove, Calanthus veratifolia and Tillandia zebrina[11] all in flower.

Medinella magnifica[12] also showing very promising. Put in this week a rare batch of scarlet Geraniums which think will prove acceptable after autumn stock are all gone.

---

[9]Dahlias would be cuttings at this time of year.

[10]Acacia longifolia, the 'Sidney Golden Wattle' from Australia, was introduced in 1791 and grown in the greenhouse as a large bush laden with pale yellow blossoms.

[11]Tillandia zebrina, a conservatory plant, is now called Tradescantia zebrina and was introduced in 1849.

[12]Medinella magnifica is one of the most beautiful shrubs of tropical evergreens, grown for its rose-pink panicles of flowers which bloom in May. The plant comes from tropical Africa and needs a minimum temperature of 15–20° C.

Plant list progressing slowly but no hurry as I want Turner's[13] spring list before publishing. Have taken this week 2/- in £ for Dillistone's debt thus making rather more than £80 by him in three years.

9th June 58

Lowton gone to Chiswick Show, T Clark potting Verbenas and Petunias. J Papworth arranging greenhouse. Ingles tying up and arranging Achimines[14] and Stove plants, Ted planting out best Dahlias[15] which he finished today. Smart hoeing.

Dixon and Warren plunging Cupressus macrocarpus, Smith potting off small Cupressus rooted from cuttings, Peter and Knight finished cleaning shop and dressing seeds etc, since last writing all bedding plants have been planted out, the trade from which by the by is very dull, Cucumbers got out at Hartford Lane 3 & 4 days ago, where Roses seem growing admirably.

At Brampton everything doing well except Quick which has been mildewed. Grafts, Buds etc very prosperous and have been all secured against wind, Our old friend Cherry Aphis just begins to appear and should much like to know how to give him quietness. Ranunculus, Anemones and American plants finally in bloom, Peaches etc in Orchard House promising well.

Several times in the Diary John Ingram mentioned his visits to London but during June 1858 he recorded an important visit to the capital which sparked off his interest to grow fine roses, the plant the nursery became renowned for in the twentieth century:–

June 18th 58

Friday

Went to London on Tuesday last and had a tremendously hot ride up on this day.

Dixon and Smart mowed lawns, Ted cleaning Walks and Borders and sowing cabbage, Warren pricking out broccoli etc, Lowton potting specimens of greenhouse plants. Ingle cutting flower sticks, Smith potting Junipers struck from cuttings, Ian washing pots, Clarke painting glazing etc.

On the 16th went with my wife to Crystal Palace Show which was a very fine exhibition, the Monster Fountains played and I was pretty nearly melted with

---

[13]Turners was a nursery at Slough, Berkshire.

[14]Achimines are commonly known as the 'Hot Water Plant'

[15]Dahlias were planted out in July in order to cut flowers and display them later in September in the nursery for orders for the following year.

the intense heat and noted down the following as good things:–

Roses, Madame Payne China, Hyb Perpetuals Souvenir des Braves, Gloire de Moscow, Cardinal Paluzzi, Comtesse d'Orleans, Theodora Madame Milterrinoz, Provence Belle de Legus, Cripiani, Dracophyllum gracile and Erica ventricosa magnifica.

At home Lowton placing hardwood plants out of doors in beds, Ingle potting stove plants, Smith putting in Epacris cuttings, Jim washing glass, Clarke painting and glazing, Ted and Dixon tying Carnations and Picotees, Ward and Smart planting out Brassicas for seed and cleaning walks.

On the 17th went to Somerset House and ascertained our land was redeemed, afternoon to Cremore Gardens to see Waterer's American plants which were past their best, the following seemed good –

Rhodns Broughtonii, Brayanum, Nero, Maculatum grandiflorum, Nigrum, Onslowianum, Hayworth, Desdemona, Currieanum and Kalmia myrtifolia.

Lowton still potting hardwooded plants and sowed Calceolaria seed, James crocking pots and washing glass, Smith pitting in Azalea cuttings, Ingle trimming sticks and tying stove plants, Clarke painting and glazing.

Bye the bye went with wife and friends to Olympia. I saw Robson and others in 'Going to the Bad' which showing the peculiar genius of Robson seemed to hang rather tediously in parts. This day returned leaving my wife behind till tomorrow. Should have said that yesterday Ted and Dixon put up Carnation Stand No 2 and filled the same, also potted Globe Amaranthus[16].

Warren and Smart were cleaning this day, Lowton and Jim cleaning and arranging plants in large greenhouse, Ingle arranging and tying stove plants, Smith potting hardwooded cuttings

The Rhododendrons recorded by John Ingram were raised by Waterer's Knapp Hill Nursery in Surrey before 1851 and *Rhododendron maculata grandiflorum* was listed by Standish and Noble in 1850. In Frederick Street's Hardy Rhododendrons published in 1955 he mentions that *R. Broughtonii* was a crimson, old Arboreum hybrid, suitable for planting in tubs in a greenhouse in December where it would flower in early April the following year. He refers to a catalogue dated 1886 when this plant cost 2s 6d.

Paxton's Great Exhibition building was erected at Hyde Park in 1851. Following this successful exhibition Paxton organised a limited company to reassemble it in another

---

[16] Globe amaranth is Gomphrena globosa, an annual which was introduced from India in 1714, it was grown as a cut flower for drying. Amaranthus is Love-lies-bleeding.

park on Sydenham Hill in south London in 1854. Mr and Mrs Ingram were lucky to see the fine gardens filled with roses planted only a few years earlier. Various gardening journals of 1854 described the gardens around the Crystal Palace: –

'Paxton's elaborate scheme for over 12,000 jets, fountains and cascades for the park necessitated a complex and costly system to circulate the water. A deep bore was sunk at the lowest level of the park from which the water was pumped into a large reservoir; from here the water could be driven into an intermediate level lake to supply the smaller waterworks. In all, 120,000 gallons of water a minute would be used when all the waterworks were in play'.

Vauxhall Gardens in South London, once a popular pleasure garden with shaded walks and bandstands, had been showing signs of decline and was closed in 1859 as a result of persistent rowdyism and immorality. By then much of its custom had been stolen by Cremore Gardens (situated off the King's Road near the Thames in Chelsea), which had been from 1846 onwards offering nightly masquerades, dancing, puppet shows, circus acts, side shows and cheap suppers. Waterer's Knap Hill Nursery mounted flower shows at Cremore Gardens and in the Botanic Gardens, Regent's Park for several years. A further show was held in the gardens of Ashburnham House in King's Road, Chelsea, in connection with the Cremore Gardens Flower Show. Here its tent was 365 feet long and 95 feet wide; members of the Royal Family were among the visitors and music was played.

John Ingram was impressed by what he saw in London that swelteringly hot day in June 1858. He noted down the roses at the Crystal Palace that he did not grow in his nursery. He also noticed the standard of the Waterer's plants in their displays, although the heat had taken its toll in the great marquee at Cremore Gardens. His reaction established the need to plan for a successful future in the nursery and his interest in growing roses was awakened. A further weekly report in the diary notes his dismay for few orders at shows and his need to pay more attention to mounting the displays:–

9th July 58

> *Friday*
>
> *Weather still very dry and has been so since last writing, carried the remaining hay from meadows, being coarse stuff left by the horses, on Wednesday or Thursday week –*

Thursday 1st July 58

> *Ted tied Carnations and preparing for Chatteris Show. Dixon, Warren and Smart manuring, digging about Dahlias, watering shrubs and planting*

Celery. Lowton and Ingle tying plants for Chatteris Show, Jim and Tom glazing and painting.

2nd July 58

Lowton and Smart at Chatteris Show where we did tolerably well, Ingle potting Roses and Lycopods for specimens, Smith potting Bouvardias[17] and cleaning cuttings, Papworth and Clarke glazing, Ted and Dixon putting in pink piping, Warren planting out Celery, forgot to say that on the 1st I went to the National Rose Show and was much delighted

3rd July 58

Lowton taking netting of Geranium house, Ingle trimming sticks and tying Heaths, Smith putting in hardwooded cuttings, Jim arranging in greenhouse, Tom glazing, Ted and Dixon still at pink pipings, Warren and Smart getting up Anemones, Wright and King taking down flue on the 2nd.

5th July 58

Lowton and Jim placing scarlet Geraniums from pit into beds, Ingle and Wright carting water pipes from station, Smith still hardwooded cuttings, Ted and Dixon planting Celery for house and mulching around Dahlias, Warren and Clarke pulling down flues etc at long house.[18]

6th July 58

All engaged getting ready for Stamford Show – I should say that on 5th I went to Hemingford and settled Gidding's hailstorm affair for which he gets something more than £50.00.

7th July 58

Lowton, Wright and self at Stamford Show where we did well except with Roses which must try and alter. Ingle and Smith moving plants in Orchid House and taking down brickwork, Ted tying Carnations and Dahlias, Dixon and Smart cleaning borders, Warren cleaning bricks. We had 2 horses in our van and Gidding's horse and van to Stamford. Myself though there at 11.00 too late to adjust my roses.

---

[17]Bouvardias are winter flowering evergreen greenhouse shrubs with white and red scented flowers. They were introduced from Mexico in 1794. 'Piping' cuttings is the term used when many thousands of cuttings are required in the nursery. Staff would simply pull the cuttings out at a joint, but they had to always be in the correct condition i.e. rooted.

B.S. Williams, who owned The Victoria and Paradise Nurseries, Upper Holloway Road, London at this time, kept a large range of rare exotics which they claimed to be 'unequalled' in this country.

[18]Glasshouse chimney stacks were cleaned annually during summer months.

8th July 58

> *Lowton and Jim arranging greenhouse, Ingle arranging stove plants, Smith at hardwooded cuttings, Ted tying Carnations and Dahlias, Dixon and Smart cleaning borders, Warren cleaning bricks.*

9th July 58

> *Today Lowton potting seedling Cinerarias and clearing Cineraria bed, Clarke painting and glazing, Ted and Ingle and the rest digging stoke hole in which respect to say we are much touched with water and fear we have our work cut out for us.*

John Ingram was no lover of holidays with the family, and missed the daily running of the nursery and keeping plants free of pests and diseases and, as the season progressed, the work became more intense:–

7th Aug 58

> *Ted and Smart layering Wisteria and digging trenches, Dixon and Warren getting off Strawberry runners, Lowton and Ingle clearing and arranging stove plants, Smith putting tiles and sand in Heath house.*
>
> *I on this day myself and wife returned from Lincolnshire after a ten day's journey, heartily glad to get home and fully convinced that it don't pay I resolved to have no more such long and wearisome trips.*

16th Aug 58

> *Ted tying Dahlias and layering Carnations, Dixon layering Carnations, Warren and Smart digging Celery trenches and clearing round the Long House, – out of door Cucumbers are becoming a matter of history and our frame Cucumbers and Melons are a most melancholy spectacle from Red Spider – surely we can devise some plan for monitoring it another season.*

17th Aug 58

> *Tuesday Lowton and Staff putting in Petunia cuttings and putting down platform in stove, Ted layering and thinning Dahlias, Dixon layering and emptying Potatoes, Warren clearing up round Long House, Smart and Charles Papworth and Mr Herberts, Searle budding Roses, Beale pulling up Pea sticks, Joe weeding amongst Stools.*
>
> *Brampton all hands getting up Potatoes. The weather has been wonderfully dry and hot. There was a nice rain at Boston and I believe here on the 4th*

inst, then no more till last Saturday evening when we had a most magnificent storm but not accompanied with much thunder and lightning, the influence of this has been most beneficial – all nature seems revived.

4th Oct 58

Ted and Staff potting Carnations and Evergreen Oaks, clipping hedges and cleaning, Lowton and Smith filling Orchard house saving Aurucaria[19] and potting variegated Geraniums, Smith cleaning and plunging cuttings, remainder painting Stove stage and lights.

7th Oct 58

Ted and Staff planting Violets and potting and plunging Evergreens, Lowton and Smith potting scarlet and variegated Geraniums, Tom glazing and washing glass and placing up variegated Geraniums, Smith putting in cuttings of scarlet and variegated Geraniums, Berberis and Ceanothus[20], Jim cleaning greenhouse plants and tying Climbers, Ingle cleaning and potting variegated Geraniums.

8th Oct 58

Lowton and Smart potting Pampas Grass and placing in Heath house, Papworth tying climbers and placing in pit, Smith putting in Heliotrope[21] and Verbena cuttings Tom mending greenhouses, Ted and staff potting and plunging evergreens[22] and cleaning Hollyhock seed.

As the days became shorter the hive of industry continued:–

10th Nov 58

Lowton and Jim watering, cleaning and arranging plants in large greenhouse, Smith and Ingle putting in cuttings of Myrtle leafed Box, weeping

---

[19] Auraucaria araucana, the Monkey Puzzle Tree was introduced by Archibald Menzies in 1795 and plants were offered by Messrs Youell & Co., Great Yarmouth ' four years old and 8 or 9 in. high' at £5 per 1,000'. (Gardeners' Chronicle 25th November 1843.)

[20] Ceanothus were grown for sale in the nursery and had been ordered by Colonel Clark at Farm Hall, Godmanchester in the 18th century.

[21] Heliotrope or "Cherry Pie" used in summer bedding of which there are numerous forms, all varieties of H. peruvianum introduced in 1757. Autumn cuttings were often more successful than those taken in the spring and require a temperature of 60°. If trained up a greenhouse wall they could reach 10 or 12 feet high. Verbenas were grown mainly as bedding plants, increased in the spring by cuttings. To keep the plants neat in shape, shoots were pegged down and new growth nipped out to form a bushy habit with more abundant flowers.

[22] 'Plunging evergreens' refers to placing pots in trenches, then covering each pot with ash or soil to protect them during the winter.

> do, Euonymus and Collettia spinosa[23], Tom glazing hand glasses and watering, Ted and staff putting moulds in Cucumber house, writing labels, digging and barrowing soil and sifting do, planting Tulips[24] and packing.

11th Nov 58

> Ted and Staff same as yesterday, Lowton tying specimens, Smith preparing cuttings, Ingle helping to draw at Hartford Lane, Clarke glazing, and trimming sticks, Jim potting herbaceous Calceolarias[25] large Cytisus, Abutilon, Eugenia and Brugmansia

12th Nov 58

> Lowton, Clarke and Jim potting Calceolarias and unloading straw, Ingle putting in hardy cuttings, Smith taking cuttings of Alyssum, new Phlox's, Jasminum nudiflorum, Thuja chiliensis, Ted and Staff getting up Dahlias and packing.

13th Nov 58

> Ted and Staff dressing seeds, planting red Cedars from Cornwall, plunging hardy evergreens and packing, Lowton and Ingle moving Stove plants, cleaning and watering, Clarke and Jim watering and potting Calceolarias, Smith putting in cuttings of Lechemanias[26] and Verbenas.

The weather turned very cold towards the end of November, and on the 23rd 12 degrees of frost were experienced and the following day Wood recorded *'thirteen degrees of frost last night and a magnificent crystal morning, every tree and bush adorned with the most beautiful network of rhime'*. The period before Christmas saw a great deal of activity for the nursery staff:–

16th Dec 58

> Potting seedling Hollyhocks[27], moving Fruit trees, cleaning borders and

---

[23]Colletias, the Anchor Plant was a half hardy evergreen introduced from South America in 1823. It occurs in Chile, Uruguay and Peru.

[24]Tulips were planted late in the year to avoid fire blight.

[25]Introduced from Chile c.1820, Calceolarias were raised from seed sown in summer and required regular repotting from three inch to eight inch pots. In May they provide a brilliant display of flowers for eight to ten weeks in the glasshouse. Eugenia is a fragrant fruiting Myrtle and Stove houseplant introduced from Asia in 1768. With our warmer winters it does not need such temperatures today. Brugmansia (Datura) is a perennial shrub from South America.

[26]Lachenalia are bulbs from South Africa with vibrant flowers often for early blooming at Christmas or the New Year.

[27]Hollyhocks appeared in large numbers at flower shows at the time.

packing, Lowton cleaning, tying and washing stove plants, glazing, Jim labels making and painting wooden labels, propagating Dillwynnias[28] etc.

17th Dec 58

Cleaning and tying Lechemanias etc, potting seedling Ferns, cleaning scarlet Geraniums, potting Geraniums, cleaning potted Roses, potting and trellising Tropaeoleums, propagating Primulas and cleaning, sulphuring Azalea[29] cuttings, Ted moving fruit trees, cleaning walks, saving wood for labels, packing and getting home underwood, Rec'd of Hemingford (not John) tells me to wash Cucumber seed in new milk if of a bad colour and if not then quite white to bleach it by putting in a tub then a pan of lighted sulphur on top and cover over with socks till morning.

18th Dec 58

Ted staking and wiring Raspberries twisting bands to, Lowton tying Azaleas, sulphuring Verbenas, cleaning scarlet Geraniums, washing Eriostemon and propagating Acacias.

20th Dec 58

Tying Epacris[30] miniata specimen, cleaning Roses, scarlet Geraniums and Cinerarias in long pit and glazing, propagating Acacia grandis and Hibbertias, Ted tying and manuring Raspberries, getting home underwood and packing.

21st Dec 58

Cutting shreds, making labels and packing, Lowton plunging cuttings, cleaning potting scarlet Geraniums and tying specimens.

22nd Dec 58

Tying specimens, cleaning scarlet Geraniums, tying other Geraniums, propagating Bossiacas and cleaning Alyssums, Ted making and writing labels, digging and packing.

---

[28] Dillwynia is an Australian evergreen shrub with red and orange flowers requiring 45° F during the winter, and introduced in 1794.

[29] Sulphuring Azaleas was carried out to avoid mildew. Cucumbers were washed in milk in order to keep the seeds viable until the following spring.

[30] Epacris is an Australian Heath with red/white flowers introduced in 1803 requiring 45° in winter. Hibbertia is an Australian greenhouse climber with yellow flowers introduced in 1816.

23rd Dec 58

Emptying pots, making and writing labels, packing, Lowton tying specimens, stacking up pots, staging Gardenias[31], tying Geraniums, cleaning Verbenas and attending to cuttings.

24th Dec 58

Tying Dillywinnias, washing stove plants, cleaning Acacia armata, Verbenas and attending to cuttings, Ted manuring herbaceous plants, making labels and packing.

Xmas Day – Weather mild and rainy, wife arrived down stairs today, rather backward with bills must work hard to get them done in time.

Not exactly the Christmas one might have imagined for such a tired nursery owner, but one where there was just a slot in his busy timetable for reflection on the past year's trade and perhaps thoughts for the future. But after one day's holiday everyone is back at work as plants need regular attention at all times:–

27th Dec 58

A fine open morning sun shining after a heavy fall of rain, yesterday Ted and staff planting Carnations and Pinks, fetching hay from Brampton and Loam from railway, Lowton at home, Ingle making orchid baskets, harrowing loam, glazing Iron labels and painting labels or tickets rather for Brampton, Smith cleaning Verbenas, Jim preparing sticks, watering and potting Jasminum nudiflorum.

28th Dec 58

Lowton potting Fuchias, rest of his men as yesterday, Ted barrowing loam, cutting Privet hedge, turning potatoes and packing.

On New Year's Eve after many days of toil there was time to reflect quietly on the passing year's work:–

31st Dec 58

Turning soil, fetching cinders, thrashing Sweet Peas and packing, Lowton tying and cleaning Heaths, cleaning Heliotropes, potting Hydrangeas, glazing labels, lifting cinders, cleaning bedding and bedding plants in long house,

---

[31]Gardenias are tropical Old World evergreen shrubs cultivated for their fragrant creamy white flowers from summer to winter, requiring 50–60° F.

have this day according to ancient custom started off all Xmas Bills by post and have the town ones and named ones in the neighbourhood ready for tomorrow and so ends the year. One of considerable worry and expense but one marked by many blessings, may its successor be as good if not better.

By now the Nursery employed several members of staff – J. Papworth, Charles Papworth, J. Clark, Ward, Smart, Ingle, Lowton, Smith, Searle, Dixon, Beale, Wright, Musk, Knight and others mentioned by their Christian names; Jim, Tom who looked after the glasshouses, Peter, Joe and Ted who worked with other staff.

In 1859 the Diary continued in the same manner as nursery work tended to be repetitive and seasonal. Some entries shed light on how the nursery carried out different work and others indicate the dedication or not of John Wood's diary keeping:–

7th March 1859

Have this day brought my Diary up from about 25th January not having had time since then to write in it, seems to have had a very busy month in February and are going on pretty well even now, weather still very mild but dry, glass going down today so that hope for rain, there is reported to have been a great deal of rain during February but more scarce here, though meadows have been flooded from the flush from up country

Everything in greenhouses looking well, cleaning out barn, carrying to timber yard, passing turf at Hartford and packing, Lowton naming Verbenas and grafting Epiphyllums[32], glazing, making and painting labels, planting Strawberries propagating Chowzemas etc, and making up cutting pots.

8th March 59

A very rough stormy day, hail and the nearest approach to snow we have had during the winter. Naming Verbenas, plunging and arranging stove plants, glazing, making labels, propagating Somphotobums[33], Ted staking pyramid trees, moving potted fruit trees to Orchard House and packing.

9th March 59

Grafting Elms at Brampton and planting Quick, arranging plants in Orchard House, propagating Dahlias and sowing Frame Radish and packing, Lowton

---

[32]Epiphyllum is a succulent from Brazil introduced in 1818 for the greenhouse and produces violet/scarlet flowers in mid-winter and grafted standard high on to Pereskia aculeata. Chowzemas are evergreen greenhouse plants introduced in 1803 from Australia, and grow to 3ft high with red and yellow flowers. During a warm summer potted plants can stand outside from March to September.

[33]Somphotobum is the plant Sophronitis, a scarlet flowered orchid introduced from Brazil in 1837 and used in hanging baskets.

naming Verbenas, Antirhinums and stacking up pots, smoking[34], making and painting labels, propagating Ericas, Epacris and sowing Hovea Celsi[35] Seed.

2nd April 59

The effects of Thursday nights frost now begin to appear, Apricots seem most of them killed young Quick and indeed all young growths, more or less injured and I think the effects will be more or less felt all through the season. Cleaning Geraniums and Camellias and potting Petunias. Ted earthing Cucumbers and Melons, planting and packing.

4th April 59

Lowering passage in house, sowing Broccoli etc and planting, Lowton naming Verbenas, Fuchsias and Heliotropes and potting and training shrubby Calceolarias[36].

5th April 59

Potting Roses and Vines and numbering the latter[37], potting Flower of the day[38] and azaleas and nailing netting on retarding house, Ted planting Arborvitae[39], Cupressus and Junipers, cleaning Alpines and packing.

22nd April 59 Good Friday

Weather very severe and has been for the last week, days sunny and nights very sharp which must have a very trying effect on vegetation, everything looks nipped and miserable, all young shrubs seem settled for the present and are either black or brown. Digging, cleaning, making and writing labels, fetching grass from the cemetery, sorting pots etc, Lowton tying, cleaning and arranging Calceolarias, smoking houses, cleaning and arranging plants in large house, attending to cuttings.

---

[34] 'Smoking' is the term used for fumigating greenhouses to kill unwanted pests, by spraying with sulphur.

[35] Hovea celsi is a greenhouse shrub introduced from Australia in 1815 growing to 3 ft with blue flowers.

[36] Shrubby Calceolarias were used mainly for bedding purposes and propagated by cuttings or layers in August, and were placed under a north wall, then when rooted they were transferred to a south facing frame throughout the winter and pinched back in February to obtain numerous flowers. Special care was taken not to water the leaves. Hardened off in April, and if weather conditions were favourable the plants could be planted out in May.

[37] Numbering vines varieties may have been used as the vine may not have been named. Some staff may not have been able to read labels so numbers were used.

[38] Potted roses would have been sold to decorate Conservatories.

[39] Arborvitae are now called Thuja.

23rd April 59

Potting and manuring Chrysanthemums, propagating Chimonanthus, Acacia and tying greenhouse climbers, Ted digging and cleaning, lining frames, barrowing soil and packing.

25th April 59

A nice gentle rain yesterday (Easter) and is keeping on beautifully this morning, I fear the prospect of the hardy fruit crop are very discouraging, Potting Dahlias, making labels, packing up, Lowton cleaning Geraniums, potting Heliotropes, trellising Hoya[40] and naming Roses, potting Azaleas and smoking.

28th April 59

Weather still very cold and stormy, a downfall just now of a curious kind seeming part rain, part hail, and part sleet. Still gravelling walks, three Cucumbers in today, hoping even yet to get some in the house. Shifting scarlet Geraniums, Camellias, Azaleas and Fuchsias, untying grafts etc, Ted planting Potatoes and gravelling the walks, rolling Lawn and packing.

29th April 59

Still at walks, mowing lawn and packing, Lowton cleaning and arranging plants in large Greenhouses, potting Lobelia speciosa, smoking, barrowing and stoking coke, cleaning plants in Geranium House, propagating Flower of the Day.

30th April 59

Cleaning and arranging plants in Show House, placing Roses in Heath House, potting Vine eyes[41], cleaning Geraniums and Potting variegated Geraniums, Ted still at walks and packing.

16th May 59

Wind still keeps in the old quarter varying from east to north and vice versa, Bedding plants trade very brisk during the last fortnight, seem likely to sell out of everything except Verbenas which are a slow sale, looking up orders and fetching bedding stuff from St Neots, potting Tobacco, tying stove plants, potting Geraniums and Epacris, Ted cleaning out ponds and packing.

---

[40]Hoya is an evergreen climber suitable for a stove or greenhouse with white-flushed pink scented flowers. It was introduced in 1802 from the Far East, Burma and China.

[41]Internodal one eyed cuttings were common when propagating vines at that time.

17th May 59

This morning a beautiful rain which is much wanted and for which all vegetation must be grateful, trimming sticks, raking and rolling walks, packing and loading van for Cambridge, Lowton cleaning geraniums and tying plants for Cambridge, potting Epacris.

18th May 59

At Cambridge Show, potting Roses and taking Geraniums into long house, cleaning scarlet Geraniums etc, Ted rolling gravel, catching snails, potting Dahlias and packing.

3rd June 59

For the last three or four days tremendous rains with much lightning and occasional thunder, the meadows and low-lands are getting flooded. Tying Calceolarias, tying and potting stove plants, Geraniums. Mowing lawn, propagating Gloxinias etc, Ted mowing lawn, planting Box Pansies and Celery. Flush of water has filled stoke hole great treat, Cucumbers planted at Hartford Lane this week – One year transplants at Brampton dreadfully impaired.

6th June 59

At Brampton today, Warren disbudding and forcing Peaches etc, Others securing grafts and moulding up Radishes which look well, Turnip seed beaten down at one end by the heavy rains, the weather still looks unsettled. Lowton tying Heaths, potting Vines, Fuchias, making labels, cleaning training Roses, Ted planting Celery, tying Pinks, lining out Dahlia Piece, staking and tying Hollyhocks, weeding beds etc.

22nd June 59

Eight haymaking at bell Close and others at Bell's, Lowton preparing for Cambridge Show, Ted pruning wall trees, Searle sticking Sweet Peas, Smith attending to cuttings, Ted clipping hedges also cleaning Nursery.

25th June 59

Pruning pyramid Apple trees and Pears, watering and mulching Roses, potting Fuchias, plunging cuttings, potting Camellias, glazing and finishing haymaking

28th June 59

Mowing lawn, potting Balsams, cleaning Tulips, cutting herbaceous flowers etc, Lowton getting ready for March Show, sponging stove plants and glazing.

4th July 59

Barrowing peat, turning manure, cleaning Geraniums, tying Vines, propagating Epacris and painting and glazing, Ted cutting hooks and hooking down dahlias, getting up Ranunculus, weeding walks and barrowing peat.

5th July 59

Putting in Penstemon cuttings, cleaning nursery, and preparing for Stamford Show, propagating hardwoods and glazing.

27th July 59

Planting Celery, loading Van for Blisworth,[42] putting in Hollyhock cuttings.

28th July 59

Cleaning Nursery and Cucumbers out of House, tying Dahlias, Lowton at Blisworth others trellising Torenias.[43]

29th August 59

Preparing for Banbury Show, clearing and counting Ranunculus, Lowton propagating Greenhouse plants, tying Stove plants, cleaning ferns.

30th August 59

Tying and thinning Dahlias, opening drains for gas pipes, and getting up bulbs.

31st August 59

Thinning Asters, cleaning Bulbs in the Nursery, Lowton propagating heaths and Greenhouse plants, making flower stakes.

1st September 59

Did nothing at Banbury on the 30th ult., weather has changed to dull cold at

---

[42]Blisworth is a small village south of Northampton.

[43]Victorian gardeners grew Torenias (Wishbone Flower) in their greenhouses; they were planted in suspended baskets and were useful for flowering throughout both summer and winter. Torenia fournieri with its trumpet shaped blue flowers was a particular favourite. The plant was introduced from Asia in 1811 and is named after an 18th century Swedish clergyman.

Brampton, getting on with training and trimming up for drawing season, Peaches much mildewed at Hartford Lane, dressing Endive Seed and Lettuce seed mostly cut, all the last year's Radish now thrashed out, and have about 10 Bushels which hope will carry us through next season or nearly.

14th Sept 59

Preparing for Cambridge Show, potting scarlet Geraniums and propagating Verbenas.

19th Sept 59

Preparing for Wellingborough Show. Planting hardy trees and putting in hardy cuttings

18th October 59

After a long cessation have just got this Diary straight again, have got the Catalogues in hand and proofed, Trade one in today. Not much yet done in the way of business, but hope for a good season.

4th November 59

Not to be forgotten that a frost of the most severe description commenced about the 23rd ult. which has turned the young shoots of Laurels and Hollies quite black shrivelled the leaves upon the trees in a most unusual manner and altogether astonishingly. Today incessant rain. Lowton sponging, cleaning and arranging Ferns, turning them and plunging cuttings. Ted tying mats, putting up seeds in shop for trial, making and writing labels and packing.

The nursery shop sold tomatoes and cucumbers to local customers. The arranging of flowering plants in a greenhouse was an important part of the nursery's trade and the display was constantly changed to show exotic indoor plants for sale when flowering. Visitors to the nursery in 1748 had already been noted in James Wood's Ledger. Much effort was given at this time to keeping the glasshouses in good repair and free from pest and diseases.

1860

4th January 60

Weather now very mild and have been since the breaking up of the tremendous frost last Thursday week, it caught again once or twice, but did not hold. My Aunt died (Mrs Ingram, Wigan) last week thought last time I saw

her, her end was near, Lowton tying specimens, making bouquets, fetching
cinders and cleaning bedding plants.

The Diary entries are now often written in brief, and several days omitted. By now the management of the nursery took more and more of John Ingram's time. There was an extensive range of plants to maintain and also large numbers of plants to propagate for sale.

11th May 60

House, potting Dahlias.

14th May 60

Home planting Cypresses, putting in Rose cuttings.

25th May 60

Turning in and tying Roses.

11th June 60

Cheerful day and fine, arranged Dahlias today for planting Marrows, preparing for Saffron Walden Show forgot to organise on the 8th, that several Apples are severely injured by the frost, no mention of April being very busy and the man not liking the trouble of reporting themselves, Cucumbers in house have been over and taken out some time, don't seem to get on so much with them in the frames. Dahlia plants have been small this year and scarce, must remember this next season. Bedding plants trade getting over, sold pretty well out, seemed to have just about enough.

26th July 60

Budding Roses and carting earth from Hartford Road and wheeling it on Rose piece, Smith has been putting in hardwood cuttings for some days. Thomas thrown off the horse and small bone of ankle broken.

There is now a break in the Diary and it is continued some two years later in 1862:–

19th April 1862

Big Mare foaled, a fine filly, young Quicksilver. On beginning of this month planted Conifers on mounds on the lawn.

1st May 62

Poppet foaled, small filly with good points.

The Diary was left to one side for a further year and then continued with only one entry in 1863:–

12th May 1863

> On the 1st inst. A tremendous frost and other minor ones at interval since that of the 1st, cutting back all Potatoes, Spruce and Silver Firs, Spanish Chestnuts, Ash, Oaks, Beech etc. etc., an unusually dry spring and arid in the extreme, Agricultural Seed trade depressingly bad, bedding plants do very slow, just removing and rearranging Conifers etc at home, at the Hartford Lane securing Roses and watering Stocks.
>
> At Brampton finished planting but some things looked very queer with the frost and drought. Set a lot of men to kill the Caterpillars on the young apple trees, which proved very destructive last year.
>
> Foals whose births was noted last year lying out at Brampton and looking very promising especially the larger one.
>
> Grape vines were planted in near border of Greenhouse about latter end of last month.

John Ingram left the Diary aside for a further two years and described the year's work in 1865 in one entry:–

1st May 1865

> Just such a frost as recorded above but I think severer the thermometer registering 13 degrees. Much behind at this time with work of all kinds, but have nearly finished planting. Bedding stuff still potting off ought to have been all ready, means that Sims should have an additional man from the new year to May Day –
>
> Cutting in[44] roses at Hartford Lane which should have been done a fortnight since, others turning in there.
>
> At Brampton still cutting in, planting and turning in, everything much behind and obliged to employ an unusual quantity of labour. Did not notice if Spruce was injured or not, but all the other things named in last notice are in addition Vines, Planes, Acacias, Mulberries, Sumacs, Walnuts and many other things have their young growth to all appearance quite destroyed – singular

---

[44] 'Cutting in' refers to when an erect spade is pushed into the soil, taken out and put in again at 45 degrees to the first insert. A wedge of soil is then removed, the plant placed against the erect face and the wedge is replaced turning in, taking a thin layer of weedy soil and turning the weeds into the soil. Sometimes called 'Cut and Covering'.

to say Filberts and Vines seemed to escaped, Aucubas on Snow Hill with pea sticks amongst them are comparatively little injured.

A further break in the Diary, this time for seven years and the next entry, described in detail the prevailing weather conditions in 1872:–

10th August 1872

Upwards of 7 years since last entry and had I not happened accidentally of this book another perhaps would not have been made, as this however has been a very exceptional season, it seems worth recording the winter was severe though not excessively so, still causing great hindrance in business, this spring awfully severe cutting everything to bits and the summer has been the rainiest I think I ever remember, hay can scarcely pay the expense of making, corn has been under water, and there was a flood over the Brampton area and Thursday morning up to horses' bellies, flowers no where, grounds literally smothered with weeds and the aspect of affairs in general most unprofitable.

My dear Aunt died just before midnight on the 8th inst. 'Requiescat in Pace'

By now John Ingram must have lost interest in keeping up his Diary. He no longer noted the tasks carried out by his staff in the Nursery and did not mention the extensive collection of plants which his Nursery had amassed to show visitors throughout the year in his cool and heated glasshouses. He was still occupied by the state of the weather. The next entry was written three years later in 1875:–

21st July 1875

The heaviest rain I ever remember, having scarcely ceased with the exception of the 18th for ten days, a memorable year the Race Course being flooded so that no Races could take place, and the rain still coming down very heavily, great quantities of hay destroyed, our own part got well, remainder badly, but still much better than many peoples, great floods reported all over the country.

John's final entry was written the next day, his writing in faint lines barely decipherable recalled for the last time the plants he had nurtured for a lifetime in his nursery:–

22nd July 75

The highest flood season, I remember three feet of water about the wine cellar, and seven feet of Bor. Walk flooded, which I have never seen before – Carnations, Picotees have done well this year but being only covered with . injured the flowers.

His son, John Wood Ingram, wrote the following entry on the last page of his father's Diary:–

John Ingram, the writer of the previous notes
Died Dec 10th 1876. Aged 54 years
Was Mayor of the Borough of Huntingdon
For the year 1875–6

An obituary to John Ingram was published in the Gardener's Year Book and Almanac in 1878:–

Dec 10 1876 Mr John Ingram of Huntingdon aged 54. Mr Ingram was the head of the old-established nursery long conducted by the family of his uncle, Mr Wood and subsequently carried on very successfully by himself under the name of Wood and Ingram. The year before his death he filled the office of Mayor of Huntingdon.

CHAPTER 5

JOHN WOOD INGRAM CONTINUES THE DIARY

John Wood Ingram continued the diary:–

Calender of Operations
Commencing Jan 1st 1877
John Wood Ingram

General Foreman	J Sims
Outdoor Foreman Home Nursery	Edmund Papworth
Hartford Lane Nursery Foreman	Chas. Papworth
Brampton Foreman	George Warren
Brampton Acting Foreman	Harry Warren
In-door Home Nursery, Acting Foreman	Thomas Clark
Outdoor Home Nursery Acting Foreman	Wm Warren
William Ratchelous	Manager at St Neots Branch
Peter Samuel	Guarnerio Clerk

My father died (as shown at the end of his diary)
On December 10th 1876. Age 54 years.
He left the business to my mother, brother (George Wood Ingram) & myself, & it will still be carried on under the style of Wood & Ingram

Each entry is commenced with 'Sims Calender' and ended with remarks by John Wood Ingram:–

1st January 1877 'Sims Calender'
   First Peach blossom open in Peach House, clearing out and cleaning Tan[1] *pits,*

---
[1] Tan (a bi-product from the tanning industry) was used in hot-bed pits for forcing pineapple plants.

overhauling and rearranging Greenhouse plants, potting Stock plants of Fuchsias for cuttings, Sims round with Mr Protheroe taking valuation.

E Papworth is still ill and has been for some time past with a bad leg. Brian in charge, rubbing through Leek seed in Stokehole, cutting basket sticks in shed. Packing in afternoon.

C Papworth planting Manettii Stocks[2], Warren clearing waste trees and taking up trees for orders. Horses at manure cart.

My own remarks are – Mr Protheroe[3] is valuing nursery stock etc., he commenced Dec 18th 1876 and Sims men cleaning out Stoke hole (Water).

2nd January 77 'Sim's Calender'

Fine day, wind N. looking over Ericas and taking out damp and decayed shoots, repotting Herb. Calceolarias for seed and sale. E Brown trenching, digging etc., packing in afternoon. C P Orders (taking up) only.

Warren, same as yesterday, horses and men at hedge – work in field

My own remarks are – Warren ought to be preparing land for stocks, but cannot on account of the water being so high and the land so wet. Slater and Shepherd at hedge work in the field.

5th January 77 'Sim's Calender'

Repotting Pelargoniums for sale in 5 inch pots. Making room in small houses for geraniums to admit of potting being proceeded with, Sims with Mr Protheroe taking valuation, last day.

Brown tying up Ivies outdoors, emptying cellar and packing in afternoon.

C P planting Manettii Stocks and trenching.

Warren clearing waste trees, trimming Pear and Plum stocks etc, taking up orders.

My own remarks are – Emptying Stoke hole, shifting Ericas from pit to south house. Weather more settled, water 2 feet deep on Brampton Road yesterday. Horses and men at hedge work in field. Slater with Sims and Mr Protheroe.

6th January 77 'Sim's Calender'

Floods at their highest up to this date, 9 inches of water in Stoke hole of high

---

[2] From 1835 onwards Manettii stocks were obtained via Messrs Rivers Nursery in Sawbridgeworth, Hertfordshire from Mr Crivelli in Italy, and were successful as root stock for roses as they seldom produced 'suckers'.

[3] Mr Protheroe (1846–1899) was the son of A. Prothero, Horticultural Auctioneer of Cheapside, London and a committee member of The Nursery and Seed Trade Association Ltd of 30, Wood Street, London, E.C.

level boiler which had to be got out twice during the day. Repotting Pelargoniums for sale, repotted and started Fuchsia for cuttings.

Brown tying up Ivies and packing in afternoon, C P taking up and doing away with Lime stools and preparing Grape vines.

Warren clearing waste trees, cutting hedges, trimming Crab stocks etc, wet day yesterday.

My own remarks are – Weather still wet, Horses and men (Slater and Shepherd included), at hedge work in field and manure cart, Warren trimming stocks budded last summer and carrying away refuse from the same. Sunday a very rough day and a deal of rain.

7th Sunday (see above)

8th January 1877 'Sim's Calender'

Floods somewhat lower today, but still 8 in of water in high level stoke hole. Repotting Pelargoniums etc. Sims went to Brampton to make out list of seedling forest and other trees required to be brought in.

Brown emptying cellar, tying up Ivies, cleaning up frame yard, barrowing manure and potting Xmas trees.

C P planting Mahonias, trenching and trimming, Warren clearing waste trees, trimming Plum and Pear stocks etc.

My own remarks are – I went to London and returned on the evening of the 10th. The remarks above should have been just to the 9th the following are for the 8th. Writing Fisher Holmes Ltd, Stewart and Co., Little & Ballantyne, Laird and Sinclair and Lawsons for samples of seedlings. Have received Hazels and Chestnuts for seed from Jas Dear.

Horses, hedge work and manure cart. Slater working in his shop. Pony taken with stud fever (did not last long).

10th January 77 'Sim's Calender'

Repotting Pelargoniums, cleaning and arranging Stove house plants and Ferns, at Hinchingbrook cutting Laurels to decorate Triumphal Arches for an expected visit of H.R.H.Prince of Wales to Hinchingbrook and Kimbolton Castle. Heavy fog all day, raining very fast now 9.30pm.

E P cutting sticks and cutting Laurels at Hinchingbrook with Sim's men.

C P planting Mahonias and to Godmanchester to plant shrubs.

Warren clearing waste trees and preparing land for Briars etc.

I had no remarks at home, Was in London all day and very wet it was towards evening.

11th January 77 'Sim's Calender'

Decorating Arches with Laurel etc in the town and making wreathing for festoons which was placed on Market Hill.

E P cutting sticks and decorating Arches.

C P decorating Arches.

Warren clearing waste trees and preparing land for briars. Horses at manure cart.

My remarks of no account.

Further decorating of the Triumphal Arches takes place over the next few days:–

15th January (Monday) 77 'Sim's Calender'

Sims and men the same as yesterday until 1 pm. and decorating houses outside with evergreens and festoons of Ivy in the town. The Prince and Princess arrived at about 1.30pm and passed through the town with the hearty greetings of the citizens; a fine day, bright sunshine.

E P same as yesterday up to one o'clock and then joining in the festivities of the day.

C P same as E P

Warren taking up orders and trenching.

My remarks are long – I with the whole staff at Huntingdon and assisted by Mr Ratchelous[4] were at the Triumphal Arches as soon as day light appeared and before, all worked hard and well and got the whole finished in time; never knew men to work better; after they had finished they all went where they liked and I believe enjoyed the holiday very much.

The Prince and Princess passed through the town about 2pm, the Amateur Brass Band was in attendance on the platform of the G. E. R. Station under my direction and had the honour of performing "God Bless The Prince of Wales" and "God save The Queen" before their Royal Highness'. There was an escort of the whole of the A Troop of the Duke of Manchester's 1st Light Horse Volunteers, about 40 men and 2 Officers.

The town was splendidly decorated with 4 Triumphal Arches (by us) and a

---

[4]Mr Ratchelous was later Secretary of the St Neots Chrysanthemum Show and the St Neots Amateur and Cottage Horticultural Society.

large number of Venetian Poles, Festoons, Banners etc. The Mayor of Huntingdon (T J Howson) and the Mayor of Godmanchester (R Bates) had the honour of being presented to their Royal Highness' at the station by the Earl of Sandwich. The Duke of Manchester, one of his sons, and the Hon. Oliver Montagu were present. They (their Royal Highness') lunched at Hinchingbrook and drove from there about 4pm for Kimbolton Castle. Everything passed off first rate.

Was a splendid day.

Horses at coke cart.

John Wood Ingram had only two weeks to prepare for the Royal visit.

On 20th January 1877 a lengthy report of the arrival at Huntingdon Station by the Prince and Princess of Wales on their visit to Hinchingbrooke and Kimbolton Castle, appeared in the Cambridge Chronicle, University Journal and the Isle of Ely and Huntingdon Gazette.

> *'In modern times the ancient and loyal town of Huntingdon has been honoured with three visits from Royalty. The first was on the 28th August 1856, when Her Majesty the Queen passed the Great Northern Railway Station en route for the north, on which occasion the station was gaily decorated. The second visit took place on 4th February 1868, when His Highness the Prince of Wales, unaccompanied by the Princess, proceeded through the town from the Great Eastern Railway Station to Hinchingbrooke, and thence to Kimbolton. The streets on that occasion were 'dressed in flowers and fennel grey'. But the visit of the Prince and Princess of Wales on Monday last far eclipsed either of the former visits in point of decoration and display of loyalty. And the day is one long to be remembered not only in the town of Huntingdon but the county also'.*

The report covers in detail decorations in the town:–

> *'To commence at Bridge Place there was a grand triumphal arch, erected by the committee, clothed with evergreens, and decorated with flags and suitable mottoes, placed over the gate lading to the Great Eastern Railway Station, with garlands and flags extending across the road.*
>
> *The next triumphal arch was erected at Orchard Lane. This was clothed with evergreens; at the summit were placed the initials "A.E." and lower down "God Bless the Prince of Wales". On the other side "A.E."*

and "Albert Edward." These were inscribed in colours on wood. This arch had a very good effect from both ends of the street.

Past the Town Hall and Post Office a grand triumphal arch was also erected by Mr Windover in imitation of grey marble, decked with evergreens, and ornamented with the Royal arms, the Prince's plumes, and emblems of Church and State and the Masonic order. At Mr Windover's establishment a platform was erected for the band in connection with his works, and this body on the arrival of the carriage containing the Prince and Princess, commenced playing. The children belonging to the schools were accommodated with platforms along the route. The bells of both churches rang merry peals during the day.

We may here mention that the public decorations of the town were erected by Mr George Thackeray, builder, Huntingdon and Messrs Wood and Ingram supplied the evergreens'.

18th January 1877 'Sim's Calender'

Propagating Verbenas, making bouquets of flowers for Ladies hair for Kimbolton Castle Ball, potting Tricolor Geraniums for specimens, fertilizing Peach and Nectarine blossom to ensure the fruit setting etc.

E P dressing seeds in shop, sorting Carrots, pruning fruit trees, pumping water from cellar and packing in shed.

C P moving Box and at Trinity Church, Warren taking up orders, trenching, getting Poplar cuttings, barrowing manure, trimming Crab and Plum stocks.

I have no remarks.

19th January 77 'Sim's Calender'

Pruning Grapes in Greenhouse (rather late this year, like to prune about Xmas) Propagating Verbena and other bedding plants.

E P making hot bed, pruning wall trees, turning manure, packing in shed.

C P moving Box, work at Trinity Chapel, orders etc.

Warren taking up orders, trenching and barrowing manure onto land.

My remarks are – Horses at manure cart. Still very wet weather. I have been hunting in pony cart, with Prince of Wales, had a jolly day.

The Cambridge Chronicle also reported that on the 19th January 1877:–

'Yesterday (Friday) the Royal Party attended the meet of the Cambridgeshire Hunt at Gaynes Hall'

20th January 77 'Sim's Calender'

> Propagating bedding plants, attending to the fertilization of peaches and Nectarines which are now in full bloom in bottom house, made floral wreaths and cross for the decoration of Dion Willie Boucicault's grave at Cemetery, and placed them thereon, attending to planting at Trinity Chapel, potted on a few Tricolor Geraniums for large plants.
>
> E P dressing Asparagus beds, pruning wall trees, cleaning in Nursery, Packing in shed.
>
> C P trenching etc., work at Trinity Chapel, taking up orders etc.
>
> Warren taking up orders, clearing waste trees and trenching.
>
> My remarks are – Slater mending sundry lights and pits, Horses at straw and coke cart.

21st January 77 Sunday –

22nd January 77 'Sim's Calender'

> Cleansing Grape vine in greenhouse, washing same with hot water and soft soap to destroy mealy bug; propagating bedding plants, cleaning over Centaureas, and spend a few hours in Peach houses with camel hair brush.
>
> E P turning manure, burning rubbish, cleaning in Nursery, pruning trees on dwelling house and packing in shed.
>
> C P planting shrubs at Mr S Smith's, pruning trees at my house, taking up orders etc.
>
> Warren taking up orders, clearing waste trees, trenching and planting Lilac and Berberis for stools.
>
> My remarks are – Last two nights frosty, samples of seedlings all in, P S G at St Neots going through books with Ratchelous.
>
> I went in the evening via G N R to Retford for Brigg in the morning of the 23rd and from there to Sheffield, looked over Fisher, Holmes and Co's nurseries on the 24th, returning home at night.

26th January 77 'Sim's Calender'

> Potting off Ericas as yesterday, cleaning over store pots cuttings., repotting Gardenias and other (a few) stove plants, cleaning over Centaureas, fertilizing Peaches etc.
>
> E P sorting Potatoes, packing in shed,
>
> C P moving manure, trimming and planting cuttings, earthing up Manettii Stocks etc,

> Warren taking up orders, barrowing manure onto land, trenching. Horses manure cart, clearing waste trees for Betts.
>
> My remarks are – I took Sims to Brampton to make out, with me, special list of surplus trees. P S G sending out seed catalogues. George very busy with seed orders and has been for some time.

27th January 77 'Sim's Calender'

> Potting off Ericas and other greenhouse plants from cutting pots. Put a few Azaleas in the stove to force into bloom, being very short of flowers. Cleaned over Japan Lilies and gave them the first watering to encourage them to start into growth, filled up shelves with centaureas.
>
> E P making hot-bed, potting Irish Ivy, packing in shed.
>
> C P Trimming briars, trenching, stopping gaps in hedge, taking up orders etc.
>
> Warren taking up orders, trenching, clearing waste trees for Betts.
>
> My remarks are – Market Day; again very wet, Warren in hovels part of day, cutting sticks etc, Sims removing Centaureas from Heath House shelves to put on stove.

28th January 77 Sunday

29th January 77 'Sim's Calender'

> A little more time than usual for reporting – had a thorough clean over in the Greenhouse and rearranging the plants, the principal object being to make the most use of the room so much needed at this time of the year; threw away a batch of Libonia floribunda[5] being over and unsold, scarcely worth growing, cut down Eupatorium odoratissimum and placed them under stage in Pelargonium house; placed Ferns and other plants that are not over particular about light, under platform in Greenhouse; cleared south platform for geraniums (which turned out a bad place) and Cyclamen; cleared over and rearranged Erica Wilmoreana in heath house which are just coming nicely into flower, taking care to set the plants that are most forward next to the path, so as to reach them quickly and easily when required; began clearing over and turned round Show Pelargoniums to prevent them getting drawn, washing pots etc.
>
> E P planting Dahlia roots in frame, potting Ivies, packing in shed.

---

[5] Libonia floribunda now called Jacobinia pauciflora is a winter flowering evergreen greenhouse shrub, 2ft high with yellow flowers. The plant was first introduced from Brazil in 1864. Eupatorium odoratissimum now called Eupatorium odoratum is a greenhouse plant introduced from Mexico.

C P moving manure, taking off Nectarine layers, cuttings etc.

Warren taking up Trees for orders, cleaning waste trees for Betts, trenching, steam thrashing (Radish Seed) etc.

My remarks are – Commenced steam thrashing Radish seed "Wet as usual".

30th January 77 'Sim's Calender'

Finished cleaning Erica Wilmoreana, emptied Hunnybuns house for reception of Verbenas, putting Geraniums from there into Greenhouse, filled up Greenhouse with Geranium, Cyclamen, etc., cleaned and turned Pelargoniums, commenced potting of Verbenas into Hunnybuns house and I hope to get a good batch as they are cleaner then they have been for years, which I attribute to the free growth, made the summer previous, when planted on a specially prepared bed, thoroughly manured with rotten manure, and last but not least, ground bone or bone dust, about ½ bush. to 1 pole of land, just pricked in with a fork, then planted the verbenas immediately, they started off into good strong growth and kept clean, and I believe out grew the disease entirely, (hope so). Fertilised and watered Peaches etc., a few set and swelling off.

E P tying Mats, plunging Ivies, dressing Radish seed in Warehouse, Packing in shed, very windy, top of straw stacks blown off.

C P Trimming and planting Ligustrums, moving Box etc.,

Warren taking up orders, clearing waste trees for Betts, and trenching.

My remarks are – went to Ramsey to try and settle claims as compensation for inferior Carrot seed supplied by us to G Rowell, Seedsman, Ramsey and Mr Rose, Boat Inn Ramsey, but could do nothing with them. Rowell having sold his to so many little customers; we had the seed from Hurst and they had not up to that time given us authority to pay anything like the amount claimed; we got home very late, was a beautiful clear frosty night.

1st February 77 'Sim's Calender'

Potted off bedding plants Lobelias into long thumb pots; cleared and turned Tricolor Geraniums, cleared over Herbaceous Calceolarias. Kept strict watch to Peaches as weather is very changeable, and when the fruits are setting an hour's chill would probably destroy the crop, this is I think the most critical time for Early Peaches.

E P Felling Pear trees, dressing Radish seed in shop, turning manure, packing in shed.

C P Moving Roses at Brampton, layering, orders etc.,

Warren Getting up orders, clearing waste trees and thrashing.

J W I's remarks are – Still thrashing Radish Seed. P S Guarnerio in London to see Hurst & Son[6] to get authority to settle the Carrot claims, which he succeeded in doing as far as Mr Rowell's customers go, customer Mr Rose who claims a lot too much.

2nd February 77

Potted off Coleus etc into large thumbs; cleared over Tricolors and Calceolarias (Sim's Calender)

E P Felling Pear trees, dressing Radish seed in shop, measuring ditto for London; packing in shed. C P Tying Roses at Brampton, layering, orders. Warren Getting up orders, thrashing, trenching, clearing waste trees etc.,

6th February 77 'Sim's Calender'

Putting in cuttings of Bedding Plants, cleaning over Variegated, Bronze and Gold Geraniums, attended to Peaches which are setting satisfactorily, but found many small grubs or weevils, which get in the decaying flowers and would prove very destructive if not watered as they bite off the fruit as clean as though it were without a knife, it is very small and very similar (if not the same as) the Rose grub, which all Rosarians know to well.

E P Digging, emptying straw, weighing Bran and Maize, finishing Maize, finishing Herbaceous plants, packing in shed.

C P Tying Roses at Brampton, layering, orders etc.

Warren Getting up orders, trenching, Radish, straw and bringing afterwards to Huntingdon.

7th February 77

Potting off Bedding Plants and a few Zonal Pelargoniums, into 48s[7] for window boxes etc., (Sim's Calender)

E P Emptying dust hole[8] at Mr Wood's houses, carting pots from Station, packing in shed.

C P Tying Roses at Brampton, layering, orders etc.,

Warren Getting up orders, cutting stakes for Briars, barrowing manure,

---

[6] William Hurst (1799–1868) established a famous seed and florist shop at 6 Leadenhall Street in London which was continued by his son William Hurst (1831–1882) at Houndsditch, London. Nathaniel Newman Sherwood (1846–1916) was proprietor of the firm from 1890.

[7] 48s are 5inch pots.

[8] 'Dust hole' is a polite name for an outside toilet, contents were collected as a valuable source of manure.

clearing waste trees, layering Huntingdon Elms.

J W I's remarks – Carling Radish straw to Huntingdon and a Pot cart from station. I W I and P S G at Ramsey succeeded in settling claims for compensation for inferior Carrot seed, amounting to £82 0s 6d

8th February 77

Potting off bedding plants, cleaning over small Ericas, cleaning over and stopping Zonal Geraniums in span roofed Pit, disbudding Peaches and Nectarines, watering the same and looking after the Peach grub. (Sim's Calender)

E P Fetching pots from station and barrowing into Shed, barrowing manure and packing in Shed.

C P Tying Roses at Brampton, layering, orders etc.,

Warren Getting up orders, Radish straw cart, layering Huntingdon Elms and barrowing manure.

J W I's remarks – Slater erecting cart sheds at Brampton, Warren taking up orders and clearing up waste trees, Horses as yesterday..

9th February 77

Sowing Pyrethrum G Feather, Liptospermum, Cinneraria maritime, and C. M. candidissima, new Begonias of sorts, Cobaea scandens, Maurandya[9], Ageratum Imp. Dwf etc., etc.

Cleaning over and stopping Zonal Geraniums in span roofed pit; removing half hardy plants, Veronica, Daphne, Onethera etc., from glass pit on north side of Peach house to temporary pit on south side of do. To get room for potting bedding Calceolarias. Weeding and clearing over tops of Peaches and Nectarines, to prevent soil from becoming sour, disbudding trained trees in Peach house (Sim's Calender)

E P Barrowing flower pots, digging, sowing Hollyhock seed, planting Ranunculus and packing in shed.

C P Tying Roses at Brampton, layering, orders etc.,

Warren Getting up orders, straw cart, barrowing manure and trenching.

J W I's remarks – Slater as yesterday, horses still clearing up Radish straw, manure Cart.

---

[9] Maurandia is a half-hardy climbing perennial with violet-purple flowers, and first introduced in 1796 from Mexico.

14th February 77 'Sim's Calender'

> *Grafting new Roses (Sims went to Peterborough on 12th to buy some Roses to plant out for budding for coming season, bought some good plants 40/- 100), potted Gloxinias and placed in Stove to start into growth potted tuberous varieties of Begonias, potted off a few White Verbenas, sent 10 doz Erica Wilmoreana[10] to Mr T James for sale having a rather strong stock of them, syringed Peaches.*
>
> *E P Clearing square behind greenhouse (north side) packing.*
>
> *C P Planting Roses, trenching, layering etc., at H Lane.*
>
> *Warren Getting up orders, trenching, barrowing manure, layering Limes, Planes and Elms.*
>
> *J W I's remarks – are that he went to Royston after Amen's a/c no success, rode young horse to Brampton.*

24th February 77 'Sim's Calender'

> *Putting in Verbenas and other bedding plant cuttings, repotting Ericas. Sims to Cambridge market with van load of Ericas.*
>
> *E P Making hot bed, turning hot manure, planting Potatoes, sowing radish seed, planting Box edging, packing in shed.*
>
> *C P Trenching, digging, making Pea sticks, sowing peas, cutting in Gooseberries, planting Lilacs, Elder cuttings etc.,*
>
> *Warren Getting up orders, planting Huntingdon Elms and Willow cuttings, planting Apricots and nectarines for training, layering Planes, digging and layering stocks in.*
>
> *J W I's remarks – Up at 5 o'clock in morning to see Sims off to Cambridge market, sent carrier home for first quarter being late gave orders to commence at a quarter to six in future.*

25th February 77 Sunday

26th February 77

> *Putting in cuttings of Bedding Plants, repotting Ericas, disbudding Peach trees and thinning fruit of peaches and nectarines (Sim's Calender)*
>
> *E P Trimming basket sticks, making labels, lining hot beds, chitting Potatoes, packing Carnations in shed.*

---

[10] Erica Wilmoreana is a hybrid which required greenhouse temperatures to produce its red flowers in July. Similar Ericas of this type were obtained from South Africa.

C P Snow. Trenching, making Pea sticks, cutting in Gooseberries, moving Acacias.

Warren Getting up orders, laying stocks in, trenching, planting large Huntingdon Elms.

27th February 77

Putting in Tricolor Geranium cuttings, repotting Ericas, watering Peaches, thinning and disbudding (Sim's Calender)

E P Barrowing manure, propagating Dahlias, clearing Carnation stands, sowing Onion seed, pruning Gooseberries, packing in shed.

C P Barrowing road scrapings on land, making Pea sticks, sowing Cytisus seed of sorts also Spanish Broom, while do, and Laburnum, trenching.

Warren Getting up orders, barrowing manure, trenching, clearing waste trees, horses manure cart parson's Field.

J W I's remarks – Very bad weather with a lot of snow and wet, just a little frost last night and snowing fast this morning. Cow should have calved on 23rd so is much over her time.

28th February 77 'Sim's Calender'

Putting in cuttings of Tricolor Geraniums, repotting Ericas, watering peaches etc.,

E P Trenching, barrowing manure, chopping stakes, making labels for Brampton.

C P Barrowing manure, making Pea sticks, sawing wood for making number sticks, frosty.

Warren Cutting Osiers, barrowing, repairing

Here the Diary ended, without stating why John Wood Ingram no longer continued to record the daily workings of his nursery.

What is known is that he was a committee member of the Nursery and Seed Trade Association Ltd of 30, Wood Street, Cheapside, London E.C., incorporated in 1877. John Wood Ingram had been invited to join the Association's committee and was now mixing in elite horticultural company, as only owners of the most important nurseries in the country were elected to its first committee.

The
Nursery and Seed Trade Association
Ltd
30, Wood Street, Cheapside, London, E.C.
Incorporated 1877

President:
Mr N. N. Sherwood (Hurst and Son), 152, Houndsditch, E C

Treasurer:
Mr W. J. Nutting (Nutting and Sons)

Trustees:
Mr T. A. Dickson, Mr J. Hayes,
Mr Harry J. Veitch

Committee:

Barr, Peter	Hayes, J.	Simpson, H.
Baker, W. Y.	Ingram, J. Wood	Turner, Harry
Bunyard, George	Jeffries, W. J.	Veitch, Harry J.
Cutbush, Herbert	Laing, John	Wood, Mr
Dickson, T. A.	May, E. H.	Watkins, Mr
Fell, Francis	Paul, William	Williams, H.
Harrison, J.	Protheroe, Mr	Wynne, B.
	Rivers, T. F.	

Solicitor:
Mr Charles Butcher, 30 Wood Street, Cheapside. E.C.

Bankers:
The London Joint Stock Bank, 5, Princess Street, E.C.

Secretary:
Mr G. Worrell

The President, Mr Nathaniel N Sherwood later became Master of the Gardener's Company from 1896 to 1898. He was awarded the Victoria Medal for Horticulture in 1897. This prestigious award, conferred by the Royal Horticultural Society, was established in 1897 in perpetual remembrance of Her Majesty Queen Victoria's glorious reign to enable the RHS Council to confer conspicuous honour on those British Horticulturalists resident in the United Kingdom. It is limited to 63 recipients in memory of the full number of years of her reign. The Treasurer, Mr William J. Nutting was the proprietor of the famous seed firm, Nutting and Son, Southwark Street,

London. T. A. Dickson, a trustee, was a florist of Centre Row, Covent Garden, London. Mr Harry J. Veitch, son of James Veitch, was admitted into partnership in the Veitch firm in 1865.

Of the committee members, Peter Barr was a Florist with Sugden at Covent Garden and a specialist in Narcissus. George Bunyard was a fruit grower at the Royal Nurseries, The Triangle, Maidstone, Kent and was awarded the VMH. John Laing took over the London branch of Stanstead Park Nursery in 1875. He hybridised tuberous Begonias and was awarded the VMH. William Paul founded the Royal Nurseries at Waltham Cross 1860 and specialised in Roses. He became a Fellow of the Linnean Society in 1875 and was awarded the VMH. Mr William Protheroe was a Horticultural auctioneer at Cheapside London 1883. Mr T. Francis Rivers (1831–1899) succeeded his father Thomas as manager of the nursery at Sawbridgeworth, Hertfordshire specialising in Fruit and Roses. He was awarded the VMH. Mr Harry Turner was nurseryman at the Royal Nurseries, Slough, Buckinghamshire, and was awarded the VMH. Mr Brian Wynne was on the Editorial Staff of the Gardeners' Chronicle 1868 and was Editor of Gardening World until 1895. The above members of the committee were awarded the VMH Medal in the same year, 1897.

The objects of the Association were:–

'To protect the business of Nurserymen, Florists and Seedsmen in the United Kingdom and abroad.

To collect and disseminate information beneficial to Members of the Association and establishment of unity amongst the Trades.

Speedy and economical collection of debts due to Members.

Investigation and arrangement of Bankruptcies and Assignments.

Making trade enquiries, and giving information generally.

One of the special benefits derived from connection with this Association is that its Members afford to each other, through the Secretary, mutual private information as to the financial position and character of and the extent of credit which may be safely given to old or intending customers.

These objectives show the concerns of the leading nursery firms of the time.

CHAPTER 6

THE NURSERY EXPANDS 1880–1903

The second half of the 19th century had seen a rapid expansion of affluent families; this new social class made up the growing ranks of customers for whom nurseries strove to produce exotic plants for their gardens and glasshouses. Cactus, orchids, ferns and exotic fruit were required by every gardener to show they could compete with the large established landowners. Vying also for their custom were the fruit importers. English table apple crops were passed over in favour of the bushels of cheap attractive, tasteless 'North American' apples which arrived on our quaysides and swiftly appeared on sale in large towns. Imports quadrupled between 1875 and 1879. Garden Journals of the 1880s reported 'go where you will American apples are in the fruit shop windows the unattractive crab-like produce of the home grown orchards have been driven out by the cherry bright, clear skins of the red Baldwins and Northern Spy, not to mention the Newtown Pippins'.

Estate owners were still able to satisfy their own needs but as enthusiasts, patriots and farmers they were as much concerned as anyone over the threat to their fruit industry. British Agriculture had gone into a severe depression in the late 1870s and it was to fruit – and apples in particular – that farmers looked for their future success. In 1883 the National Apple Congress was held in the Great Vinery of the Chiswick Gardens of the Royal Horticultural Society, following a 'fruit crusade' organised by head gardeners, farmers, nurserymen and market gardeners. Its aim was to modernise old orchards, guide new fruit growers, beat the 'Yankies' and persuade fruiterers and their customers to buy English apples before it was too late. Confusion over identities was resolved and competitive selections for the best cooker and desert apple were arranged. This event culminated with a triumphant display of the diversity of apples grown throughout the country. Visitors marvelled at 10,500 separate dishes of apples, grouped by county, and representing 236 different exhibitors and over 1,500 varieties. '500 visitors attended each day, and the Congress had to be kept open an extra week to accommodate all those who wanted to see it'.

Wood & Ingram, not wishing to be left behind, started expanding their range of apple trees for sale. James Wood had already propagated an apple in 1790 and sent it out under the name of 'Wood's Huntingdon', having obtained seed from a Golden Pippin from Court of Wick, near Yatton in Somerset. It was widely grown in 19th century gardens and in the West Country was said to withstand the 'most severe blasts form the

Welsh Mountains'. This apple is still available today from specialist nurseries under the name of 'Court of Wick'. Wood & Ingram introduced three other apples which all date from 1883. They are listed in *The Fruit Manual, A Guide to The Fruits and Fruit Trees of Great Britain*, Thomas Hogg, 1884 and *The Book of Apples*. Joan Morgan, and Alison Richards for the Brogdale Horticultural Trust, 1993.

Thomas Hogg recorded the following:–

> 'Huntingdon Codlin' – Fruit, odorous, large, three inches wide, round and prominently ribbed on the sides. Skin greasy to handle, deep yellow. Flesh, tender, mildly acid, with a pleasant perfume.
>
> An early cooking apple; ripe in August and September. The tree is a great bearer, and is well suited for orcharding for market.
>
> It was sent out by Messrs. Wood & Ingram, of Huntingdon.
>
> 'Murfitt's Seedling' – Fruit, large, three inches wide, round and depressed, rather angular in outline. Skin, very greasy to handle, green, becoming yellowish towards ripening; on the sun side it has a dull brown blush, and the surface is strewed with large russet dots. Flesh, tender, crisp, and very juicy, with a fine brisk flavour.
>
> A fine large apple for culinary use; in use from October till Christmas.
>
> I received it from Wood & Ingram, of Huntingdon.
>
> 'Woodley's Favourite' – Fruit, medium sized, three inches wide, bluntly angular.
>
> Skin, rather greasy when handled, deep yellow, and with a faint blush of crimson where exposed to the sun. Flesh, yellowish, tender, juicy, and with a pleasant mild acidity.
>
> An excellent cooking apple; in use from October to Christmas.
>
> Sent me by Messrs. Wood & Ingram, of Huntingdon.

Kelly's Directory of Huntingdon in 1885 included the following entry about the Nursery:–

> 'Wood and Ingram's nurseries in St Germain Street and the adjoining village of Brampton and at St Neots are about 100 acres in extent, and contain an immense stock of fruit and forest trees, ornamental trees and shrubs, evergreens, roses, stove and greenhouse plants of the choicest kinds, the market for which has to be found not merely in this and surrounding counties, but in nearly all parts of the world: they were established 150 years ago by a Mr Wood of the same family who raised the celebrated Huntingdon Elm: in addition to their large

nursery business, this firm has an extensive agricultural and horticultural seed trade, and has erected a range of warehouses for its development'.

By 1885 Wood & Ingram had sold the Hartford Lane Nursery in Huntingdon, now occupied by a new development of houses and two new roads named Wood Street and Ingram Street.

John Ingram had noted in his Diary for 18th October 1859 that he was preparing a nursery catalogue. But the earliest surviving catalogue of Nursery Stock, dated 1887, is now deposited in the RHS Lindley Library. On the front cover is the Seal of Huntingdon 'SIGILLVM COMMVNITAS DE HVNTIRISOVNE 1628' and there are statements that the nursery was patronised by H.R.H. The Prince of Wales, they were Horticultural Valuers, and were established 'a century and a half'. It is unusual to find a Nursery catalogue which incorporated the local town's seal. John Wood Ingram was a Councillor of Huntingdon in 1885, and probably presumed he had the right to use the seal on his catalogues.

The format of earlier 19th century catalogues always started with a list of seeds and vegetables followed by fruit trees. Although Wood & Ingram's 1887 catalogue did not include seeds, it started with 16 pages of various fruit trees and filled 41 pages covering 14 sections:–

ESTABLISHED A CENTURY AND A HALF
Patronised by H.R.H. The Prince of Wales.
1887-88
NURSERY STOCK
Fruit Trees, Forest Trees
Hardy Coniferous and Taxaceous Plants
Evergreens, Ornamental Trees & Shrubs
Hardy Climbers Roses etc
WOOD & INGRAM
THE NURSERIES, HUNTINGDON
Horticultural Valuers

'FRUIT TREES'

'Special quotations for large quantities, on application'.

Listed are 63 Dessert varieties of Apples and 85 Kitchen varieties of Apples, including the 'Huntingdon Codlin' and 'Murfitt's Seedling'. The list also included 'Lady Sandwich' now no longer available, 'Histon Favourite' raised by John Chivers of Histon, Cambridge, and 'Radford Beauty', a Nottinghamshire raised apple which was planted extensively in Cambridgeshire orchards during the 1930s.

Standard trees	18s. per doz, 125s. per 100
Half-Standards 3 to 4ft stems	12s. per doz, 90s. per 100
Dwarf fan-trained for espalier	24s per doz
Pyramids on Crab stock	18s per doz
Pyramids in a bearing state	2s.6d to 5s.0d each

The nursery offered 12 varieties of Apricot trees, 27 varieties of Cherries, 23 varieties of Currants, 63 varieties of Gooseberries, 13 varieties of Grapes, 17 varieties of Nectarines, 31 varieties of Peaches, 86 varieties of Pears, including the variety 'Swan's Egg' which James Wood had sold to Mr Jackson of Godmanchester in November 1770, 50 varieties of Plums, and 13 varieties of Strawberries. 16 pages of the catalogue were needed to list their complete range and the final page lists the 'Proper Distances for Planting Fruit Trees' – standards for orchards needed to be 20 to 24 feet apart, Pyramids for apples, Pears, Plums and Cherries needed to be 6 to 8 feet apart.

'PLANTS SUITABLE FOR GAME COVERTS, UNDERWOOD AND HEDGES'

Berberis aquifolium was listed at 10/6 per 100 plants, American Arborvitae for 6/- per dozen and 40/- per 100, British Oak 2ft–3ft for 5/- per 100 and 40/- per 1,000, Mirabolen Plum 1ft – 2ft (for hedges) for 5/- per 100 and 40/- per 1000. White Thorn or Quick 2 years' seedling were 10/6 per 1,000 and 2 years' transplanted were 15/- per 1,000. Extra strong plants of White Thorn, available for gapping, were priced 4/- per 100. Also included in this list were Beech, Blackthorn, Box, Spanish Chestnut, Elm, Gorse, Hazel, Portugal laurel, Larch, Privet and Snowberry.

'FOREST TREES'

These included British Oak – 4ft to 5ft cost £20.00 per hundred. Wood & Ingram obviously wanted to cash in on their own introduction and priced their Huntingdon Elm, (from layers) – 6ft to 7ft trees cost 6s 0d per dozen and 45s.0d per hundred, selected specimens 14ft to 16 ft were individually priced between 3s 6d to 10s 6d. John Wood Ingram had recorded in his Diary that on 24th February 1877 they were planting Huntingdon Elms out on the nursery. Balsam poplars – 3 to 4ft were 4/- a dozen. (6d each in 1776 when sent to Colonel Clark, Godmanchester but in 1887 cost 4d each.)

Listed amongst Firs, Limes, Poplars, Sycamores is the Huntingdon Elm which the Nursery had been selling for several years for a higher price than English Elms:–

Elm, Huntingdon, from layers-
6ft to 7ft	per doz 6/-, 45/- per 100
7ft to 8ft	per doz 8/-, 50/- per 100
8ft to 10ft	per doz 10/-, 75/- per 100
10ft to 12ft	per doz 15/-
12ft to 14ft	per doz 30/-
14ft to 16ft	each 3/6d
Selected specimens	each 3/6 to 10/6

Elm, Narrow-leaved English:–
2 to 3ft	3/6 per 100, 30/- per 1000
4ft to 5ft	5/0 per 100, 45/- per 1000
5ft to 6ft	6/- per 100
14ft to 16ft	each 2/6 to 3/6
Selected specimens	Each 3/6 to 10/6

'HARDY CONIFEROUS AND TAXACEOUS PLANTS'

The list included Araucaria, Cryptomeria, Retinospora, Taxodium, Wellingtonia as well as Abies, Cedrus, Cupressus, Picea, Pinus, Taxus, Thuja and Thujopsis. Prices per plant ranged from 6d to 10s.6d. except for a single specimen of *Taxus baccata elegantissima* standard which cost 21s 0d.

'EVERGREENS'

The list included Azalea, Bamboos, *Eugenia ugni* the 'Chilean Guava' introduced in 1844, *Griselinia littoralis* a New Zealand hedging plant suitable for maritime exposures introduced c1850, and an extensive range of Hollies.

'DECIDUOUS ORNAMENTAL TREES AND SHRUBS'

Five pages were required to list the 'Deciduous Ornamental Trees and Shrubs' offered by the nursery. Included were a wide range of plants from all over the world:– *Amorpha fruticosa* 'False Indigo' from S. United States, *Calycanthus carolina* 'Allspice' from North America, *Robinia hispida* 'Rose Acacia' from the S E United States, *Catalpa kaempferi (ovata)* from China introduced in 1849, *Caragana chamlagu (sinica)* from China, *Gymnocladus canadensis (dioicus)* the 'Kentucky Coffee Tree', *Magnolia acuminata* 'Cucumber Tree' from the Eastern United States sent originally by John Bartram to Peter Collinson, *Myrica cerifera* 'Wax Myrtle' Eastern United States, *Prunus* 'Pissardii' discovered before 1880 by Monsieur Pissard, gardener to the Shah of Persia, and *Halesia carolina* the 'Snowdrop Tree' named after Dr. Stephen Hales, a pioneer physiologist, and member of Corpus Christi College, Cambridge (1671–1761). Most trees were available for under 3s 0d, but a *Sophora japonica pendula* the 'Japanese Pagoda Tree was priced at 7s.6d per plant.

Wood & Ingram listed under this category a selection of Elms:–

Ulmus campestris folius aureus crispa	1s 6d
Ulmus Cornish	1s 6d
Ulmus crispa 7ft to 8ft	1s 0d
Ulmus Dampieri Wredei aurea a beautiful new golden variety	2s 0d
Ulmus gigantic	1s 0d to 1s 6d
Ulmus Hertfordshire (true broad-leaved English) 8ft to 9ft	1s 0d
Ulmus medio-variegatus	1s 6d
Ulmus Montana pendula (weeping standards)	2s 6d to 3s 6d
Ulmus paradox	1s 0d to 3s 6d
Ulmus purpled leaved	1s 0d to 2s 6d
Ulmus suberosa pendula (weeping cork-barked)	3s 6d
Ulmus variegated	1s 6d
Ulmus weeping standards	2s 6d to 3s 6d

'HARDY CLIMBERS'

The list included *Ampelopsis 'Veitchii'*, *the smallest leaved variety and the most useful and beautiful, requires no nailing* priced at 1s 6d each or 12s 0d per dozen. This plant is now named *Parthenocissus tricuspidata 'Veitchii'* and was introduced by J. G. Veitch from Japan in 1862, and was once known as the 'Boston Ivy'. *Magnolia grandiflora 'Exonensis'* is a magnificent evergreen wall shrub with fragrant creamy-white flowers in late summer appearing when the shrub is at an early age, and is the most expensive plant in this list costing between 5s 0d and 7s. 6d. A single *Passiflora caerulea* (Passion Flower) cost 1s 0d to 1s 6d, compared with the cost of 1s 0d for a Passion Flower for Mr Jackson in November 1768, over 120 years before.

'CLEMATIS'

The nursery offered 65 hybrids. Prices ranged from 1s 0d to 2s 6d for a single clematis which included *Clematis 'Jackmanii'* priced at 1s 6d, or 12s 0d per dozen. *Clematis 'Beauty of Worcester'*, *quite a novelty, said to produce both double and single flowers on the same plant for its earlier bloom; lovely blueish violet shade, with prominent pure white stamens, which greatly add to its beauty, very robust,* priced at 2s 6d per plant.

Wood & Ingram obtained new hybrids from clematis breeders and raised large quantities on their nursery. Included were *Clematis 'Madame Grange'* raised in 1875 by T. H. L. Grange, Orleans France; *Clematis 'The President'* raised in 1876 by Charles Noble, Sunningdale; Thomas Crisp & Son raised *Clematis 'Gipsy Queen'* in 1877 and

Clematis 'Jackmanii superba' in 1880. *Clematis 'Beauty of Worcester'* was raised in 1886 by Richard Smith of Worcester.

'ROSES'

A total of 295 named roses covers 7 pages of the catalogue. Many roses listed were obtained from established growers on the continent. In France rose breeders had their own nurseries, mostly near Lyons in the Rhone valley.

Prices varied:–

Hybrid Perpetuals	1s 6d for a standard, 105s per 100
	1s 3d for half-standards
	9d for dwarfs 45s per 100
Hybrid Perpetuals established in Pots for Forcing	2s 6d to 5s 0d each
A Select selection can be supplied ON OWN ROOTS	1s 0d each; 9s 0d per dozen.
Tea–Scented roses	2s 0d for a standard, 21s 0d per dozen
	1s 6d for half-standards 12s 0d per dozen
Bourbons	1s 6d for a standard
	1s 0d for dwarfs
Noisettes	2s 0d each
	1s 6d for dwarfs
Tea-Scented & Niosette	1s 6d to 5s 0d each
Moss roses	1s 6d for a standard
Climbing roses	9d each, 6s 0d per doz
Banksian roses	1s 6d each

'HARDY PERENNIAL HERBACEOUS, BULBOUS AND ALPINE PLANTS'

The complete list was available in a separate catalogue (this catalogue no longer survives), and plants were priced:–

100 plants in 100 varieties	£1 10s 0d
50 plants in 50 varieties	15s 0d
100 plants in 100 superior varieties	£2 10s 0d
50 plants in 50 superior varieties	£1 5s 0d
W & I's selection	per dozen 4s, 6s, 9s, and 12s
50 good dwarf varieties, suitable for rockwork,	15s to 20s per dozen, or per dozen 4s to 6s.

'HERBS'

The list priced herbs at 3s to 4s per dozen, 20s to 25s per 100 assorted.

'MISCELLANEOUS ROOTS &c'

Asparagus Giant	5s 0d per 100, 3 years old
Sea Kale	8s 0d per 100, 2 years old
Globe Artichokes	2s 0d per peck
Rhubarb	9d to 1s each, 6s to 9s per dozen

'FOR EDGING'

Dwarf Box, (1 yard estimated to plant 3 yards) .... 6d per yard
Thrift .... 4d per yard

'SUNDRIES'

Then followed four pages which list *Wooden Labels; Flower Sticks*; a range of Sundries included *Appleby's Registered Fumigators, Aimes' Horticultural Manure (highly recommended), Fowler's Insecticide, Gishurstine for dressing boots, Large Archangel Mats, Tobacco Paper, Pooley's Tobacco Powder, Wolff's Solid Ink Pencils and Flower Pots and Pans.* Finally, under Garden & Horticultural requisites are *Saynor, Cooke and Ridal's Pruning & Budding Knives* illustrated by a pull-out page of garden tools; and an illustration of *Yeats' Zinc labels* which were claimed to be – *'Indestructible, being Frost and Wet Proof* they *cannot Break or Rot,* they are *Cheap,* and will *bend to any angle for reading'.*

Wood & Ingram kept handwritten reference books or Stock Books listing the complete range of plants they had acquired. In them they kept an up to date list of every variety of plant. The nursery's earliest Stock Book that still exists is dated 1890 and contained over 400 pages, listing every plant Wood & Ingram held on their various nurseries. Every plant in a particular group was assigned a number throughout the stock book. The lists were not alphabetical but numerical, whereas in the catalogue the plants were listed alphabetically. Amongst the extensive list of Apples were *'Woodley's Favourite', 'Merfit's Seedlin', 'Huntingdon Codlin'* the nursery's own introductions; *'Lady Sandwich', 'Squire Fellowes', 'Lord Burleigh'* named after local patrons; *'Brampton Seedling', 'Cambridge Pippin', 'Histon Favorite'* and *'Emneth Early'* given local place names. This list was added to when the nursery obtained further apple trees. *'Bismark' (Veitch & Son '89), 'Beaumann's Reinette' (ex G.Bunyard & Co. 1893), 'September Beauty' (ex Laxton Jan 1887), 'Bramley Seedling' (Rivers 1890) , 'Beauty of Bath' (Cooling & Sons 1890).* The total number of apple varieties grown in the nursery at this time was 216.

89 Plums, 37 Cherries, 142 Pears (still including 'Swan's Egg'), 25 Grapes, 59 Peaches, 39 Nectarines, 23 Apricots, 12 Quinces, 11 Figs, and 4 Walnuts are included in the Stock Book.

On page 265 is the list of 18 elms Wood & Ingram keep for propagating purposes on their nursery:–

The Elm (Ulmus)
1. Campestris cornubiemnsis(Cornish)(Wheatleys)
2. Campestris folius variegates
3. Campestris Hertfordshire

4. Campestris Huntingdon
5. montana pendula (Weeping)
6. montana fastigiata (Paradox)
7. montana crispa (Curled leaved)
8. gigantic
9. purple-leaved
10. Dampierii Wredei aura
11. viminalis variegata
12. Narrow-leaved English (Campestris)
13. Medis variegata
14. Campestris folius auriis
15. elegantissima pendula
16. suberoas pendula (Cork ?) (Weeping ex Girton Coll. 1887)
17 Weeping Camperdown (ex Cobbett 1891)
18. Montana (Scotch. True Wych)

Over 500 roses are listed taking up 48 pages in the Stock Book, divided into groups. Only just over a half of these were included in the catalogue. At the end of this Stock Book are two pages devoted to Strawberries, the only group of plants assessed by the nursery with the following comments:–

Inspection 1890
STRAWBERRY
Dr. Hogg.............................very large, next in flavour to B Queen
John Ruskin 1890 ....very early, but not a fair trial
V Hericoat de Thury ....great cropper, early, small, good preserving
Myatt's Eleanor...................fine, conical full flared, but acid, very prolific and late
Elton Pine...........................good flavour round, late, strong grower
Noble (Laxtons)..................very early, rich, very prolific
Commander (do)..............fine flavour, large
King of the Earlies ....good colour, very rich, early, nice shape
A.F.Barron ....large, first class, mid-season, fine colour
Waterloo.............................large, very dark colour, late
All-Round (Atherton) ....medium size, gold colour & cropper, fine
President ....one of the best, great cropper
Jas. Veitch Handsome ......good cropper & flavour
Admiral Dundas.................out of date
Black Prince ....do
Sir Chas. Napier.................fine flavour, prolific, good colour
Keen's Seedling..................a good old round, very sweet
British Queen ....Still the best flavoured
Sir Joseph Paxton ....very good & prolific, fine flavour, large

Further catalogues were printed. Wood & Ingram published their 'Spring Catalogue of

Plants, for 1896' which listed Bedding Plants – 96 Geraniums which included 'Huntingdonian', an introduction of Wood & Ingram, *'the finest white for bedding'*, 43 Pelargoniums, 31 Cannas, 14 Verbenas, 165 Dahlias, 25 Fuchsias, 22 Penstemons, 56 Paeonies. Plus a large range of Stove and Greenhouse Plants including *'Rhododendron Lady Alice Fitzwilliam with white scented flowers 2s 6d – 3s 6d each'* which was named after the 4th daughter of the 6th Earl Fitzwilliam, who resided at Wentworth Woodhouse in Yorkshire and died in 1922. This pale yellow Rhododendron was awarded a First Class Certificate (FCC) by the Royal Horticultural Society when it was first exhibited in 1881 by Fisher, Son & Sibray, who were based at the Handsworth Nurseries, Sheffield. Specimens of this highly scented plant are still grown today in the conservatory at Milton Park near Peterborough.

The back page of this catalogue informed the reader that the nursery offered the following:–

STREET AND ROAD AVENUES
Handsome Trees Supplied and Planted by Contract or Otherwise

BULB CATALOGUE
Including Dutch and other Bulbs

SEED CATALOGUE
Including
Garden, Farm and Flower Seeds, Seed Potatoes, etc

PLANTS, SHRUBS & TREES
in pots for furnishing
Wedding and other Boquets

FUNERAL WREATHS & CROSSES
And cut flowers on the shortest notice
New Grounds laid out and planted.
(estimates given and contracts undertaken)

EXPERIENCED GARDENERS RECOMMENDED

There followed a further catalogue for:–

CARNATIONS, PICOTEES & PINKS

Offered for sale at
"THE NURSERIES,"
HUNTINGDON

A Branch at St NEOTS. A Branch at ST IVES, open on Mondays only.
And Attendance at CORN EXCHANGE, BEDFORD, on Saturdays.
AUTUMN 1897 & SPRING 1898
N.B. – Carnations, Picotees and Pinks are ready for delivery from October to March, inclusive, but the Autumn Season is recommended.

In the section of Clove, Self and Fancy Carnations, seven introductions by Wood & Ingram were listed:–

'Captain Selah', deep rose, of finest form 1s 6d,	per plant
'Geisha', scarlet suffused with salmon, very pretty and distinct 1s 6d,	" "
'King of the Scarlets' very vivid scarlet self 6d,	" "
'Royal Record' delicate soft rose, one of the most beautiful...........1s 6d,	" "
'Surprise' bright scarlet, a very full and fine flower, does not burst its calyx, ...1s 6d,	" "
'Sweet Marie' spotted, salmon-pink, quite distinct 1s 6d,	" "
'The Shah' cherry, splashed with bright scarlet, fine........................1s 0d	" "

By the end of the 19th century Wood & Ingram had established a nursery which ranked as one of the most important in the country. To have established such an extensive range of plants available for sale was a great achievement. As a result of astute planning and foresight, the family business expanded at a great speed between 1850 and 1900 and achieved such a good reputation that orders flowed in to their nursery. To have such a lengthy stock book of the plants held on their nursery and propagated at such a rate, and to be able to offer trees, shrubs, roses for sale at quantities sometimes reaching over a thousand required a reliable and well trained staff. Both the Huntingdon and Brampton nursery sites were stocked with plants and maintained to a high standard. Everything looked in good order and the family could look forward to moving successfully into the next century.

CHAPTER 7

WOOD & INGRAM UNDER NEW OWNERSHIP

At the height of their reputation, in 1903 surprisingly the nursery changed hands but still traded under the name of Wood & Ingram. The new owner was John Edward Perkins, who came from an established family nursery in Northampton. His grandfather, Thomas Perkins had started a nursery and seed firm at the beginning of the 19th century. His shop was in the centre of the town and his nursery was to the east along the Billing Road near St Andrew's Hospital. The family resided in a fine house nearby called 'The Priory', which still stands today.

John E. Perkins was a gentleman of substantial means and sent his five sons to be educated at private schools to enable them to prosper in the business world. His astute business sense and his shrewd cautiousness in the study of stocks and shares in which he speculated rarely led him astray. He was often in demand as a judge at agricultural and horticultural shows. The acquisition of Wood & Ingram gave John E. Perkins a suitable thriving business to oversee, whilst his eldest son Henry was introduced to nursery management.

Mr Perkins senior built a sizeable house for himself on the Buckden Road Nursery site in Brampton, appropriately named 'Nursery House'. Meanwhile his son managed the 'Old Nurseries' site in Huntingdon.

The continuity of the firm is shown in a further stock book produced on 29th August 1908, the front page of which reads:–

Wood & Ingram Huntingdon, J. E. Perkins (Sole Proprieter) of The Old Nurseries.

The layout of this stock book of 270 pages was identical to the earlier one produced by Wood & Ingram. There are gaps in the lists where a plant has been discontinued and additions are listed in copper-plate handwriting:– 17 species of conifer, 34 tree species, 80 shrub species, 216 varieties of apples, 88 varieties of plum, 142 varieties of pear and 329 varieties of hybrid perpetual roses, together with 161 scented tea roses. This extensive list of roses was one of the largest held by a nursery of this date. The stock book also listed 120 named clematis plants. These were kept at the Huntingdon Nursery site where two glasshouses could each hold 5,000 new plants. Within the next few years Wood & Ingram were to become the largest supplier of clematis in the country, their telegraphic address being 'CLEMATIS' HUNTINGDON. The majority of their other plants were kept at the Brampton Nursery.

In 1909 John E. Perkins obtained 200 acres along the Thrapston Road in the village of Brampton for growing roses to meet the new demand. Here he erected two cottages for his staff and outbuildings for nursery needs. These included a long brick barn for packing the large number of orders, stabling for 4 horses and a bothy for his employees. A large bell was kept to summon his workforce for a midday meal break from the nursery fields. Two men were employed solely to look after the horses and it was their responsibility to lead the horses when they hoed between the rows of newly budded rose bushes.

During this period of peaceful prosperity, locally as elsewhere, new gardens were being laid out and older ones expanded. On the high ground overlooking the Great Ouse as it flowed from Godmanchester towards St Ives, the garden at Houghton Grange was extended by a further 6 acres towards the river frontage between 1897 and 1905. The new garden at Houghton Grange was laid out in 1905 with topiary and several circular flower beds. To the west of Huntingdon, Howard Coote, the new owner of Great Stukely Hall, had formalised the terrace and ha-ha overlooking the park. Upon his return from a successful visit to Japan, the Earl of Sandwich had embarked on laying out a new Japanese garden at Hinchingbrooke. Wood & Ingram had, by the turn of the century, an extensive range of Japanese plants in the nursery for him to choose from.

The expansion of the nursery and the high standard attained by the new owners of Wood & Ingram were recorded in a contemporary account in the Huntingdon Post of 17th June 1912 by a local reporter:–

HUNTINGDON INDUSTRIES

MESSRS WOOD AND INGRAM

NURSERYMEN

HOW A FAMOUS TREE ORIGINATED

("Hunts. Post" Special)

The firm of Messrs. Wood and Ingram, nurserymen, of Huntingdon, Brampton and St. Neots, ranks among the oldest in Huntingdonshire, dating back to 1740, when the founder John Wood, originally no doubt, a market gardener, commenced business in a small way in St Germain's Street, Huntingdon. Out of that has grown a firm whose name is known throughout the British Isles as specialists in many varieties of trees and plants. The firm's telegraphic address is "Clematis, Huntingdon" and as growers of that beautiful climbing flower, Messrs Wood and Ingram stand unrivalled in the trade, their output of this plant amounting to many thousand a year.

The nursery at Huntingdon is in itself a model of perfection, being under the personal control of Mr Henry Perkins, son of the sole proprietor, Mr John E. Perkins, of Northampton, who acquired the business then, as now, conducted under the style of Wood and Ingram, ten years ago. Since then the nursery at Brampton has been greatly extended, that in the Thrapston Road having been added three years ago. Here have been erected modern cottages, and a full set of buildings to meet the requirements of the trade. On this portion many acres are devoted to the growing of garden and farm seeds, one of the firm's specialities being short-topped Kohl Rabi. The aim of the firm is "good quality," and they do not lay themselves out for a common cheap trade.

It was our pleasant privilege the other day to have a look over the nursery at Huntingdon, where there was every indication of a busy season, this being the particular time of the year when bedding plants are being sent out by tens of thousands. For this purpose alone Messrs Wood and Ingram have stacked on the premises a mountain of orange boxes and wooden cases, in which the plants are sent by rail, and not infrequently by sea.

In the matter of buildings there is an extensive range of stores for seed purposes, and garden requisites, with a retail department and a counting house. In a chat with Mr Henry Perkins, some interesting particulars concerning the history of the firm were gleaned.

One of the most cherished relics is the original business book, kept by the founder, John Wood. This contains a curious mixture of business and domestic affairs, but among the customers whose names are recorded are many whose descendants still maintain their confidence in the firm. Spelling was not one of John's accomplishments, but the names are easily recognised under such style as Lord Sandwig, Lrd Ludlo, Squire Geare, Curnell Clark, John Langle, Mr Cater (Huntingdon) Squir Jackson, Squir Thornel, Duke of Manchester, Mr Maul, Bishop of Lincoln, Earl of Hardwick etc.

It was this John Wood whose name has been handed down to posterity as the originator of the Huntingdon Elm, a well-known species, which is to be seen quoted in most nurserymen's catalogues at the present day. This elm, which was raised from seed, collected in the neighbourhood by John Wood, at Huntingdon, about 1746, is described in a technical work as "by far the most vigorous growing amongst all the elms propagated in British nurseries."

At the Old Nurseries, at Huntingdon, Messrs Wood and Ingram have an extensive range of glass, and employ a good number of hands throughout the year in propagating plants, and in the various stages of re-potting. Our first introduction was to one of these propagating 'pits', entirely devoted to clematis of which Messrs Wood and Ingram are the largest growers in the world. Here were the plants in their first stage. In another house they had been re-potted and staked, no less than five thousand being staged in one group.

Chief among the varieties are "Lady Northcliffe" a beautiful deep lavender tinted bright blue, with purple bar and white stamens, which gained an award of merit at the Royal Horticultural Show in 1906; "Papa Christen" a delicate mauve with broad band of deep carmine down the centre of each petal; Montana rubens, a fine new pink from China; "Mrs Quilter" a fine pure white; "Lord Neville" a bright blue; "Lasurstern" a deep blue with very large flowers, and regarded as one of the finest new clematis introduced for many years. The firm catalogues over sixty varieties of this showy climber, which does so well on verandahs, arches, trellis work and walls.

Bedding geraniums are another leading speciality at the Old Nurseries, and of these tens of thousands were to be seen, although early orders had commenced to make an inroad into the stock. We gathered that one of the most popular varieties for bedding purposes is "Paul Crampel", a very brilliant crimson scarlet, which stands the rain well and does not burn in the sun. "Henry Jacoby" is a beautiful deep crimson; "Queen of the Belgians" a very free flowering white; "West Brighton Gem" one of the best; "Mrs Robert Cannell" a popular salmon with a constitution like "Paul Crampel"; and many others might also be named.

Messrs Wood & Ingram claim to be the largest growers of foliage geranium bedding plants in the country, some of the newer introductions being simply gorgeous in colour, the most brilliant of the golden tri-colours including "Mr Henry Cox". "Masterpiece" is another good specimen, being very much the same colour, but not quite so brilliant; "Lass O'Gowrie" a silver tricolour; "Black Douglas" a bronze, "Mrs Pollock" an old favourite; "Sir John Holder" with silver edge; "Snow Queen" a new silver-edged double white-flowering variety; "Sophia Dumaresque" and many others of the best types.

Other effective bedding plants largely grown here, include "Salvia Bavaria" with bright scarlet flowers, that stand the weather well; heliotropes, summer bedding chrysanthemums, very useful for cut *flowers and table decorations, lemon scented verbenas, border carnations (another of the firm's specialities) etc. In one house over two thousand pots of solanums were staged, Messrs Wood and Ingram holding the finest strain in this country of this plant which is so very popular at Christmas time when the berries are a brilliant red.*

More space than we have at command might be devoted to the roses, which are cultivated in tens of thousands at Brampton. At the home nurseries just now, special care is being given to a new sort named "Sunburst", considered to be one of the best deep orange varieties sent out. At present this rose is being grown for stock buds.

One greenhouse was devoted to new varieties of roses. Among the new bedding roses are "Annie Maria Jacobs", "Countess of Shaftesbury", "Dad Sterling", "Edward Mawley", "Leslie Holland", "Rayon d'Or" etc.

A feature of the Huntingdon Nursery is the attention which is being given to hardy herbaceous plants suitable for borders and rock gardens, and this makes a most interesting department. Herbaceous plants have become extremely popular in recent years, and with a judicious choice, flowers may be seen in bloom nearly the whole of the year. Those of Alpine origin are particularly fascinating. In this section of the nursery Aubretia, Campanula, Iberis, Paeonies, Saxifrages and Thalictrums were specially noteworthy.

In the above we have only dealt with a few of the more striking features and with regard to the St Neots and Brampton branches have merely to add that at St Neots chiefly climbers were grown. At their Brampton nurseries a first class stock of fruit trees, conifers, deciduous and evergreen, ornamental, and flowering trees and shrubs is maintained, such things as quicks, larch, and other forest trees being grown very largely. Whilst giving personal attention to the large and growing business, Mr Perkins finds time to serve as a member of the Huntingdon Town Council, and he was also for several years honorary Secretary of the Huntingdon Horticultural Society. In connection with the Huntingdonshire Agricultural Society, Mr Perkins yearly undertakes the duties of poultry steward. – A. H. G.

Such was the extent of the Nursery in 1912. The above report indicates that here was a business which was well established and able to supply large orders of plants. Messrs John and Henry Perkins, father and son, had successfully raised the profile of their nursery which was involved in propagation of thousands of clematis, bedding plants and roses. This is revealed in the surviving ledgers which were needed to record the nursery's organisation until the business was sold in 1950. These unique ledgers, dating from 1916 to 1950, describe in great detail the wide range of activities which the office staff dealt with.

Each *Order Ledger* has an alphabetical index of customers and their addresses and then, on every page, a copy of the order. The nursery's trade had so increased by this time that the office required two such ledgers each year to record their orders, each ledger containing one thousand orders. Orders for plants received and correspondence from customers have not survived. Only copies of orders and personally addressed letters of reply remain. Each copy of the order is in copper plate handwriting. The cost and the number of plants are entered and the means of transport via private railway companies is added. Each order is numbered and the *Order Ledger* was given a code. Under the direction of Mr John Perkins, and later of his son Henry, the office staff were able to keep accurate copies of all orders for ease of reference. On average the nursery sent out two thousand orders every year, relying greatly on the efficient railway system of the time.

The 71 *Order Books* that survive today, which contain over 71,000 orders, provide evidence of the extensive range of plants sent out by Wood & Ingram. Fourteen *Letter Ledgers* also survive, some with 1,000 replies to customers' letters in one ledger and some with more than one reply on a page. There also remain six large *Day Books*, each recording when customers' bills were paid during one year; five Petty Ledgers, each giving 3,000 orders; and two *Cash Books* each listing 1000 orders when a customer's order was paid. Three *Wages Ledgers* reveal the names of employees and their wage, each ledger listing wages paid over a period of six years. A large *Bought Ledger* lists every payment for goods the nursery required over a period of three years and three *Sales Invoice Ledgers* record annually many single orders for wreaths and vegetable seeds. Finally, there remain two large Ledgers; one listing the nursery's clients, their head gardener, estate manager, their head forester and the catalogues they were each sent; the other a lengthy list of their clients in alphabetical order.

Included in the list of their customers were some who had bought plants when the nursery started in the eighteenth century – the Earl of Sandwich, Mr Thornhill, the Wimpole Estate now owned by the Robarts family who also owned Landhydrock in Cornwall, the Pym family at Hazells Hall, Sandy, and the Astells at Everton. The advent of the railway now enabled orders to be sent all over the country, or shipped to Northern Ireland, the Low Countries and France. The nursery very often had to apologise to many customers if the railways were not up to scratch:–

Mr Lee
The Gardens, Langham House,
Oakham, Rutland

7 October 1919

Dear Mr Lee,

We regret, owing to the railway strike, that our Mr Wyatt was prevented from calling upon you on Tuesday last as arranged.

We hope, however to have that pleasure on Tuesday next, that the favour of your kind order will be esteemed.

Yours faithfully,
Wood & Ingram

Other commercial nurseries were sent large orders of plants, especially roses. The aristocracy of Great Britain realised that Wood & Ingram could supply at reasonable cost a wide range of plants for their parks and gardens. Local parks and private gardens in Huntingdon and Cambridge, as well as Cambridge Colleges, were supplied with trees and shrubs. Wealthy new bankers, who could afford to live in new houses designed by Sir Edwin Lutyens, ordered plants from Wood & Ingram, as did Newmarket horse trainers. The Royal Parks in the capital and New Towns to the north of London ordered their trees from the Nursery. Such was the extent of their business that Mr J. Perkins employed several commercial travellers to call regularly on head gardeners of large estates to make sure that his nursery received their orders for his plants.

The earliest Wood & Ingram Ledger to survive is dated 1911. It is a large, heavy leather-bound ledger labelled 'Retail' and was obtained from E. H. Greenfield, 256 Strand, London W.C.. On the first page is a 'Retail' list giving dates, lists and numbers of catalogues the nursery posted to its clients. The remaining 300 pages of this ledger are filled with an alphabetical list of customers, their gardeners, estate managers and foresters from 1911 until 1918, indicating which catalogues had been sent.

This particular 1911 Retail Ledger provides interesting information – Lady Battersea resided at The Pleasaunce, Overstrand, Cromer and from 1915–1918 her gardener was Mr H. Naylor; nearby resided Miss M. J. Barclay at Herne Close, Cromer and from 1914–1918, her gardener was Mr W. Lloyd; F. H. Barclay Esq resided at The Warren, Cromer and his gardener from 1915–1918 was Mr W. Daniels; His Grace the Duke of Bedford resided at Woburn Abbey, Woburn, Bedfordshire and from 1915–1918 his gardener was Mr F. Palmer, who lived at Froxfield Gardens, Woburn; his Forester from 1911–1918 was Mr F. Mitchell at Park Farm Office, Woburn; and a Mr Hall at the same Office was sent catalogues from 1912–1918. Sir Herbert Samuel Leon, Bart resided at Bletchley Park, Buckinghamshire and from 1915–1918 his gardener was Mr G. Cooper who left in 1918.

In 1911 the nursery printed 517 Bulb catalogues on 15th August and 1,551 Tree and Shrub catalogues on 24th October. During 1912 the nursery printed 144 Wholesale Seed catalogues on 1st January, 1,652 Seed catalogues on 5th January, 7,668 Bulb catalogues on 29th August and 1,786 Tree and Shrub catalogues on 14th October. During 1913 no catalogues were printed.

Towards the end of 1914 Wood & Ingram printed 199 Wholesale Seed catalogues, 2,050 Seed catalogues, 1,007 Bulb catalogues and 1,875 Retail Tree and Shrub catalogues. Surprisingly the Nursery had to request their printers for further catalogues in 1914. 197 more Wholesale Seed catalogues and 1,997 more Seed catalogues were printed for posting early in 1915. On the 13th October 1915 the nursery printed 1,986 Retail Tree and Shrub catalogues, 1,831 Retail Seed catalogues and 160 Wholesale catalogues. No new catalogues were printed or posted during 1916, but on 9th January 1917 1,798 Seed catalogues were posted.

Carbon copies survive of typed letters which were dictated by J. E. Perkins, each with his polite replies to customers. Copies of his letters to other nurseries for restocking plants, to firms for restocking tools and horticultural materials, to gardeners seeking employment in the trade and reminders for late payment also survive. His letters replied to enquiries for prizes for local horticultural shows and for Christmas Trees for local hospital wards. Upon request, employees from the nursery were sent to tend graves in local churchyards, plant orders for customers and provide floral arrangements for local Council events. All reveal Mr Perkins's astute business acumen to run an efficient and profitable nursery.

Often customers were late in paying; some thought they did not have to pay their account for two years or more and were politely reminded by a letter requesting immediate settlement of accounts. Mr J. Perkins obviously made use of the Nursery and Seed Association that Mr John Wood Ingram had been involved in setting up in 1877. The following letter is typical of many requesting payment:–

> Mrs Meade　　　　　　　　　　　　　　　　　　17 September 1919
> St Neots
>
> Madam,
>
> We thank you for your cheque received through our St Neots branch. This has been duly placed to your credit and we have pleasure in enclosing a receipt.
>
> We note your remarks, but we would respectively point out that this account has been running for nearly two-and-a-half years, the first item being for goods supplied on July 4th 1917 since which date the account has been rendered to you no fewer than 14 times. In the face of these facts we think you must agree that we have been very lenient in our terms of credit.
>
> We are, Madam, your obedient Servants
> Wood & Ingram

The office had to keep a tight control on the receipt of orders, when orders were despatched and when payment was received. With an annual turnover of two thousand orders requiring several thousands of plants for despatch by rail in the planting season, the nursery had to be set up to establish sufficient plants in advance to meet the incoming orders. All this relied on organised forward planning. Nothing could be more embarrassing than not having sufficient numbers of a plant in fashion, because if Wood & Ingram could not supply the plant the customer would order elsewhere, and the nursery's reputation would suffer. The nursery was organised in such a way as to meet the demand for plants when they were ordered and had to have sufficient space on the nursery to grow thousands of one particular plant. During 1919 the Duke of Rutland at Belvoir Castle was sent 62,000 trees for £314 15s 3d, an order which gives some indication of the scale of organisation required, the efficiency of the nursery and the space required to produce such an order immediately after the First World War.

During the First World War, the nursery obtained Nos 2 & 3, George Street, Huntingdon, an attractive green and cream tiled double-fronted property, which provided office space for its headquarters and a shop for selling garden seeds. Mr J Perkins established this office to look after all aspects of the nursery business and, in order to keep an accurate record of orders, a fool-proof system of book-keeping was established and orders were cross-referenced from one ledger to another. Clerks were employed to make copper plate written copies of all orders, but letters to clients, other nurseries, and Government departments were dictated and always typed, most of which have survived. Soon after Mr John Perkins had set up his efficient office the bureaucracy associated with the First World War increased. Paper for printing catalogues was suddenly in short supply, men working on the nursery were required for the Army, forest trees had still to be planted for props in the trenches if there were to be another future war, and transport of orders abroad ceased. During this period his son Henry Perkins found time to serve on the Town Council of Huntingdon, and he became Mayor in 1917–18. Henry was Honorary Secretary of the Huntingdon Horticultural Society for several years and undertook duties of the poultry show at the Huntingdon Agricultural Society's annual show. With the help of his father the nursery was kept open during the First World War.

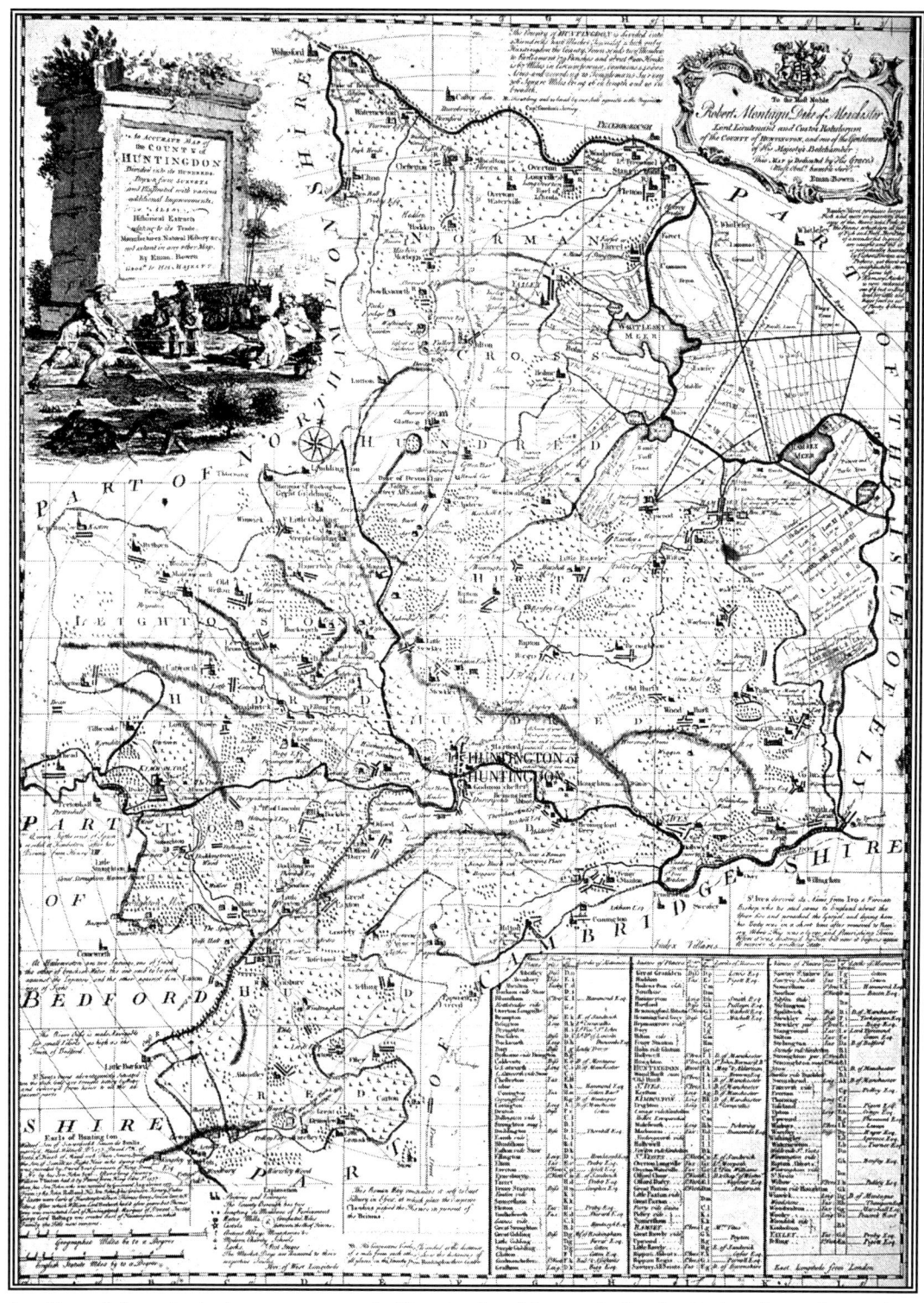

1   Map of the principal estate owners in Huntingdonshire made for the Duke of Manchester by Bowen c1750

			s	d
Exspences for y[e] year 1742				
Jan[y] 7	for Beureing my Old wife	3	3	
7	for a new coat making	0	4	6
	for a pint of Oile	0	0	4
4	for a par of Shous Soaling	0	2	
16	for caring my Sester things	0	0	
28	for a Shoue Brosh	0	0	1
feb 18	for helf a Quier of paper	0	0	4
23	for a Letter from my Brother Sam W	0	0	4
ap 28	for a par of gloves	0	1	0
ap 23	for a par of Shous Soling	0	2	0
Do	for a par of new Shous	0	5	0
may 11	for a par of Shart B[u]t[ons]	0	0	
June 21	for a par of Sharts Sleev Butons			
	a par of Sides garters	0	0	
July 4	for making 6 Shorts	0	2	
	Sharts	2	10	

2 List of James Wood's expenses 1742 in his Account Ledger

A. of Geven money for ye yea

		L	s	D
Decem 1748				
31	mr hodson	0	1	0
Jan 15	mr metchel	0	0	6
16	mess nalellon of westb	0	0	6
31	mr Thong	0	1	0
28	mr Oukle	0	1	0
feb 2, 5	mr Lucus	0	0	6
aprib	a canton with mr williams	0	0	2.2
18	mess williams	0	1	0
19	mess Nalellon of westb & har company	0	2	0
19	mr Tomes	0	1	0
22	mr Blin	0	0	6
27	mes Blan company for low young woman	0	0	6
27		0	0	6
may 1	mr Bli	0	1	0
9	mr picks company			
13	mr 71 6452	0	1	0
14	mr gick 4791	0	1	0

3 List of visitors to James Wood's Nursery in his Account Ledger

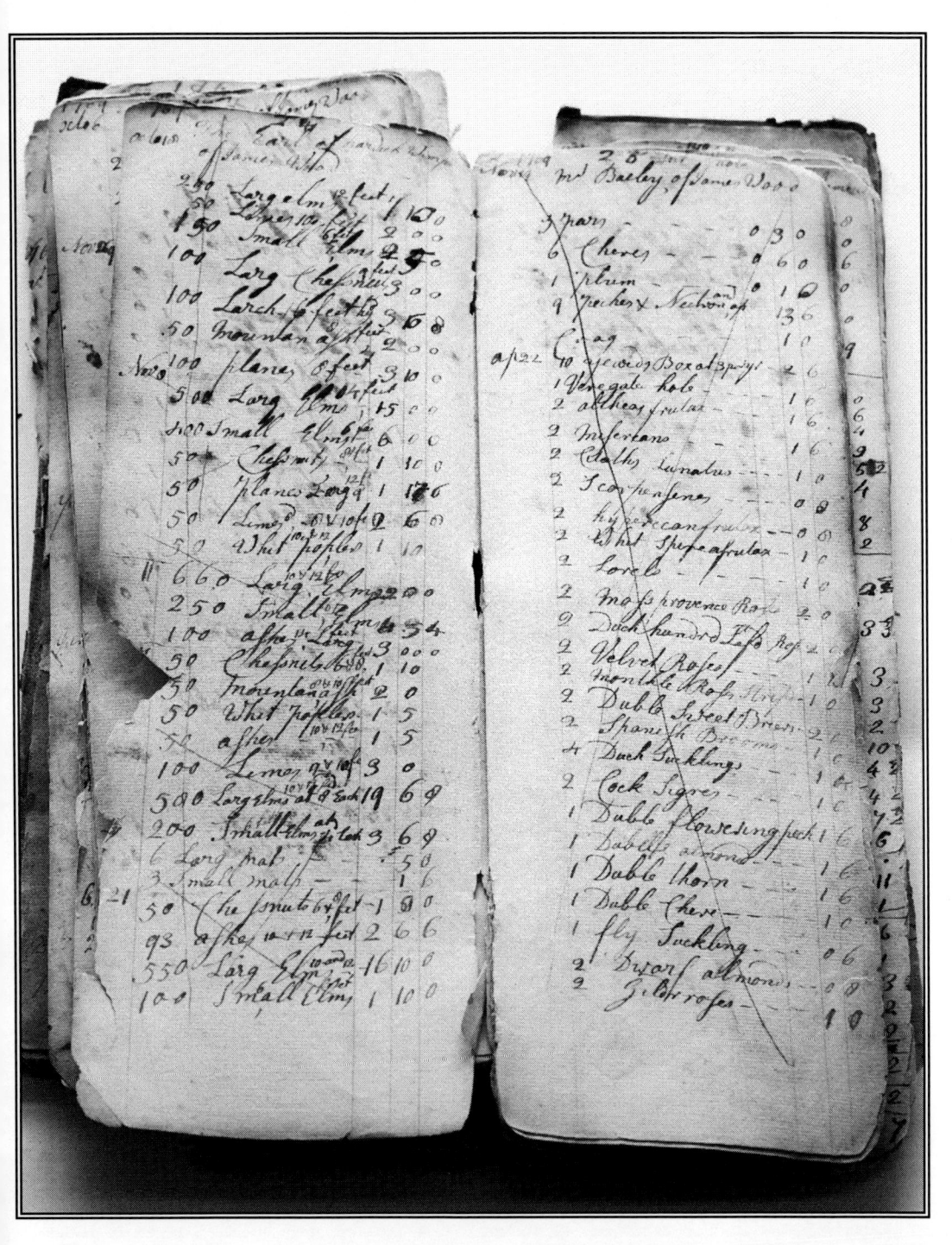

4   Two pages from James Wood's Account Ledger: left hand side shows the Earl of Hardwicke's order.

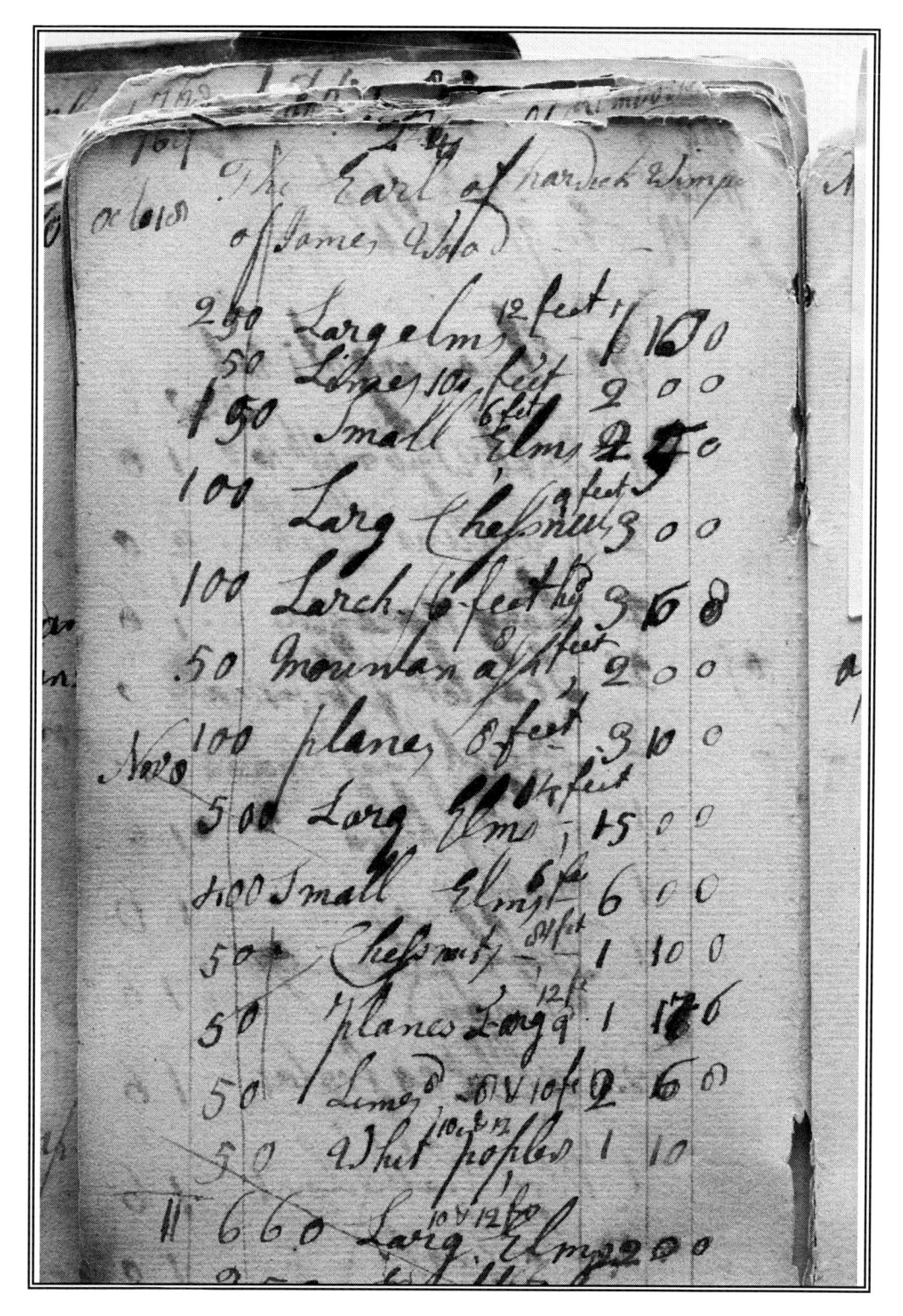

5   The Earl of Hardwicke's order for trees at Wimpole for planting the North Park.

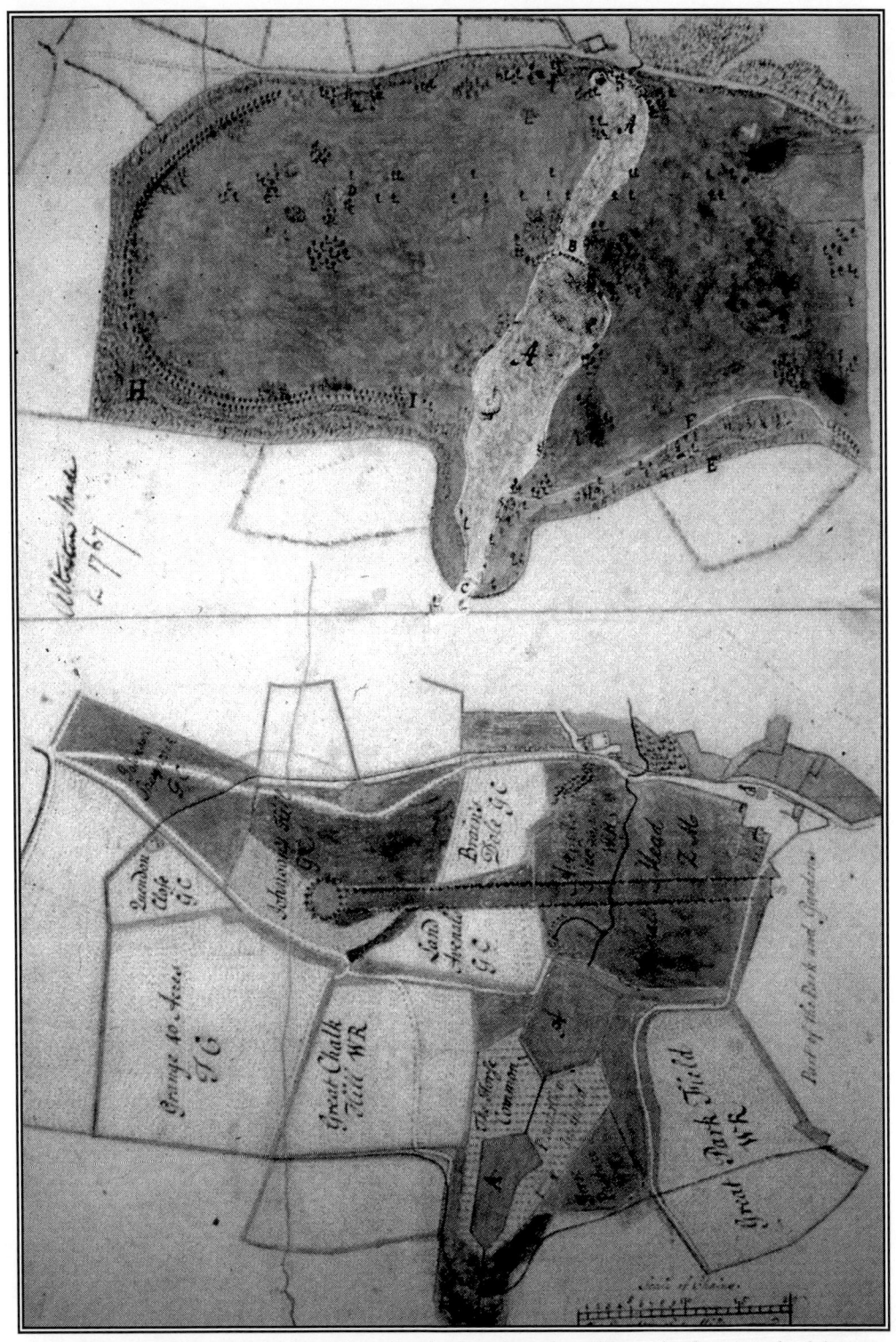

6   Anonymous 'Before' and 'After' plans for the North Park at Wimpole showing the lakes designed by Lancelot Brown.

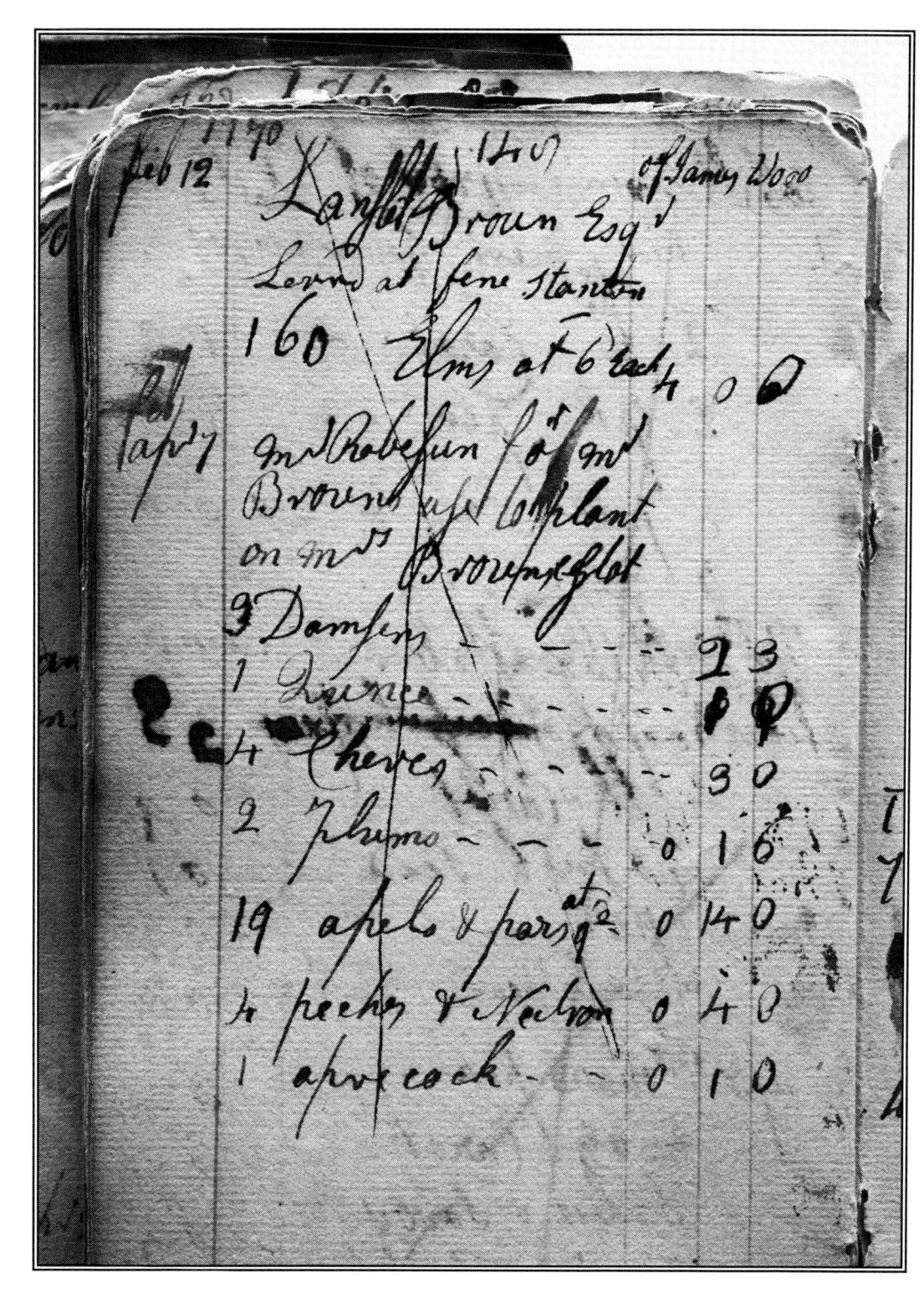

7   Lancelot 'Capability' Brown's order in James Wood's Account Ledger

8a First page of John Ingram's Diary, Monday 6th July 1857.

8b John Wood Ingram records the death of his father in the Diary.

9 Late 19th century grafting shed at Wood & Ingram's Nursery in Brampton. Now in premises of River Lane Nursery, Brampton.

73

11th Nov. 18

Mr William Bonsall.
            The Nurseries. Harrogate. Yorks.

500	Dwf. H.T. Roses in variety	7/.	17	10	.
50	Clg Roses Excelsa	1/.	2	10	
25	" " Lady Gay	1/.	1	5	
12	" " Gloire de Dijon			12	
25	" " Dorothy Perkins		1	5	.
50	Std Apples No D. varieties	2/6	6	5	.
50	Pyd " " "	2/6	6	5	.
12	" Plums " "	2/6	1	10	.
12	" Pears " "	2/6	1	10	.
100	Std & H/Std Plums Victoria		10	.	.
	Packing			6	.
		£	48	18	.

per G.N.R goods OR in through truck

10 Wood & Ingram order to William Bonsall, The Nurseries, Harrogate, Yorks, dated 11th November 1918. The only order sent out by the Nursery on Armistice Day of the First World War.

374

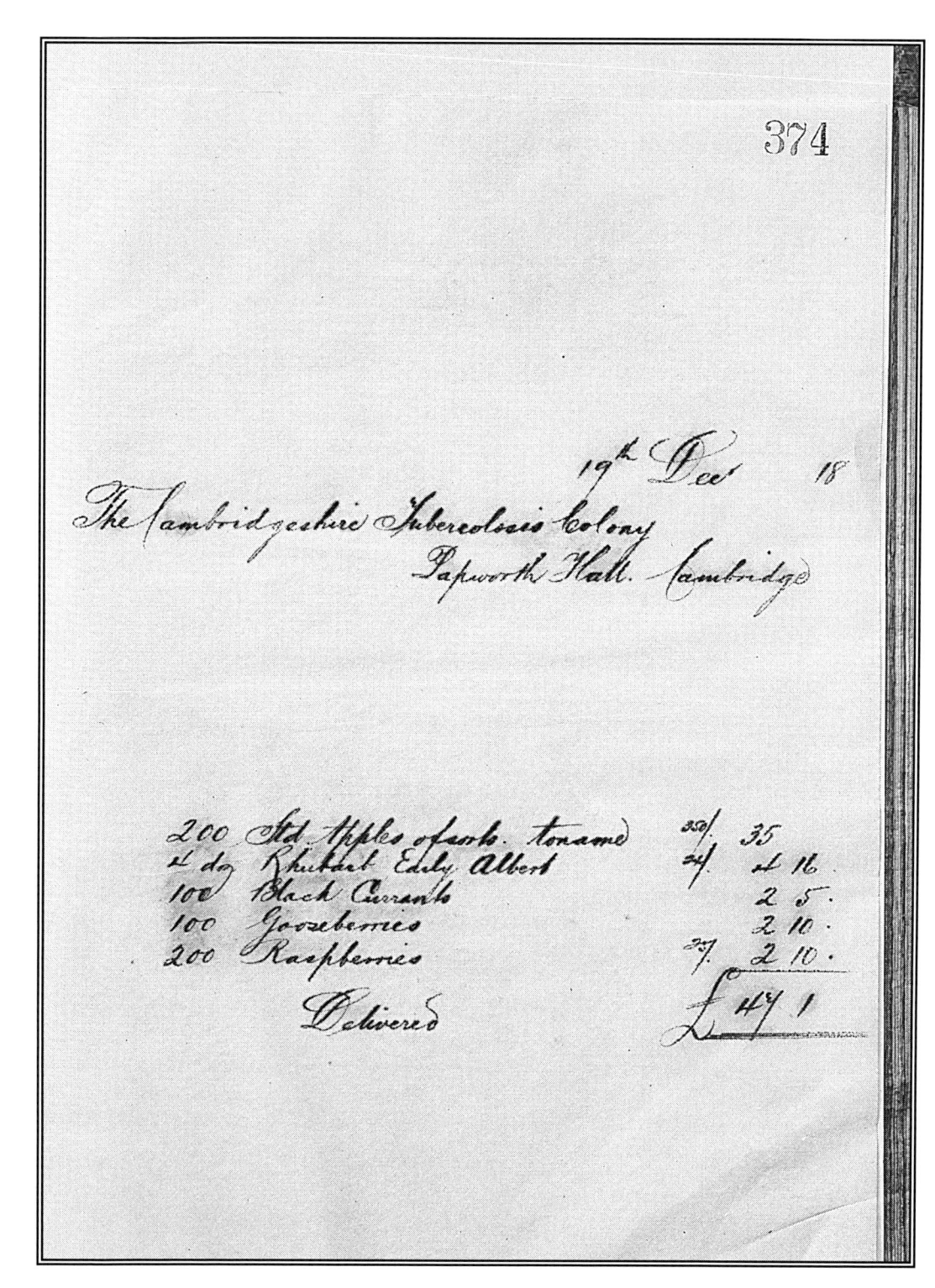

19th Dec 18

The Cambridgeshire Tuberculosis Colony
Papworth Hall. Cambridge

200	Std. Apples of sorts. to name	35/	35
1 doz	Rhubarb Early Albert	24/	1 16
100	Black Currants		2 5
100	Gooseberries		2 10
200	Raspberries	27/	2 10

Delivered £47 1

11 Wood & Ingram order to The Cambridgeshire Tuberculosis Colony, Papworth Hall, Cambridgeshire, dated 19th December 1918 for fruit trees and soft fruit.

15th Jany 19

His Grace The Duke of Rutland.
Belvoir Castle. Grantham.

15,000	Quick	50/	37	10
5,000	Native Larch, twice transpl	60/	15	.
2,000	Black Italian Poplar	7/.	7	.
1,000	Ash		3	
1,000	Spruce		5	.
18	English Yews. Selected Specimens	5/	3	15
12	Std Scarlet Oak do	12/6	7	10
6	Std Cherry Double White do	7/6	2	5
6	Std " James H. Veitch do	7/6	2	5
6	Std Copper Beech do	11/	3	3
6	Std Double Scarlet Thorns do	7/6	2	5
12	Buddleia variabilis in variety	3/	1	10
6	Broom, White Portugal		12	.
20	Azalea Mollis		3	10
3	Spiraea multiflora arguta		10	6
3	" Wilsonii		10	6
3	" Veitchii		10	6
3	" prunifolia fl pl		7	6
3	" Margaritae		10	
3	" paniculata rosea		10	
	Carried forward		97	5

12 Wood & Ingram part order to The Duke of Rutland, Belvoir Castle, Grantham, dated 15th January 1919 for large quantities of hedging and trees.

991

His Majesty's Office of Works, Buckingham Palace
per ... Hay Esq. Hyde Park, London

16th March 31

2	Garrya elliptica	1	1
12	Ceanothus in choice variety, to name	2	2
12	Buddleias in choice variety, to name	1	10
8	Jasminum officinalis major	1	4
8	Jasminum nudiflorum	1	4
8	Jasminum Stephanense	1	8
6	Azara microphylla	1	10
3	Kerria japonica		7/6
1	Myrtus		7/6
12	Escallonias in choice variety, to name	2	2
6	Forsythia spectabilis	2	5
12	Pyracanthus in choice variety, to name	3	
6	Cydonia japonica in choice variety, to name	1	1
12	Loniceras (climbing) in choice variety, to name	1	16
6	Cotoneasters in choice variety, to name	1	1
1	Viburnum rhytidophyllum		10/6
3	Shandosia undulata		15
3	Shandosia undulata fructo luteo		15
1	Solanum jasminoides		3/6
	Carried forward	24	3

13 Wood & Ingram part order to Buckingham Palace, London, dated 16th March 1931 for a collection of flowering shrubs.

1st December 1941.

Mrs Boston.
    The Old Manor. Hemingford Grey.

3 Amygdalus nana		15	-
6 Viburnum Carlesii	2	5	-
1 Cydonia Moerloesii		5	-
1 : Cardinalis		3	6
3 Std Cerasus avium	1	11	6
3 : : Hizakura	1	11	6
1 : : Gyoiko		12	6
1 Cornus Nuttallii to follow	-	-	-
1 Picea concolor	1	5	-
1 Amygdalus Georgica		7	6
1 Pourthaea Villosa		7	6
1 Std. Mountain Ash	1	2	6
3 Forsythia spectabilis		7	6
1 Stewartia pseudo-camellia	-	-	-
2 Spiraea Thunbergii to follow		15	-
3 : arguta multiflora		10	6
1 Pyrus Theifera		3	6
1 Bushel Peat		4	6
1 Bag. Balling material			
	£ 12	15	-

d/d.

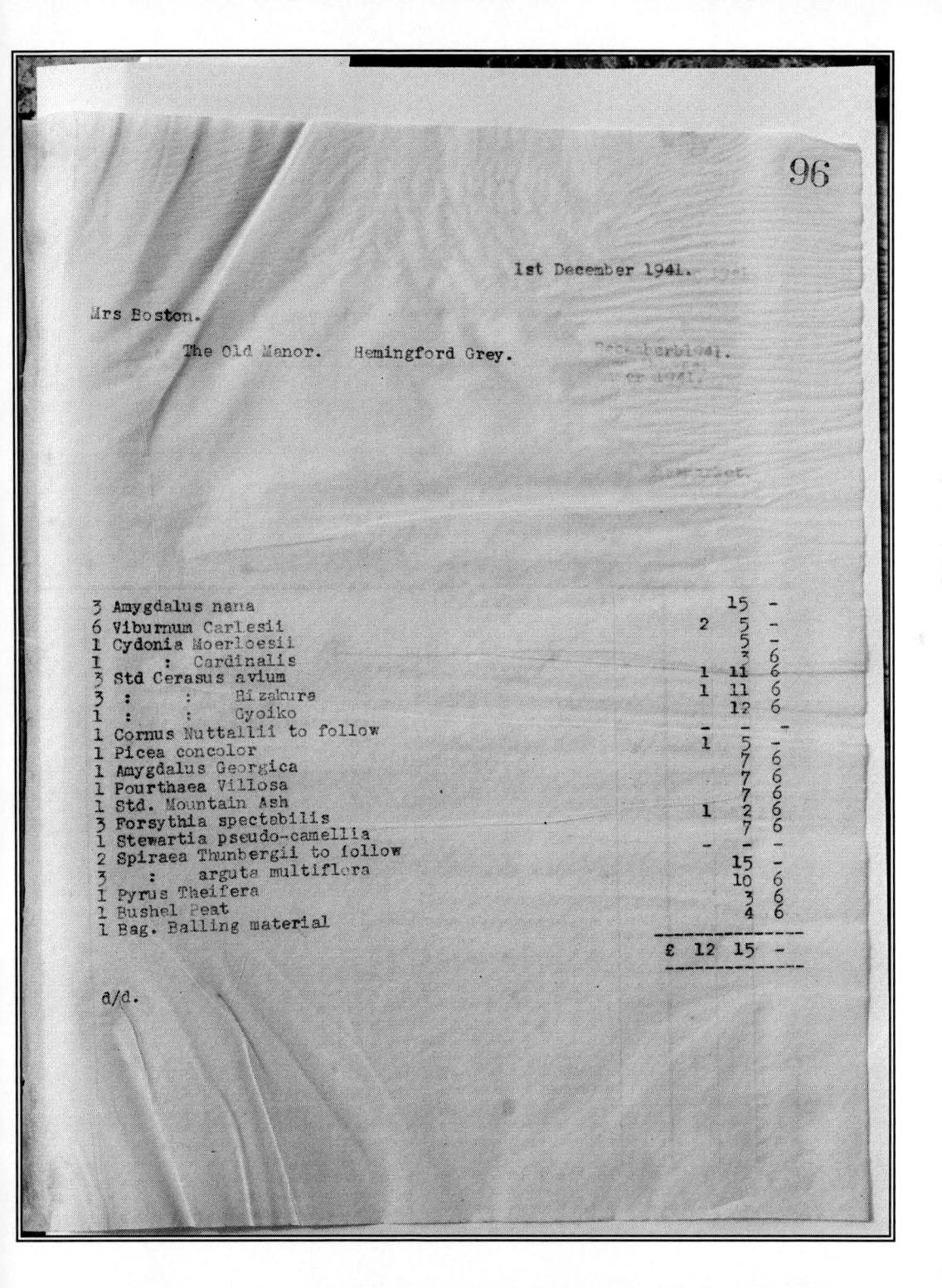

14 Wood & Ingram order to Mrs Lucy Boston, The Manor, Hemingford Grey, Cambridgeshire, dated 1st December 1941. A Second World War order for flowering shrubs.

15 Wood & Ingram's Residence and part of the Three-Storey Warehouse and House at their St Germain Street Nursery, Huntingdon. (Lot 2 of the 1950 Sale Particulars.)

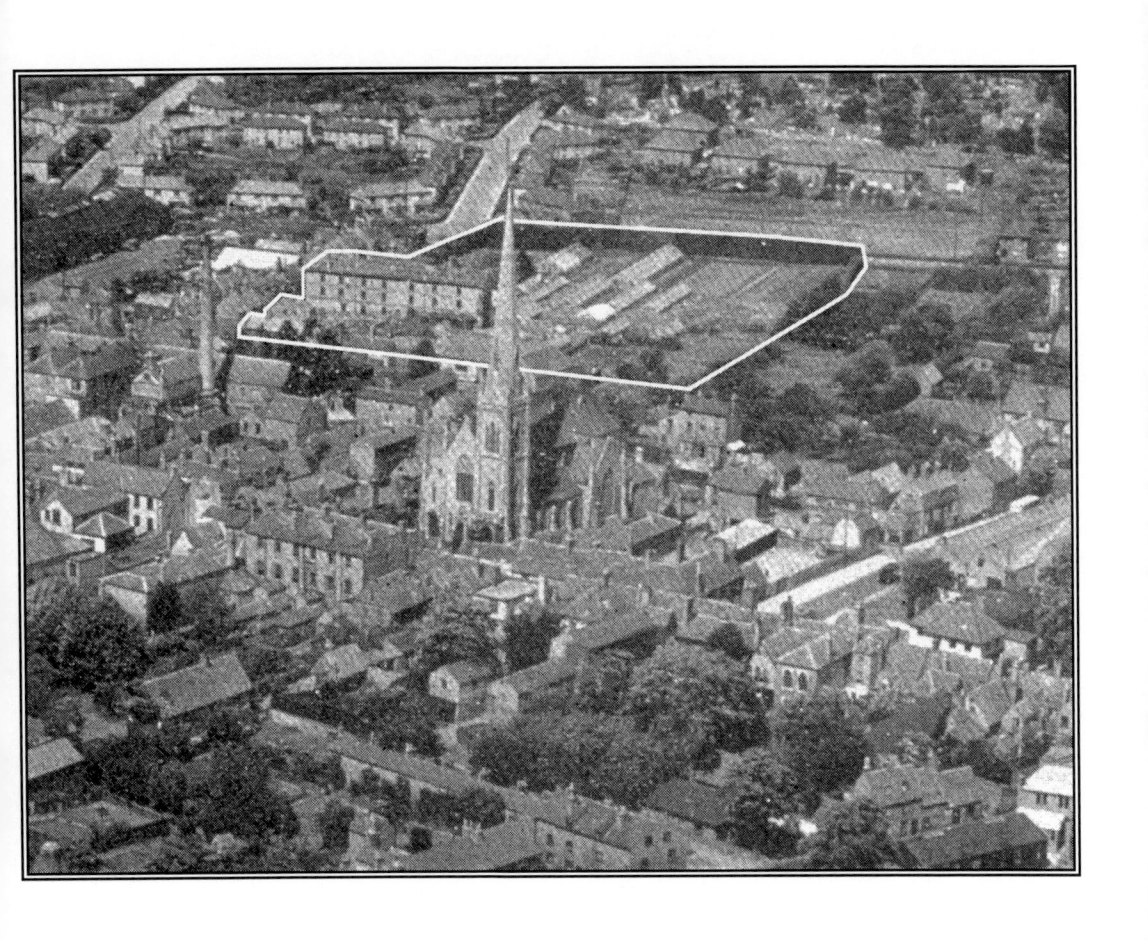

16 Aerial photograph of Huntingdon, showing the St Germain Street Nursery. Only the beech hedge alongside Sainsbury's supermarket remains today.

CHAPTER 8

OPEN FOR BUSINESS DURING THE FIRST WORLD WAR

War between Great Britain and Germany was declared on 4th August 1914. Both the government and the men of the Regular Army were confident it would be over by Christmas. That was not to be. As the war progressed, so conditions at home became ever more difficult. Coping with the bureaucracy associated with the war effort could be frustrating. However the nursery continued to grow and rose above what appeared to be important in Whitehall, but petty in Huntingdonshire. Here we find Mr John Perkins successfully steering his nursery through the First World War.

Wood and Ingram's *Order Ledger C* covers the period from 30th May 1917 until 20th February 1919 and is bound with a leather spine and leather hard covers. It measures 23cm x 28cm. Inside are 1,001 orders, of which two thirds are handwritten and one third typed all on wafer-thin copy paper. In this ledger the index is at the front, but in later ledgers the index is found at the end. Because the orders were bound during the First World War some discrepancies occur in the binding – some are bound upside down and not all numbers and names correspond with the customer index. Many of the orders in *Order Ledger C* are for local residents in the Huntingdon area and include several members of the aristocracy. Prominent, because of the several orders they sent to the Nursery, are Lady Guernsey at Abbots Ripton Hall (7 orders); the Earl of Sandwich at Hinchingbrooke (7 orders); G. C. W. Fitzwilliam at Milton Park; the Earl of Romney at Gayton Park, Norfolk; the Duke of Manchester at Kimbolton Castle; the Earl of Harrington at Elvaston Castle, Derbyshire; Viscount Clifden at Landhyrock, Cornwall; and his son the Hon. G. A. Robarts who was given the Wimpole Estate; the Hon. Mrs Cavendish at Holkham Hall, Norfolk; Lady Battersea at Overstrand, Norfolk (who orders 8 varieties of potatoes); and the Earl of Durham at Exning, Newmarket.

Most of the orders contain requests for long lists of vegetable seeds at very low prices. There are some orders for roses, flowering shrubs and fruit trees.

Mr Douglas Crossman of Gransden Hall, Sandy, ordered extensive numbers of plants covering four pages, amounting to £7 6s 6d. Mr Douglas Vickers, whose new house at Temple Dinsley in Hertfordshire was designed by Sir Edwin Lutyens, ordered 150 Pinks 'Mrs Simpkins'. Mrs Rottenberg of 5 Adams Road, Cambridge, whose husband was a passionate collector of bulbs and species tulips, sent two orders for fruit trees and plants.

More details of orders are recorded in *Day Book No 25,* which covers the period from Dec 1917 until March1918. The index of this ledger includes clients already mentioned, but also Mr Thornhill of Diddington (another 18th century family customer) who ordered 1,500 quicks for £4 10s 0d. Other orders in this Day Book are for fruit, and show that the nursery had stocks consisting of 19 apple trees, 2 apricot trees, 6 cherry trees, 1 damson, 12 pear trees, 10 plum trees, 5 peach trees.

Many orders in this Day Book request Seakale 'Solid Ivory' for forcing, often in quantities of 1,000 plants for customers all over the country. The following range of seed potato varieties were sent out by the nursery: *Sir J. Llewellyn, British Queen, Duke of York, Sharpe's Express, Myatt's Ashleaf, Mary Queen, Ninetyfold, Jerusalem White, The Factor, Beauty of Hebron, Schoolmaster, Up to Date, Midlothian Early, Evergood, King Edward VII, Sharpe's Victor, Early Puritan, Great Scott, Perkin's Snowdrop, Arran Chief, Epicure, Perkin's Early Bird, Eclipse, Sutton Flour Ball, Golden Wonder, Ringleader, Locham, Langworthy* and *Magnificent*.

Also to be noted were references for the cost of hiring 3 Palm trees for the 31st RAF Squadron at Wyton for £1.4s.6d and later that year 4 Palms cost 8/-. Cut flowers were also sold to customers – carnations were sent to the Old Bridge House, Huntingdon. Daffodils and lilies were also popular and later in the year many chrysanthemums were grown for their cut flowers. Floral arrangements were made for weddings, and funeral wreaths were supplied in various shapes – memorial tributes cost 10s.6d and choice funeral designs were charged at 12s.6d. The nursery had a very thriving business offering garden supplies to customers, a range which included Bone Meal, Manure, Kettering Loam, Horticultural Salt, Silver Sand, Nitrate of Soda, various Insecticides, Wall Nails, Labels, Canes, Raffia, Secateurs, Budding Knives, Indelible Ink and Beesom Brushes. The nursery hired their staff for gardening work at 4s.0d for 6 hours but 2s.6d for 2½ hours, and they add 2/- for the hire of a bicycle if their staff were required to travel far from the nursery. They also supplied a large quantity of onion seed (Mr A. V. Coombe, Ramsey received 6lbs for £9 0s 9d and Burwell Boys School paid 5s 0d for 2 oz), seed potatoes and carrot seed to local farmers. In 1917 the German prisoners of war at Huntingdon paid 5s 0d for their Christmas tree.

Letter Book 69 covers the period 20th October 1917 until 23rd November 1918 and includes 1004 typed letters, mostly two per page. The Index is geographically widespread and includes several nurseries and individuals. But, as one would expect, several letters were written to Government Departments dealing with the administration of the nursery. Monthly accounts are included to the Earl of Sandwich and S. Brotherhood Esq at Thornhaugh Hall, Wansford. A letter to Mr F. W. Church dated 13th November mentions that 'Our Mr Wyatt called' and 'we wish to inform you we have appointed a fresh representative, Mr. W. B. Campbell . . . '. Mr A. Pipe of Thetford receives a letter informing him of 'the list of Cordon Apples that Wood and Ingram can supply stating that the life of a cordon tree should be 20 to 30 years if kept in good condition'. A list of 18 Culinary and 23 Dessert Apples is included with this correspondence.

A letter was sent to the Ministry of Munitions requesting permission for a boiler and 3 radiators to heat a seed store. The nursery wrote on 13th November 1918 to the Officer in Charge of the Agricultural Company to notify him that Private Abbott had been admitted to hospital with influenza – an example of the terrible outbreak of lethal influenza at the time. On a somewhat brighter note the nursery wrote to both Mr Hales, head gardener at Thornaugh Hall and Mr Snell, head gardener at Wimpole Hall: 'We have been able to get hold of a nice lot of Dutch Bulbs from a vessel captured by the Admiralty'. A letter to The Olympia Agricultural & Pure Stock Farms Ltd states that 'we have 38 pigs an early despatch of the meal will greatly oblige'. Mr F. Mitchell, forester at Woburn Abbey was informed that the nursery could supply Larch Fir Native twice transplanted trees at 45s 0d per 1,000. Mr W. H. Higgins, Summerhill was requested to 'kindly send the 5,000, or whatever quantity you can do, of the Elms on order'. By September 1918 there are several letters saying 'there is a great scarcity of labour. We cannot possibly send a man to plant for you.' 'Cut flowers are getting scarce'.

The complexities of trying to maintain the nursery during these times are apparent in the following selection of letters written by Mr J. E. Perkins and later by his son Henry. It is obvious from their polite replies to both customers and government departments that the nursery always appeared to have succeeded in the face of adversity.

>R. H. Richardson Esq.,   19th July 1917
>Boston,
>U. S. A.
>
>Dear Sir,
>
>We beg to thank you for your esteemed favour of the 26th ult, but regret, owing to the severe restrictions on paper and catalogue printing, that we have not been allowed to publish a list since the date of the last copy we sent you. And we further regret, owing to the restriction on the importation of plants and bulbs, we have also not been able to keep up our usual stock of continental novelties.
>
>Directly these embargoes are removed we will keep you posted up with our list of novelties.
>
>Yours faithfully
>Wood & Ingram

Messrs Carter Page & Co. Ltd.,   11th September 1917
52 London Wall
London E.C.

CLEMATIS:– all we can supply of your esteemed order –
34 different names
+2 Lady Betty Balfour gratis
600 plants
23 Boxes,
Hay for packing £25 8 6

───•───

The Petrol Controller   3rd November 1917
19 Berkley Street
London W.1.

Dear Sir,

A fresh petrol licence has just been granted me, ostensibly for use on my car in connection with my business as a Nurseryman and Forest tree expert, under which regime I am constantly called upon to give advice upon reafforestation (in red ink) and estimates for planting.

The question now arises as to how far this term (under article No, 2- order No 2 1917) "if railway or other means of communication be reasonably available" extends.

For instance, I have an enquiry to hand now for an estimate for the replanting of 180 acres of forest. To visit this estate the return journey will take me twelve hours by rail; whereas by car it can be accomplished in four comfortably, thus saving a huge waste of time. This will be frequently occurring in the future as in the past as nearly all estates of any size are situated miles from any railway station.

Reafforestation is of the utmost National importance (again in red ink); I would respectfully make application for some form of pass to enable me to carry on this branch of my business (forest trees are grown by me by the several millions) without interference by the Police.

I remain, Dear Sir,

Yours faithfully,
Wood & Ingram

───•───

Mr W. J. Small 6th November 1917
Wimpole

Dear Sir,

We have been fortunate enough to get hold of a nice lot of Dutch Bulbs from a vessel captured by the Admiralty, comprising Hyacinths, Single early flowering Tulips, Narcissus see as list enclosed.

Should any of these be of service to you we shall be pleased to receive your kind orders to which our best attention shall be given.

Yours faithfully
Wood & Ingram

———•———

Messrs The First Garden City Ltd., 10th November 1917
Letchworth

Dear Sirs,

3 Birch	) Packed in through truck, carriage
	) paid to Letchworth station,
16 Limes red twigged, 6ft clear stems	) for the sum of
9 Ash	) £16 : 12 : 6 net.
10 Thorns 6ft clear stems	) All the trees would be 12 feet or over
12 Cornish or English Elms.(not weeping)	) excepting the Thorns, Mop-headed
18 Acacias	) Acacia and Almonds. These would all
4 Mop-headed Acacia, 6ft stems	) have 6 feet clear stems.
3 Mountain Ash	)
2 Almonds, 6ft stems	)
3 Silver Poplar	)
7 Assorted	)

Wood & Ingram

———•———

The Hon. Gerald Agar Robartes 22nd November 1917
Wimpole Hall

9 Dwarf Roses Hugh Dickson	11s	3d
9 Dwarf Roses Mr John Laing	9	0
9 Dwarf Roses Prince de Bulgarie	11	3
9 Dwarf Roses Eda Meyer	11	3
9 Dwarf Roses Mde A Chatenay	11	3
6 Liberty Dwarf	7	6
6 Dwarf Roses Papa Lambert	7	6
12 Dwarf Roses Lyon	15	0
9 Dwarf Roses Mde Rosary	11	3
2 Dwarf Roses Rayon d'Or	3	6

6 Dwarf Rose Richmond	Gratis		
8 Standard Roses Frau Karl Druschki	1	14	0
2 Standard Roses Hugh Dickson		6	0
4 Standard Roses Mde Abel Chatenay		14	0
2 Standard Roses Marquise de Sinety		7	0
100 Lilium candidum Extra Large	2	5	0
200 Tulips Golden Spire	2	5	0
2 Boxes (Postage & carriage paid)		1	0
1 Bundle and packing		1	6
	£12	2	3

―――— • ―――—

Frank F. Euren Esq.,　　　　　　　　　　　23rd November 1917
16, Bedford Square
London W C

Dear Sir,

Enclosed we have pleasure in handing you a full list of the consignment of Fruit Trees for France. In it are embodied the 1,000 trees promised by us and the extra 500 kindly ordered by you on behalf of your committee. We also enclose invoices for the last named as per your request.

The trees are well packed in 50 straw bundles and forwarded per G.N.R. & L.E. & S.C.R. to Newhaven in six trucks.

Perhaps it will be possible to clear the G.N.R. of all or any carriage charges.

With best wishes for the venture

We are, Dear Sir,

Yours faithfully,
Wood & Ingram

Contents of Consignment to Newhaven from Messrs Wood & Ingram, Huntingdon

Bundles Numbered G1to G50:–

G 1　20　Plums Rivers' Early Prolific. 10 Apples Blenheim Orange
G 2　30　Apples Blenheim Orange
G 3　30　Apples Blenheim Orange
G 4　30　Apples Blenheim Orange
G 5　30　Apples Blenheim Orange
G 6　30　Apples Cox's Orange Pippin
G 7　30　Apples Cox's Orange Pippin
G 8　30　Apples Cox's Orange Pippin 10 Ribston Pippin

G 9 30 Apples Worcester Permain
G10 30 Apples Worcester Permain
G11 10 Apples Worcester Permain 20 Allington Pippin
G12 10 Apples Allington Pippin 10 Lord Grosvenor 10 Lord Stradbrooke
G13 30 Apples Ben's Red
G14 10 Apples Hector Macdonald 20 Ben's Red
G15 10 Apples Golden Noble 20 Mr Gladstone
G16 10 Apples Sturmer Pippin 10 Lady Sudeley 10 Red Victoria
G17 30 Apples Red Victoria
G18 20 Apples Langley Pippin 5 Lane's Prince Albert 5 Lord Grosvenor
G19 30 Apples Lane's Prince Albert
G20 30 Apples Lane's Prince Albert
G21 10 Apples Ben's Red 10 Lane's Prince Albert 10 Pears Jargonelle
G22 20 Pears Jargonelle 10 Marguarite Marillat
G23 5 Pears Marguarite Marillat 5 Duchesse d'Angouleme 10 Hessle 10 Buerre de Capiament
G24 15 Pears Marie Louise 5 Buerre Easter 5 Beurre Rance 5 Gleu Morceau
G25 10 Pears Bergamot d'Esparen 20 Beurre d'Amanlis
G26 5 Pears Beurre d'Amanlis 25 Doyenne d'Ete
G27 15 Pears Josephine de Malines 15 Doyenne du Comice
G28 15 Pears Doyenne du Comice 15 Williams' Bon Chretien
G29 30 Pears Williams' Bon Chretien
G30 5 Pears Durendean 25 Williams' Bon Chretein
G31 30 Plums Czar
G32 30 Plums Czar
G33 30 Plums Czar
G34 30 Plums Czar
G35 30 Plums Czar
G36 30 Plums Czar
G37 30 Plums Czar
G38 30 Plums Czar
G39 30 Plums Czar
G40 30 Plums Czar
G41 30 Plums Czar
G42 30 Plums Czar 10 Monarch
G43 30 Plums Monarch
G44 30 Plums Monarch
G45 30 Plums Monarch
G46 30 Plums Rivers' Early Prolific
G47 10 Pears Durendean 5 Beurre Superfin 15 Pitmaston Duchess
G48 30 Pears Le Lactier
G49 5 Pears Le Lactier 10 Charles-Ernest 15 Clapp's Favorite
G50 15 Pears Charles-Ernest 15 Doyenne Beussoch

Gerald Fuller Esq., 28th November 1917
Lolworth

Dear Sir,

We beg to thank you for your esteemed order for roses.

On going into your list and comparing it with our stock we find we can do the dwarfs alright in really good stuff, but in the standard section we are sorry we cannot supply many of the sorts named.

During the last three years the labour has not been available for the collection of briars on which they are worked; consequently there is a great shortage of lots of sorts of Standard roses. And it is useless us trying to obtain them for you as every Nurseryman is in the same predicament, or worse, than ourselves.

We would therefore suggest that you leave it to us to do the very best we can for you in this section; keeping, as far as we can, to the sorts selected by you, but in cases where we are unable to supply to substitute others of equally good character and as near to your colours as possible.

We shall be glad to hear from you regarding this, and with the assurance of our best attention at all times, We are, Dear Sir,

Your obedient servants
Wood & Ingram

Please note:–
Standard Rose priced in our catalogue @ 2/- are now 2/6
        "   "   "   @ 2/6 are now 3/6
Dwarf Roses advanced 3d per tree all round.

———•———

The Rt Hon. The Earl of Sandwich 30th November 1917
Hinchingbrooke

1917

Nov 6	150	Raspberries Queen Alexander	20/-		£1	19s	6d
21	1	Cart Clay Fertiliser			1	4	0
	100	Tulips Clara Butt				14	0
	100	Tulips Pride of Haarlem				16	0
	3	Helleborus Ex strong clumps	5/-			15	0
	300	Bamboo canes 4ft	4/6			13	6
	4	Carts pots 12'	8/6		1	5	6
23	448	Dwarf Roses Choice named varieties for		25	0	0
	2	Std	"	Caroline Testout	3/6		7	0
	2	Std	"	Hugh Dickson	3/-		6	0
	2	Std	"	Mr W C Miller	3/6		7	0
	2	Std	"	Le Progres	3/6		7	0
	2	Std	"	Lady Hillingdon	3/6		7	0
	1	Dwarf	"	in pot Yellow Banksian			2	6

28	3	Dozen Birch brooms	15/-	£2	5s	0d
	1	Ream Best White Tissue		10	0
	12	Choice named Hyacinths White) Imported		12	0
	12	" " " Blue) Bulbs		12	0
	12	" " " Red)		12	0
			Forward	38	13	0
	100	Choice named Tulips scarlet)		17	6
	100	Choice " " yellow)		17	6
	100	Choice " " orange) Imported Bulbs	17	6
	100	Choice " " crimson)		17	6
	100	Choice " " white)		17	6
	200	Choice named Narcissus	10/6	1	1	0
				£44	1s	6d

———•———

Mrs Nugent   6th December 1917
Ballyedmond

Madam,

On sending your goods to the station the railway company inform us that the sailings to Ireland are suspended for the time being, so that we are unable to despatch the trees etc kindly ordered. We will, however, send them along directly they can accept goods in Ireland.

In the meantime we have sent the Strawberry plants by passenger train via Hollyhead and Dublin, as it is better they should be planted at once, now that they have been lifted.

You may rely on the remainder of your order being sent directly we are able to do so.

We are, Madam,

Your obedient servants
Wood & Ingram

There was continual unrest in Ireland during the war years, often with violent incidents in the struggle for Home Rule. This may have accounted for the suspension of acceptance of goods for shipping.

———•———

Sir Harry Veitch   2nd December 1917
South Kensington
London

Dear Sir Harry,

The fruit trees to which you refer formed my contribution to a gift organised by the Agricultural Relief of Allies Committees (per Frank F. Euren Esq., Hon. Sec.)

16 Bedford Square, London, W. C.

The consignment was addressed as follows:–

'Embarkation Commandment, Newhaven, Envoi de la Commité de Secours Agricoles aux Allies', 16 Bedford Square, Londres, A M le Ministre de l'Agriculture, Republique Française, Dieppe, France. Each tree, apart from our name tally, bore a label to the effect that it is a gift from Great Britain. These labels, as well as all address labels were provided and sent to me by the Relief Committee, so that the arrangements for despatch and conveyance to France were made by them. Perhaps therefore, your best plan would be to communicate with Mr Euren who would be in a position to give you full details.

With the season's greetings and best wishes for the coming year,

I am, Dear Sir Harry,

Yours very truly
H. Perkins

Sir Harry Veitch seems to have forgotten this communication as two years later Mr Perkins sent him the following letter:–

Sir Harry Veitch   30th August 1919
Royal Horticultural Society War Relief Fund
17 Victoria Street, London, S.W.

Dear Sir Harry,

I am sorry not to offer you any standard fruit trees wherein named. 2 years ago we gave 1,000 trees to France for the purpose of replanting and since then fruit trees are becoming scarce in this country.

Yours faithfully,
Wood & Ingram

——— • ———

R. L. Robinson Esq.,   3rd January 1918
1, Whitehall
London SW1

Dear Sir,

As members of the Agricultural Trades Association, we beg to make application for soldier labour for forest tree planting, and shall be glad if you will send us Special Form F P 71.

We are, Dear Sir,
Yours faithfully,
Wood & Ingram

Messrs – The American Express Company   3rd January 1918
84 Queen Street,
London E C

Dear Sirs,

We are in receipt of your No 9001, and herewith enclose P O 5/- for charges in connection with the bag of Vegetable Seed, consigned through you to us from Messrs Vilmorin – Andrieux & Co., Paris, numbered 68385 VA.

    Kindly send the bag along to us by Great Northern Rly, Goods Train Company's Risk Rate, at your very earliest, label enclosed herewith.

Yours faithfully
Wood & Ingram

———•———

R. L. Robinson Esq.,   15th January 1918
1 Whitehall

Your reference Labour 2

Dear Sir,

I am duly in receipt of your letter of the 14th for which I thank you.

    I note your remarks to the effect that No 43063, Pte A. Rose, cannot be spared to me for forest tree planting but that a man could be sent from the Distribution centre at Peterborough.

    I would, however, respectfully point out that I am making application for Rose, for the planting of young seedling forest trees. This is technical work and cannot be done by the ordinary labourer, hence my appeal for Rose who was with me for many years and was one of my most experienced planters; I trust therefore you will be able to reconsider your decision.

I am, Dear Sir,
Your obdt. Servant
J. E. Perkins

———•———

C/C 432 Agricultural Company   22nd January 1918
Kempton Barracks
Bedford

Dear Sir,

Replying to your communication of the 19th, I have to inform you that Army Form 3151a relating to Pte Geddes has twice been returned to you properly filled in.

    In times like these when all labour is extremely short these repetitions ought not to be necessary.

Yours faithfully
J. E. Perkins

Sir H. Veitch
South Kensington
London

30th January 1918

Dear Sir Harry,

I am sorry there has been a little delay in answering your letter of the 26th; this has been occasioned by the hunt for a label that might have been left over.

My man has now found one and I have pleasure in enclosing it herewith.

You will observe that it is indicative of a present from the Agriculturalists of England, (in red ink) so that your labels will have to be worded as to represent the Horticultural Section, together with their address.

I am very pleased to be able to supply this information which I hope will assist you in your endeavours.

I am Dear Sir Harry,
Yours faithfully
H. Perkins

——— • ———

Miss Nerontsos
39 Portman Square
London

4th February 1918

Madam,

In reply to your letter of the 1st we shall have very great pleasure in acceding to your request on behalf of the Duchess of Sutherland, for a few seeds of vegetables for use in connection with her hospital in France.

We have passed an order through to our Seed department and hope to be able to send the seeds to you in a day or so. In the meantime we respectfully wish her Grace every success in her undertaking.

We are, Madam,
Your obedient Servants,
Wood & Ingram

The doughty Duchess of Sutherland was one of the first to respond to *noblesse oblige* at the outbreak of the war. Within days she was in Belgium with her "Millicent Sutherland Ambulance" and later she established "The Duchess of Sutherland Red Cross Hospital" just outside Calais. The Duchess was commandant of this highly efficient hospital throughout the duration of the war.

——— • ———

The Hon. Mrs Cavendish 27th February 1918
Sawtry

Madam,

Replying to your letter of the 25th we regret very much that we are unable to send a man to prune your roses this season, but we are so extremely short of labour, having lost nearly 50 of our men to the army, that it is quite impossible for us to spare any man for outside work.

We are, Madam,

Your obedient Servants
Wood & Ingram

———•———

Handwritten:–

Mrs Crossman 1st March 1918
Gransden Hall, Sandy

Madam,

Replying to your esteemed favour addressed to our St Neots Branch with regard to Peas and Beans suitable for drying and keeping for Winter use, we would recommend you to grow Haricot Beans or any of the Flageolet varieties and for Peas Harrison's Glory would be most suitable. We have the Flageolet Beans in stock but we have no Haricot Beans or Harrison's Glory Peas by us just now but we shall be glad to procure them for you if you will kindly let us know what quantity you require.

Assuring you of our very best care and attention to your esteemed commands. We beg to remain Madam,

Your obedient Servant
Wood & Ingram

———•———

Mr Charles Stewart 18th April 1918
Westmoors

Dear Sir,

In reference to the article appearing in this week's H.A. relative to men engaged in the planting of Forest trees, we have been advised by Mr Pearson to place our case before you with a view of taking the matter up, on our behalf, with Mr Prothero.

The men in question are:– Albert Stevens, Alberta Crescent, Huntingdon; and Mr John Allen, Bridge End, Brampton, Hunts.

These two men are expert planters and are engaged solely in the planting and handling of FOREST TREES, we shall be glad, therefore, if you will bring their cases forward with a view to getting them exempted at least until such time as substitutes can be found. They have to report themselves for service next Tuesday, so that the matter is urgent.

We are, Dear Sir,
Yours faithfully
Wood & Ingram

Captain Coleman 27th June 1918
Hunts Cyclists,
Skegness

Dear Captain Coleman,

On receipt of your order, 10,000 Early Cabbage plants, delivered to Skegness Station for the sum of £6 7s 9d

Wood & Ingram

The Hunts Cyclists' Battalion was detailed to defend the East Coast.

— • —

W. J. Stalker Esq., 3rd July 1918
Food Production Department,
72, Victoria Street
Westminster, SW1

Dear Sir,

In reply to yours of 20th ultimo. I am sorry I was away from home when you called, but I expected you the next day. However I quite understand why you did not call.

With reference to flowers for the Trafalgar Square Bazaar, I am very sorry I could not send any to the Duke of Portland as owing to the exceptional drought, we were and still are, very short ourselves.

With kind regards
J. E. Perkins

— • —

R. J. W. Dawson Esq., 2nd August 1918
Estate Office,
Temple Dinsley,
Hitchin

Dear Sir,

In reply to your esteemed enquiry as to whether we could send a man with the Walnut Trees to plant them; we much regret to inform you that our Staff of Practical men is so reduced owing to the war, that at the moment we see no chance of a man being sent, but should the position improve between now and the planting season, we will gladly acquaint you.

With reference to the Holm Oak, we shall be pleased to supply you with these, 5 to 6 ft. high in pots at 10/6 each. This is not an easy tree to transplant and should always be planted out from pots, hence the reason we quote in pots.

We should esteem your kind orders and always assuring you of our very best services at all times.

Yours faithfully
Wood & Ingram

———•———

Mr Walter C. Slocock,   2nd August 1918
Goldsworth "Old Nursery"
Woking, Surrey

Dear Sir,

Thanks for yours of the 1st. We note you can only supply 10,000 of the one year Common Ash, and that you have booked us these, and 25,000 two years.

Kindly send us as a sample of the two years as they are now, we will then decide if we shall take up any more of these.

Yours faithfully
Wood & Ingram

———•———

Lieut. W. H. Page   28th August 1918
Prisoner of War Camp
Huntingdon

Dear Sir,

We duly received your letter of the 21st, and regret through pressure of work we have not been able to reply to same before.

You ask us to give you our opinion on the work done by the prisoners who have been in our employ. Whilst we are well aware that Prisoners of War volunteer for this class of work, we regret we cannot say that we are at all satisfied with the work done by the majority of the men, neither do we think that they have worked as well the last 12 months as the majority did the first few months they were with us.

There certainly does not seem to be near the discipline there was at the start. When we have complained little notice appears to have been taken of our complaints. To take a case in point, we made a complaint this last Spring; the reply we got from you simply upheld the prisoners instead of upholding us in what was undoubtedly a perfectly legitimate complaint. If the men are to be treated like this when employed by us, we can understand farmers telling us how dissatisfied they are with a lot of the work that has been done.

If it comes to a question of cost, we have repeatedly proved that the work they did for us, in many instances, has cost at least three times what it should have done.

At the present time we have a man in the gang we have left, who certainly is one of the laziest we ever saw of any nationality. We do not speak from hearsay, but from our personal observation.

We may add that if a good guard was allowed to work with the prisoners much more work would be done.

Yours faithfully
Wood & Ingram

Entries in Wood & Ingram's *Cash Book No 5* (which covers the period from January 1918 until May 1920) reveal that weekly payments for German Labour/German Prisoners were paid from 25th January 1918 until 25th January 1919. During August 1918 the following weekly payments were made:–

August 2nd 1918 German Labour £8 7s 1d
August 9th 1918 German Labour £4 13s 9d
August 16th 1918 German Labour £4 13s 9d
August 20th 1918 German Labour £4 16s 11d
August 28th 1918 German Labour £5 5s 3d

———•———

Harcourt E. Clare Esq.,   16th August 1918
Hon. Secretary
Lancashire War Pensions Committee
County Offices
Preston

Dear Sir,

With reference to your advertisement in the "Gardeners' Chronicle", if you have any men who have had any Nursery training at all amongst the discharged soldiers, we shall be glad if you will kindly put us in communication with them.

Yours faithfully
Wood & Ingram

———•———

The Hon. Mrs G. Neville,   29th August 1918
Bluntisham Rectory
St Ives, Hunts

Dear Madam,

We are in receipt of your letter of the 25th, and in reply to same would say that we do not employ lady gardeners in our nurseries.

Mr Prowting, Head gardener, The Gardens, Hinchingbrooke, Huntingdon, employs ladies, but we cannot say if he has any vacancies at present. Perhaps you may like to write to him and make enquiries.

Yours faithfully
Wood & Ingram

As more and more men were drawn into the armed forces their places of work were taken by women, particularly in the munitions factories. Women also worked on the land, drove trams, acted as postmen, and generally undertook a variety of jobs not previously considered appropriate. The Earl of Sandwich and his head gardener obviously adapted to the changed times.

———•———

Mr Low,   10th September 1918
The Gardens,
Euston Hall,
Thetford

Dear Sir,

Sufficient English Yews 1½ to 2 ft to plant

200 feet of Hedge – 300 plants, planted 3 to the yard Per 100, 70/- net

These are very fine plants of splendid colour and well rooted.

Wood & Ingram

———•———

Mr R. Brown   12th October 1918
Nottingham

Dear Sir,

With further reference to your letter of May 23rd, we hope to be ready with our new offices, situate at Nos. 2 & 3 George Street, Huntingdon, during the early part of next week, and we shall be glad to know if it will be convenient for you to have our telephone installation removed from us at that time. An extension will be required from there to our existing offices.

We are, Dear Sir, Yours faithfully
Wood & Ingram

———•———

J. R. Board   15th October 1918
No. 9961(7?)0, ii Cpl, R.N.
B.E.F.
France.

Dear Sir,

We have duly received your letter of the 20th September with our label which you found attached to the young apple tree.

We are very much obliged to you for both, and in reply we would tell you that this young tree was one of a thousand which we gave, free of all cost, for the replanting of the devastated areas in France.

We despatched them last November, and can only hope that a good many more of them have been equally fortunate in not being destroyed, although we fear from the fact that you have found this one, that many of the others have gone under. Kindly let us know if your address is still the same, when we will see if we cannot post just a few apples out to you.

Again thanking you, and with our very best wishes. We are, yours faithfully,
Wood & Ingram

———•———

Capt. Robinson   19th October 1918
Food Department,
Westminster

Dear Sir,

When you visited us a few weeks back you very kindly intimated that you would be very pleased to render us any assistance possible.

Owing to enormous increase in demands for seeds of all kinds we found our old premises in Germain Street totally inadequate and have been obliged to move to more commodious and central premises, situate in George Street, Huntingdon. This we explained to you during conversation.

We are also in a position to move our office to our new premises, but am asking for our telephone to be transferred, for the purpose of concentrating our business. We are informed that the work cannot be undertaken without a permit from the office with which our trade is chiefly concerned. We are wondering, therefore, if you can help in this matter, and to whether you will be good enough to instruct us to the best course to pursue?

If however, it is out of your department, will you kindly pass this letter on to the department it concerns? Thanking you in anticipation,

We are, Dear Sirs, Yours faithfully,
Wood & Ingram

———•———

Arthur George Dilley Esq.,　　　　　　　　　　　　　24th October 1918
The Walks,
Huntingdon

Dear Mr Dilley

Thanks very much for your letter of 24th. I am very sorry to hear you are confined to the house with a bad cold. Take care of yourself, and I hope you will soon get rid of it.

It is very good of your firm to give £50 to the Prisoners of War Fund, but I am sure we all realise what a worthy object that is. At last night's meeting it was decided to hold a Sale with Slide Shows on the Market Hill and in and around the Town Hall, on the 27th November, after which I am certain the sum we are out to raise will have been secured, and I hope still more.

With kind regards

I am, Yours very truly
J. E. Perkins

———•———

In *Order Ledger A*, which covers the period from 28th October 1918 until 21st November 1919, there are 1,000 orders, many to nurseries, requesting very large quantities of trees and dwarf roses:–

October 1918	Fisher & Silbray, Handsworth nr Sheffield (a large tree nursery) was sent 14,000 Scotch Fir for £29 15s 0d, followed by an order in November 1918 for 10,000 Native Larch and 10,000 Scotch Fir for £41 5s 0d, followed by an order in December 1918 for 20,000 Larch for £41 2s 6d, followed by an order in March 1919 for 1,000 Native Larch and 400 Spruce for £13 11s 0d, followed by an order for 11,000 Scotch Fir for £23 7s 6d and by a final order in November 1919 for 15,000 Native Larch, 8,600 Japanese Larch, 10,000 Native Spruce and 500 Larch for £151 6s 0d – totalling 100,500 trees for £301 7s 0d
October 1918	Algrove Nursery, Langley, Slough was sent 1,038 Dwarf roses, 200 Loganberries and 330 Plum trees for £104 9s 8d, followed by an order in November 1918 for 400 Dwarf Roses for £17 6s 4d, followed by a further order in December 1918 for 306 Dwarf Roses for £17 0s 1d
November 1918	Cant & Sons, Colchester was sent 160 Dwarf Roses for £8 16s 8d, followed by an order in February 1919 for 550 Dwarf roses for £32 4s

Owners of large estates were also obtaining large quantities of trees to improve their grounds:

November 1918	Captain Briscoe, Longstowe Hall, Cambridgeshire was sent 100 Douglas Fir, 200 Larch and 50 Oaks for £7 11s 10d, an order in January 1919 of 12 Silver

		Poplars, 12 Elms and 6 Common Beech all extra large for £49 1s 0d, an order in February 1919 for 775 Scotch pine and 750 Larch for £6 2s 0d and a further order in March 1919 for 100 Laurels, 4 Cedars, 34 Abies and 36 Cornus for £37 4s 0d
	" "	Lady De Ramsey, Ramsey Abbey was sent 220 Dwarf and Standard Roses for £32 12s 0d
December 1918		The Marquis of Bristol, Ickworth, Suffolk was sent 500 Ash for £5 12s 6d followed by further orders during the same month for 1,000 Spruce, 500 Sitka Spruce, 1,000 Larch, 200 Mountain Ash, 100 Douglas Fir, 100 Beech, 100 Thuja Lobbii, 1,000 Myrobella for £18 6s 9d and 1,000 Spruce, 1,000 Larch and 1,000 Scotch Pine for £9 5s 6d, and 1cwt of potatoes, 24 Dwarf Roses and 7 Fruit Trees for £6 11s 3d
	" "	The Duke of Bedford was sent 48 Standard roses for £25 11s 0d
	" "	The Earl Fitzwilliam was sent 1,000 Raspberries 'Superlative' and 1,000 Raspberries 'Hornet' for £20 5s 0d
	" "	The Cambridge Tuberculosis Colony at Papworth Hall was sent 200 Apple Trees, 4 dozen Rhubarb 'Early Albert'. 100 Black Currants, 100 Gooseberries and 200 Raspberries for £47 1s 0d
	" "	The Earl of Harrington, was sent 12 Standard Roses and 12 Weeping Roses for £9 13s 3d
	" "	His Majesty's Office of Works in London was sent 50 Dwarf roses for Greenwich Park for £3 15s 9d

The above order for Greenwich Park, London is one of the earliest recorded orders for His Majesty's Office of Works in Wood & Ingram's 20th century Ledgers. His Majesty's Office of Works placed many orders with the Nursery up to the time when it was sold in 1950.

Not only did the Nursery have customers who ordered large numbers of trees, shrubs and roses, but they looked after the requirements of customers who had smaller gardens. An order requiring only one plant was given the same attention as an order requiring over 1,000 plants:

October 1918		Mr Key, Ramsey was sent 6 Dwarf Roses for 13s 0d
"	"	Mr Phillips, Ramsey was sent 24 Dwarf Roses for £2 8s 9d
November	"	Lady Schindler, Fenstanton was sent 300 Whitethorn Trees and 2 Fruit Trees for 19s 3d
"	"	Mr Hunnybun, (Solicitor of Godmanchester) was sent 1 Apple Tree for 7s 6d followed by a further order in December 1918 for 1 Christmas Tree for 3s 6d (Christmas Trees sold to German prisoners of war cost 5s 0d)
December	"	Miss Fuller, Hemingford Abbots was sent Fruit Trees and 6 Dwarf Roses for £2 4s 0d
October	1919	Mr Charles Ely, East Bergholt, Suffolk was sent 5 Shrubs for £1 1s 2d
November	"	Clare College, Cambridge was sent 6 Standard Roses and 6 Dwarf Roses for £2 16s 6d
"	"	The Dean of Peterborough was sent 7 Dwarf Roses, 1 Magnolia, 1 Tree Paeony, 1 Apple Tree and 2 Plum Trees for £17 12s 0d.

The Nursery's correspondence continued:

G. F. Middleton Esq., 7th November 1918
Food Production Department
72, Victoria Street
London, S. W. 1

Dear Sir,

Where the one point that did not appear to be touched upon yesterday, and that was the question of developing fruit tree planting.

As at present instructed, I understood it is the wish of your Department that people should be encouraged to plant fruit trees, and wherever possible, to crop with a timber crop in between, but I also understand that our War Agricultural Executive Committee has distinct instructions to prevent any fresh land being planted with fruit trees. In fact, last planting season, it was advertised in the local press that no fresh land was to be planted with fruit trees without consent of the War Agricultural Executive Committee.

Will you kindly tell me what the real position is, as I get asked for information, and should like to know exactly what are the views of the department.

If the views are that the Agricultural Executive Committee should encourage people to plant fruit trees rather than prevent them from doing so, I think an intimation to the War Agricultural Executive Committee, not only in this, but in other fruit growing districts, should be sent.

Esteeming your kind reply,

I am, Yours faithfully
H. Perkins

―――● ―――

Mr A. V. Coombe 14th November 1918
The Gardens
Ramsey Abbey
Ramsey

Dear Mr Coombe

With reference to your recent letter respecting a gardener for Haverland, I shall be glad to know if you are in immediate hurry for a man, or as the Armistice has been signed and we may soon begin to expect men back, is there any likelihood of Mr Terry, who was there about three years ago, coming back.

If not, and you can wait a little while, I know of one or two very decent men who, I think, would undertake it.

Kindly let me hear from you,

With kind regards, I am,
Yours faithfully
H. Perkins

―――● ―――

The Armistice, which ended the fighting, was signed on 11th November 1918. There were endless negotiations throughout Europe and the East before the peace treaty was finally signed in June 1919 at Versailles. The Perkins family, both father and son, lost no time in their endeavour to restore the Wood & Ingram Nursery to its pre-war prestige. They wrote tirelessly to Continental nurseries in an attempt to re-stock the plants, which had been difficult to obtain during the war years.

At the end of *Day Book 25* there are details of the nursery's income between December 1917 and December 1919:–

1917	December	£ 3,785 3s 1d			
1918	January	£ 874 11s 2d			
	February	£ 956 4s 9d			
	March	£ 976 10s 0d			
	April	£ 541 2s 2d			
	May	£ 550 7s 4d			
	June	£ 1,053 8s 4d	£4,952 14s 9d		
	July	£ 228 0s 0d			
	August	£ 123 19s 3d			
	September	£ 543 19s 0d			
	October	£ 458 19s 10d			
	November	£ 3,670 7s 9d			
	December	£ 2,257 6s 2d	£5,927 13s 11d	£10,880 8s 8d	
1919	January	£ 2,319 2s 9d			
	February	£ 1,330 11s 2d			
	March	£ 1,579 9s 8d			
	April	£ 853 8s 4d			
	May	£ 1,135 16s 5d			
	June	£ 264 6s 2d	£7,473 14s 8d		
	July	£ 291 18s 5d			
	August	£ 135 1s 2d			
	September	£ 260 2s 1d			
	October	£ 722 14s 4d			
	November	£ 3,687 4s 7d			
	December	£ 4,248 17s 1d	£9,345 17s 8d	£16,819 12s 4d *	

A further *Order Ledger B* covers the period from 1st November 1918 until 27th November 1919 and runs concurrently alongside *Order Ledger A*. Before Armistice Day 11th of November 1918, the nursery sent an order to Smith & Co., Nursery at Worcester of 10,000 Quicks in 40 bundles for £12 10s 0d; Dobbie and Co. at Edinburgh received 700 Dwarf Roses for £38 0s 10d; Lady Guernsey, who had turned Abbots Ripton Hall into

---

* Wages increased considerably at the end of the First World War.

a War Hospital, was sent 120 Dwarf Roses and a few Laburnums for £14 11s 6d; Mr Thornhill of Diddington obtained 2 Nectarines, 2 Sycamores, Horse Chestnuts for £3 4s 0d; Mr Robinson of Hinxton Hall, Cambridgeshire was sent 1 Cedar, 1 Judas Tree, 1 Spanish Chestnut, Apple Trees and 60 Roses for £23 8s 6d. These large orders were sent out by the nursery during this difficult period, which continued some time after the War. A letter to the Veitch Nurseries explains the nursery's difficulties at certain times:–

> Messrs Robert Veitch & Son, Exeter   11th September 1919
>
> Dear Sirs,
>
> We are in receipt of your order for Clematis for which we thank you.
>   We can do all the plants you name, with the exception of Mrs G. Jackman, Duchess of Edinburgh and La France. We can however send substitutes for these if you would like us to do so. Owing to the depletion of labour we have not been able to produce nearly the stock we have been accustomed to carry, and are not making any offer to the Trade at all, but we shall be pleased to oblige you in any way possible.
>
> Our prices this season are as follows:– (as far as we are able)
> Purchaser's selection @ 225/- per 100
> Our selection to include 50% Jackmanii @ 200/- per 100
>
> Yours faithfully
> Wood & Ingram

The head gardener at Claremont in Surrey, Jasper Kelly, was sent an order of 12 Standard Red Twigged Limes for £2 18s 0d. Messrs Murrell, The Portland Nurseries, Shrewsbury, where Vita Sackville-West obtained all her roses for Sissinghurst, was sent 50 Dwarf Roses for £3 4s 6d. Douglas Vickers of Temple Dinsley, Hitchin, Hertfordshire was sent a considerable order of fruit trees and dwarf roses for £95 17s 9d. Some 250 other orders were sent out in the few weeks between the signing of the Armistice and Christmas Day 1918. An indication of the nursery's reputation is shown here by the range of important clients who appreciated its attention to producing good quality plants for sale so soon after the First World War.

November 1918		The Duke of Bedford was sent 3,000 Larch for £11 14s 0d
January	1919	Lord Dillon, Ditchley, Oxfordshire was sent an extensive order of soft fruit and Fruit Trees for £14 17s 9d
April	"	Sir J. Jardine, The Kremlin, Newmarket was sent 320 Asparagus 'Perkins Early Giant' 3 years old and 100 Pyrethrums for £5 13s 5d
October	"	The Earl of Harrington was sent 50 Green Hollies for £27 0s 0d
"	"	The Earl of Romney was sent 200 Dwarf polyantha Roses and 28 other Roses for £24 9s 7d
November	"	The Earl of Edgcumbe at Cothele, Cornwall was sent a large order of Roses,

"   "   Lilacs and Clematis for £7 3s 9d
"   "   Lady Meyer, Shotgrove Hall, Newport, Essex was sent 750 roses for £75 6s 0d
"   "   Mr P. H. Barclay, The Warren, Cromer was sent Dwarf roses and various shrubs for £4 13s 0d

Wood & Ingram had written to Mr P. H. Barclay earlier the same year about his order for strawberry plants:–

P. H. Barclay Esq.,   19 September 1919
The Warren, Cromer

Dear Mr Barclay,

With reference to your esteemed order for Strawberry Runners, as we are already cleared out of the Laxton, we have sent The Earl in place of same.

With regards to 'Waterloo', this being such a poor grower, and it being practically impossible to procure true in the country we have discarded same and we have therefore sent Giron's Late Prolific being one of the best late kinds, in its place.

We trust that this will be satisfactory to you, and assuring you of our best attention at all times.

We are Dear Sir, your obedient servants
Wood & Ingram

Local customers continued to order from the nursery including Bursars of Cambridge Colleges:–

November 1918   Mr Foster, Foxton Hall, Cambridge was sent Fruit Trees for £27 18s 6d
"   "   Mr Payne, Bookmaker of Eaton Socon, was sent Fruit Trees and Soft Fruit for £10 13s 0d
"   "   The Master of Downing College was sent Fruit Trees £6 10s 0d
January   1919   The Bursar of Downing College was sent 100 Beech, 2 Chestnuts, and 250 Oak to be forwarded to Mr Starr at Gamlingay for £3 12 s 0d and a later order of 1 English Oak for the College and 25 Oaks for Mr G. Martin, Burrough Green for £1 19s 6d
March   "   Mr Gray, Gog Magog Hills, Cambridge was sent 12 Nut Trees for £1 11s 0d
"   "   Mr Webb, Bury Road, Ramsey was sent 4 Dwarf Fruit Trees for £1 10s 0d
November "   Mr Bevan, Island Hall, Godmanchester was sent 26 Fruit Trees for £17 19s 6d

But by far the largest orders came from well established nurseries requiring large numbers of larch in case another war required quantities of trench supports:

November 1918   Mr H. Pitt, Brecon Road Nursery, Abergavenny was sent 20,000 Native Larch, 7,000 Quick for £45 5s 0d and a further order in Decemeber 1918 for 12,500 Larix (larch) kurilensis, 7,500 Native Spruce for £35 0s 0d

January   1919   James Smith Nursery, Tansley, Derbyshire was sent 30,000 Larch, 10,000 Quick for £72 10s 0d, a further order in March 1919 for 20,000 Larch in 100 bundles for £40 0s 0d and a further order in March 1919 for 25,500 Larch in 164 bundles for £45 16s 0d.

Apart from sending large orders of larch trees to nurseries, Mr Perkins spent time getting to know local landowners and encouraged them to buy their larch trees from his nursery.

A series of letters illustrates the development of a business relationship between the nursery and Mr Mitchell, who was employed as Head Forester by the Duke of Bedford:

Mr F. Mitchell   13th November 1919
Woods Department
Park Farm Office
WOBURN, Beds

Dear Mr Mitchell,

Many thanks for your kind letter of 11th. I can manage the 2,000 Larch for you and will send them on as soon as ever the weather permits. I note the Cedar libani and Silver fir and other forest trees.

We will see how these settle down in a year or two. At the present moment the chief difficulty is to find satisfactory seedlings of many things even at very high prices that they have got to. 1919 is the third consecutive season of frosts.

I never remember myself, so many seedlings being injured by autumn frosts inthree years. However, we have always got through in the past, and shall do so in the future somehow.

I am, yours very truly,
H. Perkins

Mr F. Mitchell,   14th August 1920
The Reservoir
Knipton
Grantham

Dear Mr Mitchell,

Many thanks for your kind enquiry of the 13th, as you are probably aware, Larch Fir is extremely scarce this season, but I can offer you 40,000 1½ – 2ft, Native Larch, twice transplanted, really good stuff, at 105/- per 1,000, carriage paid to Marston Siding.

I have about 5,000 Japanese, same size which I can offer you at 105/- per 1,000.

I can also offer you two year Scotch Fir very good at 75/- per 1,000 and Spruce fir same age about 6 to 13" at the same price.

If any of the above are of service to you, I shall be glad if you will kindly let me know as quickly as possible, as I can only offer it strictly subject to remaining unsold.

The fact is, they are so scarce and there is such keen demand, that one can hardly know how to deal with the enquiries. However, I am giving you the first chance of the Larch, and will hold it a few days pending your reply.

I ought to have a a big lot now this size, but 9/10ths of the crop was a failure, not only with us, but with other Nurserymen.

Yes, this has been a trying hay season. It seems extraordinary to think there is so much with you uncut. We got ours cut and carted it two months ago, in very good weather, and I can assure you we have felt very glad a good many times that it was up.

With our kind regards, trusting Mrs Mitchell, yourself and family are well.

I am,
Yours very truly,
H. Perkins

Mr F. Mitchell   20th August 1920
The Reservoir
Knipton
Grantham

Dear Mr Mitchell

Very many thanks for your kind letter of the 19th, which I was very glad to receive. I was much interested to read your opinion therein expressed.

I am always glad to get the opinion of anyone like yourself who is practical on the subject about which they are writing.

As regards the investment money, not only now, but in the future, of course I am speaking for any of those who have any money to invest, it is a very difficult matter to say what will prove to be a good investment.

If I had the land to plant and contemplated doing it within the next few years, I should feel very much inclined to get on with it if I could get the plants. I do not think the labour, and wiring and fencing are likely to come down, and if one looks solely to the reduction in the cost of trees, I cannot see how a first class article is likely to fall in price; and presuming there is a reduction say for arguments sake it comes to as much as a Pound or 25/- a thousand in 2 or 3 years time, it is not much per acre when one reckons it out, and then there are to my mind two other important factors, whilst we are waiting for this reduction in the price of plants, the ground we are contemplating planting will probably produce nothing in many instances and become foul, which, in the long run I am sure is a false economy. The loss of plants in many cases will be infinitely greater than ever the saving will be by waiting.

The other factor I look at is this, supposing in years to come this country was by any chance at War again, so that our timber supplies were in danger, where are we going to for the timber which proved of such use for pit props, sleepers and in endless ways during the war.

Of course, we all hope that such a thing will never arise, but if someone had not planted in the past, the loss to the Nation would have been far greater than it has been and even on this score alone I think the policy of recommending people to wait a few years is wrong.

I am telling you frankly what I think, not looking at it from the point of view of the forest trees I have to sell. I have not a great lot except it may be a fair quantity of Scotch Fir to offer this season, but such as I have I am anxious to give the first refusal to old clients like your father and yourself.

Of course, the contention of some people is, that if the country is likely to require timber in the future, let the Government provide it, or that it should be provided out of Government money.

After all, I think we should realise that there is no such thing as Government money, and at the present moment I think it is a difficult matter for the Government to find money for what they already have in hand, and it strikes me that if we wait for them to make a good job of all our plantations in the country, we shall wait a long time.

If I may say so, I think the points mentioned in this letter are those to which those responsible for the planting of estates should have their attention drawn.

Again thanking for your kind letter,

I am,
Yours very truly
H. Perkins

Dear Mr Mitchell   15th September 1920

In reply to your kind letter of 24th August, one can well understand Owners selling outlying portions of their estates, and I quite think that force of circumstances made many of them look at the matter from a different aspect to what they have hitherto done, but of course, as you know, there are a great many things done on Estates and in connection with the house and establishments which are kept up in connection therewith, which the owners do not solely from the point of view as to whether it is a good investment or otherwise.

After all there is the other side of the picture, and quite apart from the monetary return it must be born in mind on a health and pleasure point of view the return on a good deal of the outlay is sufficient in itself, and a man might very well make much worse investments today than planting trees.

As a matter of fact in the investment world, far more money has been lost during the last 12 months than will ever be lost out of planting in this country. Unfortunately for us all in this country, we are taxed far too heavily whilst we are alive, and then the death duties which follow, as you say, play great havoc with Estates.

I shall be only too pleased to see you at any time, for I always think that an exchange of views does good.

After all what is spent on the average estate nowadays on planting is quite a small item compared with what is spent in other directions, and I still maintain even at the present cost, a man might do very far worse than to plant trees.

As regards the Stilton which you are good enough to offer us, what we really want is one which will be right for Christmas, if you will be good enough to send one which will answer that purpose, and as to the time of sending it, we must leave this with you, as I expect much depends upon the condition of the cheese.

With our united kind regards

I am yours very truly
H. Perkins

———•———

The Nursery sold the following quantities of trees and roses covered by *Order Ledgers A and B* between October 1918 and November 1919:

Spruce 18,025	
Scotch Fir 59,000	
Larch 286,020	
Beech............................7,800	
Ash 12,700	
Black Italian Poplars 2,000	
Hazel..............................1,000	
Quicks ....177,000 ....563,545 Total	
Roses...12,459 Total	

Three of Wood & Ingram's *Wages Books* remain. The earliest to survive covers the period of eight years from 26th May 1916 until 23rd May 1924 and consists of over 424 weekly wage accounts. The format for the first week ending 26th May 1916 (shown below) is repeated throughout the Wages Book.

The name of each employee is entered followed by the number of days worked each week. Usually every man worked 6 days a week except Sundays. Where additional hours are noted as extra, the employee may have worked on Sunday to water the glasshouse plants or worked overtime one evening. Where 'hours out' are entered, the employee was possibly unwell and did not present himself for work. The figure 4 in the next column represents 4d which was deducted for insurance, and an employee's total wage for the week is entered in the right hand column. The first page records the following employees and their weekly wage:–

Week ending May 26th 1916
Abraham	6	4	£	1s	8d
Blissell	6 +1hr 3½ out	4		18	11
Humphreys	6	4	1	2	8

Joyce	6	4	£1	14s	8d
King	6	4	1	14	8
Lord	6 +3½ out	4	1	2	5
Luniss	6 +2½	4	1	9	5 ½
Young C	6	4	1	9	8
Young J	6	4	1	0	8
Young Jnr	6 +1hr	4		9	11
Brown	6	4	1	9	8
Stevens	6	4	1	9	8
Brampton			23	5	11 ½
			£38	9	0

The 12 named male employees worked at the Huntingdon nursery. They received a total of £15 3s 0d in wages in one week. The highest paid were Mr Joyce and Mr King who both received £1 14s 8d for a week's work, which suggests that they may have held responsible positions in the nursery. Only three named men were employed throughout the eight years covered by the ledger, Mr Humphreys, Mr Joyce and Mr King. The anonymous employees at the Brampton nursery received a total of £23 5s 11½d in the same week, which by comparison might indicate that some 18 men were employed at the nursery.

Later, on 20th July 1918, a young Mr Jordan was employed by the nursery. His wage was 10 shillings a week. Another Mr Jordan, possibly his father, was first recorded as an employee commencing work the week ending 22nd August 1919. His weekly wage until May 23rd 1924 was £3 15s 0d. He was the highest paid member of staff during this period and his role may have been foreman of the nursery.

As with other firms in the country, Wood & Ingram's employees' wages increase at the end of the First World War. In fact the nursery's wages bill doubled, as labour was so scarce. This can be noted after September 1918 when the wages paid to their staff at the Brampton Nursery increased considerably:

Week ending Sept 29th 1916 Brampton £21 12s 3d
Week ending Sept 28th 1917 Brampton £31 19s 5d
Week ending Sept 27th 1918 Brampton £33 8s 11d
Week ending Sept 26th 1919 Brampton £62 18s 6d
Week ending Sept 24th 1920 Brampton £110 7s 2d
Week ending Sept 30th 1921 Brampton £92 18s 9d
Week ending Sept 29th 1922 Brampton £91 4s 11d
Week ending Sept 28th 1923 Brampton £81 14s 11d

The following year saw an increase of staff at their Huntingdon Nursery, when an additional six men were required to propagate plants for the increase in orders.

CHAPTER 9

THE NURSERY RECOVERS AFTER THE FIRST WORLD WAR

In 1920 Mr John Perkins retired from the nursery and spent his last days at his home in Northampton. He died on 12th July 1924 and his obituary in the Northampton Independent recorded *'the deceased from his youth upwards devoted himself to his business very closely, and by his industry and expert knowledge extended it considerably. He also interested himself in the raising and grazing of stock, varied with a keen study of stocks and shares in which he speculated with a shrewd cautiousness that rarely led him astray. In his younger years he used to go hunting and was in request as a judge at Horticultural Shows. He was a devout Churchman and Conservative, but shrunk from any public duties'.*

Later during the same year Henry, John Perkins' son, bought Houghton Grange to the west of St Ives. This fine residence was designed by Ransome in 1897 for Mr H. Coote, a rich coal factor. His new house in late Victorian – Elizabethan style still stands in 34 acres approached by a ¼ mile long lime avenue. The garden overlooks the River Ouse with expansive views towards the west. This extensive property could only have been afforded with funds from a successful business. The nursery was now in the sole hands of Henry Perkins. His purchase of Houghton Grange showed that he had sufficient funds to acquire a large residential property, which enabled him to move up the social scale and to mix with other local landowners.

A *Letter Book* from 24th July 1920 to 20th September 1920, contains 503 typed letters. These are mainly to other nurseries with enquiries about the availability of trees, shrubs and roses, requesting them to send the plants required. Large orders often left the nursery short on certain ranges of popular plants and Wood & Ingram lost no time in finding ways to replenish their depleted stock. Prominent in receipt of several letters are J. C. Allgrove, Fruit Tree Nursery near Slough with seven requests for fruit trees and Slocock's Nursery, Woking in Surrey with nine requests for trees and shrubs. Following an enquiry from Hilliers & Son, Winchester, Wood & Ingram replied that they could offer Hilliers 5,000 Scotch Fir @ 65/- per 1,000. Grootendorst's nursery at Boskoop was asked if they could supply plants of Polyanthus 'Novelty' and Vilmorin Andrieux Seed Co., Paris was asked to supply various seeds. The friendly goodwill between nurserymen was conveyed in the following letter:–

Mr M. Morse   12th August 1920
Westfield Nurseries,
Eaton,
Norwich

Dear Sir,

The buds are safely to hand, for which we thank you. These are certainly very much better than what we had before.

If we should require any more of the Los Angles, can you arrange them in similar wood to these, and if so how many? Can they be dispatched on next Monday? Kindly let us have your reply to this by return.

Can you manage us a few nice standards of apples, Allington Pippin, if so, kindly say quantity and price?

Do you happen to grow Wyken Pippin apple, the old true stock? Mr Morse senr. will remember that there was a very fine old tree of this variety that stood within a few yards of the front door of our Mr Perkins' old home, and he is wondering if by any chance Mr Morse senr. happens to know anyone who has it, as our Mr Perkins would like to get it.

The old tree he finds is dead.

With kind regards

Yours faithfully
Wood & Ingram

——— • ———

Other correspondence requested that the Ministry of Agriculture and Fisheries send one of their representatives to the nursery to inspect the white potatoes. The Hon. R. Fellowes was advised on the choice of a new gardener. *The Gardener's Chronicle* was contacted regarding the placing of advertisements. Mr Henry Perkins now had established himself as the new owner of the nursery and there was lengthy correspondence with The Registrar of Business Names office in London regarding the R. of B. N. Act 1916 and the change of Proprietorship. On 18th August 1920 Mr H. Perkins wrote to:–

The Registrar of Business Names,
30 Russell Square, London W.C.

Dear Sir,

Registration of Business Names Act 1916 Certificate No. 57949

A change of name having taken place in the Proprietorship of this firm we shall be glad if you would kindly send us by an early post a form of notification so that we may put the thing in order.

We are, dear sir,
Wood & Ingram

During August 1920 Mr H. Perkins wrote to many customers about the change of Proprietorship. One letter in particular, dated 30th August 1920, showed his attempt to gather outstanding money owed by one of the Nursery's long established customers:

> A. H. B. Sperling Esq.,
> Lattenbury Hill
> St Ives
>
> Dear Sir,
>
> You have probably noticed the announcement in our local and other papers to the effect that the proprietorship of this business has been transferred from Mr J.E.Perkins, senr, to Mr Henry Perkins.
>   This necessitates, as far as possible, our having to collect all outstanding debts up to and including the date of transfer, viz. June 30th last. Might we therefore ask you to be good enough to kindly favour us with a cheque for the amount of your account to that date at your convenience? (£193:1:7).
>   Thanking you for past favours and with the assurance of our best attention to your future kind orders,
>
> We are, Dear Sir, your obedient Servants,
> Wood & Ingram

———•———

A similar *Letter Book* covers the period 20th September 1920 until 16th April 1921. It contains 505 pages of typed letters, a few are handwritten and some pages contain two letters. Often the same letter is sent to more than one nursery or organisation:–

> The Curator,   26th March 1921
> The Royal Botanic Gardens,
> KEW
>
> Dear Sir,
>
> We are anxious to obtain a pinch of seed, or a few plants of Echium Wildgotti, and it has been suggested that probably you could help us in the matter.
>   If that is so, and you would kindly oblige us, we shall esteem it as a great favour, and we will willingly pay your charges or reciprocate in any way possible.
>   In the event of your not being able to help us perhaps you are in a position to inform us where we should be likely to get a piece of seed.
>
> We are,
>
> Yours faithfully
> Wood & Ingram

An identical letter of the same date was posted to F. G. Preston Esq., The Botanic Gardens, Cambridge.

————— • —————

Mr Henry Perkins never missed an opportunity of drumming up interest in his nursery. Letters often record social events which he attended:– 'Mr Perkins had the pleasure of meeting you when you were Rook shooting and recalled you were requiring Ash and Elm trees. We would be glad to see you at the nursery'.

Mr W. C. Modral,   16th August 1920
The Gardens, Old Warden Park, Biggleswade

Dear Mr Modral,

I have been wondering if one day next week would be convenient for me to send a car over for Mrs Modral, yourself, and I believe Mrs Perkins said Mrs Modral's sister would join you.

    We have been trying to fix this up for sometime past, but the weather seems to have had a fit of the miserables. As it is better now, we hope you will be able to fix (stet) it in, if not next week, sometime in the near future.

With kind regards

I am,
Yours very truly

————— • —————

Whether Mr Perkins was very attached to his horses which worked his nursery fields is open to speculation, but two letters indicated a liking for them:–

Messrs Rowland Wood Ltd   2nd October 1920
The Jungle
167, Piccadilly,
London W

Dear Sirs,

I have two Horses hoofs I want mounting. I think one into an ink pot, and probably one into a door stop, unless you can suggest anything better.

    The hoofs were cut off last night. Will you kindly tell me if they should be sent to you direct as they are, or do you wish any form of preparation beforehand, and will you give me some idea roughly of the cost of mounting same, per return.

Yours faithfully.

Messrs Rowland Wood did reply promptly and the following letter was sent to them on 15th October 1920:–

Dear Sirs,

In reply to yours of the 14th, I note you are proceeding with the inkstand, which is quite in order.
    I accept your estimate for the double candlestick in the design which I saw.

I am,

Yours faithfully
Wood & Ingram

———•———

The *Order Ledger R* from 3rd March 1922 until 16th January 1923, includes 1,000 orders, many from new customers. The vast list of customers in the index of this and other ledgers indicate that clients from all over the country now patronise the Nursery. These include members of the aristocracy, successful business men, commercial nurseries, as well as local residents. It was six years since the signing of the Armistice and a threat of another war seemed to have been forgotten. There were no orders from customers needing young Larch trees to replace their recently felled Larch trees. Hedging was still required, as shown in the orders for the Hon. C. Rothschild, Aston Wold, Oundle, who was sent 150 Oval leaf Privet for £11 18s 0d on 6th February. The Rev W. Watson at Rockingham Castle was sent 2,500 Privet for £21 13s 0d on 10th March, the Trustees of the Shuttleworth Collection, Bedfordshire were sent 1,500 Quicks for £10 1s 2d on 29th March and Messrs T. Rivers & Son at Sawbridgeworth were sent 10,000 Quick for £47 10s 0d on 9th November. But most orders were for customers who wished to plant new shrubs, fruit trees and roses. The following examples are taken from *Order Ledger R* and show the range of plants which new customers now required:

9th March 1922		The Marquess of Salisbury was sent 14 shrubs and 12 roses for £6 2s 11d.
13th " "		Lord Lilford, Oundle was sent 20 Clematis and 222 various shrubs for £9 6s 0d, followed by 48 Laurels for £5 0s 0d and 6 Ilex for £4 8s 0d..
" " "		The Duke of Bedford was sent 6 Rubus canadensis for 17s 0d followed by 100 Azaleas, 200 Laurel and 227 shrubs for £112 14s 0d followed by 2 Berberis aggregata and for 17s 0d.
" " "		Amos Perry Hardy Plant Firm, Enfield was sent 36 Buddleia globosa for £3 8s 0d.
18th " "		The Spirella Company, Letchworth was sent 100 Laurel caucasica, 1 Wisteria, 12 Lonicera nitida and 2 Golden Yews for £114 7s 6d
21st " "		Sir Philip Sassoon, Port Lympe, Kent was sent 6 Lonicera fragrantissima and 2 Lonicera mackii for £1 6s 4d.
23rd " "		Lady Battersea, Overstrand, Norfolk was sent 12 Tamarisk, 6 Oleria and 6 Osmanthus. for £5 2s 6d, followed by 2 Ceratostigma for 18s 3d, followed by 4 Roses, 12 currants and 10 fruit trees for £6 8s 0d.
" " "		Mr Harold Peto, Ilford Manor was sent 18 Bush Roses for £1 16s 5d.

30th	"	"	His Majesty's Office of Works, Regent's Park, London was sent 100 Red Dogwood, 100 Scarlet Willows for £8 0s 0d.
10th April	"		Lord Glanelly, Exning House, Newmarket was sent 2 Ampelopsis veitchii and 1 Ceanothus indigo for 12s 11d.
24th	"	"	The Duke of Northumberland, Albury Park was sent 200 fruit labels and 2 roses for 19s 7d.
7th Oct	"		The Bournville Village Trust Nursery was sent 6 Cotoneaster horizontalis for 12s 7d followed by 12 Persian Lilac, 3 Pears, 6 Acer pseudoplatanus and 12 Ampelopsis veitchii for £4 6s 0d.
4th Nov	"		Bedford College for Women, Regent's Park, London was sent 48 shrubs including 3 Hamamelis and 7 Cydonia marleii for £13 15s 6d.
9th Nov	"		The Countess of Clarendon, The Grove, Watford was sent 24 shrubs which included 5 standard Wisteria sinensis and 6 climbing Wisteria for £7 1s 0d.
"	"	"	Lady Nunburnholme, Benningborough Hall, York was sent 22 shrubs, 100 Lavendula nana and 250 Dwarf Roses for £49 7s 11d.
"	"	"	Sir Otto Beit, Trewin Water, Welwyn was sent 7 Cupressus, 36 Hollies, 2 Irish Yews and 6 English Yews for £17 9s 0, followed by 12 Yews for £2 9s 4d.
11th	"	"	Lord de Saumarez, Shrublands Park, Suffolk was sent 4 Peach Trees and 1 Apricot Tree for £5 3s 0d.
20th	"	"	Sir Fowell Buxton, Waltham Abbey was sent 84 Austrian Pines and 108 Spruce firs for £55 4s 0d.
22nd	"	"	Earl of Lindsey, Uffington House, Stamford was sent 50 Dwarf roses and 1 of each of 60 shrubs for £23 15s 0d.

(This order takes up three pages in the ledger.)

24th	"	"	Lady Huntingfield, Heveningham Hall was sent 26 shrubs including Hibiscus, Phlomis, Cistus, Lonicera and Osmanthus for £4 16s 7d.
27th	"	"	Captain Drummond, Cadland Park Southampton was sent 9 Dwarf Pears and 200 Strawberies 'Waterloo' for £5 13s 0d.
"	"	"	Mr Lawrence Johnston, Hidcote Manor was sent 3 Euonymus alatus for 13s 4d.
6th Dec	"		The Marquis of Kedleston at Hackwood Park, Basingstoke was sent 12 loganberries for £1 1s 1d.
"	"	"	The Earl of Ancaster at Grimsthorpe Castle, Lincolnshire was sent 61 English Yews, 3 Clematis, 15 Persica rosea and 12 Standard Rose for £32 6s 6d.
12th	"	"	Sir Herbert Leon, Bletchley Park, Bucks was sent 36 Laurustinus, 36 Laurel caucasica, 36 Laurel rotundifolia and 36 Berberis darwinii for £21 3s 2d.
28th	"	"	Lord Desborough, Taplow Court, Taplow was sent 100 Salix alba caerulea for £8 12s 6d.
"	"	"	Sir Walter Bagge, Stradsett Hall, King's Lynn was sent 2 Pears and 3 Plums for £2 1s 6d.
4th	Jan	1923	Mr C. Ingram, The Grange, Benenden, Kent was sent 2 Prunus, 2 Pyrus, 1 Rubus deliciosus, 1 Shropshire Prune for £2 5s 6d.

The following orders from the same *Order Ledger R* reveal new local customers who supported the Nursery with their custom:–

THE NURSERY RECOVERS AFTER THE FIRST WORLD WAR 151

3rd March 1922		Bidwells for Cambridge University Farms were sent 700 Quick for £5 10s 7d.
" " "		Mr H. Boardman, Paxton Park ws sent 12 fruit Trees for £8 2s 0d.
8th " "		Mr Smith, Manor House, Hemingford Grey was sent Fruit Trees and a specimen Holly for £3 15s 0d.
" " "		Mrs Coote, Houghton Grange was sent 18 Currants 'Seabrook Black' for 18s 0d.
27th " "		Chivers of Histon was sent 2 Golden Yews and 48 Portugal laurels for £5 19s 6d, followed by 50 Portugal Laurels for £4 15s 0d.
" " "		Mrs Frost, Cross Hall, St Neots (formerly owned by Mr Thornhill of Diddington and planted in the mid 18th century with plants obtained from James Wood) was sent 24 Flowering shrubs, 12 Box, 6 Limes and 1 Malus floribunda for £21 13s 0d.
30th " "		Mrs Rose, Umvote, Brampton was sent 2 Chestnuts, 12 Filberts, 12 Fruit Trees, 12 Dwarf Roses, 72 Lavenders, and 72 Thuja lobelli for £37 2s 0d.
" " "		G. Willers, Trumpington Road Nursery, Cambridge was sent 12 Dwarf Roses, 2 Standard Roses, 4 Fruit Trees and several climbers for £33 11s 3d.
2nd Nov "		Sir George Fordham, Odsey Grange, Ashwell was sent 12 Currants, 2 Cherry Trees and 6 Apple Trees for £3 12s 6d.
7th " "		Mr J. Binney, Pampisford Hall, Cambridge was sent 1 Pinus bungeana and 5 yards of Box hedging for £1 4s 6d.
9th " "		Sir Graham Green, Harston, Cambridge was sent 36 Quick, 12 Gooseberries, 18 Red Currants, 12 Currants, 12 Berberis, 1 Fagus and 1 Apple Tree for £5 5s 6d.
14th " "		Mr Boyes, Godmanchester was sent 27 fruit Trees for £22 2s 0d, followed by 200 various Shrubs for £24 12s 6d.
18th " "		Captain Bendyshe, Barrington Hall was sent 12 Apple trees, 2 Cherry Trees, 1 Fig, 10 Dwarf Roses, 2 Sweet Briars, 1 Jasmine and 150 Larch for £9 17s 0d.
" " "		Mr Sale, Manor Nurseries, Arbury Road, Cambridge was sent 2 Plums, 2 Apples, 2 Pears, 50 Oval Privet and 3 Clematis for £7 5s 3d.
22nd " "		Mr Brown, Castle Camps Hall, was sent 25 Strawberries 'The King' and 24 Strawberries 'King George' for 7s 3d.
24th Nov "		Mr K. Paine, Caxton Hall was sent 12 Strawberries 'The Queen' and 6 Raspberries 'Huntingdon Yellow' for 6s 3d.
29th " "		Mr Joshua Taylor, Cambridge was sent 9 Christmas Trees for £2 5s 0d.
" " "		Miss Dunscombe, Waresley Park was sent 3 Peaches, 1 Apricot, 1 Oak, 13 Roses, 24 Currants and 18 Gooseberries for £6 14s 0d.
6th Dec "		Mrs Fowke, 4 Selwyn Gardens, Cambridge was sent 1 Plum 'Red Magnum bonum' for 16s 6d.
" " "		Mr Reed Gaultier, Madingley Road, Cambridge was sent 1 Double Cherry and 1 Pyrus malus for £1 4s 7d.
9th Jan 1923		Major Francis, Quy Hall was sent 20 Yews, 20 Elms, 2 Birch, 1 Catalpa, 2 Clematis and 6 shrubs for £12 18s 19d.
11th " "		The Earl of Ellesmere, Stetchworth Park was sent 12 Pears, 4 Plums, 1 Nectarine, 2 Peaches and 1 Apple Tree for £8 15s 6d.

From one of the six remaining *Ledgers* devoted to letters (each with no title), the following correspondence, written between August 1922 and November 1922, records that when the nursery was working at full strength it was able to reply to a range of enquiries and to problems affecting the everyday running of a large nursery:

Mr Snell   August 11th 1922
The Gardens, Wimpole Hall,
Royston,

Dear Sir,

We thank you for your kind order received through our Mr Fells for Wood Wool and Wadding. The former we are sending by Goods Train to Old North Road station today. This article is put in bales of 56lbs. We have therefore taken the liberty of sending you a full bale rather than split it as by dividing it up it means that not only does it occupy a great deal more space but it is more inclined to get dirty and damp. If, however, our action does not meet with your approval we shall of course be pleased to take back half the quantity on hearing from you. We might also add that the finest quality Aspen Wood Wool which we are sending you is exceedingly difficult to get hold of and it is only by the merest stroke of luck that we have been able to have this in stock.

The Wadding will be posted to you on Monday,

Hoping you are well and with kind regards,
We are, dear sir, yours faithfully,
Wood & Ingram

———•———

Lady Edward Cecil   9th September 1922
Bodiam

My Lady,

In checking our books we find that the amount £2 15s 0d, paid to us on July 1st, had already been kindly paid by you on May 25th.
    This discrepancy probably arose through payment having been made from our Lady Day account and afterwards Your Ladyship making payment from original invoice. We therefore have pleasure in refunding the amount and enclose same herewith, which perhaps you will be good enough to kindly acknowledge at your convenience.

With thanks for past favours and with the assurance of our best services at all times, we have the honour to remain, Your Ladyship's most obedient servants,
Wood & Ingram

———•———

J. Gray Esq., 27th September 1922
Storey's Way,
Cambridge

Dear Sir,

We received the enclosed postcard this morning which evidently through an oversight you omitted to complete. If you would be good enough to inform us as to the message or instructions you wished to have conveyed we will at once see that the same has our immediate attention.

We are, dear sir, your obedient servants,
Wood & Ingram

——— • ———

Mr T. J. Watson 30th September 1922
Bletchley Park

Dear Sir,

When at the Royal Show you kindly intimated to our Mr Fells that you would be requiring some fresh Roses for this Season.

 We have just received a copy of our Catalogue from the printers, a copy of which we have pleasure in forwarding under separate cover. On pages 27–47 will be found a complete list of Roses embracing all the best of the newest kinds. You will also notice a complete revision has been made in the prices throughout.

 We hope to receive a goodly share of your order which you may rely upon us giving our best attention.

Thanking you for past favours,

We are, dear sir, yours faithfully,
Wood & Ingram

——— • ———

Mr Bertrand W. Weal October 12th 1922
Kelvedon

(original handwritten)

Dear Sir,

We thank you for yours of the 6th inst, also for specimen root of Beet this certainly appears a very good stock of Long Beet and we will bear same in mind it is however much different in foliage to the Nuttings Dark Red Beet we sell, ours is Green leaf, please leave the order cancelled for the 7th Nuttings as we have booked it elsewhere. If you have good stock of Model Globe Beet and could send us a root or two please quote price.

 We also thank you for yours of the 9th inst, and the pods of Brooklands Giant Runner Bean this looks like a very good variety and we enclose order for a bushel for trial, also 3 Bushel of Pea 'The Gladstone', which please give your attention in due course.

Yours faithfully,
Wood & Ingram

The Rt Honourable Olivia Countess Cairns   October 30th 1922
Round Hill
Lyndhurst

My Lady,

Agreeably with your esteemed request we are sending you by this post, under separate cover, a copy of our Nursery Catalogue on pages 60, 69 and 82 of which will be found a list of Berberis we can offer. We hold magnificent stocks of everything thus upholding the superlative reputation of our firm for 'Quality', a reputation that has been built up and maintained for upwards of 200 years.

Any orders entrusted to us will be esteemed and command our prompt care and attention,

We have the honour to remain,
Your Ladyship's most obedient servants,
Wood & Ingram

———•———

Messrs Nutting & Sons   October 31st 1922
106, Southwark Street
London SE1

Gentlemen,

When your Mr Nutting called, he was enquiring if we were likely to have any surplus peas to offer, of our growing.

We are enclosing you a sample of the only lot we have which are Thomas Laxton, Net Crop 1922.

Of these we have 28 Bushels as per sample, which we can offer you at 37s 6d per Bushel, subject to your favoured reply by return, which will be esteemed.

Yours faithfully,
Wood & Ingram

———•———

The Distribution Co-operative Society Ltd   6th November 1922
Raunds
Near Wellingborough

Dear Sirs,

Replying to your esteemed favour of the 4th instant and in confirmation of our conversation over the telephone this morning with your Mr Lawrence, we shall be pleased to make you up any Floral Designs at short notice and providing we get the order by phone or letter say 2hrs before any train starts from Huntingdon we could get them in the train for you.

Wreaths, Crosses and Chaplets we can supply at from 15/- upwards, or for a very small size for 10/6.

Other designs such as Harps and Anchors would be more expensive and orders should not be taken for either of these floral designs for less than 25/- as there is a great deal more work entailed in the making.

We shall be pleased to allow you a working discount of 20% on any orders entrusted to us which shall receive our prompt attention.

We are, dear sirs, yours faithfully
Wood & Ingram

The Co-operative Society ran an extensive funeral service for its members and succeeded in obtaining good terms for floral tributes from the nursery.

———•———

Mr W. Mallabar   December 15th 1922
Head Gardener's Lodge
Hatley Park
Gamlingay

Dear Sir,

Many thanks for your esteemed order of the 14th inst for Strawberry Plants.

We are sending you herewith, under separate cover, a copy of our Nursery catalogue, on page 26 of which will be found a list of the varieties we grow. We have marked the varieties we can still do in pots with a tick, those doubly ticked we can do 150 plants and over. All good runners, however, are practically cleared but can still do really good plants of Givons Late prolific which is the only variety we can offer from ground in the quantity requested. Will you kindly let us know whether you prefer these or pot plants of either of the varieties named when your kind order shall have our immediate attention and be dispatched by passenger Train on Monday. These are grown at our St Neots Branch. Perhaps, therefore, you would rather arrange to have them fetched from there as this is not far from your estate by road.

We are, dear sir, yours faithfully,
Wood & Ingram

Mr Wm. Mallabar F.R.H.S.   March 26th 1923
Hatley Park,
Gamlingay

Dear Sir,

Replying to your letter of the 22nd instant we are still on the lookout for you and anything that comes along we will at once let you know but good places are very few and far between just now.

With kind regards, we are dear sir,
Yours faithfully
Wood & Ingram

Mr Wm MallabarApril 17th 1923
Hatley Park
Gamlingay

Dear Sir,

We have an application from a gentleman in this district for a gardener and shall be glad to hear from you if you are prepared to accept a good single handed place with the help of a man during the best part of the year and, if so, we shall be glad to know what wages you are willing to accept.

We are, dear sir, yours faithfully,
Wood & Ingram

Mr Wm MallabarMay 3rd 1923
Hatley Park
Gamlingay

Dear Sir,

We are in receipt of your letter of 1st May and we are pleased to gather there from that you are now fixed up in another situation. We sincerely hope that this will prove more congenial in every way than the last. If at any future time we can be of any further assistance to you we shall be only too pleased to render our services.

With best wishes for your future comforts,

We are, dear sir, yours faithfully,
Wood & Ingram

If when you are settled in your new home you will kindly give us your address we will register same for a regular supply of catalogues.

——— • ———

Dr. A. F. R. Wollaston28th April 1923
Kings College
Cambridge

Dear Sir,

Replying to your kind favour to hand the goods under reference were ordered by Mr F. G. Peters under Kings College heading by which we presumed that they were to be charged to yourself. We herewith enclose copy of Invoice which we trust will be found in order.

With the assurance of our best endeavours at all times

We are, dear sir, yours faithfully,
Wood & Ingram

Dr. A. F. R. Wollaston 3rd May 1923
King's College
Cambridge

Dear Sir,

Please accept our best thanks for your p.c. of the 2nd instant in regard to seeds ordered by Mr F. G. Peters and booked to you in mistake. As it was written under King's College address and no mention was made of who the goods were to be charged to, coupled with the fact that Mr Peters informed us that you were coming over the same day, we concluded that they were for you. However, we have now adjusted the matter in our books and are sending corrected account to Mr Peters with an explanatory letter.

Apologising for any trouble caused you and with many thanks for past favours,

We are, dear sir, yours faithfully,
Wood & Ingram

(Dr. A. F. R. Wollaston was a famous explorer; he had accompanied Mallory to the South Pole and was also a keen botanist. 40 plants were named after him, including *Primula wollastonii*. He was a Fellow and Senior Tutor at King's College. He died tragically in 1930.)

———•———

The second *Wages Ledger* which survives continues immediately from the earlier one, commencing on May 30th 1924 and ending on 26th December 1930. The layout on each page is similar to that adopted in the earlier *Wages Ledger*. The first entry records the following:

May 30th 1924

Carter	6 +3½		£2	13s	6d
Childs	6		2	2	0
Clark	6 (Aug 24th)			15	0
Day	6 Sunday		2	6	0
Freeman	6		2	2	0
Hardwicke	6	9d	2	19	3
Head	6	+3½	2	13	6
Humphreys	6	+3½	2	13	6
Jordan	6		3	15	0
Joyce	6	9d	3	9	6
King	6	+3½	3	4	3
Lunnis	6		3	0	0
Madeley	6		3	0	0
Mason	6–1		2	9	0
Newstead	6	+3½	2	13	6

Owen	6			12	0
Rudd	6	9d	3	4	3
Webb	6		2	0	0
Brampton			87	1	3
			£132	13	3d

By May 23rd 1924 Mr Humphreys' wage had increased in 6 years from £1 2s 8d to £2 13s 6d for 6 days work and 3½ hours overtime. Similarly Mr Joyce's wage had increased from £1 14s 8d to £3 9s 3s for 6 days, which included a deduction of 9d for insurance. This was increased by 5d a week after 1924. Mr King was still employed and his wage was increased from £1 14s 8d to £2 13s 6d for 6 days and 3½ hours overtime. The Huntingdon staff had now been increased from 12 to 18 employees, reflecting the vast increase in orders received by the nursery.

In only eight years Wood & Ingram's weekly wages bill had risen from £38 9s 0d to £132 13s 3d. Mr Jordan, a junior, had been replaced by two further trainees: Mr Clark and Mr Owen. By January 25th 1925 Mr Clark was paid 19s 0d for 6 days work, Mr Owen 14s 0d for 6 days work. They were joined by Mr Scate who was paid 1s 6d for 1 days work, bringing the total of young men to four. Mr Jordan as foreman was still the highest paid member of staff.

Every week from October 31st 1924 until May 15th 1925 there was an entry of 5s 0d for Stoking, which might be a sum of money given to the particular employee whose responsibility was to stoke the boilers during cold weather. This entry re-appeared from October 23rd 1925 until 7th May 1926, and again from November 5th 1926 until May 6th 1927 and throughout the ledger until 1930.

By November 1926 Mr Clark was paid £1 2s 3d for 6 days work, including 9d deduction for insurance, and now he was a permanent member of staff. Mr Owen was no longer employed after 23rd July 1926. Mr Scate was paid 14s 3d for 6 days work, less 9d insurance. He was joined by Mr Ashley, who was paid 10s 0d for 6 days work and Mr Brown, who was paid 14s 0d for 6 days work. The average wage remained constant throughout this period, only fluctuating with overtime when the nursery was very busy or if the glasshouses had to be attended on a very hot Sunday. The *Wages Ledger* records on December 24th 1929 that Mr King, who had been employed in 1916, had died on December 7th 1929. Mr Jordan finished his employment as foreman on July 17th 1925. By the end of 1930 Mr Joyce, who had also been working for the nursery since 1916, was now the highest paid employee at the Huntingdon Nursery and had taken over the role of foreman of the nursery.

The final entry in the second *Wages Ledger* records the following employees:

December 26th 1930

Carter	6		9	£2	14s	3d
Childs	6		9	2	1	3
Dean	6				12	0
Freeman	6		9	2	1	3
George	6 + 6		9		16	0
Goodacre	6		9	1	9	9
Hardwick	6		1/4	3	8	8
Head	6		9	2	9	3
Humphreys	6		9	2	9	3
Joyce	6		1/4	3	18	8
Lunniss	6		¼	2	18	8
Madeley	6 + 8		9	3	9	3
Mason	6		9	2	9	3
Meadows	6		¼	3	8	8
Newstead	6		9	2	9	3
Pack	6		1/3		16	9
Scate	6 + 8		9	1	10	8
Watson	6 + 6		9		12	9
West	6		9		14	3
Stoking					5	0
Brampton				128	18	10
King	¼					
Walls	¼					
				£169	13	8

The only employees at the Huntingdon nursery who had been with Wood & Ingram since 1916 are Mr Humphreys, Mr Joyce and Mr Lunniss. Out of the nineteen men listed in 1930, five received less than £1 for a week's work, even if, like Mr George, they worked 6 days and on Sunday worked 6 hours overtime. There seem to be three rates of insurance for employees at this time – 9d, 1s 3d and 1s 4d.

During the 1920s Wood & Ingram increased their trade by selling directly to other commercial nurseries throughout the British Isles. Mr Henry Perkins continued in his father's footsteps, developing the nursery with a strong eye for business. The 1002 orders in *Order Ledger P,* were mainly related to the commercial trade covering the period between November 1926 until March 1927. The following list illustrates the extensive range of commercial nurseries to whom Wood & Ingram sent plants during this period:–

20th Nov 1926   Messrs G. Banyard, The Royal Nurseries, Maidstone was sent 25 Buddleia amphissemia for £3 3s 9d

24th   "   "   Messrs R. Heal & Sons Ltd, Trinity Road, Wandsworth was sent 100 Lonicera nitida for £2 10s 0d

"	"	"	Messrs Wm Cutbush & Son Ltd, Barnet, Herts was sent 100 taller Lonicera nitida for £3 15s 0d
"	"	"	Messrs Bakers, Codsall, Wolverhampton was sent 2 x 10 varieties of shrubs for £3 15s 0d, followed by a further order for 240 Lonicera nitida and 11 Spartium junceum for £15 6s 0d on 4th March 1927
26th	"	"	Messrs Chilbrass Ltd, Hale, Altrincham was sent 82 dwarf roses and 275 Berberis in 11 varieties for £19 1s 3d
"	"	"	Messrs Benjm Reed & Co., 72 Guild Street, Aberdeen was sent 225 Berberis for £11 2s 6d
1st	Dec	"	Messrs J. Cheal & Sons Ltd, Crawley, Sussex was sent 24 x 3 Berberis for £4 15s 0d
3rd	"	"	Messrs Hilling & Co., Orange Hill Nurseries, Chobham, Surrey was sent 3,000 Crab stocks for £15 0s 0d in 6 bundles and packing for 7s 6d
6th	"	"	Messrs Dobbie & Co. Ltd, Edinburgh was sent an extensive 3 page order of specified fruit trees for £103 11s 1d and later on 17th December 250 Currants 'September Black', 250 Currants 'Boskoop Giant' and 25 Standard plums for £21 7s 0d
8th	"	"	Messrs The Forest Orchard Nurseries Ltd, Melbury Heath, Falfield, Gloucestershire was sent 36 Ceanothus and 31 dwarf Roses for £4 14s 0d
10th	"	"	Messrs Samsons Ltd 8–10 Portland Street, Kilmarnock was sent 96 Berberis for £5 4s 0d
"	"	"	Messrs Wm Wood & Son Ltd, The Nurseries, Taplow was sent 100 Lonicera for £2 10s 0d
1st	Jan	1927	Mr J. C. Allgrove, The Nursery, Middle Green, Langley, Slough was sent 1 each of Fig 'White Marseilles', 'Ringo de Mel' and 'St John'
14th	"	"	Mr H. Gee, Black Hall Nurseries, Marston Ferry Road, Oxford was sent 15 Standard Limes – 10/12 ft transplanted and 12 Dutch Honeysuckle 'Late Red' for £5 8s 0d
31st	"	"	Mr George West, The Nurseries, Datchet, Buckinghamshire was sent 600 Lonicera nitida for £15 0s 0d
10th	Feb	"	Messrs Lowe and Shawyer Ltd, The Nurseries, Uxbridge, Middlesex was sent an extensive number of trees and shrubs for £38 9s 0d
15th	"	"	Messrs V. N. Gauntlett & Co. Ltd, Japanese Nurseries, Surrey was sent 25 Artemesia, 72 Spiraea for £6 17s 9d, followed by 48 shrubs for £4 1s 0d on 23rd February, followed by a large order for shrubs including 25 Perovskia for £8 14s 2d on 4th March, followed by 38 various shrubs for £3 11s 5d on 7th March, and a further shrub order for £14 8s 3d on 18th March
25th	"	"	Messrs Hilliers & Sons, West Hill, Winchester was sent 72 Berberis, 14 Choisyia and 2 Chimonanthus for £9 12s 0d, followed by a further order for 259 Berberis for £13 6s 9d on 21st March
4th	"	"	Messrs W. Treseder Ltd, Cornwall was sent 12 Berberis for £2 0s 6d
9th	"	"	Messrs Carter Page & Co. Ltd, London was sent 100 Lonicera nitida for £2 10s 0d
18th	"	"	Messrs J. Jeffries & Son Ltd, The Royal Nurseries, Cirencester was sent 200 Lonicera nitida for £4 10s 0d
"	"	"	Messrs Hugh M. Kershaw Ltd, The Nurseries, (Keighly), Yorkshire was sent 36 Berberis and 50 Lonicera nitida for £3 18s 3d

21st   "   "   Messrs Cashburn & Welch, The Cambria Nurseries, Huntingdon Road, Cambridge was sent 18 Hollies, 6 Cotoneasters, 12 Ruscus, 6 Hypericum and 3 Garrya for £5 19s 9d

Both Berberis and Lonicera were popular plants for hedging at this time. In 1928 the nursery sold over 3,158 *Lonicera nitida* plants, although the plant had been introduced into this country earlier in the century. Perennial plants were grown for sale at the nursery but do not appear in many orders. However one particular order in 1926 is of interest as it includes a large number of herbaceous plants and shrubs required for laying out a new garden:

B. E. Todhunter Esq., Kingsmoor, Great Parndon, Essex 13th December 1926

6	Aconitum wilsonii	£	6s 0d
6	Alstromeria		3s 9d
6	Anemone japonica 'Alba'		4s 6d
6	Anemone japonica rosea		4s 6d
1	Astilbe davidii		1s 0d
1	Spiraea aruncus var Kneifii		1s 6d
1	Spiraea palmatum		1s 0d
6	Aster sub-caeruleus		6s 0d
6	Campanula persicifolia 'Telham Beauty'		9s 0d
6	Campanula persicifolia grandifolia alba		6s 0d
6	Chelone barbata		5s 3d
12	Delphiniums to name	£1	10s 0d
3	Erigeron 'Amos Perry'		3s 0d
3	Coreopsis grandiflora		1s 6d
1	Echinops ritro		4s 6d
3	Helenium Hoopesi		3s 0d
6	Incarvillea Delaveyii		4s 6d
6	Heuchera		4s 6d
3	Rudbeckia purpurea		3s 0d
6	Thalictrum dipterocarpum		9s 0d
6	Tritoma 'Lord Roberts'	£1	1s 0d
3	Trollius 'Orange Globe'		6s 0d
3	Trollius 'T Smith'		4s 6d
3	Papaver 'Mrs Perry'		2s 3d
3	Papaver mahony		3s 0d
3	Statice latifolia		3s 0d
12	Carnations Allwoodii in variety		7s 6d
1	pair secateurs Aubert's patent		6s 6d
1	pair Gloves Extra Strong hedging		7s 6d
6	Lilacs to name	£1	10s 0d
1	Stranvaesia undulata		5s 0d
3	Cotoneaster frigida		10s 6d
6	Ilex 'Golden Queen'	£2	8s 0d

6	Ilex 'Silver Queen'	£2	8s	0d
3	Ceanothus 'Gloire de Versailles'		18s	0d
1	Romneya coulterii		3s	6d
1	Corylopsis pauciflora		7s	6d
3	Box gold tipped 3ft		15s	0d
1	Climbing Rose 'General McArthur'		2s	0d
2	Standard Cerasus oveeni 6ft stems	£1	1s	0d
2	Forsythia spectabilis		10s	0d
6	Hydrangea paniculata grandiflora	£1	10s	0d
1	Hydrangea hortensis Mouselline		5s	0d
2	Veronica salicifolia		7s	0d
1	Standard Weeping Elm 12/15 feet stem selected specimen	£3	3s	0d
1	Osmanthus armatus		7s	6d
1	Viburnum carlesii		7s	6d
1	Hamamelis mollis	£1	1s	0d
1	Carpenteria californica		5s	0d
1	Rubus deliciosus		7s	6d
12	Azalea mollis in variety	£3	12s	0d
3	Azaleadendrons	£1	17s	6d
8	Rhododendron 'Pink Pearl'	£4	4s	0d
12	Rhododendron 'John Walters'	£4	10s	0d
6	Rhododendron 'Viscount Powerscourt'	£2	5s	0d
5	Rhododendron 'Madame Carvallo'	£1	17s	6d
6	Rhododendron 'William Agnew'	£2	5s	0d
3	Rhododendron 'Lady Grey Egerton'	£1	2s	6d
3	Rhododendron 'Doncaster'	£1	11s	6d
300	Tulips to name	£2	15s	0d
250	Yellow Crocus 1st size	£1	2s	6d
150	Winter Aconites		6s	0d
5	Cast Flower Pots 32's	£2	7s	6d
2	Cast Flower Pots large 60's		10s	0d
2	Cast Flower Pots small		7s	0d
100	Wood labels 10"		10s	0d
100	Wood labels 6"		3s	0d
4	Veitchberry		14s	0d
	7lb tin Soft Soap (Paraffin)		10s	6d
	Box 1s 0d Packing 3s 0d		4s	0d
		£59	11s	0d

Orders continued to be received from His Majesty's Office of Works in London:

3rd March 1926   HMO of W at Regent's Park was sent 50 Standard Oaks for £26 5s 0d, followed by 36 Standard Thorns for £18 18s 0d on 24th November.

1st Dec 1926   HMO of W at Regent's Park was sent 150 Dwarf Old Pink China Roses for £10 0s 0d for the Wallace Collection at Hertford House, followed by a further

	order for 15 Bush Roses 'Independance Day' for £2 9s 8d on 11th December.
10th Jan 1927	HMO of W at Hyde Park, London was sent 3 Ceanothus dentatus, 1 Cotoneaster Henryii, 1 Forsythia spectablis, 2 Yucca recurvifolia, 1 Osmanthus armatua, 1 Viburnum rhytidophyllum, 1 Daphne for £7 4s 6d.
" " "	HMO of W at Hyde Park was sent 150 Cotoneaster acutifolia, 50 Cotoneaster applanata, 100 Cornus sanguinea, 200 Rosa rubiginosa, 100 Ribes sanguinea, 100 Symphoricarpus namely Henryii, parviflorus, conglomeratus, occidentalis, racemosus and laevigatus, 100 Prunus myrobalana, 100 Prunus spinosa and 100 Ribes grossularia for £25 0s 0d.
11th " "	HMO of W at Hyde Park was sent 12 Weigela 'Conquest', 12 Philadelphus grandiflorus, 12 Forsythia in variety, !2 Deutzia in variety, 12 Ribes atrosanguinea, 12 Spiraea in variety, 12 Lonicera maackii, 12 Symphoricarpus in variety, 12 Viburnum lanatana, 12 Hypericum patulum Henryii, 12 Cornus flaviramea, 12 Buddleia in variety for £10 0s 0d.
7th Feb "	HMO of W at Greenwich Park, London, E 10 was sent 25 Standard Cornish Elms, 25 Wych Elms, 12 Norway Maples, 45 Limes and 6 Birch (all selected specimens) for £48 6s 0d.
28th " "	HMO of W at St James's Park, London was sent 24 Rosemary Miss Jessup's Upright variety and 6 Rosemary selected specimens for £7 1s 0d.
" " "	HMO of W at St James's Park, London was sent 3 Cotoneaster applenata, 3 Cistus laurifolius, 3 Azara microphylla, 3 Pyracantha, 3 Cotoneaster harroviana, 3 Cotoneaster rugosa Henryii, 3 Cotoneaster salicifolia rugosa, 6 Ampelopsis sempervirens, 3 Ceanothus floribunda, 18 Forsythia in choice variety, 3 Viburnum rhytidophyllum, 3 Stranvesia undulatum, 3 Berberis gagnepaenii, 5 Buddleia 'Pink Pearl', 5 Buddleia veitchianus, 5 Buddleia amplissima, 5 Buddleia gigantea, 5 Buddleia perfecta, 5 Buddleia superba, 5 Buddleia 'Delight', 5 Buddleia magnifica, 5 Buddleia 'Distinction', 5 Buddleia variabilis rosea, 5 Buddleia alternifolia, 6 Forsythia -selected choice named varieties, 3 Viburnum utile, 3 Escallonia 'Edinburgh', 3 Ceanothus thyrsiflorus, 3 Escallonia 'Donard Seedling', 3 Ceanothus azureus grandiflorus for £40 0s 0d.
3rd March "	HMO of W, Duke of York's School, Dover was sent 1 Cedrus atlantica, 1 Taxus semper aurea, 3 Hollies – female – selected, 1 Cupressus Lawsoniana stewartii, 1 Wellingtonia gigantea, 1 Crataegus carnerii, 1 Crataegus oxycantha rosea plena, 1 Crataegus oxycantha punica, 1 Crataegus Gibbsii, 1 Acanthopanax picinifolia, 1 Liquidamber styraciflua, 1 Magnolia lennii, 1 Magnolia conspiceus alba superba, 1 Quercus coccinia splendens, 1 Daphne, 1 Cedrus libanii, 1 Juniperus conastii, 1 Abies nordmanniana , 1 Pyrus malus floribunda, 1 Pyrus malus atrosanguinea, 1 Pyrus malus spectabilis, 1 Pyrus malus sargentiana, 1 Pyrusa malus niedzwerzkyana, 1 Pyrus malus purpurea, 1 Pyrus malus scheideckeri, 1 Pyrus malus aldenhamensis, 1 Pyrus malus veitchii, 12 Pyrus malus atropurpurea, 1 Pyrus malus parkmanii and 1 Pyrus malus spectabilis for £23 7s 6d.

The Nursery was, by this time, sending orders abroad to Ireland. Customers were providing good recommendations of Wood & Ingram's quality plants to other members of their families and more orders arrived on Mr Henry Perkins' desk. In May 1922 Kilkenny Castle, Ireland, was occupied by the Republicans and besieged by the Free State troops for two days before the garrison was compelled to surrender. Both sides were evidently proud of having been 'defended' and 'rescued'.

Rt. Hon. The Earl of Ossory   6th December 1926
Kilkenny Castle
Kilkenny
Ireland

6 Standard Roses 'Etoile de Hollande'	£1	16s 0d
12 Dwarf Roses " "		18s 0d
12 Dwarf Roses 'Mabel Morse'	£1	4s 0d
12 Dwarf Roses 'Shot Silk'	£1	10s 0d
6 Dwarf Roses 'Albertine'		15s 0d
36 Dwarf Roses 'Angèle Pernet'	£4	10s 0d
12 Dwarf Roses 'Souvenir de Georges Pernet'		18s 0d
12 Dwarf Roses 'Betty Uprichard'		18s 0d
12 Dwarf Roses 'Mrs Henry Morse'		18s 0d
12 Dwarf Roses 'William Kordes'		18s 0d
12 Dwarf Roses 'Marcia Stanhope'	£1	4s 0d
1 Bundle and Packing		2s 6d
Carriage		8s 9d
	£16	3s 0d

Captain G. T. H. Gough   21st February 1927
Lough Cutra Castle,
Gort, County Galway, Ireland

100	Common lavender	£3	15s 0d
3	Cupressus macrocarpa lutea 2–3ft	£1	2s 6d
24	Cupressus macrocarpa 2–3ft	£3	12s 0d
150	Rhododendron ponticum	£18	15s 0d
200	Common Firs	£3	10s 0d
24	Veronica traversii	£4	4s 0d
50	Bat Willows 3–4ft (true)	£1	5s 0d
50	Alder 2–3ft		15s 0d
2	Wellingtonia gigantica 3ft	£1	1s 0d
3	Taxodium distichum 2–3ft		15s 0d
1	Cryptomeria japonicum		10s 6d
18	Golden Irish Yews 4ft selected	£18	18s 0d
12	Salix vitellina britzensis		9s 0d
6	Corylus purpurea	£1	1s 0d
12	Berberis darwinii	£2	2s 0d
12	Berberis aquifolium		10s 6d
60	Vinca	£1	7s 6d

200	Sitka Spruce 2–3ft	£8	0s	0d
2	Clematis 'Duchess of Edinburgh'		6s	0d
6	Clematis 'Gypsy Queen'		18s	0d
3	Clematis 'Jackmanii'		9s	0d
2	Clematis 'Ville de Lyon' for 'Mdme Eduard Andre' now sold out		7s	0d
2	Clematis 'Fairy Queen'		6s	0d
1	Vine Muscat Hamburgh)			
1	Vine Muscat of Alexandria)			
1	Vine Foster's Seedling) + Planting canes	£8	15s	0d
2	Vine Lady Downe's Seedling)			
1	Vine Madresfield Court)			
1	Vine Appleby Towers)			
1	Basket 3s 0d, 9 Crates £2 14s 0d, & Packing, Balling 12s 6d	£3	12s	6d
		£86	11s	6d

———•———

Local long-standing customers like the Earl of Sandwich had monthly accounts mainly for garden materials, particularly those needed for a large walled garden with glasshouses. Typical of such customers is Mr A. J. Thornhill Esq, (his family had obtained plants from the nursery in the 18th century) of Diddington Hall, Buckden, whose account dated 30th September 1928 showed items ordered over a period of three months:

July 9th	1 ream Tissue Paper 8/6, 6 Quires Greaseproof 6/-	£	14s	6d
	2 balls String finest		5	–
	½ cwt Thompson's Vine Plant Manure		18	–
	2 balls Fillis Twine 3/- 1 Truck basket 6/6		9	6
	2 balls Fillis Twine thin		2	–
	14lbs Clays Fertiliser		6	–
	4 oz Radish Olive-Shaped Scarlet		2	–
	4 Boxes Carnation Rings		6	–
	½ gall. White fly Vapour		10	6
	2 rolls Kitchen Paper		2	0
	1 Grass Edging Knife		7	6
	2 cwts. Silver Sand 10/- 2 bags 1/-		11	0
July 19th	½ gall. Cory's White Fly Death		10	6
	1 gall. Klall Insecticide	1	1	–
July 23rd	1 gall. Abel		9	6
	1 gall. Klall Insecticide	1	1	–
Aug 22nd	1 pkt Schizanthus Wisetonenels		2	6
	1 pkt. Cauliflower Perkin's Express		2	6
	2 pkts. Radish Olive-Shaped Scarlet		1	–

		£	s	d
	2 bus. Sphagnum Moss..		3	–
	½ cwt. Thomson's Vine Plant Manure.............................	1	10	–
	28lb Clay's fertiliser		10	–
	7lb Rafia @ 2/-..		14	–
	200 Bamboo Canes 3ft.		19	–
Sept 14th	100 Flower Pots 5"..		14	7
	1 bus. Coconut Fibre		3	6
	2 cwts Silver Sand		10	0
	Label:– 100 8" 1/9, 100 10" 3/-		4	9
	½ gall. Corry's White Fly Death		10	0
	½ gall. Klall Insecticide...		11	0
	3 balls Fillis Twine 1/6		4	6
	3 balls Fillis Twine 1/-		3	–
	3 bags 6d...		1	6
Sept 24th	3 balls Tarred Twine thick 1/9..		5	3
	3 balls Tarred Twine medium 1/9...................................		5	3
	1 tin Volck 4/9, 1 doz. Lamp Wicks 6d		5	3
	....	£18	5	10

Wood & Ingram's *Order Ledger Book B* records 992 orders sent between 20th October 1928 and 18th December 1928. Many orders indicate the large range of plants the nursery offered for sale by this date:

30th Oct 1928 Wezelberg & Son, Near Leiden, Holland was sent 100 Ceanothus veitchii, 150 Ceanothus dentatus, 200 Ceanothus floribundus and 50 Ceanothus rigidus to be sent via Harwich c/o Messrs Hudig, Rotterdam for £24 6s 0d.

12th Nov " The King Edward VII Sanatorium, Midhurst, Surrey was sent 12 Rhododendrons, 56 Paeonies, 48 Delphiniums, 24 Dwarf China Roses, 48 Phlox, 48 Nepeta and 12 Ghent Azaleas for £35 0s 0d.

" " " Mr Harding, Madingley Hall, Cambridge was sent two bundles consisting of 100 Privet, 6 Apple Trees, 4 Peach Trees, 2 Nectarine Trees and 170 English Yews 3/4 feet selected for £93 10s 0d.

13th " " Mrs Rothschild, Aston Wold was sent 1,000 Oval leaf privet, 180 Yews 7/8 feet, 36 Clematis and balling materials by lorry for £245 13s 6d.

15th " " Captain Broughton, Barton Stud, Bury St Edmunds was sent 460 Fir Trees, 228 Cupressus lawsoniana, 100 various shrubs, 12 Norway Maples and 12 Sycamores for £117 10s 3d.

" " " W. Finch Esq., Burghley on the Hill was sent 30 Cornish Elms, 300 Yellow Broom, 200 Ash, 200 Polyantha Roses and other shrubs for £106 2s 0d.

21st " " Sir L Brassy, Apethorpe Hall, Peterborough was sent 34 Limes, 26 Ulmus campestris, 106 Dwarf Roses, 50 privet and an extensive number of fruit trees for £68 3s 6d.

22nd " " Mr Astell, Woodbury Hall, Everton, Bedfordshire was sent various shrubs including Eucryphias and Magnolias for £3 10s 6d (The Astell family ordered from James Wood in the 18th century).

29th "	"	The Bursar, Downing College, Cambridge was sent 7 Acers, 3 Standard Hawthorns, 1 Magnolia grandiflora, 1 Liriodendron, 18 English Oaks, 4 Beech and various herbaceous plants for £12 4s 0d.
8th Dec	"	F. H. Barclay Esq., The Warren, Cromer, Norfolk was sent 12 Cytisus (in variety) for £2 9s 8d.
10th "	"	Messrs Dobbie & Co. Ltd, Edinburgh was sent 500 Black currants, 500 Lonicera nitida, 55 Standard Roses, 90 Plum Trees, 62 Berberis, 48 Weigelias and 37 Apple Trees for £62 10s 0d.
18th "	"	Cutbush & Son, Barnet Nurseries was sent 1,200 Quick, 250 Lavendula nana compacta for £9 14s 6d.

As well as providing this wide range of plants, Henry Perkins had been striving assiduously to become the largest rose-grower in the country.

CHAPTER 10

ROSES AT THE NURSERY DURING THE 20TH CENTURY

Before John Ingram and his wife travelled to London on 16th June 1858 and visited the Crystal Palace Exhibition, their nursery was not well known for roses. However, they were most impressed by both the amazing fountains at Sydenham and the fine displays of roses they saw in full bloom. Although the nursery had offered several roses for sale, it had not been successful in its attempts to produce roses to match the same standard they saw displayed at the Crystal Palace Exhibition. The Nursery up to this time had not been famous for breeding any prize winning roses. Instead it ordered from rose breeders who were established both in England and Europe, leaving that painstaking task of introducing new roses to others. Some roses had been available for many years, as noted in the Nursery's 18th century ledger (see Lord Sandwich's order 1768 for Moss roses, *Rosa gallica*, *Rosa damescena* and *Rosa centifolia*). By the end of the 19th century Wood & Ingram's catalogues listed an extensive range of roses.

Each year John Wood Ingram methodically checked through the printed lists of awards given for new roses of excellence at various prestigious Rose Shows:– The Geneva Gold Medal lists, The Bagatelle Gold Medal lists, The Rome Gold Medal lists, The Royal National Rose Society lists, The Hague Gold medal and Golden Rose Awards and the Portland (Oregon) Gold Medal lists from America. A letter was sent to the appropriate rose breeder, asking if a particular award winning new rose could be supplied in a small quantity. Upon receipt of this new rose, the nursery quickly grafted as many roses from it as possible. If the grafts succeeded, healthy plants could be available for sale within two years. By this method the nursery was able to obtain over 673 new roses from 70 rose breeders by 1887. In 1892 Wood & Ingram was able to list 728 roses available for sale in large quantities. By 1899 the nursery held the largest range of roses for sale in England.

Not every rose that was bred in the 19th century was registered. But those that were, can be traced through *The International Check List of Roses*. France was now famous throughout Europe for producing fine roses and, by the end of the 19th century, over 40 rose breeders existed in that country, the majority situated near Lyon. Their roses enjoyed the warm growing conditions of the Rhone Valley. Of the 12 rose breeders in England at the end of the 19th century, William Paul and Son from Waltham Cross,

Hertfordshire were far the most successful. By comparison America produced only 7 rose breeders worthy of the attention of Wood & Ingram *(see Appendix note on Rose Breeders)*.

John Wood Ingram had met William Paul at the Nursery and Seed Trade Association Ltd meetings from 1877 onwards and had established good relations with his fellow nurseryman. Included in his 1889-90 catalogue were:– *Rosa Paul's Carmine Pillar*, a splendid single rose with flowers 3"–4" across of the brightest rosy-carmine. Dwarfs 1/- each, in pots 1/6 to 3/6 each. *Rosa Charles Darwin*, a brownish crimson fragrant rose (1879). *Rosa Beauty of Waltham*, a bright red fragrant rose (1862), *Rosa Zenobia* (1894). Later *'Paul's Scarlet Climber'* was added to the nursery stock and was available in 1918. All these roses were raised by William Paul. The Nursery's 1890 Stock Book listed over 500 roses of which half appear in their 1898-99 catalogue *(see Appendix 1)*.

When Mr John Perkins bought the Nursery in 1903, he continued to obtain roses, following John Wood Ingram's successful route. Dwarf Roses were becoming popular and replaced annual bedding schemes in parterres and the new garden owners set about planting this new range of roses. To maintain the Nursery's high standards and to produce roses in the large quantities required, it was essential that Wood & Ingram trained their staff successfully to graft a rose on to budding stock and to grow the rose on to ensure that a saleable plant was available within two years. A large failure rate would have been disastrous and lost the nursery its reputation. Large orders of Manettii stock for grafting roses were obtained from the continent, as these were the least prone to produce wild side shoots. Wood and Ingram required most of the sixty acres along the Thrapston Road in Brampton for the sole purpose of coping with the large demands of customers requiring roses from the Nursery. Luckily the Nursery was well aware that, to maintain their reputation for high quality reliable plants, it was essential to retain their loyal staff and therefore reasonable wages and conditions were offered to their staff.

The Nursery grew roses for sale all through the First World War, albeit with depleted numbers of men. Regular customers continued to support the nursery and were ordering extensive numbers of the fashionable new Dwarf Roses. In 1917 the Earl of Sandwich was sent 448 dwarf roses, the Hon. G. A. Robarts of Wimpole Hall was sent 80 dwarf roses, Lord De Ramsey was sent 220 dwarf roses and Mrs Bevan of Island Hall, Godmanchester was sent 24 dwarf roses from the nursery.

The bulk of rose orders at the end of the First World War came from well established nurseries, others from keen rose enthusiasts:–

4th Nov 1918		Dobbie & Son, Edinburgh was sent 700 Dwarf Roses for £38 0s 10d, followed by a further order on 2nd December 1918 for 150 Dwarf roses and 100 Standard Roses for £32 18s 0d.
11th "	"	Bonsall Nurseries, Harrogate was sent 500 Dwarf Hybrid Tea Roses, 100 Climbing Roses, 100 Apple Trees and 100 Plum Trees for £48 18s 0d.
13th "	"	R. Veitch & Son, Exeter was sent 112 Dwarf Roses for £6 7s 5d, followed by a further order on 2nd December 1918 for 300 Dwarf and Standard Roses for £24 11s 0d.
12th Dec	"	Kent & Brydon, Darlington was sent 800 Dwarf Roses for £45 19s 0d.
12th March 1919		Mr S. Brotherhood, Thornhaugh, Peterborough was sent 120 Dwarf Roses for £18 2s 3d.
11th Nov	"	Lady Meyer, Shotgrove Park, Newport, Essex was sent 750 Roses for £75 6s 0d.
27th "	"	Mr L. Numburnholne, Walter Priory, York was sent 1,500 Dwarf roses in 6 Bundles for £206 6s 6d.

Shortly after sending Lady Meyer her rose order, Mr Henry Perkins wrote to her estate agent:–

> Mr Guile,   17th November 1919
> Estate Office, The Gardens,
> Shotgrove Park, Newport
>
> Dear Sir,
>
> Mr Perkins thinks it might be worthwhile looking up the gardener at Melchet Court, and I will be so obliged if you could give us the gardener's name.
>
> Also, that you tell us where Mr Lionel Rothschild's place is and anything about it.
>
> Thanking you in anticipation of a reply for which I enclose a stamped address envelope.
>
> I am, yours faithfully
> H. Perkins

One of Mr Perkins's difficulties was contacting French rose breeders after the First World War. Many sons had been lost in the war and some nurseries were forced to close. On Monday 3rd August 1914, Germany had declared war on France and rapidly made their way towards Paris. One such rose nursery which suffered in the war was owned by Joseph Pernet-Ducher, who had bred several award winning roses. His eldest son Claudius, too impatient to be called up, enlisted as a soldier of the 159th Infantry Regiment and his brother Georges joined the 357th. Claudius was mortally wounded on 23rd October 1914 at St Laurent-les-Arras and his brother died in an assault on La Fontenelle in Vosges. The grief-stricken parents and their sisters Angèle, Marie and Louise sent out a notice of this cruel loss on 2 August 1915. After the war Mr Perkins was keen to re-establish contact with Joseph Pernet of Pernet Ducher, whose nursery was near Lyon. Pernet had named two new roses in memory of his sons and in 1924 Joseph arranged for Jean Gaujard to take over his business. Jean Gaujard named his first new rose after Joseph's eldest daughter Angèle. A series of letters between Mr Perkins and Pernet Ducher illustrates the close connection between the nursery and the rose breeder. The correspondence continued for several years and in 1924 Pernet Ducher's orange Hybrid *Rosa Angèle Pernet,* became one of Wood & Ingram's most popular roses.

    Messrs J. Pernet Ducher,   10th November 1919
    Rose Grower,
    Venissieux les Lyon,
    (Rhone), France

    Dear Sir,

    We shall be glad to hear if you can offer us any more pruned plants of your new rose Souvenir de Claude Pernet, and Captaine Georges Desirier, and if so, how many can you spare of each.

    Also what you can offer of Madame Abel Chantenay, Madame Segond Weber, in dwarf budded plants.

    Kindly reply as early as possible, and oblige,

    Yours faithfully
    Wood & Ingram

    Messrs J. Pernet Ducher   19th November 1919
    Rosieriste
    A Venissieux les Lyon
    (Rhone) France

    Dear Sirs,

    Thanks for your postcard, we note you are sold out of Captain Georges Desirier, and that is not your intention to put Souvenir de Claude Pernet on the market this season.

    We note on your list which you sent us in September, that you would not send this variety out unless a minimum of 3,000 were subscribed. We shall be glad to know what size order you would require to enable you to send this variety out, as possibly we might be able to increase our order.

    Kindy let us have your views on the matter.

    Yours faithfully,
    Wood & Ingram

Mr J. Pernet Ducher   26th November 1919
Rose Grower
Venissieux les Lyon,
(Rhone) France

Dear Sir,

If you can still supply any of your new rose Severine, kindly send them on by quickest possible route. If you can do a few, please post them, and oblige.

Yours faithfully
Wood & Ingram

Mons. J. Pernet Ducher   9th December 1919
Venissieux les Lyon
(Rhone) France

Dear Sir,

Kindly say what you can still offer us in the way of plants, Souvenir de Georges Beckwith and oblige.

Yours faithfully
Wood & Ingram

Mons J. Pernet Ducher   15th December 1919
Venissiuex les Lyon
(Rhone) France

Dear Sir,

Many thanks for your kind letter of the 12th, we will take the 150 pruned plants of Souvenir de Georges Beckwith, kindly send them on with the Severine on order.

We then asked you to kindly send us a few plants of Benedictine Seguin, if you have them left, we should also like about half a dozen of Mistress Farmer and the same of Georges Basset. If you do another ½ dozen Aspirant Marcel Rouyer and Jean G.N. Forestier, we shall be obliged if you will send these on at the same time. When forwarding same, if you have any good plants on briar of Madame Abel Chantenay, kindly include them also.

With further reference to your postcard of 22nd re your new rose Sovenir de Claudius Pernet, we have been wondering if it would be worth your while to distribute these this next spring, say in the month of February. It would not perhaps be a difficult matter for you to notify those who have ordered it, that a sufficient demand having arisen for it, you have decided to distribute it then.

We feel that there are several good yellows coming along, it is a pity for the rose loving world not to have the benefit of our fine introduction as soon as possible, and as we shall be in a position to deal with a fair quantity ourselves, we should be glad to know how many more you would require to be purchased, as to enable you to distribute this novelty the coming spring.

We are anxious to help you in the matter, and shall be glad to hear your views and will you also kindly tell us at the same time if the above suggestion does not appeal to you, whether you are prepared to sell us this season's output of this novelty in one lot for cash, and if so on what conditions.

We take this opportunity of tendering our very best wishes for the approaching Christmas and New Year, and with kind regards,

Yours faithfully,
Wood & Ingram

Mons J. Pernet Ducher,   30th December 1919
Venissieux les Lyon
(Rhone) France

Dear Sir,

On the 15th December, we wrote you as per enclosed copy of letter, and so far having received no reply or acknowledgement, we wonder if you received the letter, and in case you did not, we repeat same, and shall be glad to have your reply as early as convenient.

Yours faithfully,
Wood & Ingram

———•———

Although he had been well supplied with roses from continental rose breeders before the war, Mr Perkins sometimes found that nurseries which had re-opened after the war had not built up their stock in sufficient numbers to be able to send roses to his Nursery at short notice. To have available for sale the large number of roses required to satisfy Mr Perkins's ever increasing orders sometimes became a problem. Certain requests for roses were not fulfilled. Ordering plants during the despatching season could be risky and there was always one order that seemed to cause trouble when the other nursery was unable to provide roses urgently required. Wood & Ingram had problems during the Christmas period of 1919 with Ketton Bros. of Luxembourg.

Messrs Ketton Bros.,   10th November 1919
Luxembourg,
(Grand Duchy)

Dear Sirs,

Kindly say what you can offer in Dwarf Budded Plants on briar, first class quality of Madame Segond Weber; Madame Abel Chantenay; Lady Pirrie; & Lady Hillingdon, with prices.

Yours faithfully,
Wood & Ingram

Messrs Ketton Bros., 28th November 1919
Luxembourg,
(Grand Duchy)

Dear Sirs,

Thanks for your letter and marked Catalogue, we wired you as per enclosed confirmation this morning, and shall be glad to have delivery as quickly as possible.

Kindly say if you can offer any Dwarfs of Horace Vernet and Betty.

Yours faithfully
Wood & Ingram

Messrs Ketton Bros., 9th December 1919
Luxembourg
(Grand Duchy)

Dear Sirs,

Kindly say if you can supply a few dwarf rose Mrs Harold Brocklebank, and Zépherine Drouhin, and oblige.

Yours faithfully,
Wood & Ingram

Messrs Ketton Bros., 30th December 1919
Luxembourg,
(Grand Duchy)

Dear Sirs,

With reference to your invoices of November 29th and December 4th we received three bundles of Roses on the afternoon of December 24th just as we were closing down for the Xmas holiday, and on unpacking same, we are sorry to find that you have sent us one bundle containing someone else's order.

We have nor received any of the 300 General McArthur, nor the 4 Mrs Alfred Tate; 7 Lady Battersea, 6 Weddingen, but instead of these the bundle contains Roses of the following numbers:– 868, 1036, 1836, 113, 636, 121, 753, 1027, 731, 1671, 1575, 1201, 866, 114, 70, 1673, 101, 1634, 263, 1779, 1738, 1047, 1344, 1744, 627, 383, 1829, 807.

The only variety in this bundle that is if any service to us is the last one viz: 807 Dorothy Page Roberts. We shall be glad to keep this variety if we may do so. The rest are of no service to us, and we shall be glad to know what you wish done with them, and also how you propose to put the matter right as far as the varieties we are short of are concerned.

Of course we are well aware that it is an easy matter when you are busy for the wrong address label to become attached, but unfortunately it is a serious matter for us to receive a lot of varieties we do not want and not to receive what we do want.

Kindly let us hear from you by an early post.

Yours faithfully,
Wood & Ingram

Messrs Ketton Bros., 8th January 1920
Luxembourg
(Grand Duchy)

Dear Sirs,

Thanks for yours of the 5th. We duly forwarded the entire bundle to Mr T Butcher of South Norwood in accordance with your wishes, and we regret to have to inform you we have not yet received our bundle containing 300 McArthur: 4 Mrs Alfred Tate; 7 Lady Battersea and 6 Weddingen.

Naturally, it is very annoying to us, and we fear after lying about in a manner these roses have, that they will be of little use to us when we want them. However, we will do whatever is fair by you and acquaint you of their condition as desired, as soon as they arrive.

On December 31st we sent you an order to send us by parcel post, 100 Dwarf Roses on briar Hugh Dickson, 6 Dwarf Meddingen and 3 Rembrandt (H). You do not refer to this order in your letter, but we shall be glad if you will kindly send them by first possible post, as we are most urgently in want of them.

We cannot understand why they have not been sent before, or if sent, why we have heard nothing of them.

Yours faithfully
Wood & Ingram

Messrs Ketton Bros., 14th January 1920
Luxembourg
(Grand Duchy)

Dear Sirs,

On December 31st we sent an order to you for 100 Dwarf Roses Hugh Dickson, on briar, 6 Dwarf Weddingen and 3 Rembrandt.

On Saturday last the 10th, we sent you a cable, reply paid, to know if you had sent these by parcel post, as instructed, as we are most urgently in want of these roses.

So far we have received no reply whatever from you, neither have we received the roses. Although we on the same day posted an order to another firm in Luxembourg, we may say these roses were duly posted and received here by last Saturday.

Kindly give the matter your immediate attention, and if you have not already posted the roses for us, send them by parcel post immediately.

Yours faithfully
Wood & Ingram

Messrs Ketton Bros., 14th January 1920
Luxembourg,
(Grand Duchy)

Dear Sirs,

In further reply to your letter of the 5th we duly forwarded the whole order of the wrong bundle to Mr Thomas Butcher, and we have now received in return, the 300 General McArthur, but having been out of the ground since the end of November, they have arrived in simply a useless condition.

They are extremely dry, and much too badly withered to be able to send out, we therefore intend planting them up to see what we can do with them for another season. We shall be glad to know what you suggest doing in the matter.

The 4 Mrs Alfred Tate; 7 Lady Battersea and 6 Weddingen were not included in bundle 681or 682, in fact we have not received them at all.

Kindly rectify this matter, and as soon as you have sent us the Hugh Dickson and 6 Weddingen, we shall be glad to have your statement of account, for all goods supplied, so that we can remit for the whole together.

Yours faithfully
Wood & Ingram

Difficulties with continental rose breeders caused the Nursery many headaches. Rose nurseries in England, Ireland and America had started to replace those lost in Europe. Mr Perkins turned his back on Europe and looked towards those nurseries which had been unaffected by the war. One such nursery was McGredy & Sons who had established their nursery at Portadown, Northern Ireland and already had a good stock of some Gold Medal roses, which were not available from Harkness's Nursery in nearby Hitchin, Hertfordshire. In the following correspondence Mr Perkins clearly had his eye on a certain rose and lost no time in contacting McGredy to obtain a supply.

Messrs S. McGredy & Sons 18th November 1919
Portadown
Ireland

Dear Sirs,

Kindly say if you can supply one or two odd plants (old pot plants will do) of Rosa Mrs Henry Winnett, Ophelia Supreme, also plants of Severine, and Colombia hardy plants from pots.

Yours faithfully
Wood & Ingram

The above letter was an example of how the Nursery quickly set out to obtain the latest introduction *R. Columbia*, which had in 1919 been awarded the American Rose Society

Getrude Hubbard Gold Medal and the Portland Gold Medal. Their request was so casual, hoping that McGredy would not spot Mr Perkins' real intention, to obtain a source of this award-winning rose. McGredy & Sons at Portadown in Ireland were kept on their toes by what had now become a very efficient head office in Huntingdon, masterminding rose orders from other nurseries. To satisfy eager customers with the latest award winning rose, the Nursery had to establish a stock of award-winning roses for sale before another nursery overtook them.

>Messrs S. McGredy & Sons   21st December 1919
>Portadown
>Ireland
>
>Dear Sirs
>
>We wired you this morning as per enclosed confirmation, and shall be glad if you can despatch these early next week. If you think it necessary to insure, please do so.
>
>   We have not yet received your reply to our letter respecting Severine and others. If you can supply, we shall be glad if you will include with those you despatch next week. We will wire you immediately on receipt of your reply.
>
>Yours faithfully
>Wood & Ingram

The Nursery wrote again as they were concerned about receiving the one rose they urgently needed. The mention of insurance suggested they would be prepared to do anything rather than lose *R. Columbia*. They became somewhat desperate when they did not receive the roses and feared they might have been lost or delayed in despatch. The following letter almost conceals their concern.

>Messrs S. McGredy & Sons
>Portadown,
>Ireland
>
>Dear Sirs,
>
>On Monday last you wrote us that you were despatching the Columbia roses on the following day.
>
>   We presume that they were sent turned out of pots, per passenger train in accordance with our instructions, but so far they have not arrived.
>
>   We shall be glad if you will kindly inform us per return whether they left on Tuesday last as promised, what quantity, and what they were contained in, as we are wanting to get them here this week.
>
>Yours faithfully
>Wood & Ingram

Having settled down to this efficient level of operation, Mr Perkins concentrated on expanding his sales of roses to other nurseries, hoping to corner this market in England. Meanwhile the nursery was busy planting fruit trees and soft fruit to enable gardeners to re-establish their orchards and gardens. Many orders were sent to vicarages in the district. Re-establishing the popularity of a genus often proved difficult and it was not a certainty that a new rose would become a best seller for the Nursery. However the interest in roses by English gardeners continued and, luckily for Wood & Ingram, these plants became even more popular during the 1920s. By the autumn of 1922 Wood & Ingram's rose orders greatly increased and had now overtaken the earlier need of providing larch trees. The Nursery contacted seventeen rose breeders in America to obtain more prize winning roses.

The following orders show the vast numbers of roses the Nursery was capable of supplying:

7th Nov 1919		Hunter King, Dumfries was sent 270 Dwarf Roses, 650 Berberis, 152 Clematis and 50 Shrubs for £252 15s 7d
"	" "	Dobbie & Co., Edinburgh was sent 2,800 Dwarf Roses, 450 R 'Marcel Rouyer' and 750 R 'Lady Price' for £296 5s 5d; further orders on 16th November 1919 for 3,800 Dwarf roses including many R 'Ophelia' for £252 11s 5d and on 28th December 1919 1,700 Dwarf Roses for £83 9s 1d
7th Nov 1922		Benjamin Cant & Sons, Colchester was sent 50 Dwarf Roses 'British Queen', 50 R 'Constance', 50 R 'Mrs Bertram Walker' and 24 R 'Una' for £12 19s 1d
"	" "	E. Murrell, Shrewsbury was sent 190 various Dwarf Roses for £13 9s 8d

Although the nursery was always happy to receive large orders, smaller orders for roses were given as much care and attention as larger orders and include:–

10th March 1922		Miss Measures, Bletsoe Castle, Bedfordshire was sent 1 Weeping Standard Rose 'Albéric Barbier' for 7s 6d
11th "	"	The Earl of Ancaster, Grimsthorpe Castle, Lincolnshire was sent 7 Standard Roses 'Dorothy Perkins' for £2 12s 6d

Detailed examination of many rose orders between 1924 and 1930 in Wood & Ingram's Ledgers reveal that one rose was more popular than any other rose of that time, *Rosa 'Angèle Pernet'*. Described in the catalogue as a Pernet Rose with *'reddish orange flowers shaded and bordered with chrome yellow, handsome large bronze green shiny foliage; hardy and fine constitution and good bedding habit; free and perpetual flowering; very sweetly scented; glorious in sunlight and also under artificial light.'*

29th Nov 1926	Miss Christy, Flower Farm, Bogton Cross, Chelmsford was sent 2 Dwarf Roses 'Angèle Pernet' for 5s 0d
" " "	Messrs G. Gibson & Co., Leeming Bar, Bedale was sent 50 Dwarf Roses 'Angele Pernet' for £2 15 0d
" " "	Mr Shuttleworth, Old Warden Park, Bigglewade, Bedfordshire was sent 100 Dwarf Roses 'Angèle Pernet' for £12 10s 0d
" " "	Messrs Dobbie & Co. Ltd, Edinburgh was sent 500 Dwarf Roses 'Angèle Pernet' for £30 0s 0d

One great rosarian, Mr Charles Rothschild had inherited Ashton Wold to the west of Peterborough for his Hungarian bride Rozsika von Wertheimstein. According to his daughter, the late Dame Miriam Rothschild, they were both keenly interested in the genus Rosa, and between them they established a great collection of roses which were planted in the grounds at Ashton Wold. Although Mr Charles Rothschild died in 1923, his wife continued to enlarge the collection with the help of her son Victor, until he inherited Tring Park in Hertfordshire in 1935. She died in 1940. An order listed the 1,105 roses and shrubs Victor Rothschild bought from Wood & Ingram:–

Mr Rothschild,   18th November 1926
Ashton Wold,
Oundle

Dwarf Roses:–

12	Golden Emblen		18s	0d
24	Lady Inchiquia	£1	16s	0d
6	Betty Uprichard		9s	0d
140	Madame Butterfly	£10	10s	0d
45	Los Angeles	£3	7s	6d
6	Henrietta		9s	0d
6	Sir Claudius Pernel		9s	0d
60	Christine	£4	10s	0d
150	Angèle Pernet	£18	15s	0d
54	William Rader	£4	1s	0d
3	La Tosca		4s	6d
6	Sunburst		9s	0d
25	Caroline Testout	£1	17s	0d
10	Cheerful		15s	0d
3	Ophelia		4s	0d
10	Ulrick Brunner		15s	0d
16	Red Letter Day	£1	4s	0d
6	King of Kings		9s	0d
40	George Dickson	£3	0s	0d
48	Orleans	£3	12s	0d
176	Hollandia	£13	4s	0d
12	Lady Pirrie		18s	0d

6	Victor Hugo		9s	0d
40	Etoille de Hollande	£3	0s	0d
76	Irish Elegance	£5	14s	0d
3	Sorbet		4s	6d
3	Kirsten Poulsen		6s	0d
3	Ellen Poulsen		4s	6d
2	Moyesii		7s	0d

Standard Roses:–

16	Mrs Henry Morse	£4	0s	0d
12	Etoile de Hollande	£3	12s	0d
12	George Dickson	£3	0s	0d
12	Madame Butterfly	£3	0s	0d
12	Lady Hillingdon	£3	0s	0d
2	Betty Uprichard		12s	0d
16	Madame E Herriot	£4	0s	0d
20	Frau Karl Drushki	£5	0s	0d

Half Standard Roses:–

14	Frau Karl Drushki	£3	10s	0d
225	Raspberries Lloyd George	£5	12s	6d
3	Bush Plums Victoria	£1	11s	6d
1	Dwarf trained Cherry Morello		10s	6d
8	Bush Apples to name	£4	4s	0d
1	Cedrus deodora		15s	0d
12	Spartium junceum	£1	10s	0d
1	Standard Rose Caroline Testout		5s	0d
	1 Box, 3 Bundles 2 Crates & packing	£1	4s	6d
		£137	15s	0d

Acme labels to follow, direct from factory
L&NER goods Oundle Station

Dame Miriam Rothschild described the garden at Ashton Wold in her book *'The Rothschild Gardens'* 2000:

> 'Apart from the walled garden and the grounds dividing the house from the wood and open fields, there were several discrete walled gardens including the rose garden with a stone sundial and paved paths, and a watergarden with a sunken central pool encircled by flowers – roses, iris, catmint and a great variety of other cultivated and wild species . . . alongside a 150 yard range of Morello cherries, peaches and nectarines, enclosed in a glass wooden frame ten feet high was a double row 200 yards long of hybrid tea roses, kept for cutting'.

In 1926 and 1927 the nursery began to send out large orders of roses:–

29th Nov 1926		Messrs Dobbie & Co. Ltd, Edinburgh was sent 500 Dwarf roses for £30 0s 0d
" " "		Messrs Toogood & Sons, Southampton was sent 194 Dwarf roses for £7 18s 9d
30th "	"	Messrs Alex Dickson & Sons Ltd was sent 900 Dwarf Roses for £37 0s 0d
1st Dec	"	Messrs W. & J. Brown, Rose Nurseries, Eastfield, Peterborough was sent 157 Dwarf Roses for £4 4s 3d, followed by a further order on 2nd December for 247 Dwarf Roses for £8 9s 1d
9th "	"	Messrs B. R. Cant & Son Ltd, The Old Rose Gardens, Colchester was sent 397 Dwarf Roses for £16 9s 4d, followed by a further order on 13th December for 250 Dwarf Roses for £12 10s 0d
7th Feb 1927		Messrs Dobbie & Co. Ltd, Edinburgh was sent 1,100 Dwarf Roses for £51 5s 0d, followed by a further order on 24th February for 1,087 Dwarf Roses for £44 11s 0d
4th Mar	"	Messrs Daniels Bros Ltd Norwich was sent 450 Roses for £21 6s 0d

By 1928 Wood & Ingram were supplying an even greater number of nurseries with large orders for roses on a commercial basis and their Order Ledgers reveal their growing commercial success:–

7th Mar 1928	A. J. Heal, Victoria Nursery, Harrogate	paid £3 17 8d for 112 roses.
9th Mar '28	Murrell's Nursery, Shrewsbury	paid £6 4 10d for 120 roses.
12th Mar '28	G. A. Clark's Nursery, Dover	paid £9 15 8d for 220 dwarf roses
12th Mar '28	Dobbie & Co. Ltd, Edinburgh	paid £18 6 0d for 500 dwarf roses
12th Mar '28	Daniels Bros Nursery, Norwich	paid £11 19 1d for 324 bush roses
21st Mar '28	Daniels Bros Nursery, Norwich	paid £20 11 4d for 340 dwarf roses
15th Oct '28	Dickens & Sons, Edinburgh	paid £419 8 9d for 13,000 dwarf roses
19th Oct '28	Lea Hunter & King, Dumfries	paid £68 4 8d for 1,400 dwarf roses
19th Oct '28	Darling's Nursery, Hull	paid £31 2 2d for 850 dwarf roses
19th Oct '28	Chaplin Bros Nursery, Waltham Cross	paid £124 15 2d for 2,250 roses
19th Oct '28	Brooks Nursery, Weston Super Mare	paid £12 1 5d for 300 bush roses
19th Oct '28	Parman & Co., Chard	paid £21 3 8d for 600 dwarf roses
19th Oct '28	Pearson & Sons, Lowdham, Northumb	paid £33 11 6d for 800 roses
24th Oct '28	Samson Ltd, Kilmarnock	paid £24 4 0d for 650 bush roses
24th Oct '28	Cuthbert Ltd, Southgate, London	paid £71 9 8d for 1,150 roses
24th Oct '28	Bunyard & Co., Maidstone	paid £12 15 3d for 375 dwarf roses
24th Oct '28	Hillier & Sons, Winchester	paid £215 1 9d for 4,270 bush roses
26th Oct '28	Dickson & Robinson, Manchester	paid £92 2 9d for 2,600 bush roses
26th Oct '28	W. Jones Nursery, Woodford Essex	paid £34 3 6d for 1,500 dwarf roses
5th Nov '28	Dobbie & Co. Ltd, Edinburgh	paid £20 8 1d for 518 bush roses
7th Nov '28	Reed & Sons Ltd, Loughton, Essex	paid £33 2 4d for 1,025 bush roses
6th Nov '28	Cant & Sons Ltd, Cochester	paid £144 6 11d for 3,400 dwarf roses
9th Nov '28	Spooner & Sons, Hounslow, Middlesex	paid £45 5 9d for 1,200 roses
12th Nov '28	G. Jackman & Son, Woking	paid £9 18 0d for 250 dwarf roses
12th Nov '28	Cant & Sons Ltd, Colchester	paid £32 12 11 for 670 dwarf roses

16th Nov	'28	G. Prince, Longworth, Berks	paid £21 6 10d for 500 dwarf roses
19th Nov	'28	Harkness, Hitchin	paid £23 4 4d for 660 dwarf roses
19th Nov	'28	Cadwell & Sons, Knutsford	paid £13 6 11d for 325 dwarf roses
19th Nov	'28	Austria & Kalan, Glasgow	paid £19 3 10d for 575 bush roses
23rd Nov	'28	R. Cant & Sons Ltd, Colchester	paid £45 5 0d for 730 roses
24th Nov	'28	Scottish Co-op Soc, Springside Nursery	paid £21 15 9d for 475 roses
20th Nov	'28	Dobbie & Co. Ltd, Edinburgh	paid £124 1 5d for 1,350 roses
1st Dec	'28	Veitch & Son Ltd, Exeter	paid £5 14 10d for 152 dwarf roses
4th Dec	'28	Bees, Chester	paid £14 7 6d for 200 dwarf roses
4th Dec	'28	Murrells Nursery, Shrewsbury	paid £8 3 1d for 200 dwarf roses
4th Dec	'28	Rogers, Pickering, Yorkshire	paid £8 12 5d for 187 dwarf roses
4th Dec	'28	Scottish Co-op Soc	paid £5 12 4d for 165 dwarf roses
4th Dec	'28	R. Cant & Sons Ltd, Colchester	paid £29 2 6d for 600 dwarf roses
8th Dec	'28	Bunyard & Co., Maidstone, Kent	paid £9 4 1d for 262 dwarf roses

During the above 10 months in 1928 Wood & Ingram's Nursery sent out 44,000 roses to their other nursery customers.

The Rose, which had always been the national emblem of Great Britain, was rarely out of demand in gardens. Over the years certain roses came in and out of fashion, dwarf roses were succeeded later by hybrid teas, and today there has been great interest in old fashioned varieties. The Nursery found it was difficult to plan ahead when grafting large numbers of roses. It was important to have large numbers of roses available of every variety should the fashion change. At certain times the Nursery would find they had more roses than they had orders for. Wood & Ingram attempted to sell large quantities of roses during the Depression when it was overstocked, and wrote to its printers to produce circulars of its rates for commercial nurseries:–

Messrs Holmes & Smith Ltd, 21st October 1932
Gloucester Street,
Manchester:–

Dear Sirs,

Thank you for yours of the 20th. inst., and we will have 1,000 of the Rose circulars as quoted, kindly put in hand at once and let us have a PROOF with speed.

Please add to our list in correct order Climbing Madame Butterfly, @ 75/- per 100, and please note the following alterations in prices.

Angèle Pernet	55/- per 100
Baby Betty	50/- per 100
Betty Uprichard	55/- per 100
Duchess of Atholl	50/- per 100
E.G.Hill	55/- per 100
Etoile de Hollande	50/- per 100
Gloria Mundy	50/- per 100

Golden Salmon ....50/- per 100
Julien Potin ....50/- per 100
Lady Fortevoit ....50/- per 100
Little Dorrit..50/- per 100
Mabel Morse ....55/- per 100
M. A. Baxter ....50/- per 100
Mrs R. A. Barraclough..55/- per 100
Mrs Beatty..55/- per 100
Mrs G. A. van Roossem ....50/- per 100
Orange Perfection..50/- per 100
Orleans...50/- per 100
Shot Silk...50/- per 100
Talisman ....50/- per 10

Yours faithfully
WOOD & INGRAM

―――― • ――――

On the last page of the Nursery's 1936 catalogue is a photograph depicting 10 members of their staff in the rose fields along the Thrapston Road loading packed crates of roses; an order of 160,000 roses, all raised by Wood & Ingram, destined for Waterdown, Ontario, Canada.

Correspondence relating to orders shipped to Canada is to be found in Wood & Ingram's Ledgers:–

The Manager   27th October 1932
The Royal Bank of Scotland
Bank Buildings
Princess Street
London EC2

Dear Sir,

We beg to acknowledge receipt of your letter of the 26th instant enclosing cheque value £25 (Twenty five pounds) on account of Freeburnes Ltd, Hamilton, Ontario, and for which we are obliged.

We are, Dear Sir,

Yours faithfully
WOOD & INGRAM

The Manager, 29/4/33
The Royal Bank of Scotland,
6, Lethbury,
London EC2

Dear Sir,

We beg to acknowledge receipt with many thanks of your cheque value £937 18s 7d (nine hundred and thirty seven pounds, eighteen shillings and seven pence), for our account against Messrs. Freeburnes Ltd, Hamilton, Ontario.

We are, Dear Sir,

Yours faithfully
WOOD & INGRAM
(signature) H. Perkins

If Wood & Ingram were still holding their prices for large quantities for commercial nurseries a year later, one might presume that an order costing £962 18s 7d would mean that over 37,000 roses were shipped from Liverpool to Freeburnes, in Ontario in 1933.

———•———

John Harkness, an accomplished rose grower, relates in his book *'Makers of Heavenly Roses'*, published in 1985, the events that occurred at a certain Rose Show in London during 1934. In Chapter 8 p.90 he writes about the Danish rose grower, Svend Poulsen:–

> "Rose 'Else Poulsen' and 'Kirsten Poulsen' were immediately recognised as a decided breakaway, and perhaps the advance guard of a new race of roses. Roses which flowered in heads or clusters of little flowers were quite familiar; Poulsen now offered such roses with big flowers, and subsequently a greater area of colour. Else and Kirsten grew tall and strong. They marched into beds in gardens and parks where roses had never before appeared, for want of varieties of suitable habit and growth. Although Svend's roses were putting money in the bank for every rose nursery in Britain, they were earning no pounds for the Poulsens, because no copyright or patent could apply to them. A firm from Huntingdon, Wood and Ingram, introduced the roses into England. They had been appointed because they were Poulsen's best customers in England, and imported every year large quantities of flowering trees, shrubs and conifers .
>
> Svend went to a show in London in 1934, and saw a fine display of the double 'Anne-Mette Poulsen', and Wood and Ingram doing great business

with it. He had a strong feeling that justice was not his portion. Many originators knew this experience. Gilbert and Sullivan had fought rigorously for some return from those who performed their work to their own profit. Svend wanted to tear down his roses at this English show, and take them back to Denmark.

He was stopped by Samuel Davidson McGredy, who said, "Don't make a fool of yourself, Mr Poulsen, your roses are too good for that. You'd better come with me, back to Portadown".

McGredy and Poulsen entered into an agreement, whereby McGredy would introduce the Poulsen roses in Britain, and despite the lack of legal obligation, McGredy would for a period of three years pay all royalties to Poulsen on each variety he introduced."

In the Wood & Ingram's 'Honest Opinions' 1938 Rose Catalogue, 270 roses were included for sale. In this catalogue were 30 roses which had remained favourites from their 19th century catalogues: *Rosa Amy Robsart, Rosa Anne of Geierstein*, Rosa Blanc Double de Coubert, Rosa Banquet d'Or*, Rosa Catherine Seyton, Rosa Cécile Brünner, Rosa Conrad Ferdinand Meyer, Rosa Crimson Rambler, Rosa Fabrier, Rosa Fellemberg, Rosa Flora McIvor, Rosa Gardenia, Rosa Gloire de Dijon, Rosa Green-Mantle, Rosa Grus an Teplitz, Rosa Hermosa, Rosa Jennie Deans, Rosa Julia Mannering, Rosa Lady Penzance, Rosa La France, Rosa Léonie Lamesch, Rosa Lucy Bertram*, Rosa Madame Abel Chatenay, Rosa Madame Eugène Résal, Rosa Marechal Neil, Rosa Meg Merilees, Rosa Queen Mab*, Rosa Reine Marie Henriette, Rosa Rêve d'Or and Rosa William Allen Richardson.*[1]

The Nursery also introduced its customers to various collections of roses – a ploy to encourage the smaller gardener to buy, at a bargain price, more than one or two roses. It tempted the buyer with its 'Guinea Collection'. For £1 1s 0d one could obtain 18 roses, one of each rose listed. Other collections were included:–

The Huntingdon Collection –12 choice named varieties, our selection entirely	10/6
The Brampton Collection – 25 choice named varieties, etc	20/-
The Wandi Collection – 50 choice named varieties, etc	40/-
The Scented Collection – 12 choice named varieties for their sweet scent	12/-
The Rambler Collection – 12 selected Rambler Roses	15/-
The Climber Collection – 12 selected Climbing Roses such as Climbing H.T.s	15/-
The 'Polyantha' Collection of 12 selected named varieties	10/6

---

[1] Only four roses * in this list are unavailable today.

The catalogue promoted the acquisition of Acme Labels for Roses for 3d each or 2/6 per doz. This was followed by a page of comments entitled 'What our customers say':–

> *'The Countess of .... wishes to express her thanks for all the trouble which Messrs Wood & Ingram have taken on her behalf. She is glad to hear that the plants sent for her are of a splendid variety, and have been delivered in excellent condition to Lady ...., who is delighted with them' – London, W 1*

> *"Rose trees have arrived. I should like to say I have had a good many from other firms, but these are the best and healthiest-looking trees I have ever had'. Newport, I. of W.*

The *'Honest Opinions'* Rose Catalogue represented a break from Wood & Ingram's standard format. From 1938 its rose lists were published separately and illustrated in colour. Its new introduction *Rosa 'Home Sweet Home'*, was illustrated on the cover, and had been awarded two gold medals. In the introduction, signed by Henry Perkins, Managing Director, the nursery made several claims:–

> *'The remarks we make about the different roses are our own honest opinions, formed after fully testing the varieties: if a rose is good and has succeeded with us under normal conditions, we say so; on the other hand, if a rose, however much it may have bloomed, does not give us satisfaction, we do not hesitate to say so, and to give our reasons.*

> *We annually test new varieties from all parts of the world, where they are raised, we add the best only to our collection, this is a small percentage so as to make sure of retaining those of real merit.*

> *We would call special attention to our New Rose, **Home Sweet Home**, as illustrated on the front cover and fully described on page 9.*

> *Our services, as one of the largest producing firms of Rose Growers and general Nurserymen in the World, are at your command; let us help you all we can; don't hesitate to ask, don't think anything is too much trouble; we are only too willing to do anything within reason and will gladly do our best to supply any item we do not list'.*

> *'It is with very great pleasure and confidence that we have the honour of offering this very fine New Rose to our many thousands of customers and all Rose lovers.*

> *It is a genuine seedling of our own raising, distinct from any other Rose in our collection, its colour is a pure rich velvety pink with plenty of*

life, yet a softness very pleasing in effect. The colour lasts well, until the petals drop. Under artificial light it has a brilliancy unequalled by any other pink Rose we know.

The stems are stiff, holding the beautifully-full flowers upright, the petals have plenty of substance and are of beautiful texture.

Its perfume is deliciously sweet – true old Rose; and the blooms last well, both on the tree and when cut.

It is very perpetual flowering, has large, bold, dark green, glossy foliage, and a good constitution.

Amongst the large collection we grow of more than a thousand varieties, this is one of the most outstanding of all. It is very charming, either as a bedder, as a cut flower, or for pot culture'. Strong, open-ground bushes @ 2/6 each Standards, or on English Briar @ 7/6 each

It is surprising that Wood & Ingram introduced few new roses during the period the nursery was in business. The surnames of the Wood, Ingram and Perkins families are to be found in Rose lists but this does not mean that they were new introductions by Wood and Ingram.

Rosa Charles Wood was raised by Pormeter Fils in France. *Rosa Tom Wood* was raised by Alex Dickson in 1896. *Rosa Dorothy Perkins* was raised in 1902 by Jackson & Perkins of Newport Beach, California. *Rosa Miss Ingram* is illustrated in 1874 edition of *The Amateur's Rose Book* which was compiled by Shirley Hibberd. *Rosa Nellie Perkins* was raised in 1928 by Alex Dickson.

The following roses, which were bred when the Perkins family owned the Nursery, are recognised as Wood & Ingram introductions:–

1927 **Climbing Rosa 'Wilhelm Kordes'** a very fragrant salmon pink rose.

1930 **Rosa gracilis**, a Boursalt Rose and one of a group of thornless climbers which became popular in the late 19th century and was much admired by Gertrude Jekyll. The nearest rose available today is one bred by Wood & Ingram named Rosa 'Madame Sancy de Parabere'

1934 **Rosa Starlight**, a sweetly scented deep orange Hybrid Tea Rose. It is useful for cut flower work.

1939 **Rosa 'Home Sweet Home'**, a rich velvety pink Hybrid Tea Rose. This became a favourite rose throughout the Second World War, often ordered singly to mark a special anniversary of a loved one.

CHAPTER 11

THE YEARS 1930–1939

In 1931 the whole world was struck by a terrible 'slump' in trade. Great Britain already had a scheme of unemployment insurance, and now the immense demands on the Unemployment Fund meant that its money could not meet the weekly payments. It had to borrow from the Treasury. Trade was universally bad, the 'balance of trade' suffered and revenue decreased. A demand was made for drastic economies. The Labour Government could not by itself deal with so serious a situation and the Prime Minister, Ramsay Macdonald, asked Conservatives and Liberals to join him in a National Government.

The new National Government had first to restore confidence, which it did by very drastic measures. Taxation was increased sharply, the wages of all government officials and employees were reduced and unemployment benefit was cut. Great Britain abandoned Free Trade. Tariffs were put on goods coming into the country with the idea of reducing purchases from abroad. Gradually panic subsided and trade began to revive.

It is against this economic background that the continuation of Wood & Ingram's nursery must be seen. In *Bought Ledger No 4* were entered the wages paid by the Nursery to their staff between January 1927 until September 1932. The average annual wage bill from 1927 until 1931 was £9,500 and it dropped to £5,000 in 1932. How soon the 'slump' hit the Nursery and when it recovered is hard to pinpoint as ledgers covering this period do not reveal that the nursery suffered badly during the recession.

Wood & Ingram's *Order Ledger P* covered the period from October 1930 until March 1932 and shows that orders to commercial nurseries and private clients continued to be similar in numbers to previous years. Orders from garden designers and writers appear in this ledger.

Major Daniel was one such garden designer (working for rich clients at Diddington Park, Herstmonceaux and Heveningham Hall). He lived at Moulton House near Newmarket. Some of his large orders for plants were for design commissions which he was working on. Other orders were sent directly to his home. He was known for his expertise in designing large herbaceous borders of which those at Anglesey Abbey for Lord Fairhaven were a fine example. The grounds and Abbey now belong to the National Trust.

21st October 1930	Major Daniel was sent an extensive shrub order for £53 17s 0d; this was followed by a further large order in November for 1,180 Bush Roses for £82 7s 7d and a further order for shrubs for £4 11s 1d
10th November 1930	Beverley Nicholls was sent 40 trees for his wood plus a Foreman's time for planting for £26 10s 6d, a further order for 60 Trees for £26 6s 9d and a further order for 25 yards of Box Hedging for £2 12s 0d.

Beverley Nicholls, who wrote Gardening Books and articles for Women's Magazines which were famous all over the British Commonwealth, lived in a thatched cottage called 'Allways' in the village of Glatton, situated west of The Great North Road, north of Huntingdon. In his book '*Down the Garden Path*', 1932, he recalls a visit to Wood & Ingram's Nursery. He mentions his first order of November 1930 on page 84:–

> *"I went to the nearest nursery gardens – which are fortunately only ten miles away, and are very large and reputable.*
>
> *It was a lovely day when I first entered those gardens. A yellow September day that smelt like the rind of a lemon. My heart beat fast with excitement as I drew up at the gate and walked down the empty drive. All around me were flourishing shrubs and trees. In my pocket was a fat wad of notes. All that was lacking was someone to come and take my order.*
>
> *I wandered about, down empty avenues, through deserted shrubberies. I have since discovered that one always does this when one goes to a nursery garden. Nobody is ever there. However, on this, my first visit, the absence of human life struck me as a little odd. I felt like pulling a branch of a weeping willow and crying 'Miss'. At last, turning a corner, I saw an enormous young man crushed in a peculiar position in a small green bush.*
>
> *I told the young man that I would like to order a wood, if it pleased him, and it appeared to please him so much that he put his fingers in his mouth and produced an ear-splitting whistle.*
>
> *Instantly the gardens came to life. It seemed as though the managers slid down trunks of trees and clerks dropped like walnuts from the topmost branches. Eventually from the gathering there detached himself a small man of evident authority, who was the top man of all. We will call him Mr Honey, because it is very like his real name, and it fits him perfectly.*
>
> *Mr Honey spoke exclusively in Latin.*
>
> *The first thing I said to him, after explaining that I wanted to buy a*

wood, was that I liked 'that big bush with red berries over there'. 'Crataegus Pyracantha crenuklata Yunnanensis' crooned Mr Honey. I took a deep breath and was about to reply when Mr Honey waved his arm to the right and murmured. 'Ribes sanguineum splendens'. This, I felt, was enchanting. One had a sense of being a young disciple walking by the side of his master. Overhead there was the clear enamelled sky, all around were flowers and bushes, exquisitely displayed. And through the still air, as he walked, came the dulcet tones of Mr Honey, speaking in Latin. And here is the bill for the first list of trees which I ever ordered:–

4	Standard Limes	£2	10s	0d
4	Standard Silver Birch	£2	10s	0d
2	Standard Laburnums	£1	1s	0d
2	Standard Mountain Ash	£1	1s	0d
2	Standard English Elms	£3	3s	0d
6	Austrian Pines	£2	5s	0d
4	Douglas Fir, Colorado variety	£1	0s	0d
2	Rosa Moyesii		7s	0d
1	Horse Chestnut	£1	1s	0d
2	Standard cut leaf Birch	£1	11s	6d
2	Standard Walnuts	£2	2s	0d
2	Abico Colorado	£1	1s	0d
6	Nuts Merveille de Boluryller	£1	10s	0d
1	Standard Sycamore		10s	0d
1	Standard Maple dasycarpum		10s	6d
1	Standard Thorn Double Crimson		10s	6d
20	Stakes, Tar Cord and Hessian	£1	1s	0d
	Foreman's time preparing and planting		15s	0d
	Bus fare and out of pocket expenses		2s	9d
	Special delivery by road, Calling	£1	4s	9d
	1 bundle and packing		10s	6d
	3 Stakes		3s	0d
		£26	10s	6d

Writing in 1932 Beveley Nicholls continued:–

'It sounds very modest. It was. For, in those days, I had myself well in hand. Today, it is different. I have a dreadful suspicion that before I have finished with my wood, it will cost every penny of five hundred pounds'

Mid November 1930   Beverley Nicholls was sent a further 60 trees for £26 6s 9d, and a further order for 25 yards of Box Hedging for £2 12s 0d

Continuing through Wood & Ingram's *Order Ledger P* it becomes apparent that Henry Perkins still maintained his business links with other commercial nurseries and large estates. These indicate that economic problems were not experienced as might be thought in gardens:–

4th Nov 1930		Dobbie and Co. Ltd was sent 72 Dwarf Roses, 150 Gooseberries, 1250 Currants and 24 Forsythia for £19 2s 2d
5th Nov 1930		Viscount Dunford of Eastwell, Ashford, Kent was sent 5,815 Dwarf Roses in 61 bundles for £263 1s 6d
" " "		Murrells of Shrewsbury was sent 112 Dwarf roses for £5 10s 8d
" " "		V. N. Gauntlet & Co. Ltd Japanese Nurseries, Chiddingfold, Surrey was sent 260 Dwarf Roses for £12 12s 10d
7th Nov 1930		T. K. Ingram, Parkstone Nurseries, Dorset was sent 100 Dwarf Roses and 40 Climbing Roses for £7 4s 0d
" " "		Dobie & Co. Ltd was sent 150 Dwarf Roses for £6 11s 7d
10th " "		Harkness of Hitchin was sent 200 Dwarf Roses for £6 19s 5d
11th " "		Mr Yarnold, Westwood Park, Peterborough was sent 55 Cupressus macrocarpa, 2,000 Daffodils, 55 Privet and 20 Roses for £24 4s 0d
" " "		Sir W Prescot, Chestnuts, Godmanchester was sent 65 Dwarf Roses and 50 Quick for £5 18s 9d
12th " "		Boston Rose Farms was sent 450 Dwarf Roses for £16 12s 9d
" " "		Gauntlett & Co. Ltd, Japanese Nurseries was sent 42 Roses for £4 8s 11
13th " "		Hillier & Sons was sent 300 Dwarf Roses for £10 6s 10d
14th " "		Dobbie & Co. was sent 100 red Limes 9 ft for £23 10s 0d
" " "		Cant & Sons, Ltd was sent 200 Dwarf Roses 'Else Poulsen' and 100 Dwarf Roses 'Karen Poulsen' for £9 9s 2d
17th " "		Capt. Briscoe, Longstowe Hall, Cambridge was sent 60 trees by lorry, and planted by Wood & Ingram for £20 8s 8d
17th " "		Railway Convalescent Home, Par, Cornwall was sent 50 Dwarf Roses for £3 7s 4d
18th " "		Lord Fairhaven was sent 26 Limes, 24 Spruce, 24 Abies, 8 Black Italian Poplars, 6 Scotch Firs and other trees by special delivery with motor lorry for £42 15s 0d
19th " "		Harkness & Co., Hitchin was sent 274 Dwarf Roses for £10 16s 4d (all original plants from Denmark)
21st " "		Beckwith & Son, Hoddesdon, Hertfordshire was sent 525 Dwarf Roses for £17 14 10d
22nd " "		Captain Wigam, Loudham Hall, Woodbridge was sent 56 Yews and 105 Dwarf Roses for £36 16s 3d
17th Nov 1930		The Junior Bursar, Queens' College, Cambridge was sent 2 Salix babalonica and 4 Cricket Bat Willows for £1 8s 0d

This order for the Bursar of Queens' College was the first of several orders supplied to Cambridge colleges during the 1930s. The size of the University of Cambridge was much smaller than it is today and, being a tight community, every college master and gardener knew each other. Often, as in this case, a recommendation for obtaining plants from a certain nursery spread to other colleges, who all kept fine gardens within their grounds.

21st Nov 1930		Mrs Fitzpatrick, The Lodge, Queens' College, Cambridge was sent 12 Dwarf Roses 'Leoni Lamesch' and 4 Dwarf Roses 'Perle d'Or' for £1 13s 9d.
24th "	"	Mr Line, Steward, Emmanuel College, Cambridge was sent 2 Willows, 1 Horse Chestnut, 1 Silver Birch and 1 Sorbus aria for £3 4s 1d.
" "	"	The Bursar, King's College, Cambridge was sent 12 Aucuba male, 12 Aucuba female, 24 Laurustinus, 14 Dwarf Roses and 2,000 Bluebells for £23 18s 10d.
26th "	"	The Junior Bursar, Queens' College, Cambridge was sent 5 Dwarf Cherries for £2 7s 7d.
12th Jan 1931		Mr J. Burnaby, Junior Bursar, Trinity College, Cambridge was sent 1 Portugal Quince for 15s 9d.
16th March "		Miss E. M. Crystal, Newnham College, Cambridge was sent 1 Pyrus japonica, 1 Myrtle and 1 Passiflora caerulea for 14s 3d.

Running in parallel with orders from the Cambridge Colleges were orders from academics and their wives, who resided in large houses to the west of the city:–

10th Nov 1930		Mrs Clay, Upton House, Grange Road, Cambridge was sent 6 Climbing Roses for 11s 2d.
14th "	"	Mr E. Clark, The Bin Brook, Cambridge was sent 24 Dwarf Roses for £1 17s 10d.
17th Nov	"	Mr Gutteridge, The Rydings, Sylvester Road, Cambridge was sent 73 Bush Roses 22 Climbing Roses, and Fruit Trees for £38 1s 10d, followed by a further order for 8 Cupressus, 19 Climbing Roses, 12 Kentish Cob Nuts, 2 Pears and 5 Plums delivered by road for £13 3s 0d.
" "	"	Mrs Rottenburg, 5 Adams Road, Cambridge was sent 40 Dwarf Polyantha Roses, 8 Climbing Roses, 12 Oval privet, 14 Lonicera nitida and 12 Rosa rugosa alba for £6 14s 6d followed by a further order for 2 Junipers and 1 Viburnum carlesii for 15s 6d.
" "	"	Miss E. Turner, Half Way Cottage, Storey's Way, Cambridge was sent 1 Rosa moyesii for 4s 0d.
27th "	"	Mrs Shillington Scales, 4 Adams Road, Cambridge was sent 12 Bush Roses for 18s 0d.
27th Dec	"	Mr S. Campbell, 64 Storey's Way, Cambridge was sent 3 Silver Birch for £1 6s 3d.
30th Dec	"	Miss Herbert, Holmleigh, West Road, Cambridge was sent 1 Cedrus atlantica glauca and 3 Standard Pyrus for £2 3s 0d.
16th March 1931		Mrs Boughly, 4 Cranmer Road was sent 6 Bush Roses for 12s 3d.
" "	"	Mrs F. Jonas, Wychfield House, Huntingdon Road, Cambridge was sent 1 Garrya elliptica, 2 Calycanthus praecox and 2 Clematis jackmanii superba for £1 5s 7d.
18th "	"	Mrs T. M. Blanch, 11 Cranmer Road, Cambridge was sent 1 Weigela, 3 Berberis, 1 Rosemary and 1 Philadelphus for £1 8s 0d.
" "	"	Mrs Valliamy, Amwell House, Millington Road, Cambridge was sent 4 Ash, 3 Silver birch and 1 Euonymus europaeus for 13s 1d.

Trade with other commercial nurseries continued, with extensive orders mainly for Dwarf Roses, whose popularity went from strength to strength. Henry Perkins having been in charge of the Nursery for ten years, still maintained its position in the horticultural trade as the leading supplier of Dwarf Roses throughout the country.

26th Nov	1930	R. Veitch & Son, Exeter was sent 108 Dwarf roses for £4 16s 9d
" "	"	Edwin Murrell's Nursery, Shrewsbury was sent 62 Dwarf Roses for £2 10 0d
27th "	"	Chivers & Sons, Histon, Cambridge was sent 20 larch, 12 Silver Birch, 12 Sycamore and 12 Italian Poplar for £1 0s 0d and a further order of 300 Privet for £4 14s 0d.
" "	"	J. Cheal & Son, Crawley, Sussex was sent 100 Dwarf Roses 'Kirsten Poulsen' for £3 5s 2d, a further order of 200 Dwarf Polyantha Roses 'Else Poulsen' for £6 7s 7d, and a further order of 123 Roses for £4 7s 6d.
4th Dec	"	Dicksons & Sons, Chester was sent 750 Dwarf Roses for £24 6s 2d.
6th "	"	John Warterer & Sons, Twyford, Berkshire was sent 200 Dwarf Roses 'Kirsten Poulsen' for £6 6s 9d.
12nd "	"	Dobbie & Sons, Edinburgh was sent an extensive shrub order, including 1,000 Lonicera nitida, 1,035 Standard Roses, 259 Dwarf Roses 'Mrs G. A. Van Rossen' for £284 14s 0d.
18th Jan	1931	Hillier & Sons, Winchester was sent 1,445 Dwarf Roses for £36 15s 0d and a further order of 122 Dwarf Roses for £4 6s 4d.

Private clients continued to place large orders with the Nursery despite the economic problems.

21st Nov 1930		Mr W. Finch, Burley on the Hill, Oakham was sent 1500 Ash, 2000 Larch, 900 Ash, 200 Oak, 36 Bush Roses, 96 Hybrid Sweet briars and an extensive order of shrubs for £130 1s 0d.
" "	"	Mrs Hunnybun, Old Court Hall, Godmanchester was sent 6 Limes, 3 Sorbus and 3 Lombardy Poplars for £10 15s 9d.
27th "	"	Lt. Col. Goldie, The Old Rectory, Brampton was sent 192 Dwarf Polyantha Roses, 2 Acer negundo and 6 clumps of Rhubarb 'Earl Albert' for £18 16s 6d.
" "	"	Lady Walston, Newton Hall, Cambridge was sent 2 Birch, 2 Horse Chestnut, 1 Golden Privet and 3 Pears for £4 5s 6d.
" "	"	The Trustees of Rockingham Castle were sent a large order of fruit trees and soft fruit for £7 5s 0d.
" "	"	Mr S. Whitbread, Southill Park, Bedfordshire was sent 12 Yews, 2 Dwarf Roses, 2 Passiflora and several Fruit Trees for £24 9s 0d.
6th Dec	"	Sir L. Brassey, Apethorpe Hall, Peterborough was sent 18 Sweet Briars, 6 Sage, 6 Thyme and 2 Japanese Maples for £2 15s 8d.
" "	"	Viscount Clifden, Landhydrock, Devon was sent 36 bush Roses for £2 17s 2d.
8th "	"	Madresfield Gardens, Malvern were sent 148 Bush Roses for £ 6 16s 0d.
" "	"	Maj. Harrison, Kings Walden Bury, Hertfordshire was sent 5 Pears, 12 Raspberries and other shrubs for £ 8 12s 9d.
9th "	"	Sir Balfour Gourlay, Cambridge Preservation Society was sent a large shrub

" " "	order to plant around a bungalow in Madingley Road, Cambridge for £30 0s 0d and a further extensive order of shrubs for £23 4s 6d.
" " "	Mr Nall-Cain, Brocket Hall, Hertfordshire was sent 120 Standard White Horse Chestnuts for £81 0s 0d.
12th " "	Mrs C. Rothschild, Tring Park, Hertfordshire was sent 6 English Yews (selected specimens) balling and special delivery by motor lorry for £20 4s 0d.
18th " "	Lady Battersea, Overstrand, Norfolk was sent Fruit Trees, Roses and Herbaceous plants for £23 10s 11d.
31st " "	The Duke of Bedford was sent fruit trees and soft fruit for the Pleasure Grounds for £2 12s 9d and 18 Gooseberries for the Kitchen Department at Woburn for £1 10s 2d.
16th Feb "	Viscount Cowdray was sent 6 Double Cherries, 3 Muscat 'Alexandra' Vines, 2 dwarf peaches, 12 Black Currants and 1 Nectarine for £10 13s 0d
19th " "	Mrs Harker, Blofield Hall, Norfolk was sent 36 Berberis, 12 Philadelpus, 12 Kalmia, 12 Ceanothus, 24 Acer palmatum and other shrubs for £23 11s 1d.
18th Mar "	Capt. Cunningham Reid, The Hall, Six Mile Bottom, Newmarket was sent 4 Cordon Pears, 24 Globe Artichokes and 50 Zinc Labels for £3 17s 3d.

Also between October 1930 and March 1931 are several important orders from His Majesty's Office of Works which indicate the extensive replanting that was being undertaken at this time in The Royal Parks:–

9th Nov 1930	His Majesty's Office of Works was sent 18 Cornish Elms and 2 Elms 'Van Houteu' for £25 0s 0d to be delivered to Hyde Park.
19th Dece "	His Majesty's Office of Works was sent 100 Buddleia – 5 varieties in pots, and 30 Buddleia prostrata for £13 0s 0d to be delivered to St James Park.
" " "	His Majesty's Office of Works was sent 6 Cydonia 'Simone' and 3 Exocorda albertii macrantha for £2 12s 6d to be delivered to Hyde Park.
29th " "	His Majesty's Office of Works was sent 75 Philadelphus, 100 Euonymus, 50 Weigela, 100 Spiraea, 100 Lycestera, 25 Syringa and other shrubs for £48 12s 6d to be delivered to Regents Park.
20th Jan 1931	His Majesty's Office of Works was sent 4,700 plants consisting of Rambler Roses and Shrubs in quantities of 100, 200 and 500 for £95 0s 0d to be delivered to Regents Park.
10th Feb "	His Majesty's Office of Works was sent 12 Acer, 12 Golden Elms, 12 Red twigged Limes, 6 Populus nigra and 50 Dwarf Roses for £23 18s 0d to be delivered to Hyde Park.

The most prestigious order Wood and Ingram received during 1931 is possibly the order for plants to be planted in the grounds of Buckingham Palace:–

Order Ledger P, p.991

His Majesty's Office of Works, Buckingham Palace 16th March 1931
Per T. Hay Esq., Hyde Park, London.

2	Garrya elliptica	£1	1s	0d
12	Ceanothus in choice variety, to name	2	2	0
12	Buddleias in choice variety, to name	1	10	0
8	Jasminum officinalis major	1	4	0
8	Jasminum nudiflorum	1	4	0
8	Jasminum stephanense	1	8	0
6	Azara microphylla	1	10	0
3	Kerria japonica		7	6
1	Myrtus		7	6
12	Escallonias in choice variety, to name	2	2	0
6	Forsythia spectabilis	2	5	0
12	Pyracantha in choice variety, to name	3	0	0
6	Cydonia japonica in choice variety, to name	1	1	0
12	Lonicera (climbing) in choice variety, to name	1	16	0
6	Cotoneasters, in choice variety, to name	1	1	0
1	Viburnum rhytidophyllum		10	6
3	Stranvesia undulata		15	0
3	Stranvesia undulata fructo luteo		15	0
1	Solanum jasminoides		3	6
	Carried forward	23	3	0

Order continued on page 992:

1	Vitis cognettiae		10	6
1	Vitis vinifolia purpurea		7	6
24	Clematis in choice variety, to name	4	4	0
1	Actinidia kolomitka		5	0
1	Actinidia rubrucaulis		5	0
		£29	15	0d

In through truck. Carriage Paid Home

16th March 1931	His Majesty's Office of Works was sent 2 Acers, 1 Aesculus indica and 1 Euonymus latifolius for £5 19s 6d to be delivered to Mr Hay at Hyde Park.
" " "	His Majesty's Office of Works was sent 300 Crataegus, including 200 Crataegus 'Paul's Scarlet' for £32 0s 0d to be delivered to Mr Marlow at Bushy Park.
18th " "	His Majesty's Office of Works was sent 50 Standard Horse Chestnuts for £13 0s 0d to be delivered to Bushy Park, Hampton Court.

There are 996 handwritten orders in Wood & Ingram's *Order Ledger R* which cover the period from 28th January until 5th December 1931. This Ledger partly covers the period to be found in the previous *Order Ledger P*, whilst the majority of orders are for single customers; the trend, commenced in the previous year, continued with Cambridge College orders, landed gentry orders, and further orders from His Majesty's Office of Works. Also included in the same ledger are extensive repeat orders to other nurseries:–

Austin & McAslan, Glasgow	5 orders
W. Brown, Eastfield, Peterborough	11 orders
G. Beckwith and Son, Hoddesdon	7 orders
Barnham Nurseries Ltd, Barnham	4 orders,
Blackhouse Nurseries, York	3 orders
Chaplin Bros, Waltham Cross	2 orders
A. Charlton & Sons, Tunbridge Wells	10 orders
Carter Page & Co., London	5 orders
W. Cutbush & Son, Barnet	7 orders
W. Crowther & Son Ltd, Horncastle	4 orders
Chilbrans Ltd, Hale	5 orders
Dickson & Robinson Ltd, Manchester	7 orders
Dicksons Nurseries Ltd, Chester	12 orders
Dobbie & Co. L:td , Edinburgh	37 orders
A. Dickson & Sons, Newtonards	8 orders
Fisher & Silbray Ltd, Sheffield	5 orders
A. Goatcher & Son, Washington	7 orders
V. N. Gauntlet & Co., Chiddingford	11 orders
R. Harkness & Co., Hitchin	4 orders
Hillier & Sons, Winchester	10 orders
J. Jeffries & Son, Cirencester	7 orders
Kent & Brydon Ltd. Darlington	4 orders
Laxton Bros, Bedford	7 orders
Lane's Nurseries Ltd, Berkhamsted	7 orders
E. Murrell Ltd, Shrewsbury	4 orders
R. C. Notcutt, Woodbridge	4 orders
Peed & Son, Mitcham	8 orders
Ramsbotham & Co., Bletchley	8 orders
R. V. Roger, Pickering	5 orders
T. Rivers & Son Ltd, Sawbridgeworth	4 orders

Cambridge Colleges placed further orders with the nursery:–

Downing College ordered a mixed range of plants for £3 6s 0d
Clare College ordered a mixed range of shrubs for £2 6s 9d
Trinity College ordered 1,020 Perkins' Early Giant Asparagus Plants and 6ozs of Silver or Seakale Beet for £5 18s 8d
Queens' College ordered 100 Roses for £7 7s 2d
King's College ordered Silver birches and standard limes for £8 7s 9d
Ridley Hall ordered 3 Cotoneaster frigida for 9s 0d

Both Lady Battersea with 3 orders and Lady Macmillan with a single order still continued to patronise the nursery from Overstrand, Norfolk. Lady Battersea resided at The

Pleasaunce (now a Christian Endeavour Holiday Home), which was designed by Sir Edwin Lutyens in 1897–9. It was adapted from two existing seaside villas of the 1880s for Cyril Flower, First Lord Battersea, who had married a daughter of Sir Anthony de Rothschild. The garden was laid out by Lutyens but there is no evidence of any contribution by Gertrude Jekyll. The brick walling for the beds and semicircular steps remain today.

The Duke of Bedford had two large orders for £93 13s 9d (partly illegible) but included 54 Berberis shrubs, and £50 17s 7d for Box and Laurels for his Pleasure Grounds. B. Drage Esq., Lingfield, Kent had a large shrub order for £278 12 9d which included a special visit from W & I's representative, travelling expenses at 9d a mile for 199 miles and professional advice with regards to planting. Douglas Crossman Esq. ordered 4,000 Snowberry shrubs, 2,000 Berberis and 3,000 Hazel for £266 4s 0d. Captain Le Strange, Hunstanton Hall, Norfolk ordered 1,000 English Oak, 1,000 native Larch, 250 Spanish Chestnuts and Ash, Spruce, Firs and Privet for £34 17s 6d. Col. W. A. Harding, Madingley Hall, Cambridge requested shrubs and poplars amounting to £37 7s 3d. The Rt. Hon. Lord Fairhaven, Anglesey Abbey ordered 24 various rose bushes for £14 1s 8d.

Further orders to His Majesty's Office of Works were supplied:–

2nd Feb 1931	His Majesty's Office of Works at Regent's Park, London was sent 112 Dwarf Roses Karen Poulsen – Original Danish Plants for £21 0s 0d.
5th Feb 1931	His Majesty's Office of Works, for T. Hay Esq., M.V.O. Superintendent, Hyde Park, London was sent 170 specimen Standard limes for £212 10s 0d for the New Houses of Parliament, Belfast.
23rd Mar 1931	His Majesty's Office of Works at Hyde Park was sent 6 selected Cornish Elms for £3 3s 0d.
23rd Apr 1931	His Majesty's Office of Work at Hyde Park was sent Clematis, Jasminum, Ceanothus, Azara and Escallonias (total 25) for £4 18s 0d.
30th Jun 1931	His Majesty's Office of Works at Hyde Park was sent 100 Perovskia for £12 10s 0d.

The nursery continued to maintain its position as the country's main supplier of roses throughout the 1930s. In *Order Ledger O* which covered the period November 1934 until February 1935, existing clients would appear to be completely satisfied with the standard of service they received from the nursery, and they continued to stay with Wood & Ingram.

Captain Daniels, the garden designer from Moulton, near Newmarket, was very busy at this time. Here are examples of orders sent by Wood & Ingram for the gardens he designed:

4th Dec 1934	large order for Park Close, Englefield Green, Egham, Surrey for £38 9s 0d (list illegible)
" " "	Order for Bakenham House, Englefield Green for £15 5s 0d (list illegible)

17th " "		further order for £54 15s 9d (list illegible).
17th Jan 1935		Shrub Order for Anglesey Abbey, Cambridge for £8 5s 4d.
12th Feb "		Rose and Apple order for Herstmonceaux Castle for £3 0s 0d.

More orders from His Majesty's Office of Works included:

3rd Dec 1934	His Majesty's Office of Works at Hyde Park was sent 24 Dwarf Roses for £1 7s 0d.
" " "	His Majesty's Office of Works at Hyde Park was sent 278 Dwarf Roses for £22 3s 6d.
4th " "	His Majesty's Office of Works at Regents Park was sent various 13 trees for £16 7s 0d.
5th Feb 1935	His Majesty's Office of Works at Hyde Park was sent 8 Cornish Elms, 6 Acers and 2 Pyrus for £13 13s 0d.

Wood & Ingram received two further orders for Buckingham Palace Gardens:

Order Ledger O, p.845

His Majesty's Office of Works at Hyde Park, London W2   17th January 1935
For Buckingham Palace Gardens
150 Dwarf Roses as under

10 (illegible)	10 (illegible)
10 "	10 Madame Butterfly
10 Etoile de Hollande	10 Elizabeth of York
10 Shot Silk	10 Flamingo
10 Emma Wright	10 Edith Nellie Perkins
10 Angèle Pernet	10 Mrs (illegible)
10 (illegible)	10 Lady Sylvia
10 "	

....£9 0s 0d

Order Ledger O, p.924

His Majesty's Office of Works Buckingham Palace   5th February 1935

50 Evergreen Shrubs £12 10s 0d
per L & N E Rly Goods Through Wagon carriage Paid Home

In 1936 Wood & Ingram applied to the Royal Horticultural Society to be granted a site to display their roses at the Chelsea Flower Show at the end of May. This request was granted and they were located a stand in the Rose Tent, but not in the large Marquee. The large Marquee, at that time, occupied the area east of the Great Monument in the grounds of the Royal Hospital. The Nursery was amongst other rose nurseries, which included Frank Cant and Co. Ltd Colchester, Ben R. Cant & Sons Ltd, Colchester, Alex

Dickson & Sons Ltd, Newtonards, Northern Ireland, Laxton Bros (Bedford)) Ltd, Bedford, and Wheatcroft Bros Ltd, Ruddingford, Nottinghamshire. In the same marquee were displays of new plants. Completing this group were two further marquees for orchids, tulips, violas and strawberries.

There was no mention in the Royal Horticultural Society's lists of awards of Wood & Ingram being awarded a Gold or Silver-Guilt Medal at this show. But the Society must have been impressed with their stand of roses in 1936, because they were back at a following Chelsea Flower Show in 1938 where they had been given an island site 59a in the West Marquee. The show had increased in size and the floral displays were now held in two similar large Marquees, one to the east and the other to the west of the Monument. In the West Marquee Wood & Ingram's stand was next to Dobbies Ltd of Edinburgh, a Nursery to whom it had supplied thousands of plants. Luckily Dobbies had chosen to show a large display of tulips, so there was no competition between the two nurseries.

The third surviving Wood & Ingram *Wages Ledger* covers the period from the week ending 28th April 1939 until the week ending 9th January 1945. By 28th April 1939 there were 57 people employed on the nursery plus a further four who were employed on piecework turning the headlands. Staff were paid either £3.0s 0d for 6 days work less insurance of 1s 2d or £1 14s 0d for 6 days work less insurance for 1s 2d. Young men straight from school were paid 17s 4d for 6 days work less insurance of 3d. The four men on piecework were paid 9d for every pole of headland that was turned. Three hundred and fifteen poles were turned during the week, which meant their combined wages came to £11 16s 3d less insurance of 5s 10d, each receiving £2 16s 4d. The total wages bill for the week was £110 19s 2d.

Between July and the outbreak of war, while the nursery turnover slackened, 23 members of staff were employed budding roses. The remaining 45 members of staff were all working a full 6 days a week. The entry in the ledger for the week ending 25th August 1939 records that:

Crow and Reedman emptying Cesspool	....	10s 0d
Baxter Hoeing in Mdn Roses	398.72 chains @ 11/4d less 1s 1d.......£2	0s 5d
Budding Rose Stocks @ 14s 0d		
Leverton Jnr, A. Allen, J. Reedman & Butler	17,000 less 4s 3d £11	13s 8d
Leverton, J. Allen & J. Reedman	1,284..	18s 0d
Brown Jnr, Will Smith, Headland & J. Allen	19,000 less 4s 4d £13	1s 8d
Blunt & F. Mills	9,500 less 2s 2d £6	10s 10d
Searle & Sewell	9,500 less 2s 2d £6	10s 10d
Papworth & Childery	9,500 less 2s 2d £6	10s 10d
W. P. Smith, M. E. Curtis, Townsend, Shatton	16,000 less 4s 2d £10	19s 10d
Burton & S. Allen	9,500 less 2s 1d £6	10s 10d

E. A. Smith & H. Smith   9,500 less 2s 2d £6 10s 10d

Such was the demand for roses until the start of the Second World War: approximately 100,700 roses were being grafted each week. Over a period of 9 weeks almost 1 million roses were grafted during the summer slack period.

CHAPTER 12

THE FINAL YEARS

A young Master Wady first worked for Wood & Ingram at the nursery's Brampton site in 1939 during his summer holidays, just before the start of the Second World War. He had walked to the nursery from his home in Brampton and, upon arrival, plucked up courage and asked to see Mr Henry Perkins to enquire if he had a job for him. He was in luck and was employed during his summer holiday, and at the same time the following year. Whilst at the Brampton nursery he was employed doing general jobs, but was soon allowed to tie up clematis and honeysuckle plants. Master Wady was then 13 years old and earned 15s 0d a week. By December 1939 the staff had been reduced from 68 men to 32 men. Summers during the period of the war never recorded the dizzy heights of a mass production of roses in the nursery. During 1940 Master Wady also worked at the nursery's shop in George Street, Huntingdon on Saturdays for 5s 0d a day (or 2s 6d a morning if he had to leave and play cricket for his team in the afternoon). He was told that 100 staff were employed in the rose fields before the war and that the 'Rose Foreman' checked every rose that was sent out in an order. Eventually, when he was 15 years old, Mr Wady left school and worked in the nursery full time, starting in the summer of 1941. His daily routine was to walk to the nursery and arrive before 7.00am and then to walk home for breakfast at 8.00am, returning to the nursery by 8.30am. Lunch break was between 1.00pm and 2.00pm and the day's work finished at 5.30pm. He also worked until 5.30pm on Saturdays. Holidays had to be taken during the summer before the busy autumn order season. Mr Wady's wages for his first week's work, ending 1st August 1941, for 27 hours amounted to 7s 10d. The following week he worked 6 days and was paid 14s 6d.

Mr Wady recalled that during 1942 Mr Roberts was the foreman at the Thrapston site; Mr Percy Last brought the weekly wages for the staff in a large bag and Mr Clarke was in charge of the horses the nursery used for ploughing. Mr Davy gardened at the foreman's house at Brampton. They were all Brampton residents. Mr Wady thought Mr Henry Perkins was a real old gentleman, who thought more of his horses than of his men. According to Mr Wady, Mr Perkins was considered to be a millionaire whilst living at Houghton Grange. He had to move to the house adjoining his nursery in Brampton when he lost money in a Matches business. Mr Perkins was also very interested in racehorses and enjoyed attending meetings at Newmarket. He was friendly with Sir Humphrey Trafford, the owner of land in Manchester on which Old Trafford football and cricket pitches are sited. Sir Humphrey ordered plants from the nursery and kept his own racehorses in Royston.

Most of Wady's time in the nursery was during wartime. He recalls that the Thrapston Road rose-growing grounds were reduced and grew crops of clover seed and corn. The supply of briar-grafting stocks, which had always been obtained from the continent, now stopped as many nurseries had been over-run by the German army. The Nursery carefully kept a few specimens of each rose bush for future use as stock plants. Mr Alf Brown senior, the 'Rose Foreman', was employed throughout the duration of the war. Mr Wady was called up when he was 18 years old in May 1945, but, by the time he had finished his army training, the war was over. He was sent across the Channel to France, by train to Toulouse and by ship to Port Said and Palestine.

Wood & Ingram's *Order Ledger W* covers the period from 28th February 1940 until 7th September 1940 and contains 998 pages, each page having one typed order. Orders in this ledger are mostly for local clients from Huntingdonshire, Cambridgeshire and Bedfordshire. Unlike the trend recorded during the First World War, the nursery's orders were no longer for great estates, but were concerned with supplying vegetable seeds in March and April. Of interest are the number of local schools that ordered quantities of seeds etc. through the Huntingdon Education Committee: Huntingdon Grammar School, Huntingdon Council School, Earith British School, Great Stukely School, Brampton School, Godmanchester School, Upton Church of England School, Stilton Church of England School, Ramsey St Mary's School and Abbots Ripton School to name but a few.

Hunts Education Committee Gt Stukeley School			14th March 1940	
"Gardening"				
1 pint	Beans Perkins' Prizewinner		1s	3d
1 "	" Canadian Wonder		1s	6d
½ oz	Savoy Drumhead			6d
½ oz	Broccoli Veitch's Self-Protecting			10d
½ oz	Cabbage Christmas Drumhead			6d
½ oz	Beet Covent Garden			6d
½ oz	Cabbage Flower of Spring			4d
½ oz	Lettuce Perkins' Pompadour		1s	0d
1 oz	Onion Ailsa Craig		1s	6d
1 oz	Parsley Moss Curled		1s	0d
2 pts	Peas Perkins' Little Marvel		2s	6d
½ oz	Savoy Tom Thumb			9d
2oz	Radish French Breakfast		1s	0d
2pkts	Veg.Marrow Bush White		1s	0d
14lb	Potatoes Duke of York CL 2102		4s	0d

14lb	Potatoes Sharpe's Express CL.146	3s	0d
1oz	Sprouts Harrison's XXX	1s	4d
2pkts	Flower Seeds	1s	6d
	£1	4s	2d

The Governors of Huntingdon Grammar School
Huntingdon

12th March 1940

1pair	Felcut Secateurs	9s	6d
3oz	Virginian Steel	3s	9d
1 tin	RENADINE	4s	6d
1 ball	Fillis String	1s	6d
	£1	19s	3d

The Governors of Huntingdon Grammar School
Huntingdon

11th April 1940

2lbs.	Lawn Grass Perkins' Special Mixture	7s	0d
5lbs	" " " " "	17s	6d
1 ball	Fillis String	1s	6d
	£1	6s	0d

The Governors of Huntingdon Grammar School
Huntingdon

10th May 1940

6	Bamboo Canes 8ft	2s	0d
1½lb	Lawn Grass Perkins' Special Mixture	5s	3d
		7s	3d

The Governors of Huntingdon Grammar School
Huntingdon

3rd June 1940

Supplying:–
38   Geraniums Paul Cramper in pots
42   Lobelia in pots
42   Alyssum
124   Antirrhinums
                                               £2 16s 6d

(note: written in pencil across this order; Noel Thornhill Esq.)

Miss Branson, Head teacher, Tollington Park School,

at the Old Grammar School, Huntingdon

4th April 1940

1 doz.	Wire Guards	4s	6d
½ oz	Beet Crimson Globe		6d
1pkt	Cabbage Milams' Early Dwarf		6d
4pkts	Broccoli	1s	0d
1 pkt	Kale Tall Green Curled		3d
1 "	Savoy Drumhead		3d
1 "	Cauliflower Early London		3d
1 "	Radish French Breakfast		3d
1 ball	Tarred Twine	1s	0d
1 ball	Thick String	1s	0d
14lb	Potatoes Epicure Class 1 Scotch	3s	0d
		12s	6d

There were two orders for The Boys' Council School, St Ives (Evacuees A/c), for Mr S. Frith on 26th February 1940, a long list of 29 vegetable seeds costing £2 4s 5d; again for Mr S. Frith on 11th March 1940, a shorter list of vegetable seeds and seed potatoes costing £1 18s 2d.

———•———

There were continuous orders for wreaths, usually for 'a choice floral wreath' required from the Royal Air Force Stations at Upwood and RAF Wyton. The cost of wreaths ranged from 15s to £3 0s 0d.

Wood & Ingram's *Order Ledger U* covers the period between 21st October 1939 until 28th March 1940 and contains 768 typed orders.

Orders continued to His Majesty's Office of Works during the Second World War:–

21st December 1939

His Majesty's Office of Works
Kirby Hall, per Mr T. Hay, Hyde Park

Bush Roses:–

30	General Mc Arthur	)		
9	Angèle Pernet	)		
15	Ville de Paris	)	£5	0s 0d
7	Etoile de Hollande	)		
25	Talisman	)		
18	Lady Sylvia	)		
250	Dickson's Perfection		£10	0s 0d
			£15	0s 0d

Delivered to Kirby Hall

2nd March 1940

His Majesty's Office of Works
per Mr D. Campbell, Park Superintendent's Office, Inner Circle, Regent's Park, London NW1

41	various Shrubs 3 of each	£41	18s	6d
60	Bush Roses	£5	7s	6d
	Carriage		12s	6d
		£47	18s	6d

Sent to Mr E. A. Gaskin
The Gardens
The Duke of York's School, Dover

The Duke of York's School was still a Royal Military School.

20th March 1940

His Majesty's Office of Works
per Mr T. Hay, Hyde Park Gardens
Hyde Park a/c

Collection of Shrubs £12 10s 0d
(27 varieties totalling 67 shrubs)

20th March 1940

His Majesty's Office of Works
No 10 Downing Street
via Hyde Park Gardens

1	Eucryphia pinnitifolia specimen	£1	0s	0d
1	Cotoneaster perkinsii		7s	6d
1	Buddleia alternifolia		7s	6d
1	Viburnum Burkwoodii trained for a wall	£1	1s	0d
1	Solanum jasminoides		3s	6d
1	Rhyncospernum jasminoides		7s	6d
12	Verbascum Pink Domingo		18s	0d
	Total	£4	6s	0d

Collected

27th March 1940

His Majesty's Office of Works
per Mr T. Hay, Hyde Park Gardens
Buckingham Palace Gardens a/c

	Collection of shrubs as under ....)
2	Lonicera syringantha ....)
2	Philadelphus Virginal............................)
2	" tartarica rosea ....)

2	Prunus incisa...................................)		
4	Ribes astrisanguineum ....)		
4	Osmanthus illicifolius.........................)		
2	Syringa Wilsonii ....)		
2	" reflexa.......................................)		
2	Berberis Darwinii................................)		
4	Stephanandra Tanakae ....)		
2	Prunus myroboleana mume pink ....)		
2	Philadelphus Favourite ....)		
2	" brachybotrys.................)		
2	Althaea rubis ....)	£17	1s 6d
2	" Coeleste...................................)		
4	Forsythia spectablilis ....)		
2	Euonymus coccineus ....)		
2	" Yedoensis ....)		
2	Deutzia crenata magnifica ....)		
2	Cotoneaster Perkinsii ....)		
2	Berberis dictiophylla ....)		
2	" Stenophylla ....)		
2	" purpurea ....)		
4	Amaygdalus Pollardii ....)		
4	Lilacs in variety...................................)		
3	Osmanthus in variety ....)		
2	Weigelia profusion...............................)		
3	Magnolia Stellata.................................)		
12	Pyrus japonoca in variety, extra strong)		

———•———

There was now a marked change in the range of plants customers required. Many would have remembered the food shortages during the First World War when families relied on their own source of vegetables and fruit to survive. Lawns and parks were being cultivated for produce, albeit some Royal Parks continued to plant shrubs for displays.

10th February 1940

Bryant Bulb Co. Ltd, London NW1

2,000 Black Currants £7 10s 0d

Order no 565 is typical of many during this period:

G. R. B. Loch Esq., West Malling, Kent
5th March 1940

1	H T Apple James Grieve	7s	6d
1	" Pear Marie Louise..................................	7s	6d
2	Loganberries	3s	0d
1	Blackberry Parsley Leaved	1s	6d

1	D T Peach Hale's Early	10s 6d
24	Strawberries Royal Sovereign Elvaston Improved	4s 0d
2	Lavender Twickle Purple	1s 6d
		£1 17s 0d

To be sent to Mr Thrussell, Wratton Cottage, Wratton Road, Hitchin, Herts

There are 6 orders from nurseries requesting 4,700 Clematis vitalba stocks, who were charged at the rate of £2 8s 2d per thousand. The nursery was offering Plant Lots which were bought by both nurseries and individuals. Several accounts were sent, just listing the men's time for packing and cost of packing materials used. The nursery was, at this time, rather anxious to sell off many of its roses in order to pay wages and to give more room for urgently required food crops.

Order 548

Superintendent Parks Department, Town Hall, Torquay
1st March 1940

Men's time lifting and packing 108 Lots £15 0s 0d

Order 726

F. W. Jekyll Esq., Munstead Wood, Godalming, Surrey
23rd March 1940

Man's time lifting 1 Lot 3s 0d

Gertrude Jekyll's nephew was at this time about to sell Munstead Wood.

——— • ———

Large orders to nurseries were rare during the Second World War, but the following two examples show that the nursery still kept large stocks of plants for sale:

20th November 1940

Hilling & Co., Chobham, Woking, Surrey

250	Polygonatum baldschuanicum	£11 5s 0d
500	Ampelopsis Veitchii	£22 10s 0d
1,000	Pyracantha in variety	£45 0s 0d
500	Cydonia in variety	£30 0s 0d
50	Garrya eliptica	£4 7s 6d
122	crates and packing	£1 10s 6d
		£114 13s 0d

By Goods Train in 3 through wagons

Forest Products Ltd, Huntley, Glos

22nd November 1940

4,500	Privet ovalifolium	£20	5s	0d
250	Cornish Elms	£28	15s	0d
		£49	0s	0d

Goods train in through track to Blaisdon siding.

———•———

By now the nursery was employing staff to take grafts of *Clematis vitalba* in large quantities. 4,700 plants were sent out to other nurseries, like Hilliers and Joffrey Bros Nursery. The rose trade continued well in the early period of the war; 550 plants of Rose 'Home Sweet Home' were sold by March 1940. Other nurseries continued to place large orders for roses:

Stanfield Nurseries, Wisbech, Cambs
14th March 1940

| 5,000 | Polyantha Roses in variety | £32 | 5s | 0d |

Collected

Stanfield Nurseries, Wisbech, Cambs
28th March 1940

2,000	Polyantha Roses ....)			
2,000	H T Roses ....)	£31	5s	0d
500	Climbing Roses ....)			
	To men's time lifting above roses	£3	10s	0d
		£34	15s	0d

Burscough Nurseries, Burscough Bridge, Lancs
18th March 1940

| 10,000 | Bush Roses as list attached | £75 | 0s | 0d |

———•———

Hidden in *Order Ledger U*, was Major J. A. Codrington's order no 569 dated 7th March 1940:

Major J. A. Codrington
Park House, Onslow Square, London S.W.7

| 36 Bush and Climbing Roses to name | £2 | 15s | 3d |

per pass train in 1 Bundle
Packed free and carriage paid

In 1931 John Codrington was a captain in the Coldstream Guards when he met Primrose Harley, daughter of an eminent physician. Codrington was thirty-eight and had spent most of his time abroad in Smyrna and Syria. Both shared a streak of wanderlust and their marriage, with eight bridesmaids, in the Royal Military Chapel of Wellington Barracks took place on Monday 21st December 1936. They found a delightful property, occupying a left over patch at the end of Pelham Place, fell in love with it and bought Park House, Onslow Square. Here they both gardened, creating a green jungle in the heart of the city. In 1942 they decided to go their separate ways. He moved to Gibraltar, later becoming a garden designer and plantsman, eventually living in Northamptonshire. He designed the interesting formal garden at Emmanuel College, Cambridge and the shrub borders for Bartlow Hall in south Cambridgeshire. She, a flower painter, later married Lanning Roper, a patriotic American, who also created gardens in Cambridgeshire for Lord De Ramsey at Abbots Ripton Hall and advised the National Trust on the management of Anglesey Abbey.

———•———

By 1942, well into the war, the nursery was still going strong. Mr Perkins's ingenuity in keeping a reduced staff fully employed is now evident. Seven acres of peas were pulled during the week ending 31st July 1942, 6 acres of peas were pulled the next week, and 4 acres of peas were pulled the following week. His men were paid 55/- an acre for this piece work, which substituted for grafting roses normally taking place during the same months.

From Wood & Ingram's *Order Ledger C*, covering the period 17th April 1941 until 6th October 1942, examples abound of the nursery's efforts in trying to sell off as many roses as possible. Several staff at the Thrapston Road rose fields were laid off and were never re-employed. A further order was sent to Canada when the nursery realised that the war might severely reduce orders for roses in England.

> The Avon Valley Green Houses, Falmouth, Nova Scotia
> 3rd February 1942
>
> > 1,000 Bush Roses, Orange Triumph £30 0s 0d
> > 1,000 Bush Roses, Eileen Poulsen £30 0s 0d
> > 2 Cases. Moss and Mossing. Inspection of
> > Roses by Ministry of Agriculture, Inspection
> > of Moss by Veterinary Surgeon
> > Issuing certificates etc., etc., ...£22 10s 0d
>
> To: The American Express Co. Inc.
>   at Alexander Dock, Liverpool
>   for Shipment per SS Stuart Prince

Amazingly the SS Stuart Prince crossed the Atlantic Ocean safely and the American Express Co. Inc paid the account. Even more surprising is that space should be found for roses at such a time.

The Horticultural Botanical Association Ltd.,
1st January 1942
Caldecot House, Goff's Oak, Hertfordshire

8,000 Bush Roses 'Home Sweet Home'	£240	0s	0d
100 Standard Almonds)	...£21	17s	0d
50 Fan trained Morello Cherries)			
	£261	17s	0d

(Waltham Cross Station)

Messrs Austin & McAslan Ltd
91 to 95, Mitchell Street, Glasgow C.1.
6th December 1941

Bush Roses:–

250 Else Poulsen	£7	10s	0d
250 Karen Poulsen	£7	10s	0d
250 Kirsten Poulsen	£7	10s	0d
100 Nurse Cavell	£3	0s	0d
50 Poulsen's Yellow	£2	0s	0d
150 Van Nas (all can)	£4	10s	0d
100 American Pillar	£3	11s	0d
25 Dorothy Perkins.		18s	9d
25 Easlea's Golden Wonder		18s	9d
50 Excelsa	£1	15s	0d
12 Elegance		14s	0d
12 Albertine		9s	0d
250 Anne Poulsen	£7	10s	0d
200 Etoile de Hollande	£6	0s	0d
200 Madame Butterfly	£6	0s	0d
50 General McArthur	£1	10s	0d
200 Mrs Sam McGredy	£6	0s	0d
100 Mrs G A Van Rossem	£3	0s	0d
4 Bundles & Packing NET		16s	0d
	£71	1s	6d

Goods Train Cathcart Station.

During this period many nurseries remained open, buying plants to grow on to sell to their own customers. Following their success two years earlier, Wood & Ingram increased their sale of clematis stocks. In their *Order Ledger C*, over 14,250 *Clematis vitalba* stocks were sent out to eight other nurseries on 18th February 1942 followed by a further 4,000 *Clematis vitalba* stocks to two nurseries one week later. Wood & Ingram charged £3 0s 0d for 1,000 clematis stocks. An increase of 11s 10d per thousand had occurred in under two years. Many individuals ordered large numbers of fruit trees and soft fruit for their vegetable gardens or allotments. A very lengthy order no. 313, for various lots of fruit trees was sent to Messrs Dickson Brown and Tait Ltd, Manchester. It covers 10 pages in the Order Ledger and includes 155 different lots each separately numbered, packed and priced, for a total of £149 13s 4d.

His Majesty's Office of Works was sent a large order of shrubs to be delivered to Mr D. Campbell, Store Yard, Hyde Park, London W2 on 18th March 1942 for £45 7s 6d. The order included 37 different shrubs in various numbers totalling 220 plants.

Surprisingly, quicks were still wanted during the Second World War. The Boughton Estates, Kettering were sent 4,000 quicks for £17 0s 0d on 16th March 1942. Papworth Industries at Papworth Everard were sent 26 Larch, 50 Ornamental trees and two further lots of trees for £40 17s 6d on 10th March 1942. Messrs S. A. Whittome Ltd, Ramsey, Huntingdon were sent 31 tons of Dunbar Standard White potatoes for £170 10s 0d; 30 tons of King Edward potatoes for £195 0s 0d totalling £365 10s 0d on 31st March 1942; 15 tons of Mangels, Goldern Tankard for £24 7s 6d on 9th April 1942 and 7½ tons of White Ware potatoes. A few days later, Whittome was sent more Dunbar Standard for £43 2s 6d on 21st April 1942. Mr L. Mann, Buckden was sent 3 tons of Mangels, Goldern Tankard for £5 5s 0d on 24th April 1942. Mrs Don, Pepys House, Brampton was sent 3 doz yellow Antirrhinums, 3 doz red Antirrhinums, 4 doz Stocks, and 3 Globe Artichokes for £1 0s 0d on 24th May 1942.

Wood & Ingram's last *Wage Ledger* indicates that before the Second World War over 75 men were employed on the nursery. Their total wages came to approximately £110 0s 0d each week. By 22nd May 1942 the men employed had dropped to 20 and the wages came to £65 0s 0d a week. But average weekly wages had risen from £2 a week in 1939 to £3 a week in 1945. During the war the staff were employed for growing and harvesting oats and barley, pulling peas, planting and harvesting swedes. A small typed note, dated 6th May 1943, reveals the age of each member of staff and, as recollected by Mr. Wady, the job they carried out.

Name	Age	Wage	Mr Wady's recollections
Ball	44	4s 6d	Worked on the Farm at the Thrapston Road
Brown, A.B.	31	£3 0s 8d	
Brown, A.	58	£3 10s 8d	Rose Foreman
Clark, A.	55	£3 0s 8d	In charge of Horses (lived on farm site)
Crow	67	£3 4s 7d	
Curtis	37	4s 9d	
Davey		£2 18s 8d	
Eustace	55	£3 5s 8d	Could do everything on nursery
Gale	43	£3 5s 8d	Packed orders in winter

Headland	29	4s 6d	
Humphrey	42	£2 18s 8d	General Nurseryman
Last	65	£2 18s 2d	Despatch Clerk, produced all the labels
Leverton	58	£3 10s 8d	General Foreman
Papworth		£3 2s 2d	
Redman	60	£2 18s 8d	General Nurseryman
Rosamond	46	£3 5s 8d	In charge of Greenhouses and Potting Shed
See	35	£2 15s 8d	Lorry driver when old enough
Smith	49	£3 3s 2d	General Nurseryman
Summers	51	£3 0s 8d	Like Eustace he lived on the Green in Brampton in one of the Nursery's cottages

Mr Summers was paid an extra 9s 0d for working in Cambridge

(Mr Summers is often noted as receiving extra wages for working away from the nursery perhaps planting trees and shrubs for clients.) He was paid £1 2s 6d for 9 days work in Newmarket in December 1940, 2s 6d for 1 days work at Broughton in March 1941, 2s 6d for 1 days work at Spaldwick in March 1941, 9s 0d for 3 days work in Newmarket in July 1941, 2s 6d for 1 days work at Glatton in August 1941, 12s 0d for working 4 days at Wimpole in October 1941, 9s 0d for working 3 days at Wimpole in December 1941, 3s 0d for working 1 day at Peterborough and 3s 0d for working 1 day at March in April 1942.

Mr Leverton, the General Foreman, showed visitors round the nursery and it was his responsibility to accompany important visitors, like HRH The Duchess of Gloucester, when they came to look at the nursery. But while visitors came to inspect the plants, there was the nursery's typical way of processing their orders which could not stop during the packing season. All the packers were in one shed and the foreman would come in with a bundle of orders. An order number was given to each order, which would be attached to the bundle, and the list of plants would be checked against the number and original order. The plants were then packed in straw and tied up. It was Mr Last's responsibility to look at the order number and write out the customer's address on the label. At 5 o'clock all packed orders were taken by horse trolley to Buckden Station, which was half way along the Cambridge to Kettering Line.

During his time at the nursery Mr Wady learnt to bud 2,000 roses a day; he first started by tying the rose round with raffia but, later, roses were budded with a square rubber clip with a pin, which was so much quicker and easier. During the war the nursery stopped posting catalogues, which meant that one of Mr Wady's jobs was to cycle round the district delivering them.

Luckily, most of the thousands of roses which were grafted during the Second World War were sold. Nursery sales dropped after 1945 when the country started to pay back the money owed during the war. Some time after the war, when funds were still short, the nursery changed their leather-bound ledgers containing stitched copies of orders to a cheaper system of hard cardboard covers, where each typed invoice had two holes punched into it. These invoices mainly cover plant and vegetable seed orders, garden tools, chemicals and wreaths. As there is no address index for ease of reference, and invoices had been hastily filed in batches from different offices, a careful appraisal of the invoices reveals that most customers were local and placed small orders with the nursery.

One such surviving hard-covered green file includes *Sales Invoices* 1001–2000 sent out between July 1947 and August 1948.

8th August 1947	14 different orders for wreaths in memory of Mr George Ashpole, Huntingdon.
12th August 1947	RAF Brampton ordered 2 x 2lbs of D.D.T. Dusting Powder for 8s 0d.
21st August 1947	Major Montgomery, 'The Hurst' Hartford, Hunts ordered 1 tin of D.D.T. Powder for 1s 9d and a further order on 28th August '47 for D.D.T. Powder for 8s 0d.
1st Sept 1947	H. C. Barnes, Ramsey Abbey School ordered 7lbs of Perkins Special Lawn Sand Mixture for £16 0s 0d.
25th Sept 1947	W. H. Halsam, Great Missinden, Bucks ordered 200 named Darwin Tulips, 50 named Hyacinths, and 50 named Narcissus for £13 5s 6d.
Sept 47–Jan 48	Several orders for the Executors of the Late J. A. Fielden, Esq., Holmewood Estate Office, Holme, near Peterborough included 28lbs of Tomorite for 14s 9d, 6 x 7lbs of Tomorite and Tomato plants for £2 14s 6d, Raffia, and 2 x 5 gallons of Mortegg (Tar Oil Winter Wash).
Sept–Oct 1947	Capt., The Hon. J. J. Astor, Hatley Park, Hatley St George ordered various vegetable seeds and 10 tins of Wasperd for £10 12s 9d, and a large order of named bulbs £22 9s 6d.
6th Oct–Dec 47	The Rt. Hon. Vicountess Hinchingbrooke ordered several orders of bulbs, 23 different species for £ 2 18s 9d.*
27th Oct 1947	Mrs Walston, Thriplow Farm ordered a large number of bulbs for £13 17s 0d.

During November 1947 there are several simple orders for *Aster yunnanensis 'Napsbury'*, which might indicate that this was a popular plant for borders immediately after the Second World War.

14th Nov 1947	Large order of various farm seeds including Red Clover was sent to Messsrs Grimbby in Lincolnshire for £38 15s 4d.
23rd Dec 1947	Moxon Bros, Farmers and Root Merchants, Chatteris was sent 28 lbs of Onions – Suttons, A1 English grown in 2 bags for £73 16s 7d and a further order on 6th January 1948 for 12lbs of Onions for £31 10s 0d and on 22nd December 1947 4lbs of Shallots for 6s 0d.
3rd Jan 1948	The Catering Manageress, Civil Service Luncheon Cafe, Marston Road, Oxford ordered 3lbs of Garlic for £1 12s 3d.
5th Jan 1948	Mr Shaw, Head Gardener, Diddington Hall ordered Arran Pilot seed potatoes*
14th Jan 1948	The Governors of Huntingdon Grammar School ordered 2 cwt of Bone Meal for £3 15s 0d.

19th Jan 1948		Miss Morton, Harcourt, Hemingford Grey ordered 2 x 56lb of Garden Lime and 1cwt of Bone Meal for £2 7s 6d.
5th Feb 1948		G Jones Esq., Ramsey was sent 100 lbs of Onions 'Giant Eittan' for £262 17s 0d.
Feb 1948		Messrs Brand, Warboys ordered 5cwt of Carrot Chantenay Red for £356 5s 0d.

*The Sandwich family at Hinchingbrooke and the Thornhill family at Diddington Hall had ordered from Wood & Ingram for almost 200 years.

Many nurseries suffered from similar problems as those that had been experienced after the First World War, and in a few years Wood & Ingram's business changed from that of selling their own propagated plants to a business similar to garden centres of today. Smaller orders and various garden requisites were now the order of the day. The *Sales Day Book* from March 1949–February 1950 covers 77 pages in the Ledger and reveals the following income during the last months of trading:

Total for March 1949	£ 2,664	10s 11d
" " April "	£1,251	19s 1d
" " May "	£ 838	18s 11d
" " June "	£ 378	18s 0d
" " July "	£ 350	6s 11d
" " August "	£ 357	0s 9d
" " Sept. "	£ 889	16s 3d
" " October "	£ 2,770	14s 11d
" " Nov. "	£ 6,400	6s 1d
" " Dec. "	£ 4,032	3s 0d
" " January 1950	£ 3,158	8s 3d
" " February "	£ 2,142	9s 8d
Total	£25,215	12s 9d

Comparing the nursery's earlier income between the two World Wars for identical periods a surprising pattern emerges:

March 1928 – Feb 1929 total income £14,864 12s 11d

March 1936 – Feb 1937 total income £ 4,270 5s 9d

March 1949 – Feb 1950 total income £25,215 12s 9d

By 1950 Henry Perkins had been the owner of Wood & Ingram's Nursery for nearly 30 years, having taken over the business when his father retired in 1920. With healthy sales Henry Perkins was in a favourable position to offer the nursery for sale.

In April 1950 the Huntingdon Post carried an advertisement stating:

> Re Wood & Ingram Ltd
> County of Huntingdon
>
> Announcement of sale by Public Auction of
>
> ## THE OLD-ESTABLISHED WELL-KNOWN WOOD & INGRAM NURSERIES
>
> (Mainly with VACANT POSSESSION)
> comprising:
>
> ### Lot 1 – The Nurseries, Brampton
>
> with attractive Residence, Four Cottages, Offices, and Nursery premises,
> in all about 45A. 1R. 9P.
> together with the goodwill and valuable growing stock
>
> ### Lot 2 – The Old Nurseries,
> ### St Germaine Street, Huntingdon
>
> with superior Residence, commodious three-storey warehouse
> and Nursery garden with an
> extensive area under glass.
>
> ### Lot 3 – Nos 16 and 18,
> ### Cambridge Street, St Neots
>
> Nursery Garden and Residence,
> Glasshouses and Florist's Sale Shop
>
> ### Lot 4 – Nos 2 and 3 George Street, Huntingdon.
>
> Double-fronted Sale Shop,
> Suite of Offices and Store Accommodation
>
> For sale by auction Wednesday 19th April 1950 at The George Hotel, Huntingdon
> at 2.30 o'clock in the afternoon punctually.

The following sale particulars offer more information about the nursery's land and property: The auctioneers were Dilley, Theakston & Beardmore, Market Hill, Huntingdon and the solicitors were Hunnybun & Sykes, Ferrar House, Huntingdon.

The Firm:
The business of Messrs. Wood & Ingram Ltd can be traced back over 200 years and throughout such lengthy period of time the production of quality has prevailed and the stock remains of the highest standard.

The name:
The use of the name of 'Wood & Ingram' will be granted to the Purchaser of Lot 1 (the Brampton Nurseries), but the use of such name will not be allowed to a separate purchaser of Lots 2, 3, & 4

PARTICULARS

Lot 1
To be offered as a going concern

THE NURSERIES, BRAMPTON

The well-known and Old Established Nursery Business together with the Freehold Nursery Premises which comprise

A DESIRABLE DETACHED RESIDENCE
SUITE OF OFFICES, NURSERY BUILDINGS
AND LAND

together with

FOUR COTTAGES

the whole extending to an area of about

45 Acres 1 Rood 9 Poles

The Nursery Premises are very well situated in the Parish of Brampton, have a long and valuable frontage to the road leading from Brampton to the Great North Road and being about two miles distant from the County Town of Huntingdon

The very attractive Brick and Tiled
RESIDENCE
stands conveniently distant from the road, was built in 1903, and is fronted by a pleasant Rose Garden enclosed by shaped Yew Hedge. There is also an enclosed Lawn. The House, the interior of which has been tastefully decorated and is in excellent order, is approached by a crazy paved pathway to a tiled ENTRANCE PORCH and contains Entrance Hall, Drawing Room, Dining Room, Breakfast Room, Back Kitchen, Two Pantries and a staircase leading to Three Bedrooms and Bathroom
Outside
Paved Yard, Three Store Rooms, Coal Store and Two W.C's

Brick and Tiled Garage to house three cars and having Loft over and concrete wash
Large store with partition enclosing electric water pump.
Over part of this building are installed Two Large Galvanised Water Storage Tanks.

The well built
SUITE OF OFFICES
which include Manager's Office; Typists' Office, Two Clerks' Offices
and a Telephone Room.
Enclosed Orchard planted with choice varieties of Fruit Trees

THE TWO SETS OF NURSERY BUILDINGS
include
Long timber and tiled Range of Store Places and
packing Sheds with Lean-to Store Place
Walled-in Store or Stock Yard with Tractor House and Covered Store Place
Large 6-bay Implement and Cart Hovel
Foreman's Office, Rose Sorting Shed, Cutting Shed
Glasshouse 69 feet long, Glasshouse 40 feet long with water tanks
Eleven Light Frames
Glasshouse 40 feet long with stoke hole adjoining
Potting and Store Sheds and Store Place

THE LAND
which lies in a ring fence averages a good depth of light loam with gravel sub-soil, has
been well cared for and is in a good state of cultivation.
THE VALUABLE GROWING NURSERY STOCK
is included in the sale of the freehold and includes
BUSH ROSES including the latest novelties and choice varieties
STANDARD AND CLIMBING ROSES all on briar stock
BUSH, HALF-STANDARD AND TRAINED FRUIT TREES in the leading varieties
FRUIT BUSHES including Black and Red Currants, Gooseberry, etc.
Selection of STANDARD, FLOWERING AND ORNAMENTAL TREES
including rare and valuable specimens
FLOWERING SHRUBS in choice varieties
HEDGING PLANTS including English Yew, Privet, etc.
HERBACEOUS BORDER PLANTS, etc., etc., etc.

Also included in the sale are
FOUR COTTAGES

Situate in the High Street and The Green, Brampton, all such cottages being at present occupied by service Occupiers and more particularly described as follows

"The LAURELS", HIGH STREET

A brick and slated double-fronted

DWELLING HOUSE

converted into two dwellings and in the occupation
of Messrs Leverton and Brown

Water Supply from well, but main supply is available

This property is approached by a driveway entrance from the High Street and there are good gardens

THE GREEN

A Pair of excellent Semi-detached Brick and Tiled Cottages facing The Green and fronted by small gardens with pale fencing
and in the occupation of Messrs Summers and Eustace

Main water laid on

Large and productive gardens

Fee: Farm Rent payable to Vicar and Churchwardens of Brampton 13s 4d.

Lot 2
HUNTINGDON
THE OLD NURSERIES
ST GERMAINE STREET

With Superior Residence, Commodious Storage Accommodation and Nurseries with an extensive area under glass.

The property has long and valuable frontage to St Germaine Street and Nursery Road, is approached by a large double gate entrance to wide gravelled drive and comprises: the Substantially Built Brick and Slated

RESIDENCE

which has the following accommodation

Basement with Cellar with fitted meat safe

Ground Floor with Entrance Hall, Lounge, Dining Room, Breakfast Room, Kitchen, Two Larders, Scullery, Store Room

Two Staircases

First Floor with three Bedrooms, Bathroom,

Second Floor with four Bedrooms, Large Dressing Room and Tank Room

Tennis lawn with flower and rose beds, Ornamental
Garden, Rose Arbor, Lily Pond, Yew and Muabella Hedges

THE NURSERY BUILDINGS

include

a very Valuable Brick and Tiled

THREE-STOREY WAREHOUSE

125 feet by 16ft 4inches

(producing upwards of 6,000 sq ft of floor space)

and which has the following accommodation

Ground Floor with Front Sale Shop, Two Floral Rooms, Large Store, Spacious Garage
and Two-Stall Stable

First Floor with Store Room (over stable), Three Warehouses

Second Floor with Four Warehouses with Roof Lofts over

Range of timber and tiled buildings comprising

Garage, 3-Bay Open Shed and Store Room with Loft

Carpenter's Shop with Loft

Potting Shed, Pot Storage Shed,

Pigsty and run, Fowl House

Potting Shed and Store with Loft over

An area of approximately **15,000** sq feet under glass, mostly heated comprising:

Five fitted Propagating Houses approached from the Potting Shed measuring in length
respectively: 40 ft, 30 ft, 30 ft, 24 ft and 24 ft.

A brick Plant House 13 ft by 13 ft.(not heated)

A Glass House 85 ft by 10 ft (heated)

Five heated Glass Houses measuring respectively: 64 ft by 24 ft, 117 ft by 21 ft,
82 ft by 21 ft, 80 ft by 13 ft, 79 ft by 13 ft.

Fern House 33 ft by 18 ft (heated)

Glass House 41 ft by 11 ft (heated)

Five further heated Glass Houses measuring respectively; 29 ft by 19 ft, 71 ft by 10 ft,
62 ft by 11ft, 39 ft by 11ft, 39 ft by 10 ft

Fixed and portable garden frames are included in the sale.

The water supply is pumped from a well by a Moorlands water pump driven by
Ruston & Hornsby 4 h.p. petrol/paraffin engine and housed in a brick built building
which has a large galvanised storage tank over. The heated water for the glasshouses
is provided by three "Robin Hood" boilers.

THE NURSERIES

are of a convenient size and there is a Small Orchard

The whole property containing

3 Acres 0 Rood 9 Poles

(more or less)

is screened from Nursery Road by a magnificent tall beech hedge and from St Germaine Street along most of its 289 ft. frontage by a high wall and poplar trees. Included in the sale are the wall, bush and standard trees and all plants or shrubs growing in the ground

VACANT POSSESSION

will be given upon completion of the purchase (or by earlier arrangement) of the land and buildings. The residence is occupied by a Service Occupier and Notice to Quit has been given

Outgoings – Title Redemption Annuity as assessed.

The stock-in-trade, plants in pots, tools and other effects may be taken over by valuation, if required, by the Purchaser provided notification is given to the Vendor's Solicitors immediately after the sale

The property above described is coloured red and green on the plan attached to these particulars of sale. The area of land coloured green on such plan is the property of the Governors of the Huntingdon School Foundation and has been occupied upon a yearly tenancy by Messrs. Wood & Ingram Ltd. and their predecessors for over one hundred years and the said Board of Governors have intimated that they will be prepared to grant a similar tenancy at a rent of £10 per annum to the Purchaser for the purpose of a Nurseryman's business or other purpose approved by them. The remainder of the property is freehold.

LOT 3

The Valuable Freehold

NURSERIES

with

RESIDENCE, GLASSHOUSES and FLORIST'S SALE SHOP

situate and being

Nos. 16 and 18 CAMBRIDGE STREET, ST NEOTS

(adjoining the main shopping centre of the busy Market Town)

and comprising

THE DOUBLE FRONTED BRICK AND SLATED RESIDENCE

containing

On the Ground Floor, Entrance Hall, Dining Room, Drawing Room, Kitchen and Pantry

On the First Floor, Four Bedrooms, Bathroom and Separate W.C.

Basement with Cellar

Outbuildings comprising Wash House now used as a Coal Store and W.C.

Adjoining and communicating with the Residence is

THE CONVENIENT FRONT SALE SHOP

having a frontage of 16 feet 10 inches to Cambridge Street

The following Fixtures are included in the sale

Large nest of 162 drawers; mahogany topped counter and shelving

There is a Loft over the shop

THE SPACIOUS WALLED-IN NURSERIES

approached by a double iron gate entrance from Cambridge Street has the following equipment erected thereon

LEAN-TO GLASSHOUSE 36 ft by 12 ft with fitted staging, hot water piping and underground soft water storage tank

Timber built BOILER HOUSE fitted with "Robin Hood" boiler and piping

LARGE GLASSHOUSE 125 ft by 20 ft with hot water piping and underground soft water storage tank

GLASSHOUSE 100 ft by 14 ft with fitted staging, hot water piping, underground soft water storage tank and adjoining range of twenty-two built in frames

Sunken BOILER HOUSE of brick with "Robin Hood" horticultural boiler and piping

GLASS PROPAGATING HOUSE 55 ft by 9 ft with frames

GARDEN FRAME with fourteen lights

GARDEN FRAME

TWO STORE PLACES, GARAGE, TOOL SHED and LOOSE BOX with rooms over (formerly used as a cottage)

Four-bay brick and tiled HOVEL

POT SHED

Newly constructed STATIC WATER SUPPLY TANK

The growing of fruit trees and bushes, the numerous tulip, daffodil and iris bulbs and any growing plants or shrubs are included in the sale. The stock-in-trade, plants in pots, loose effects, etc., may be taken over by the Purchaser at valuation (if required), provided notification is given to the Vendor's Solicitors immediately after the sale.

The whole property embraces an area of
1 Acre 0 Rood 34 Poles
(more or less)
and has a frontage of 140 ft 10 inches to Cambridge Street
VACANT POSSESSION
will be given upon completion of purchase, with the exception of the Residence which is held upon a service occupation. Notice to Quit has been given to the present occupier.
Outgoings – None Paid
Inspection will show that the land is in good heart and has been well cultivated and stocked
The Property occupies an exceptional and commanding position and is of such size and lay-out that labour is reduced to a minimum.
The wall to the east, south and southern portion of west boundaries is a party wall

LOT 4
HUNTINGDON
This Excellent Double-Fronted
SALE SHOP
SUITE OF OFFICES
and
STORAGE ACCOMMODATION
being
Nos. 2 and 3 GEORGE STREET
(in close proximity to the Market Hill, Post Office and main shopping centre of the County Town and directly opposite The George Hotel)
Well designed and of pleasing appearance, the property is substantially built of brick (part of the front being of glazed green brick) with tiled roof and in excellent structural
condition, and has a frontage of 35 feet to George Street and a depth of approximately 41 feet and comprises

THE ATTRACTIVE DOUBLE-FRONTED SALE SHOP

33 ft 4 in. by 25 ft., with two plate glass display windows, window display stands, oak service counters with seed drawers and pigeonholes, counter desk, two large oak nests containing 481 seed drawers, shelving, two large hot water radiators, wood block floor

The central oak staircase, having hot water radiator, gives access to the landing and
EXCELLENT SUITE OF FIRST FLOOR OFFICES
CLERK'S SPACIOUS OFFICE with tiled fireplace, mahogany desks and cupboards under stairs
MANAGING DIRECTOR'S OFFICE with tiled fireplace
SECRETARY'S OFFICE with tiled fireplace
Approached by a Staircase the second floor comprises
Two rooms, together measuring 33 ft 4 ins. by 25 ft and having shelving and cupboards.
At present used for storage purposes
OUTSIDE
STOREPLACE with a right of way along a pathway four feet wide over the adjoining yard to and from the rear of the property
SHED housing a "Robin Hood Junior" boiler which provides central heating to the shop premises
COALHOUSE and W.C. adjoining
W.C. and STORE
STORE ROOM with sink, cupboards and pigeonholes, with loft over and access to shop
Electricity and main water are laid on

VACANT POSSESSION
of the property will be given upon completion of purchase
Outgoings – Land Tax £1 8s 2d
The stock of seeds, garden requisites and tools may be taken over at valuation by the purchaser, provided notification is given to the Vendor's Solicitors immediately after the sale.

Conditions of Sale in the Sale Particulars
As to the greater part of Lot 1 with a Deed of Conveyance and Covenant to Surrender for the value dated the 5th January 1903 and made between John Wood Ingram and George Wood Ingram of the one part and John Edward Perkins of the other part.
As to further part (which formerly formed part of the ancient possessions of Clare College in the University of Cambridge) with a Conveyance for value and dated 6th April 1925 and made between the Master and Fellows and Scholars of that College of the one part and Henry Perkins of the other part.
And as to the remainder thereof with a Conveyance for value dated the
31st December 1918 and made between the Most Noble William Angus Drogo Duke of Manchester of the first part The Honourable Arthur George Keith Falconer and
The Most Honourable the Marquess of Tweeddale (the grandson of the 9th Earl of Tweeddale who married the 3rd Daughter of the 5th Duke of Manchester in 1816), of the second part and the said Henry Perkins of the third part.

· · ● · ·

All four lots were sold at the auction on April 19th 1950 and Wood & Ingram's famous nursery finally closed its gates to customers after 200 years trading.

Wood & Ingram

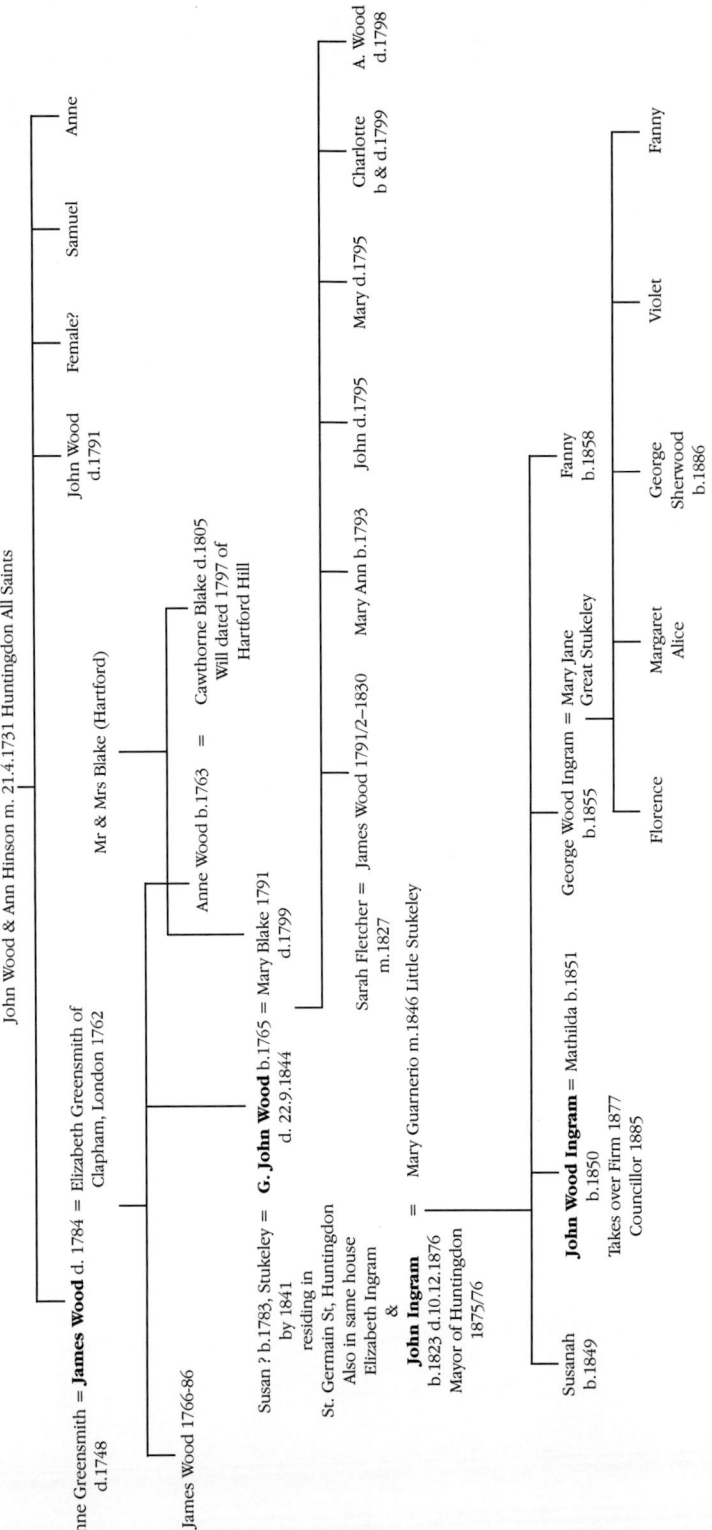

Mr & Mrs John Wood
John Wood & Ann Hinson m. 21.4.1731 Huntingdon All Saints

```
                                              John Wood    Female?    Samuel    Anne
                                              d.1791
                Mr & Mrs Blake (Hartford)

                                    Cawthorne Blake d.1805
                                    Will dated 1797 of
                                    Hartford Hill
                Anne Wood b.1763 =
                                d.1799
                                                                                        A. Wood
                                                                                        d.1798
                                                               Mary d.1795    Charlotte
                                                                              b & d.1799
                Sarah Fletcher = James Wood 1791/2-1830
                m.1827
                                            Mary Ann b.1793   John d.1795
```

Anne Greensmith = **James Wood** d. 1784 = Elizabeth Greensmith of
d.1748   Clapham, London 1762

James Wood 1766-86

Susan ? b.1783, Stukeley = **G. John Wood** b.1765 = Mary Blake 1791
residing in   d. 22.9.1844
by 1841
St. Germain St, Huntingdon
Also in same house
Elizabeth Ingram
&
John Ingram = Mary Guarnerio m.1846 Little Stukeley
b.1823 d.10.12.1876
Mayor of Huntingdon
1875/76

```
                                                            Fanny
                                                            b.1858
                        George Wood Ingram = Mary Jane
                        b.1855                Great Stukeley
                                                                           Violet        Fanny
Susanah   John Wood Ingram = Mathilda b.1851
b.1849    b.1850
          Takes over Firm 1877    Florence   Margaret   George
          Councillor 1885                    Alice     Sherwood
                                                       b.1886
```

This family tree traces the ownership of Wood & Ingram's Nursery prior to
John Edward Perkins buying the nursery in 1903.

APPENDIX 1
THE LIST OF 740 ROSES IN
WOOD & INGRAM'S STOCK LIST OF 1890

THE ROSE (Rosa)

Class 1 Provence
1. Anemoneflora
2. Blush
3. Cabbage or Common
4. Cristata or Crested
5. Dutch
6. Evelina
7. Rachel
8. Red Double
9. Stadholder
10. Triomphe d'Abberville
11. Unique or White
12. Grande Agathe
13. La Reine de Provance
14. Comte Plater

Class 2 Provence Dwarf
1. Burgundy
2. De Meux
3. Sponge

Class 3 Moss
1. Blush
2. Common
3. Crimson Double
4. Du Luxembourg
5. Moussue Partout
6. Old White or Bath
7. Perpetual White
8. Prolifere or Mottled
9. Prolifie or Gracilis
10. Comtesse de Murinais
11. Unique de Murinais
12. Alice Leroy
13. Elsia
14. French Crimson or Ecarlate
15. Laucel
16. Lanei
17. Perpetual Crimson
18. Princess Alice
19. Salet Perpetual
20. James Veitch
21. Baron Wassener
22. Madame Blanche Moreau
23. Zenobia, ex W. Paul & Son/94

C 4 Hybrid Provence
1. Aspasie
2. Blance Fleur
3. Globe Hip
4. Leah
5. Princess Clementine

C5 French
1. Amiable Queen
2. Bizarre Marbre
3. Black Frizzled
4. Boula de Nauteuil
5. Buonaparte
6. Cynthia
7. Eclâtante
8. Duchesse de Cleves
9. Fanny Parissot
10. Favorite
11. Grandpapa
12. —
13. Les 10th
14. Louis Phillipe
15. Mundi
16. Nelly
17. Octave Corelli
18. Oriflamme
19. Roi de Naples
20. Sable (good)
21. Sir Walter Scott
22. Village Maid
23. OEillet Parfait
24. Cambroune
25. Cerise Superb
26. Dr. Dieltheur
27. William Tell
28. Guerin's Gift
29. Triomphe de Jaussons
30. Hebe
31. D'Aguesseau
32. Julie d' Etanges
33. La tour d' Auvergne
34. Schonbrunn
35. Je me maintiendrai
36. Pashot

C 6 Hybrid China
1. A l' Odier de Pate d'Amande
2. Aurora
3. Belle Parabere
4. Bizarre de Brabant
5. Blairii
6. Bouquet Blanc
7. Brennus
8. Charles Foucquier
9. Comtesse d'Iacepede
10. Coupe d' Amour
11. Coutard
12. Franklin
13. Fulgens
14. Gen Kleber
15. La Dauphine
16. Lauzezeur
17. Madame Pisaroui
18. Mad Plantier
19. Sky Hybrid
20. Smith's Seedling
21. Stadtholder sinensis (Crowders)
22. Victor Hugo
23. Victor Tracy
24. Becquet
25. Chenedole
26. Leopold de Bauffremout
27. General Lemarque
28. General Jacqueminot
29. Descartes
30. Magna Rosea
31. Juno
32. George the 4th

C 7 Hybrid Bourbon
1. Athelin
2. Charles Duval
3. Coupe d'Hebe
4. Hortense Leroy

APPENDIX 1   227

5   Comte Boubert
6   Paul Ricaut
7   Belle de St Cyr
8   Frederick 2nd
9   Paul Perras
10 Charles Lawson
11 Henri Barbert

C 8 Alba
1   Celestial
2   Maidens Blush
3   Princesse de Lamballe
4   Sophie de Marsilly
5   Felicite (Parmentier)
6   Madame Audot
7   Madame Legras

C 9 Damask
1   La Ville de Bruxelles
2   Leda or Painted
3   Madame Hardy
4   Old or Common
5   Madame Zoutman
6   Madame Stoltz
7   Napoleon
8   Ohl
9   York and Lancaster

C 10 Sweet briar
1   Celestial
2   Doubled Marbled
3   Doubled Red
4   Red Provence Seedling
5   Common

C11 Hybrid Sweet briar
1   Double Margined Hip
2   Hebes Lip or Margined Hip

This entry is crossed out and 320 written across it

C12 Sulphurea Dble Yellow
1   Yellow or cabbage

C13 Scotch
1   Blush
2   Dark Velvet
3   Ladies Blush
4   Large Red
5   Light Red
6   Marbled

7   Marbled Pink
8   Double White (ex Bunyard)
9   Double Yellow (ex Bunyard)
10 —
11 Provence Blush
12 —
13 Semi Double Shaded red
14 Suphur Yellow
15 —
16 White Provence Seedling

C 14 Austrian Briars
1   Copper
2   Yellow Single
3   Yellow Double
4   Persian Yellow
5   Harissonii

C 15 Ayrshire
1   Bennetts Seedling
2   Elegans or Double White
3   Ruga
4   Williams Evergreen

C 16 Multiflora
1   Frasers Climbing
2   Hybrida or Laura Davoust
3   Russelliana
4   De la Grifferie

C 17 Sempervirens Evergreen
1   Adelaide d'Orleans
2   Felicité Perpetualle
3   Myrianthes
4   Princess Louise
5   Princess Marie
6   Scandens or Alice Grey
7   Banksiae flora

C18 Banksian
1   White
2   Yellow
3   Jaune Serin
4   Jaune Vif Serin
5   Anemoneflora
6   Fortuniana

C 19 Boursalt
1   Blush or De Lille

2   Drummonds Thornless
3   Gracilis
4   Red
5   Crimson

C 20 Hybrid Climbing
1   —
2   —
3   Madame d'Arblay
4   The Garland

C 21 Damask Perpetual
1   Blush or Palmyre
2   Four Seasons Scarlet
3   Portland Blanc
4   La Capriciense

C 22 Hydrid Perpetual
1   Baronne Prevost
2   Duc de Rohan
3   François Louvat
4   Madame Furtards
5   Marèchal Vaillaut
6   Mademoiselle Bonnaire
7   Comtesse de Kergolay
8   Geant des Batailles
9   Madame Heraud
10 Prince Famille de Rohan
11 Charles Lefebore
12 Louis Darzens
13 Professor Koch
14 Queen Victoria
15 Jules Margottin
16 Caroline de Sansal
17 Duchesse de Norfolk
18 Beauty of Waltham
19 Olivier Delhomme
20 William Griffiths
21 Maurice Bernadin
22 Alexandre Fontaine
23 Alpaide de Rotalier
24 General E Jaqueminot
25 Alphonse Belin
26 Eugine Verdier
27 Gabriel de Peyronny
28 Madame Campbell d'Islay
29 Jean Touvais
30 Kate Hausburg
31 Duchesse de Morny
32 Leopold 1st

33	Madame de Canrobert	80	Mademoiselle Eleanor Grier	127	Richard Wallace
34	Gloire de Vitry			128	Madame Lefebvre Bernard
35	Madame Victor Verdier	81	Ville de Lyon	129	Madame Scipion Cochet
36	Madame Vidot	82	Paul Verdier	130	Souvenir de Julie Gonod
37	Duchesse d'Orleans	83	Souvenir de Monsieur Boll	131	Comtesse de Palikas
38	Marèchal Suchet	84	Charles Verdier	132	Charles Lee
39	Mrs Rivers	85	Francois Fontaine	133	Charles Margottin
40	Pierre Notting	86	Baroness Rosthchild	134	Felix Genero
41	John Hopper	87	Madame Gondier	135	Thérèse Levet
42	Madame Bouttin	88	Clothilde Roland	136	Princess Mary of Cambridge
43	Louise Peyronny	89	La France	137	Abbe Giraudier
44	La Ville de St Denis	90	Madame Noman	138	Duhamel de Monceau
45	Dr. Audry	91	Pitord	139	Madame Lacharme
46	Charles Wood	92	Prince Humbert	140	Madame Moreau
47	Anna de Diesbach	93	Viscountesse de Vesins	141	Mademoiselle Julie Pareard
48	Prince de Joinville	94	Miss Ingram		
49	Comtesse de Chabrillant	95	Edouard Morren	142	Mrs Laing
50	Victor Verdier	96	Duke of Edinburgh	143	Madame Marius Cote
51	Senateur Vaisse	97	Berthe Baron	144	Souvenir de la Princesse Amelia des Pays Bas
52	Madame Boll	98	Julie Louvais		
53	Madame Charles Frapelet	99	Madame Decour	145	Monsieur Woolfield
54	Duchesse de Caylus	100	Madame Creyton	146	Bessie Johnson
55	Achille Gonod	101	Reine Blanche	147	Reynolds Hole
56	Comtesse de Paris	102	Victor Trouillard Pere	148	Felicien David
57	Madame Moreau	103	John Keynes	149	Mrs Veitch
58	Marguerite de St Armand	104	Xavier Olibo	150	Pierre Seletzky
59	Kings Acre	105	Marie Baumann	151	Claude Levet
60	Duke of Wellington	106	Comtesse d'Oxford	152	Madame Emma Combey
61	Lord Macauley	107	Ferdinand de Lesseps	153	Mademoiselle Fermande de la Foreste
62	Jean Lambert	108	Louis Van Houtte		
63	John Grier	109	La Motte Sanguine	154	The Shah
64	Gloire de Ducher	110	Mademoiselle Eugene Verdier	155	Madame Louise Levêque
65	Jean Cherpin			156	Etiennne Dupuy
66	Comte Alphonse de Seringe	111	Paul Neron	157	Duchess of Edinburgh
		112	Leopold Hausburg	158	Marie Finger
67	Exposition de Brie	113	Elie Morel	159	Captain Christy
68	Camille Bernardin	114	Abel Grand	160	Francois Courtin
69	Fisher Holmes	115	Henri Pages	161	Antoine Mouton
70	Black Prince	116	Climbing Victor Verdier	162	Colonel de Sausal
71	Charles Rouillard	117	Princess of Wales	163	Monsieur E. Y. Teas
72	Mademoiselle Marie Rady	118	Captain Lamure	164	May Turner
73	Professor Ducharte	119	Princess Christain	165	Hippolyte Jamain
74	Mademoiselle Margueritte Dombrain	120	Princess Louise	166	Baronne Louis Uxkell
		121	Lyonnaise	167	Antoine Ducher
75	Prince de Porcia	122	Andre Dunand	168	Francois Michelon
76	Alfred Colomb	123	Baronne de Prailly	169	Miss Hassard
77	Comte Litta	124	Baron de Bonstettin	170	Revd J. B. M. Camm
78	Madame Rival	125	Etienne Levet	171	General Cissy
79	Mademoiselle Annie Wood	126	President Thiers	172	Jean Libaud

173 Madame Prosper Laugier
174 President Leon de St Jean
175 Mademoiselle Emilie Verdier
176 Mademoiselle Bertha Sacavin
177 John Stuart Mill
178 Sir Garnet Wolseley
179 Horace Vernet
180 Madame Hachary
181 Star of Waltham
182 Perle des Blanches
183 Jean Rosenkrantz
184 Perfection de Lyon
185 Empress of India
186 Royal Standard
187 Dr. Hooker
188 Souvenir de Baron de Semur
189 Marguerite Brassac
190 Duke of Connaught
191 Oxonian
192 Boieldieu
193 Eduoard Pynaert
194 Fontonelle
195 La Saumonce
196 Madame Anna de Besobrasoff
197 Madame Dorlia
198 Madame Francois Pittet
199 Madame Gabriel Laizet
200 Madame de Laboulaye
201 Madame la Marquise d'Hervey
202 Madame Roger
203 Princesse Charlotte de la Tremouille
204 Princesse Lise Troubetskoi
205 Duchesse de Vallombrosa
206 Abel Carriere
207 Comtesse de Serenafe
208 Sultan of Zanzibar
209 Henri Bennett
210 Marchioness of Exeter
211 Comtesse de Choiseuil
212 Deuil de Colonel Denfer

213 Docteur Braillon
214 John Bright
215 Louis Doré
216 May Quennell
217 Rosy Morn

New Hybrid Perpetuals
218 Ambrogio Maggi
219 Charles Darwin
220 Countess of Rosebery
221 Comte de Mortemart
222 Gloire de Bourg-la-Reine
223 Harrison Weir
224 Henriette Petit
225 Julius Finger
226 Leon Duval
227 Mon Alfred Dumesnil
228 Madame Ducher
229 Madame Oswald de Kerchove
230 Marquis of Salisbury

New Climbing Rose
231 Satina
232 Baron Gaylor
233 Mrs Laxton
234 Geant des Batailles
235 Duchess of Bedford
236 Climbing Jules Margottin
237 Climbing Bessie Johnson
238 Annie Laxton
239 Duke of Teck
240 George Baker
241 La Rosiére
242 Mabel Morrison
243 Magna Charta
244 Prince Arthur
245 Princess Beatrice
246 A K Williams
247 Mrs Harry Turner
248 Egeria
249 Avocat Duvivier
250 Prefect Limbourg
251 Dupuy Jamain
252 Glory of Cheshunt
253 Dr. Hogg
254 Wilhelm Koëlle

255 Penelope Mayo
256 Paul Jamain
257 William Warden
258 Souvenir d'Arthur de Sansal
259 Mademoiselle Catherine Soupert
260 Emily Laxton
261 Lord Frederick Cavendish
262 Violette Bouyer
263 Merville de Lyon
264 Mademoiselle Alfred de Rougement
265 Lord Bacon
266 Queen of Queens
267 Gloire Lyonnaise
268 Her Majesty
269 Empress
270 Mrs Baker
271 Baron Hausmann
272 Eclair
273 Ali Pasha Cherif
274 Vicomtesse de Serves
275 Sir Roland Hill
276 Duchess of Leeds
277 Grand Mogul
278 Lady E Stewart
279 Earl of Dufferin
280 —
281 Queen of Autumn
282 Lady Alice
283 Mrs John Laing
284 Ulrich Brunner
285 —
286 Victor Hugo
287 Lady Sheffield
288 Margaret Dickson
289 Suzanne Marie Rodocanachi
290 Bruce Findley
291 T. W. Girdlestone
292 Danmark
293 Paul's Single White
294 Salamander
295 Augustine Guinoisseau
296 Marguerite Boudet
297 Le Havre
298 Marchioness of Dufferin

299 Madame Eugene Verdier
300 Francis Bloxham
301 Violet Queen
302 Paul's Early Blush
303 Marchioness of Londonderry
304 Charles Gater
305 Gustave Piganeau
306 Duke of Fife
307 Duchess of Fife
308 Jeannie Dickson
309 La France de '89
310 Madame E Michel
311 Caroline Testout
312 Spenser
313 Dr. Sewell
314 Laurence Allen
315 Bladud
316 Carmine Pillar
317 Climbing Earl of Pembroke
318 Mrs Rumsey
319 Ton Wood
320 Ards Rover
321 Bardou Job
322 Berthe Gemen
323 Clio
324 Helen Killen
325 Captain Hayward
326 Charles Lamb
327 Heingrich Schultheis
328 Baron Hausmann
329 Mrs R G Sharman Crawford

C 23 China
1 Mrs Bosanquet
2 Louis Phillipe
3 Cramoisie Superieure
4 Purple China
5 Old Blush
6 Old Dark
7 White
8 Viridiflora
9 Madame E Resal
10 Duke of York
11 Queen Mab
12 Irene Watts
13 Madame L Messimy
14 Marjolin
15 Cora
16 Jean Bach Sisley

C 24 Bourbon
1 Baronne de Noirmont
2 Baron Gonella
3 Comtesse de Barbantanne
4 Emotion
5 Louise Margottin
6 Modèle de Perfection
7 Rev D Dombrain
8 Madame Desprez
9 Reine de Castille
10 Souvenir de la Malmaison
11 Acidalie
12 Madame Jeannine Joubert
13 Queen of Bedders
14 Jules Jurgesen
15 Red Malmaison
16 Madame Issac Pereire
17 Mrs Paul
18 Climbing S de la Malmaison

C 25 Tea Scented
1 Belle Chartronnaise
2 Duc de Magenta
3 Gloire de Bordeaux
4 Laurette
5 Bougère
6 Madame Damaizin
7 Madame Joseph Halfshen
8 Devoniensis
9 Homère
10 Sombrieul
11 Climbing Devoniensis
12 Marèchal Niel
13 Louise de Savoie
14 Julie Mausais
15 Lutescens
16 Souvenir d'un Ami
17 Adrienne Christophle
18 La Tulip
19 Marie Sisley
20 Marie Ducher
21 Montplaisir
22 Madame Falcot
23 Niphetos
24 Madame Willermoz
25 Narcisse
26 Safrano
27 Madame Bravy
28 La Pactole
29 Auguste Vaucher
30 Adam
31 Mademoiselle Jenny Pernet
32 Rubens
33 President
34 Jaune d'Or
35 Socrate
36 Madame Margottin
37 Reine de Portugal
38 Gloire de Dijon
39 Cheshunt Hybrid
40 Duchess of Edinburgh
41 Madame Tartas
42 Belle Lyonnaise
43 Souvenir de Paul Neron
44 Madame Van Houtte
45 Madame Berard
46 La Boule d'Or
47 Aline Sisley
48 Jean Ducher
49 Marie Guillot
50 Clothilde
51 David Pradel
52 Perle de Lyon
53 Reine de Pays Bas
54 Souvenir d'Elise
55 Louis Richards
56 Madame Blanche Durrschmidt
57 Madame Lambard
58 Letty Coles
59 Madame Velemortez
60 Bon Silene
61 Jules Finger
62 Madame Barthelemy Levet
63 Madame Angele Jacquier
64 Madame Mathilde Lenaerts
65 Reine Marie Henriette
66 Comtessee Rizco du Parc
67 Ma Capucine
68 Catherine Mermet
69 Isabella Sprunt
70 Madame Camille
71 Madame de St Joseph
72 Perle des Jardins

APPENDIX 1

73 Safrano a fleur Rouge
74 Madame Etienne Levet
75 Reine Maria Pia
76 American Banner
77 Madame Denis
78 Etoile de Lyon
79 Anna Ollivier
80 Comtesse de Nadaillae
81 Moiré
82 Mademoiselle C Soupert
83 Sunset
84 Souvenir de Therése Level
85 Etandard de Jeanne d'Arc
86 Madame de Watteville
87 The Bride
88 Dr. Berthet
89 May Rivers
90 Climbing Niphetos
91 Princess Beatrice
92 Hon. Edith Gifford
93 Ma Capucine
94 Souvenir d'Elise Varden
95 Madame Cusin
96 Sounenir de S A Prince
97 Mons Desir
98 Vicomtesse Folkestone
99 Madame Hoste
100 Medea
101 Waban
102 Souvenir de Lady
103 Ernest Metz
104 Cleopatra
105 Climbing Perle des Jardins
106 La Soliel
107 Fransisca Kruger
108 Corinna
109 Princess May
110 Madame Pernet Ducher
111 Christine de Noue
112 Kaiserin Augusta Victoria
113 Ethel Brownslow
114 Dr. Grill
115 Elise Fugier
116 Dulce Belle
117 Rainbow
118 Luciole
119 Waltham Climber
120 David d'Angus

121 Papa Goutier
122 White M. Niel
123 White Lady
124 Souvenir de Catherine Guillot
125 Muriel Grahame
126 Marquise Sitta
127 G Nabonnand
128 Francis Dubreuil
129 Belle Siebrecht
130 Antoine Rivoire
131 Sylph
132 Enchantress
133 Empress Alexa of Russia
134 Beryl
135 Meta
136 Grace Darling
137 Climbing Kaiserin Augusta Victoria
138 Souvenir de Madame Metral
139 Madame Bouland
140 Souvenir de Charles Gargend
141 White Bougere
142 Bridesmaid
143 Mrs Robert Garratt
144 Grossherz of Ernst Ludwig
145 Climbing Belle Siebrecht
146 Duchess d'Anerstadt
147 Longworth Rambler
148 Reine Olga de Wurtenburg
149 Maman Cochet
150 White Maman Cochet
151 Sunrise
152 Soliel d'Or
153 Liberty
154 Bessie Brown
155 Corallina
156 Grusan Tiplitz
157 Gustav Regis
158 Mrs Edward Mawley
159 Claire Jaquier
160 Madame Charles
161 Souvenir de G. Drevet

C 26 Noisette
1 Amie Vibert
2 Blush
3 Cerise
4 Fellemberg

5 Jaune Desprez
6 La Biche
7 Lamarke
8 Red, or Wells' Pink
9 Solfaterre
10 Cloth of God
11 Isabella Erly
12 Triomphe de Rennes
13 Celine Forestier
14 Margarita
15 Madame Caroline Kuster
16 Bouquet d'Or
17 Reve d'Or
18 Ophelia
19 Madame Louise Henri
20 Madame Alfred Carrière
21 William Allen Richardson
22 L'Ideal
23 Madame Pierre Couchet

C 27 Musk
1 Purple

C 28 Miniature China
1 Blush or Pumilla
2 Crimson
3 Minima or Fairy

C 29 Microphilla
1 Alba Odorata

C 30 Macartney
1 Double Blush
2 Marie Leonida
3 Single

C 31 Hybrid Tea
1 Beauty of Stapleford
2 Duke of Connaught
3 Duchess of Connaught
4 Duchess of Westminster
5 Hon. George Bancroft
6 Jean Sisley
7 Michael Saunders
8 Nancy Lee
9 Pearl
10 Viscomtess Falmouth
11 Pierre Guillot
12 Souvenir de M. Favre

(C 31 Hybrid Teas is crossed out)

C 32 Rose Stocks
1. Common Briar
2. Briar cuttings
3. Seedling Briar
4. Manettii
5. Multiflora de la Grifferail

C 33 Lucida
1. Rose Button

C 34 Rugosa
1. Alba
2. Madama George Bruant
3. Rubra

C 35 Rosa Indica
1. Gigantea

C 36 Rosa Abysinian
1. Ecae

C37 Polyantha (Hybrids)
1. White Pet
2. Ma Paquerette
3. Mignonette
4. Crimson Rambler
5. Alister Stelle Grey
6. Madame E Nolte
7. Thalia
8. Aglaia
9. Euphrosyne
10. Dundee Rambler
11. Psyche

APPENDIX 2

The following rose breeders were contacted by Wood & Ingram and the roses they bred appeared in Wood & Ingram's catalogues by 1900. The year in which a new rose was introduced by the breeder is recorded in the International Check List of Roses.

French Rose Breeders:–

A. N. Baumann, Bolwyller, *Rosa Maria Baumann* 1863

Jean Beluze, Lyon, Rhone, *Rosa Souvenir de la Malmaison* 1843

A. Bernaix, Villeurbanne, Lyon, Rhone, *Rosa Abbe Girandin* 1881

Bernede, Bordeaux, *Rosa Madame Tartas* 1858

Bonnaire, Lyon, Rhone, *Rosa Dr. Gill* 1886

Bougere, *Rosa Niphetos* (once a very famous fragrant white greenhouse rose)

Bruante, Poitiers, *Rosa rugosa Madame George Bruante* 1887 *Rosa Blanc Double de Coubert* 1892

Scipion Cochet, Coubert, Seine-et-Marne, *Rosa Madame Pierre Cochet* 1891

Damaizin, Lyon, Rhone, *Rosa Madame Damaizin* 1858

Desprez, Yebles, *Rosa Baronne Prevost* 1842

Dubreuil, Lyon, Rhone, *Rosa Francois Dubreuil* 1843, *Rosa Perle d'Or* 1884

Ducher & Vivienne Ducher (widow) Ducher, Lyon, Rhone, (succeeded by Pernet-Ducher) *Rosa Gloire de Ducher* 1865, *Rosa Marie van Houtte* 1872, *Rosa Bouquet d'Or* 1872, *Rosa William Allan Richardson* 1878

Garcon, Rouen, Seine-Inf, *Rosa Madame Issac Pereire* 1881

Granger, Grisy-Suisnes, Seine-et-Marne, *Rosa Caroline de Sansal* 1849, *Rosa Edward Morren* 1868

Modeste Guerin, Paris, *Rosa Louis Phillipe* 1834

J. B. Guillot Fils, Montpelier, Lyon, Rhone, *Rosa La France* 1867 – first Hybrid tea introduced. *Rosa Madame Laurette Messiny* 1887, *Rosa Mignonette* 1889. *Rosa Ma Paquerette* 1875 – first Polyantha rose

Guillot Pere, Lyon, Rhone, *Rosa Senateur Vaisse* 1859

B. Guinoisseau, Angers, *Rosa Angustine Guinisseau* 1889

M. Hardy, one time gardener at the Luxembourg Gardens in Paris, *Rosa Madame Hardy* 1832

Jacotot, Dijon, *Rosa Gloire de Dijon* 1853

A. A. Jacques, one time gardener at the Chateau de Neuilly, *Rosa Adelaide d'Orleans* 1826

Hippolyte Jamain, Paris, *Rosa Dupuy Jamain* 1868

Francois Lacharme, Lyon, Rhone, Rosa Alfred Colomb 1865, *Rosa Louis Van Houtte* 1869

M. Laffay, Bellevue, *Rosa Coupe d'Hebe* 1840, *Rosa Fabrier* 1832

Jean Liaband, Lyon, Rhone, *Rosa Francois Michelon* 1871, *Rosa Baron de Bonstetten* 1871
Antoine Levet, Lyon, Rhone, *Rosa Ulrich Brunner* 1881
Antoine Leveque, Ivry near Paris, *Rosa Madame Louise Leveque* 1874 cont/d
Marechal, Angers, *Rosa La Marque* 1830
Marest, Paris, *Rosa Souvenir d'Elise Varden* 1885
M. Margottin, Bourg-La-Reine, *Rosa Comte de Mortemart* 1880
Moreau-Robert, Angers, *Rosa Blanche Moreau* 1880
Gilbert G Nabonnand, Golfe Juan, Alpes-Maritimes, *Rosa Papa Goutier* 1883
Joseph Pernet-Ducher, Venissieux-Les-Lyon, Rhone, (Successor to Ducher, succeeded by J Gaujard) *Rosa Cecile Brunner* 1881
Pernet Pere, *Rosa Baroness Rothschild* 1868
Plantier, Lyon, Rhone, *Rosa Madame Plantier* 1835
Portemer, Gentilly, *Rosa Pierre Notting* 1863
Henri Pradel, Lyon, Rhone, *Rosa Marechal Niel* 1864
M. Robert, Biarritz, Basses-Pyrenees, *Rosa Blush Boursalt* 1829
Robert & Moreau, Angers, *Rosa Reine Blanche* 1858
Roussel, Montpelier, *Rosa General Jacqueminot* 1853
J. Schwartz, Lyons, *Rosa Madame Alfred Carriere* 1879, *Rosa Victor Hugo* 1884
Trouillard, Angers, *Rosa Celine Forestier* 1842
E. Verdier, Paris, *Rosa Abel Carriere* 1875
Vibert, Angers, *Rosa Aimee Vibert* 1828

English Rose Breeders:–
Henry Bennett, Shepperton, *Rosa Mrs John Laing* 1887, *Climbing Rosa Souvenir de la Malmaison* 1893
B. R. Cant, Colchester, *Rosa Prince Arthur* 1875
A. H. Gray, Bath, *Rosa Alister Stella Gray* 1894
Lane, Berkhamsted, *Rosa Lanei* 1854
George Paul (Paul & Son), Cheshunt, Hertfordshire, *Rosa Rosy Morn* 1878
Keynes & Williams & Co., Salisbury, *Rosa Amy Robart* 1894, *Rosa Flora McIvoor* 1894, *Rosa Meg Merilees* 1894
W. Paul & Son Ltd, Waltham Cross, Hertfordshire, (succeeded by Chaplin Bros) *Rosa Beauty of Waltham* 1862, *Rosa Charles Darwin* 1879, *Rosa Zenobia* 1894
Rev. J. H. Pemberton, Havering-atte-Bower, Nr. Romford, Essex, *Rosa Lord Penzance* 1894, *Rosa Lucy Alister* 1894, *Rosa Bradwardine* 1894, *Rosa Green Mantle* 1895
George Prince & Co., Longworth, Berkshire, *Rosa Devonensis* 1841
Rivers, Sawbridgeworth, *Rosa Manettii* 1835
J. Veitch & Sons, King's Road, Chelsea, London, *Rosa Duchesse of Edinburgh* 1874
Wells, Tunbridge Wells, Kent, *Rosa The Garland* 1836
Ward, Ipswich, *Rosa John Hopper* 1862
Williams & Co., Horsham, Sussex, *Climbing Rosa Niphetos* 1889

American Rose Breeders:–
Cutis, Dallas, *Climbing Rosa Devonensis* 1838
John Cook, Baltimore, Maryland, *Rosa Maman Cochet* 1896
Ellwanger & Barry, Rochester, N Y, *Rosa Crimson Rambler* 1895
E. G. Hill & Co., Richmond, Indiana, *Climbing Rosa Belle Siebrecht* 1889
Peter Henderson & Co., New York, N. Y., *Rosa Setina* 1879
W. A. Manda South Orange New Jersey, *Rosa Gardenia* 1899
H. P. May, Summit, New Jersey, *Rosa The Bride* 1885

German Rose Breeders:–
Peter Lambert, Trier, *Rosa Kaiserin Augusta Victoria* 1891, *Rosa Gruss an Teplitz* 1897, *Rosa Eugenie Lamesch* 1899
Dr. F. Muller Weingarten, *Rosa Conrad Ferdinand Meyer* 1899

Dutch Rose Breeder:–
G. A. H. Buisman & Son, Heerde *Rosa Princess Beatrice*

Irish Rose Breeder:–
Alex Dickson & Sons Ltd, Hawlmark, Newtownards, County Down, NI, *Rosa Mrs W J Grant* (R. Belle Siebrecht) 1869, *Rosa Earl of Dufferin* 1887

Grand Duchy of Luxembourg Rose Breeder:–
Soupert & Notting, *Rosa Clothilde* 1890

APPENDIX 3

List of rose breeders and the roses they supplied to Mr Perkins after he had taken over the nursery of Wood & Ingram in 1904.

French Rose Breeders:–
Barbier & Co., Orleans, *Rosa Frau Karl Druscki* 1901, *Rosa Alberic Barbier* 1900, *Rosa Francois Juranville* 1906, *Rosa Albertine* 1921

M. Chambard, Lyon, Monplaisir, Rhone, *Rosa Comtesse de Castilleja* 1926

Jean Gaujard, Isere (successor to Pernet-Ducher) *Rosa Madame Joseph Perrand* 1934

Levasseur, Orleans, *Rosa Mrs W H Cutbush* 1907

Mallerin, Alliers-et-Risset, Isere, *Rosa Simone Guerin* 1929

G. Nabonnard, Golfe Juan, Alpes Maritimes, *Rosa Lady Waterlow* 1903

Joseph Pernet-Ducher Vennissieux-les-Lyon, Rhone, *Rosa Chateau de Clos Vougeot* 1908, *Rosa Severine* 1918, *Rosa Angele Pernet* 1924

Rosiers Pierre Guillot, Saint-Priest, Isere, *Rosa Comtesse du Cayla* 1902

Turbat & Co., 67 Route d'Olivet, Orleans, *Rosa Eblouissant* 1918, *Rosa Bonfire* 1928

American Rose Breeders:–
L. B. Coddington, Murray Hill Nursery, New Jersey, *Rosa Mrs L B Coddington* 1931

The Conrad-Pyle Co. Ltd, West Grove, Pennsylvania, *Rosa Madame Gregoire Staechelin* 1929, *Rosa Comtesse de Sastago* 1932, *Rosa Luis Brinas* 1934 (New)

Dixie Rose Nursery, Tyler, Texas, *Rosa President Hoover* 1931

Domer & Sons Co., Lafayette, Indiana, *Rosa Hoosier Beauty* 1915, *Rosa Marie* 1918

Henry A. Dreer Inc, Philadelphia, Pennsylvania, *Rosa McGredy's Ivory* 1930, *Rosa The New Dawn* 1930, *Rosa Primrose* 1930, *Rosa Crimson Glory* 1935, *Rosa Rosenalfe* 1939

Dr. Walter van Fleet, Glenn Dale, Massachusetts, *Rosa American Pillar* 1902

C. J. Groen, Montebello, California, *Rosa Sylvia Leyvre* 1935

Henderson & Co., New York, N Y, *Rosa Dr. W Van Fleet* 1910

E. G. Hill, Richmond, Indiana, *Rosa General McArthur* 1905, *Rosa Columbia* 1916, *Rosa Madame Butterfly* 1918

Howard & Smith, Montebello, California, *Rosa Los Angeles* 1916

Jackson & Perkins Co., Newport Beach, California, *Rosa Betty Prior* 1938 (New), *Rosa Matador* 1934 (New), *Rosa McGredy's Sunset* 1936 (New)

Joseph W. Kallay, Painesville, Ohio, *Rosa Blaze* 1932

Alex Montgomery Co., Hadley, Massachusetts, *Rosa Talisman* 1929

P. M. Peierson, Ossining, New York, NY, *Rosa Briarcliff* 1926

Charles H. Totty Co. Ltd, Madison, New Jersey, *Rosa Easlea's Golden Rambler* 1932

E. Towill, Roslyn, Penn., *Rosa Roslyn* 1929

Walsh, Woods Hole, Massachusetts, *Rosa Minnehaha* 1905

Danish Rose Breeder:–
Svend Poulsen, Copenhagen, *Rosa Anne Poulsen* 1935 (New), *Poulsen's Yellow* 1939 (New)

English Rose Breeders:–
W. E. B. Archer & Daughter, Sellinge, Ashford, Kent, *Rosa Dainty Bess* 1925, *Rosa Ellen Willmot* 1936 (New), *Rosa Folkstone* 1936

Beckwith, Hoddesdon, Herts, *Rosa Polly* 1927

Bees, Seakland Nurseries, Chester, *Rosa Independence Day* 1919, *Rosa Lady Rachel Verney* 1925 (New), *Rosa Madge Whipp* 1936 (New)

Burbage, Hinkley, Leicestershire, *Rosa Baby Betty* 1928

B. R. Cant & Sons Ltd, The Old Rose Gardens, Colchester, *Rosa Blush Rambler* 1903, *Rosa Covent Garden* 1919
Chaplin Bros, Waltham Cross, Hertfordshire, *Rosa Chaplin's Pink Climber* 1928, *Rosa Gwyneth* 1928
Cutbush, Barnet, Hertfordshire, *Rosa Sunshine* 1927
Dobbie & Co. Ltd, Edinburgh, *Rosa Duchess of Atholl* 1928
Walter Easlea & Sons Ltd, Eastwoood, Leigh-on-Sea, Essex, *Rosa Lavinia* 1918, *Rosa Lal* 19333 (New)
Laxton Bros, Bedford, *Rosa Violet Simpson* 1930
Lowe & Shawyer, Uxbridge, *Rosa Lady Hillingdon* 1910, *Rosa Rselandia* 1924
McGredy & G. Beckwith & Son, Hoddesdon, Herts, *Rosa Frazer Annesley* 1935 (New), *Rosa Fred Walker* 1935 (New)
Merryweather, Southwell, Nottinghamshire, *Rosa Jessie* 1909
R. Murrell, Rose Acre, Bedmont Hill, Hemel-Hempstead, Herts, *Rosa Coral Cluster* 1920
Paul, Cheshunt, Herts, *Rosa Lady Codiva* 1908
Rev J. H. Pemberton, Havering-atte-Bower, Romford, Essex, *Rosa Penelope* 1924, *Rosa Cornelia* 1925, *Rosa Aurora* 1928
George Prince & Co., Longworth, Berkshire, *Rosa Allen Chandler* 1923, *Rosa Elizabeth Arden* 1929
D. Prior & Son, Colchester, Essex, *Rosa Madge Prior* 1934
A. Reeves & Co., Old Catton, Norwich, *Rosa Little Dorrit* 1930
Snaders & Sons, St Albans, *Rosa Sander's White* 1912
Thomas Smith & Co., Stranraer, Scotland, *Rosa Margaret Anne Baxter* 1927
W. Stevens, Hoddesdon, Herts, *Rosa Lady Sylvia* 1926
Harry Wheatcroft & Sons Ltd, Edwalton, Nottingham, *Rosa Christopher Stone* 1935 (New)

Irish Rose Breeders:–
Alex Dickson & Sons Ltd, Hawlmark, Newtownards, Co. Down, *Rosa Aureate* 1932, *Rosa Betty Uprichard* 1922, *Rosa Leading Lady* 1935 (New)
Hugh Dickson, Belfast, N I, *Rosa Gorgeous* 1915
Sam McGredy, Portadown, N I, *Rosa Christine* 1918, *Rosa McGredy's Yellow* 1933 (New), *Rosa McGredy's Wonder* 1934 (New)
Walsh, Portadown, N I, *Rosa Hiawatha* 1904, *Rosa Excelsa* 1909

German Rose Breeders:–
M. Krause, Hasloh, Holstein, *Rosa Kardinel* 1924
P. Lambert, Trier, *Rosa Frau Karl Druschki (Snow Queen)* 1901
J. C. Schmidt, Erfurt, *Rosa Tansendschon* 1906
Kordes, Sohne, Spanieshoop, Holstein, *Rosa Fortschritt* 1933 (New), *Rosa Golden Romance* 1933 (New)
Matthew Tantan, Ueterson, Holstein, *Rosa Heros* 1933 (New)
Victor Teschendorff, Dresden, *Rosa Ellen Poulsen* 1911, *Rosa Rodhatte* 1911

Dutch Rose Breeders:–
Kersbergen, Boskoop, *Rosa Paul Crampel* 1930
M. Leenders, Tegelan, *Rosa Nathalie Nypels*
Sliedrecht & Co., Boskoop, *Rosa Gloria Mundi* 1929
Jan Spek, Boskoop, *Rosa Miss Edith Cavell* 1917, *Rosa Ideal* 1921
Jacques Verschuren & Sons, Haps, *Rosa Etoile de Hollande* 1919, *Rosa Miss C E van Rossen* 1919

Australian Rose Breeder:–
Hazlewood Bros & Pty Ltd, Epping, N S W, *Rosa Golden Dawn* 1929

Spanish Rose Breeder:–
Pedro Dot, San Feliu de Llobregat, Barcelona, *Rosa Angels Mateu* 1934, *Rosa Sunrise* 1939 (Wood & Ingram list this rose in 1892 Stock List)

(Modern Roses 7 The International Check List of Roses 1969. The McFarland Company, Harrisburg, Pennsylvania U S A.)

SELECT BIBLIOGRAPHY

Adshead, David *'Wimpole, Architectural drawings and topographical views'* , The National Trust, 2007

Bean, W. J. *'Trees and Shrubs hardy in the British Isles', Vols 1–4 8th Edition,* John Murray, 1976

Brett-Jones, Norman *'Life of Peter Collinson'*, 1925

Brown, Jane *'Lanning Roper and His Garden',* Weidenfield & Nicholson, London 1987

Burke, John *'An Illustrated History of England'*, 1980

Clifford, Thomas and Arthur *'Description of the Parish of Tixall'*, 1827

Colquhoun, Kate *'A Thing in Disguise – The Visionary Life of Joseph Paxton'*, 2003

Conner, T. P. *'Architecture and Planting at Goodwood 1723-1750',* Sussex Archaeological Collections Volume 117, 979.

Cook, E. T. *'The Century Book of Gardening',* The Country Life Library, George Newnes Ltd

de Crevecoeur, J Hector St. John *'Letters from an American Farmer',* E P Dutton & Co Inc, 1st Published 1782, Reprinted 1957

Curtler, W. H. R. *'The Enclosure and Redistribution of our Land',* 1820

Desmond, Ray *'British and Irish Botanist and Nurserymen'*, 1977

Duthie, Ruth *'Florists' Flowers and Societies',* Shire Garden History, 1988

Gerard, John *'The Herbal or History of Plants'* 1596, Enlarged and Revised by Thomas Johnson 1633

Godber, Joyce *'The Marchioness Grey of Wrest Park'*, Bedfordshire Historical Record Society, 1968

Harkness, John *'Makers of Heavenly Roses'*, 1985

Harvey, John *'Early Garden Catalogues',* Philimore & Co. Ltd, 1972

Harvey, John *'Early Nurseries'*, 1974

Henrey, Blanche *'British Botanical and Horticultural Literature before 1800',* 1975

Hibberd, Shirley *'Amateur's Book of Roses',* 1874

Hogg, Thomas *'The Fruit Manual, A Guide to The Fruits and Fruit Trees of Great Britain'*, 1884

Kingston, Alfred *'Fragments of Two Centuries, Glimpses of Country Life when George III was King'*, Warren Bros & Cooke Ltd, Royston, 1893, reprinted 1990

Laird, Mark *'The Flowering of the Landscape Garden, English Pleasure Grounds, 1720 –1800',* Harvard University Press

Leith Ross, Prudence *'John Evelyn's new garden at Sayes Court'*, Journal of The Garden History Society, Spring 2004

Loudon, John *'Arboretum et Fruiticetum Britanicum' or 'Trees and Shrubs of Britain'*, 1838

Loudon, John *'The Suburban Gardener and Villa Companion',* 1838

Meyers, Amy R. W. & Pritchard, Margaret Beck *'Empire's Nature, Mark Catesby's New World Vision'*, University of North Carolina Press, 1998

Mingey, G. E. *'English Landed Society in the 18th Century',* 1963

Minter, Sue *'The Apothecaries Garden, A History of the Chelsea Physic Garden'*, Sutton Publishing Ltd, 2000

Montgomery-Massingberd, Hugh *'Burke's & Savills Guide to Country Houses, Vol III: East Anglia'*, 1981

Morgan, Joan and Richards, Alison *'Book of Apples'*, Brogdale Horticultural Trust, 1993

Nicholls, Beverley *'Down the Garden Path'*, 1932

Pevsner, Nikolas and Watson, Bill *'Norfolk 1: Norwich and North-East'*, Penguin Books, 2nd Edition, 1997

Pym, Francis *'Sentimental Journey'*, 1998

Robertson, R. P. *'The Book of the Carnation'*, 1903

Rothschild, Dame Miriam *'The Rothschild Gardens'*, 2000

Seddon, George and Radecka Helena *'Your Kitchen Garden'*, Mitchell Beazley/Edenlite, 1975

Souden, David *'Wimpole Hall'*, The National Trust, 1991

Stuart, David *'Georgian Gardens'*, Robert Hale Ltd, 1979

Sweet, Robert *'The Ornamental Flower Garden, Vol III'*, 1854

Taylor, Patrick *'The Oxford Companion to the Garden'*, Oxford University Press, 2006

Tebbutt, C. F. *'St Neots, The History of a Huntingdonshire Town'*, 1978

Terraine, John *'To Win a War, 1918, The Year of Victory'*, Macmillan Publishers Ltd, 1986

Turner, Roger *'Capability Brown and the 18th Century English Landscape'*, 1999

Whitely, Peter *'Lord North, The Prime Minister who Lost America'*, The Hambledon Press, 1996

Wilson, E. J. *'Nurserymen of the World'*, 1989

Wilson, Richard and Macklet, Alan *'Creating Paradise, The Building of the English Country House, 1660–1880'*, 2000

Cambridgeshire Gardens Trust *'The Gardens of Cambridgeshire, A Gazetteer'*, 2000

Harkness Rose Catalogue, 1912

Hillier's Manual of Trees and Shrubs, 1974

The International Check List of Roses, The MacFarland Company, Harrisburg, Pennsylvania, U S A

Transactions of the American Philosophical Society, M5.33.pt 1, Philadelphia, 1942

INDEX

People

Abbott, Private 118
Abraham, Mr (W&I employee) 143
Adam, Robert 22
Aislabie, John 23
Allan, Mr John 128
Allan, Mr A. (W&I employee) 199
Allen, Mr J. (W&I employee) 199
Allen, Mr S. (W&I employee) 199
Ammann, Dr 2
Ancaster, 2nd Earl of 150, 178
Aragon, Catherine of 32
Arundel, Mr 14
Ashley, Mr (W&I employee) 158
Ashpole, Mr George 213
Astell, Mr 166
Astell, Richard Esq (1717–1777) 21, 40
Astell, William 38, 39, 40
Astor, Hon J. J. 213
Bagge, Sir Walter (1875–1939) 150
Baker, Mr W. Y. 94
Balfour Gourlay, Sir 193
Ball, Mr (W&I employee) 211
Banks, Sir Joseph 24
Barclay, Mr F. H. 113, 167
Barclay, Mr P. H. 139
Barclay, Miss M. J. 113
Barnes, H. C. 213
Britten, Baron 39
Barr, Mr Peter 94, 95
Barret, Thomas 17th Baron Dacre 47
Bartram, Mr John 1, 2, 4, 100
Bates, R. 85
Battersea, Lady (1843–1931) 113, 116, 149, 194, 196
Baxter, Mr (W&I employee) 199
Beale, Mr (J. Ingram employee) 59, 66, 71
Bedford, 1st Duke of (1616–1670) 2–4
Bedford, 4th Duke of (1710–1771) 2, 3, 21, 23
Bedford, 12th Duke of (1888–1953) 113, 135, 138, 140, 149, 194, 197
Beit, Sir Otto (1865–1930) 150

Bendyshe, Capt 151
Bernard, Sir John 21, 36
Bernard, Sir Robert 34, 36
Bevan, Mr 139
Bevan, Mrs 169
Binney, Mr J. 151
Blake, Mr Cawthorne 50
Blake, Mary 50
Blanche, Mrs T. M. 192
Blissell, Mr (W&I employee) 143
Blunt, Mr (W&I employee) 199
Board, Cpl, J. R R.N. No 9961(7)0 133
Boardman, Mr H. 151
Bonfoys, Mr 21, 43, 51
Bonfoys, Mr Hugh 43
Bonfoy Rooper, Mr 51
Boucicault, Mr Dion Willie 87
Boughly, Mrs 192
Boyes, Mr 151
Bowen, Mr Emanuel 20
Branson, Miss 204
Brand, Messrs 214
Brassey, Sir Leon (1905–1967) 166, 193
Brazier, Mr 41
Breadalban, 3rd Earl of (1695–1782) 27
Breintnall, Mr Joseph 1, 2
Bridgeman, Charles 27, 46
Briscoe, Capt 134, 191
Bristol, Marquess of 135
Brotherhood, Mr S. 117, 170
Broughton, Capt 166
Brown, Mr 151
Brown, Mr R. 132
Brown, Lancelot 'Capability' 20, 21, 24–31, 37, 39, 46–49, 51
Brown, Lancelot (son of 'Capability') 24, 49
Brown, John (son of 'Capability') 49
Brown, Bridget (daughter of 'Capability') 49
Brown, Mrs (wife of 'Capability') 48, 49
Brown, Mr A. B. (W&I employee) 211

Brown, Mr Alf (W&I employee) 202, 211
Brown Jnr., Mr (W&I employee) 199
Brown, Mr (W&I employee) 144, 158
Browning, Mr E. (W&I employee) 82
Buckingham, Lord 31
Bunyard, Mr George 94, 95
Burnaby, Mr J. 192
Butcher, Mr Charles 94
Butler, Mr (W&I employee) 199
Burton, Mr (W&I employee) 199
Buxton, Sir Fowell (1889–1945) 150
Cairns, Countess Olivia 154
Campbell, Mr (W&I commercial traveller) 118
Campbell, Mr D. 205
Campbell, Mrs S. 192
Caroline, Queen 22
Catesby, Mr Mark 36
Cater, Mr 100, 109
Carter, Mr (J. Ingram employee) 58, 59
Carter, Mr (W&I employee) 157, 159
Cavendish, Hon Mrs 116, 128
Cecil, Brownlow, 9th Earl of Exeter (1725–1794) 26, 27
Cecil, Lady Edward 152
Chambers, Sir William (1723–1796) 20, 23
Charlotte, Queen 22
Chew, Dr Samuel 1
Childs, Mr (W&I employee) 157, 159
Childery, Mr (W&I employee) 199
Christy, Miss 179
Church, Mr F. W. 118
Clare, Mr Harcourt E. 131
Clarendon, Countess of 150
Clarke, Alured 37
Clarke, Curnel Alured 37, 67, 100, 109
Clarke, Charles 37

INDEX – PEOPLE

Clarke, Mr (W&I employee) 157, 158
Clarke, Mr A. (W&I employee) 201, 211
Clarke, Mr E. 192
Clark, Mr Thomas (J. Ingram & J. W. Ingram employee) 58, 60, 62, 63, 66, 68, 71, 81
Clay, Mrs 192
Clifden, Viscount 193
Cobham, Lord 46
Codrington, Major J. A. 208
Cole, Elizabeth 44
Coleman, Captain 129
Collinson, Mr Peter 1–5, 100
Cook, Captain 24
Coombe, Mr A. V. 117, 136
Cooper, Mr G. 113
Coote, Mr Howard 108, 145
Coote, Mrs 151
Cowdray, Viscount, of Midhurst, Sussex 194
Creasey, Mr D. 52
Crivelli, Mr 82
Crossman, Mr Douglas 116, 197
Crossman, Mrs 128
Crow, Mr (W&I employee) 199, 211
Crystal, Miss E. M. 192
Cunningham Reid, Captain 194
Curtis, Mr M. E. (W&I employee) 199, 211
Custance, Mr William 17
Cutbush, Mr Herbert 94
Dacre, 17th Baron 47
Daniels, Mr W. 113
Daniels Major 188, 197
Davey, Mr (W&I employee) 201, 211
Dawson, Mr R. J. W. 129
Day, Mr (W&I employee) 157
De Ramsey, Lady 135
De Ramsey, Lord 169, 209
De Saumarez, 5th Baron 150
De la Warr, 5th Earl of (1791–1869) 51
Dean, Mr (W&I employee) 159
Dear, Mr Jas 83
Demidorff, Mr 2
Desborough, 1st Baron (1855–1945) 150

Devonshire, Duke of 21
Dickson, Mr T. A. 94, 95
Dilley, Mr Arthur George 134
Dilley, Theakston & Beardmore 215
Dillistone, Mr (J. Ingram employee) 59, 62
Dillon, Lord (1868–1947) 138
Dixon, Mr (J. Ingram employee) 60, 62–66, 71
Don, Mrs 211
Dowsing, Sarah 44
Drage, Mr B. 197
Drummond, Captain 150
Drummond, Mr 47
Dumbleton, Mr 13
Dunford, Viscount 191
Dunscombe, Miss 151
Durham, Earl of (1855–1929) 116
Edgcumbe, Earl of 138
Edward I 32
Ellesmere, Earl of 151
Ellis, Mr John 24
Eley, Mr Charles (1872–1960) 135
Euren, Mr Frank F. 121
Eustace, Mr (W&I employee) 211
Evelyn, Mr John 26, 46
Exeter, 9th Earl of (1725–1794) 26, 27, 47
Fairhaven, Lord 188, 191, 197
Falconer, Arthur George Keith 224
Fell, Mr Francis 94
Fellows, Edward 51
Fellowes, William Henry 43
Fells, Mr (W&I commercial traveller) 152
Finch, Mr W. 166, 193
Fielden, Mr J. A. 213
Fitzpatrick, Mrs 192
Fitzwilliam, 3rd Earl (1786-1857) 51
Fitzwilliam, 6th Earl (1815-1902) 105
Fitzwilliam, 7th Earl (1918) 116, 135
Fitzwilliam, Lady Alice 105
Fletcher, Miss Sarah 52
Flower, Cyril 1st Lord Battersea 197
Fordham, Sir George 151

Foster, Mr 139
Fowke, Mrs 151
Fox, Mr Charles James 24
Francis, Major 151
Freeman, Mr (W&I employee) 157, 159
Frith, Mr S. 204
Frost, Mrs 151
Fuller, Miss 135
Fuller, Mr Gerald 4, 123
Gale, Mr (W&I employee) 212
Galilei, Alessandro 1
Garrick, Mr 33
Gaskin, Mr E. A. 205
Gaujard, Monsieur Jean 171
Gaultier, Mr Reed 151
Geare, Squire 100, 109
Geddes, Private 126
Gee, Mr H. 160
George III 12, 19, 20, 47, 51
George, Mr (W&I employee) 159
Gerard, Mr John 3, 4, 23
Giddings, Mr 59
Glanelly, Lord 150
Gloucester, H.R.H. Duchess of (1901–2004) 212
Gmelin, Professor 2
Goldie, Lt Col 193
Goodacre, Mr (W&I employee) 159
Gordon, Mr James 3
Gough, Capt G. T. H. 164
Grafton, 2nd Duke of (1683–1757) 31, 47
Gray, Mr 139
Gray, Mr J. 153
Green, John Bishop of Lincoln (1706–1779) 32, 33
Greene, Sir Graham 151
Greenfield, Mr E. H. 113
Greensmith, Miss Elizabeth (later Mrs James Wood) 8, 11
Grey, Jemima, Marchioness (1722–1797) 27, 31
Grimbby, Messrs 213
Gronovius, Dr Matchel 4
Groun, Mr Richd 13
Guarnerio, Mary 56
Guarnerio, Mr Peter Samuel (J. W. Ingram employee) 90
Guernsey, Lady 116, 137

Guile, Mr 170
Gutteridge, Mr 192
Hales, Mr 118
Hales, Dr Stephen (1671–1761) 100
Hall, Mr 113
Halsam, Mr W. H. 213
Harding, Col W. A. 166, 197
Hardwicke, 1st Earl of (1690–1764) 5, 20, 21, 27–29
Hardwicke, 2nd Earl of (1720–1790) 30–33, 42, 100, 109
Hardwicke, Mr (W&I employee) 157, 159
Harker, Mrs 194
Harkness, Mr John 184
Harley, Primrose 208
Harrington, 8th Earl of (1844–1919) 116, 135, 138
Harrington, Miss Elizabeth 19
Harrison, Major 193
Harrison, Mr J. 94
Hastings, Warren 22
Hatfield, Mr 13
Hatfield, Mr James 56
Hay, Mr T. 195, 197, 204, 205
Hayes, Mr J. 94
Head, Mr (W&I employee) 157, 159
Headland, Mr (W&I employee) 199, 212
Heding, Mr 13
Herberts, Mr (J. Ingram employee) 66
Hebertstein, Monsieur Pere 5
Heding, Mr 14
Henry III 32
Henry VIII 32
Herbert, Miss 192
Herberts, Mr 59
Hewit, Mr 13
Hewitt, Mr Samuel 14
Hewitt, Mr Thomas 14, 15, 21
Hibberd, Mr Shirley 187
Hicklam, Mr White 13
Higgins, Mr W. H. 118
Hinchingbrooke, Lord 34
Hinchingbrooke, Viscountess 213
Hogg, Mr Thomas 97
Holland, Mr Henry 49

Honey, Mr 190
Howson, Mr T. J. 85
Humphreys, Mr (W&I employee) 144, 157–159
Humphrey, Mr (W&I employee) 212
Hunnybun, Mr 135
Hunnybun, Mrs 193
Huntingfield, Lady 150
Hurst, Mr 27
Hurst, Mr William (1799–1868) 90
Hurst, Mr William (1831–1882) 90
Ingle, Mr (J. Ingram employee) 62, 66–68, 70, 71
Ingram, Mr C. 150
Ingram, Mrs Elizabeth 56
Ingram, Mr George Wood 81
Ingram, Mr John 56–60, 64, 77–80, 98, 168
Ingram, Mr John Wood 80, 81, 84, 90, 91, 93, 94, 98
Jackson, Mr George 44
Jackson, Mr John 43, 44, 45, 46, 99, 100, 101
Jackson, Mr Original 44
Jackson, Mrs 45
James I 32, 44
James, Mr T. 92
Jardine, Sir J. 138
Jeffries, Mr W. J. 94
Jekyll, Mr F. W. 207
Jekyll, Gertrude 197, 207
Jenkins, Mr 13
Jenkins, Mrs 13
Johnson, Mr. B. 33
Johnson, Mr Thomas 3
Johnston, Mr Lawrence (1871–1958) 150
Jordan, Mr (W&I employee) 144, 157, 158
Jordan Jnr, Mr (W&I employee) 144
Jonas, Mrs F. 192
Jones, Mr G. 214
Joyce, Mr (W&I employee) 144, 157–159
Kedleston, Marquess Curzon of (1859–1925) 150
Kelly, Mr Jasper 138
Kennedy, John 15
Kent, Duke of (1671–1740) 27

Kent, William 31, 46
Key, Mr 135
King, Mr (J. Ingram employee) 65
King, Mr (W&I employee) 144, 157, 158, 159
Kingsley, Elizabeth 38
Kingsley, Mr Heylock 39
Kingston, Mr William 40
Knight, Mr (J. Ingram employee) 58, 60, 62, 71
Laing, Mr John 94, 95
Langle, John 100, 109
Lapidge, Mr Samuel 49
Last, Mr Percy (W&I employee) 201, 212
Lee, Mr 113
Lennox, Charles, 2nd Duke of Richmond (1701–1750) 1–3
Leon, Sir Herbert Samuel (1850–1926) 113, 150
Le Strange, Capt 197
Leverton, Mr (W&I employee) 199, 212, 213
Leverton, Jnr, Mr (W&I employee) 199
Lilford, Lord 149
Lincoln, Lord Bishop of (1706–1779) 21, 32, 41, 100, 109
Lindsey, Earl of 150
Line, Mr 192
Lloyd, Mr W. 113
Lock, Mr G. R. B. 206
London, Mr George 14
Lord, Mr (W&I employee) 144
Loudon, Mr John C. (1783–1843) 54, 57
Lovit, Mr Ted 13
Low, Mr 132
Lowton, Mr (J. Ingram employee) 58–63, 65–72, 74–77
Ludlow, Peter (later Earl Ludlow) (1730–1803) 34, 35, 100, 109
Lunniss, Mr (W&I employee) 144, 157, 159
Lutyens, Sir Ewin 113, 116, 197
Macdonald, Mr Ramsey (1866–1937) 188
Mackie, Mr John 4
Macmillan, Lady 196
Madeley, Mr (W&I employee) 157
Manchester, Duchess of 23, 35, 38

INDEX – PEOPLE

Manchester, George, 4th Duke of (1737–1788) 1, 3, 5, 14, 20–23, 34, 44, 100, 109
Manchester, 8th Duke of 84, 85
Manchester, 9th Duke of 116, 224
Mandeville, Lord, later 2nd Duke of Manchester (1700–1739) 1
Mallabar, Mr W. 155, 156
Mann, Mr L. 211
Marlow, Mr 195
Martain, Mr 13
Martin, Mr G. 139
Mason, Mr (W&I employee) 157, 159
Matchel, Dr 3,
Maul, Mr 100, 109
Maules, Mr E. 58
May, Mr E. H. 94
Meade, Mrs 114
Meadows, Mr (W&I employee) 159
Measures, Miss 178
Menzies, Mr Archibald (1754–1842) 67
Meyer, Lady (1862/3–1930) 139, 170
Middleton, Mr G. F. 136
Miller, Mr Charles 3,17
Miller, Mr Philip 3–5, 36
Miller, Mr Sanderson 28
Mills, Mr F. (W&I employee) 199
Mitchell, Mr F. 113, 118, 140–142
Mitchell, Mrs Margaret 141
Modral, Mr W. C. 148
Montagu, Sir Edward (1530–1602) 19
Montagu, George, 4th Duke of Manchester (1737–1788) 21–23
Montagu, Henry, 1st Earl of Manchester (1563–1642) 19
Montagu, Hon Oliver (1844–1893) 84, 85
Montagu, Ralph, 1st Duke of Montagu (1638–1709) 19
Montagu, Robert, 3rd Duke of Manchester (1710–1761) 20, 22
Montagu, Sir Sidney (d.1644) 19
Montgomery, Major 213
Morse, Mr M. 146
Mosle, Mr 11
Morton, Miss 214

Moxon Bros, 213
Musk, Mr (J. Ingram employee) 60, 71
Nall-Cain, Mr 194
Naylor, Mr H. 113
Nerontsos, Miss 127
Neville, Hon Mrs G. 131
Newcastle, Duke of 33
Newstead, Mr (W&I employee) 157, 159
Nicholls, Mr Beverley 189, 190
North, Lord (1732–1792) 23, 24, 44
Northampton, 7th Earl of 47
Northumberland, Duke of 37, 150
Nugent, Mrs 124
Nunburnholme, Lady 150, 170
Nutting, Mr W. J. 94
Ossory, Lord 164
Ossory, Lady 164
Owen, Mr (W&I employee) 158
Pack, Mr (W&I employee) 159
Page, Lieut W. H.130
Papworth, Mr Charles (J. W. Ingram employee) 59, 60, 66, 71, 81–84, 86–90, 92, 93
Papworth, Mr E. (J. Ingram & J. W. Ingram employee) 58–60, 81–84, 86–90, 92, 93
Papworth, Mr J. (J. Ingram employee) 60, 62, 71
Papworth, Mr (W&I employee) 199, 212
Paine, Sir Giles 13, 14
Paine, Mr K. 151
Palmer, Mr F. 113
Pamer, Mr 14
Parvin, Mr 13, 14
Paul, Mr William 94, 95
Paxton, Mr Joseph (1803–1865) 64
Payne, Mr 139
Peacock, Mr Reed 9, 10
Peet, Mr 13
Perkins, Mr Henry 99, 100, 109, 111, 113, 115, 118, 141–148, 159, 164, 167, 170, 178, 186, 191, 193, 201, 214, 224
Perkins, Mr John Edward 97, 98, 102, 107–109, 111, 113–116, 118, 127, 134, 138, 145, 147, 209
Pernet-Ducher, Claudius 170
Pernet-Ducher, Joseph 170, 171
Pernet, Madamoiselle Angele 171

Persia, Shah of 100
Peterborough, Dean of 135
Peto, Mr Harold (1854–1933) 149
Petre, Lord (1713–1742) 2, 3
Phillips, Mr 135
Pigot, Lord 49
Pipe, Mr A. 118
Pissard, Monsieur 100
Pitt, Mr H. 140
Pitt, William "The Younger" (1759–1806) 19
Plat, Mr 23
Portland, Duke of 129
Poulsen, Mr Svend 184
Prescot, Sir W. 191
Preston, Mr F. G. 148
Price, Mr 59
Protheroe, Mr A. 82, 94, 95, 128
Prowting, Mr 132
Pym, Mr Francis (1756–1833) 40
Pym, Catherine 40
Pym, Mr William (1723–1788) 38, 39
Ratchelous, Mr William (J. W. Ingram employee) 81, 84, 87
Re(e)dman, Mr (W&I employee) 199, 212
Repton, Mr Humphry 40
Richardson, Mr R. H. 118
Richmond, Mr Nathaniel 39, 40
Rivers, Mr T. F. 94, 95
Robartes, Hon G. A. (became 7th Viscount Cliveden in 1920) 116, 120, 169
Roberts, Mr (W&I employee) 201
Robinson, Capt. 133
Robinson, Mr 125, 126, 138
Robeson, Mr 48
Robson, Mr 63
Romney, 6th Earl (1864–1933) 116, 138
Roper, Mr Lanning 209
Rosamund, Mr (W&I employee) 212
Rose, Mr 89
Rose, Mrs 151
Rose, Pte A. No 43063 126
Rothschild, Hon C. (1877–1923) 149, 179
Rothschild, Sir Anthony de 197
Rothschild, Dame Miriam 179, 180

Rothschild, Mr L. 170
Rothschild, Mrs 166
Rothschild, Mr Victor 179
Rothschild, Mrs C. 194
Rottenburg, Mrs 116, 192
Rowe, Mr (J. Ingram employee) 58
Rowell, Mr G. 89
Rowland Wood 148
Rudd, Mr (W&I employee) 158
Rust, Mr 14
Rutland, 8th Duke of (1852–1925) 115
Sackville-West, Vita 138
Sale, Mr 151
Salisbury, 4th Marquess of 149
Salter, Mr 17
Salton, Mr 17
Samuel, Mr Peter 81
Sandwich, John Montagu, 4th Earl of (1718–1792) 1, 3, 13, 14, 16, 20, 21, 23–26, 34, 44, 49, 109
Sandwich, 9th Earl of (1874–1917) 85, 99
Sandwich, 10th Earl of (1874–1962) 108, 116, 117, 123, 132, 166, 169
Sassoon, Sir Philip (1888–1939) 149
Scate, Mr (W&I employee) 158, 159
Schindler, Lady 135
Searle Mr (J. Ingram employee) 58, 59, 66
Searle, Mr (W&I employee) 71
Searle, Mr (W&I employee) 199
See, Mr (W&I employee) 212
Sewell, Mr (W&I employee) 199
Shatton, Mr (W&I employee) 199
Shaw, Mr 213
Shepherd, Mr (J. W. Ingram employee) 82, 83
Sigesbeck, Professor 2
Sims, Mr J. (J. W. Ingram employee) 82, 83
Shelburne, Earl of 48
Shatton, Mr (W&I employee) 199
Sherwood, Mr Nathaniel Newman (1846–1916) 90, 94
Shillington Scales, Mrs 192
Shuttleworth, Mr 179
Sims, Mr J. (J. W. Ingram employee) 78, 81–84, 88, 89, 92, 93

Simpson, Mr H. 94
Slater, Mr (J. W. Ingram employee) 82, 83, 91
Slocock, Mr William C. (1853–1926) 130
Small, Mr W. J. 120
Smart, Mr (J. Ingram employee) 62–65, 67, 68, 71
Smith, Mr (J. Ingram employee) 62, 63, 66, 67, 70, 71, 74
Smith, Mr E. A. (W&I employee) 200
Smith, Mr H. (W&I employee) 200
Smith, Mr Will (W&I employee) General nurseryman 199, 212
Smith, Mr W. P. (W&I employee) 199
Snell, Mr 118, 152
Somerset, Duke of 33
Sparrow, Mr William 49
Spearling, Mr A. H. B. 147
Stalker, Mr W. J. 129
Stanford, Mr Abraham (apprentice to James Wood) 10
Starr, Mr 139
Stevens, Mr (W&I employee) 144
Stevens, Mr Albert 128
Stewart, Mr Charles 128
Stroud, Dorothy 28, 29, 49
Sutherland, Duchess of 127
Sweet, Mr Robert 54
Sweeting, Mr H. 52
Summers, Mr (W&I employee) 212
Taylor, Mr Joshua 151
Thackeray, Mr George 86
Thornhill, Mr A. J. 165
Thornhill, Mr George (1681–1754) 21, 41, 42, 51, 100, 109, 151
Thornhill, Mr George (1738–1827) 41, 51
Thornhill, Mr Noel (1882–1955) 117, 138, 203
Thornton, Mr William 40
Thrussell, Mr 207
Ting, Mr 13
Todhunter, Mr B. E. 161
Townsend, Mr (W&I employee) 199
Trafford, Sir Humphrey 202
Turland, Mr John (apprentice to James Wood) 10
Turner, Miss E. 192

Turner, Mr Harry 94, 95
Tweeddale, 11th Marquess of 224
Veitch, Mr Harry J. (1853–1924) 94, 95, 124, 125, 127
Veitch, Mr J. G. 101
Vickers, Mr Douglas 116, 138
Valliamy, Mrs 192
Victoria, Queen 57, 85
Vintner, Mrs 8, 9
Von Wertheimstein, Rozsika 179
Wady, Mr (W&I employee) 201, 202, 211, 212
Wales, Edward, H.R.H. Prince of (1841–1910) 83–86, 98
Wales, Alexandra, H.R.H. Princess of (1844–1925) 84–86
Wallace, Cosmo 22, 23
Walls, Mr (W&I employee) 159
Walpole, Mr Horace (1717–1797) 27, 31
Walston, Lady 193, 213
Ward, Mr (J. Ingram employee) 63, 71
Warren, Mr G. (J. Ingram & J. W. Ingram employee) 59, 60, 62–66, 74, 81
Warren, Mr H. (J. W. Ingram employee) 81, 93
Watkins, Mr 94
Watson, Mr (W&I employee) 195
Watson, Mr 6
Watson, Mr T. J. 153
Watson, Rev W. 149
Webb, Mr 139
Webb, Mr (W&I employee) 158
Weal, Mr Bertrand W. 153
Weddell, Mr 54
West, Mr (W&I employee) 159
Westminster, Dean and Chapter of 21
Wigam, Captain 191
Williams, Mr H. 94
Williams, Mr B. S. 65
Williams, Bishop John 32
Williers, Mr G. 151
Windover, Mr 86
Whitbread, Mr S. 193
Whittome Bros, S. A. 211
Wollaston, Dr F. R. 156, 157
Wolly, Mr 14
Wood, Mr 90, 94

Wood, Anne (daughter of James Wood) 7, 11, 49, 50
Wood, Elizabeth (2nd wife of James Wood) 11
Wood, Mr James 1, 3–16, 21–24, 26–29, 32–36, 38, 40, 41, 43, 45, 48, 50–54, 96, 99
Wood, James (son of Mr James Wood) 11, 50
Wood, Mr John (son of Mr James Wood) 7, 11, 14, 50, 54–56, 85
Wood, John (brother of James Wood) 11
Wood, Samuel (brother of James Wood) 11
Wood, Mrs Susan 56
Wood Ingram, Mr George 81, 224
Wood Ingram, Mr John 93, 99, 114, 224
Worrell, Mr G. 94
Wright, Mr (J. Ingram employee) 65, 71
Wyatt, Mr (W&I commercial traveller) 113, 118
Wynne, Mr B. 94, 95
Yarnold, Mr 191
York, Rev James, Bishop of Ely 32
Yorke, Philip, 2nd Earl of Hardwicke (1720–1790) 27, 30
Young, Mr C. (W&I employee) 144
Young Jnr, Mr J. (W&I employee)

Places

Abbots Ripton Hall, (Hunts) Cambridgeshire 21, 43 116, 137, 209
Abbots Ripton School, (Hunts) Cambridgeshire 202
Albury Park, Surrey 150
Alexander Dock, Liverpool 209
Althorp, Northamptonshire 31
Anglesey Abbey, Cambridgeshire 188, 197, 198, 209
Apethorpe Hall, Northamptonshire 166, 193
Ashridge, Hertfordshire 48
Aston Wold, Oundle, Northamptonshire 166, 179

Ballyedmond, Ireland 124
Bartlow Hall, Cambridgeshire 209
Barrington Hall, Cambridgeshire 151
Barton Stud, Bury St Edmunds, Suffolk 166
Bedford, Corn Exchange, Bedfordshire 106
Belhouse, Avely, Essex 47
Belfast, New Houses of Parliament, Northern Ireland 197
Belvoir Castle, Nottinghamshire 31, 115
Benenden, The Grange, Kent 150
Benningborough Hall, Yorkshire 150
Biggleswade, Grammar School, Bedfordshire 50, 53

Bletchley Park, Buckinghamshire 113, 150, 153
Bletsoe Castle, Bedfordshire 178
Blickling Hall, Norfolk 31
Blisworth, Northamptonshire 75
Blofield Hall, Norfolk 194
Bluntisham, Rectory, (Hunts) Cambridgeshire 131
Bodiam, Kent 152
Boston, U.S.A. 118
Boughton Estates Kettering, Northamptonshire 211
Boughton House, Northamptonshire 19
Bramham Park, Yorkshire 31
Brampton, (Hunts) Cambridgeshire 1, 11, 21, 56, 89, 90, 97
Brampton, 'Bridge End' (Hunts) Cambridgeshire
Brampton Park, (Hunts) Cambridgeshire 36
Brampton, Pepys House, (Hunts) Cambridgeshire 211
Brampton, R.A.F. Station (Hunts) Cambridgeshire 213
Brampton School, (Hunts) Cambridgeshire 202
Brampton, Bridge End (Hunts) Cambridgeshire 128
Brampton, 'The Green' (Hunts) Cambridgeshire 212, 218

Brampton, 'The Laurels', High Street (Hunts) Cambridgeshire 218
Brampton, 'The Old Rectory', (Hunts) Cambridgeshire 193
Brampton, 'Umvote', (Hunts) Cambridgeshire 151
British Embassy, St Petersburg 2
Brocket Hall, Hertfordshire 194
Broughton, (Hunts) Cambridgeshire 212
Buckden, (Hunts) Cambridgeshire 21, 41, 212
Buckden, Stirtloe House (Hunts) Cambridgeshire 24
Buckden Palace, (Hunts) Cambridgeshire 32, 33
Buntingford, Hertfordshire 59
Burghley House, (Northants) Cambridgeshire 26, 27, 47, 166
Burghley on the Hill, Oakham, Leicestershire 193
Burrough Green, Cambridgeshire 32, 139
Burwell Boys School, Cambridgeshire 117
Bury St Edmunds, Suffolk 31

Cadland Park, Southampton, Hampshire 150
Caldecote (Hunts) Cambridgeshire 21
Cambridge 31, 212
Cambridge University 33

Cambridge University Farms 151
Cambridge University Botanic Garden 18, 148
Cambridge University Physic Garden 1, 3, 17, 18
Cambridge, Clare College 40, 135, 196, 224
Cambridge, Corpus Christi College 33, 101
Cambridge, Downing College 139, 196
Cambridge, Emmanuel College 192, 209
Cambridge, King's College 156, 157, 192, 196
Cambridge, Newnham College 192
Cambridge, Queens' College 191, 192, 196
Cambrisge, Ridley Hall 196
Cam,bridge, St John's College 32
Cambridge, Trinity College 23, 192, 196
Cambridge, 4 Adams Road 192
Cambridge, 5 Adams Road 116, 192
Cambridge, 4 Cranmer Road 192
Cambridge, 11 Cranmer Road 192
Cambridge, Upton House, Grange Road 192
Cambridge, Wytchfield House, Huntingdon Road 192
Cambridge, Madingley Road 151
Cambridge, Amwell House, Millington Road 192
Cambridge, 4 Selwyn Gardens 151
Cambridge, Storey's Way 153
Cambridge, 64 Storey's Way 192
Cambridge, Half Way Cottage, Storey's Way 192
Cambridge, The Bin Brook 192
Cambridge, The Rydings, Sylvester Road 192
Cambridge, Holmleigh, West Road 192
Cambridge, Hoop Hotel 51
Cambridge, Market 92
Castle Ashby, Northamptonshire 47
Castle Camps Hall, Cambridgeshire 151
Catforth, (Hunts) Cambridgeshire 21
Caxton Hall, Cambridgeshire 151

Chatteris, Cambridgeshire 213
Chiswick Gardens, Royal Horticultural Society, London 96
Civil Service Luncheon Club, Marston Road, Oxford 213
Claremont, Surrey 138
Copingford, (Hunts) Cambridgeshire 21
Cothele, Cornwall, 138
Court of Wick, Yatton, Somerset 96
Covington, (Hunts) Cambridgeshire 21
Cromer, Herne Close, Norfolk 113
Cromer, The Warren, Norfolk 113, 139, 167
Cross Hall, St Neots, (Hunts) Cambridgeshire 41, 151
Culford Hall, Suffolk 31
Crystal Palace Exhibition, Sydenham, London 62, 64, 168

Darby, Philadelphia, America 11
Diddington Hall, (Hunts) Cambridgeshire 21, 41, 42, 117, 138, 165, 188, 213
Ditchley Park, Oxfordshire 138
Duke of York's School, Dover, Kent 163, 205

Earith British School, Cambridgeshire 202
East Bergholt, Suffolk 135
Easton Neston, Northamptonshire 31
Eastwell, Ashford, Kent 191
Eaton Socon, Bedfordshire 139
Ellington, (Hunts) Cambridgeshire 13
Elvaston Castle, Derbyshire 116
Engerfield Green, Surrey 197
Everton, Bedfordshire 21
Everton House, Bedfordshire 39, 40
Euston Hall, Suffolk 31, 132
Exning, Newmarket, Sufolk 116, 150
Eynesbury, (Hunts) Cambridgeshire 21

Fenstanton, (Hunts) Cambridgeshire 26, 27, 47–49
Fixby, Yorkshire 41
Fountains Abbey, Yorkshire 31
Foxton Hall, Cambridgeshire 139

Gamlingay, Cambridgeshire 139
Gaynes Hall, (Hunts) Cambridgeshire 86
Gayton Hall, Norfolk 116
Glatton, 'Allways', (Hunts) Cambridgeshire 189, 212
Godmanchester, (Hunts) Cambridgeshire 22, 44, 83, 151
Godmanchester, 'Chestnuts', (Hunts) Cambridgeshire 191
Godmanchester, Farm Hall (Hunts) Cambridgeshire 37, 67
Godmanchester, Island Hall (Hunts) Cambridgeshire 44, 99, 139, 169
Godmanchester, Old Court Hall (Hunts) Cambridgeshire 193
Godmanchester School (Hunts) Cambridgeshire 44, 202
Goff's Oak, Horticultural Botanical Association Ltd, Hertfordshire
Gog Magog Hills, Cambridge 139
Goodwood, Sussex 1
Gransden Hall, Sandy, Bedfordshire 117, 128
Great Missenden, Buckinghamshire 213
Great Staughton, (Hunts) Cambridgeshire 34, 35
Great Stukely Hall, (Hunts) Cambridgeshire 108
Great Stukely School (Hunts) Cambridgeshire 202
Grimsthorpe Castle, Lincolnshire 150, 178

Hackwood Park, Basingstoke, Hampshire 150
Hampton Court, Middlesex 47, 49
Harston, Cambridgeshire 151
Hartford, (Hunts) Cambridgeshire 50, 213
Hartford, The Hurst (Hunts) Cambridgeshire 213
Hatley Park, Cambridgeshire 155, 1566
Hazells Hall, Bedfordshire 38, 39
Hemingford Abbots, (Hunts) Cambridgeshire 59, 135
Hemingford Grey, Harcourt, (Hunts) Cambridgeshire 213
Hemingford Grey, The Manor House, Cambridgeshire 151
Herstmonceaux Castle, Sussex 188, 198

INDEX – PLACES

Heveningham Hall, Suffolk 150, 188

Hidcote Manor, Gloucestershire 150

Hilton, Fenstanton, (Hunts) Cambridgeshire 48, 49

Hinchingbrooke, (Hunts) Cambridgeshire 1, 19, 20, 23, 26, 45, 83–85, 116, 123, 132

Hinxton Hall, Cambridgeshire 33, 138

Histon, Cambridgeshire 151, 193

Hitchin, Temple Dinsley, Hertfordshire 116, 129, 138

Holkham Hall, Norfolk 31, 116

Hollywell, (Hunts) Cambridgeshire 21

Holmewood Hall, Holme, (Hunts) Cambridgeshire 213

Houghton Grange, (Hunts) Cambridgeshire 21, 98, 108, 145, 151, 201

Houghton Hall, Norfolk 31

Hunstanton Hall, Norfolk 197

Huntingdon, (Hunts) Cambridgeshire 1, 116

Huntingdon, Alberta Crescent, (Hunts) Cambridgeshire 128

Huntingdon, California Road, (Hunts) Cambridgeshire 50

Huntingdon, Council School, (Hunts) Cambridgeshire 202

Huntingdon, Fountain Inn, (Hunts) Cambridgeshire 44

Huntingdon, 2 & 3 George Street, Offices, (Hunts) Cambridgeshire 201

Huntingdon, Grammar School, (Hunts) Cambridgeshire 202, 203, 214

Huntingdon, Hartford Lane Nursery, (Hunts) Cambridgeshire 50

Huntingdon, Hospital Lands, (Hunts) Cambridgeshire 6

Huntingdon, Mill Lane, (Hunts) Cambridgeshire 50

Huntingdon, Old Bridge House, (Hunts) Cambridgeshire 117

Huntingdon, Old Grammar School 204

Huntingdon, Priory Lane, (Hunts) Cambridgeshire 6, 56

Huntingdon, Prisoner of War Camp, (Hunts) Cambridgeshire 130

Huntingdon, Race Course, (Hunts) Cambridgeshire 79

Huntingdon, The Old Nurseries, St Germaine Street, (Hunts) Cambridgeshire 97, 108, 215

Huntingdon, The Walks, (Hunts) Cambridgeshire 52, 134

Huntingdon, Trinity Church, (Hunts) Cambridgeshire 87

Ickworth, Suffolk 135

Ilford Manor, Wiltshire 149

Kelvedon, Essex 153

Kempton Barracks, 432 Agricultural Company, Bedfordshire 126

Kenilworth Castle, Warwickshire 31

Keyston, (Hunts) Cambridgeshire 21

Kilkenny Castle, Kilkenny, Ireland 164

Kimbolton Castle, (Hunts) Cambridgeshire 1, 5, 19–23, 34, 50, 83,–86, 116

Kimbolton Castle, Farm Hall (Hunts) Cambridgeshire 38

Kimbolton, Grammar School, (Hunts) Cambridgeshire 50, 53

King Edward VII Sanatorium, Midhurst, Surrey 166

King's Lynn, Norfolk 6

Kingsmoor, Great Parndon, Essex 161

Kings Walden Bury, Hertfordshire 193

Kirby Hall, Northamptonshire 204

Landhydrock, Cornwall 19

Letchworth, The First Garden City Ltd, Hertfordshire 120

Letchworth, The Spirella Company, Hertfordshire 149

Lingfield, Kent 197

Lichfield, Grammar School, Staffordshire 33

Little Ravely (Hunts) Cambridgeshire 21

Little Stukely, (Hunts) Cambridgeshire 13, 56

Liverpool, Alexander Dock, Lancashire 209

Lolworth, Cambridgeshire 123

London, Apothecaries Garden 3

London, Ashburnham House 64

London, Bedford College for Women 150

London, Brompton Park 15

London, Buckingham Palace 20, 194, 195, 198, 205

London, Bushy Park, Hampton Court 195

London, Chelsea Flower Show 198, 199

London, Chelsea Physic Garden 3, 5

London, Clapham Rise 8

London, Covent Garden 4, 94

London, Cremore Gardens 63, 64

London, 10 Downing Street 205

London, Food Production Department, 72 Victoria Street 129, 133

London, Greenwich Park 135, 163

London, Highbury Fields 41

London, Hyde Park 24, 63, 163

London, Hyde Park, His Majesty's Office of Works 113, 150, 196–198, 204, 205, 211

London, Kew, The Royal Botanic Gardens 23, 59, 148

London, Kensington Palace 47

London, King's Cross 41

London, King's Road, Chelsea 64

London, Onslow Square 209

London, Mill Hill 2

London, Regent's Park 150, 162, 194, 197, 198, 205

London, Regent's Park, Botanic Gardens 64

London, Somerset House 63

London, St Paul's Cathedral 33

London, St James's Park 24, 163, 194

London, The Royal Society 3, 23, 24, 30

London, Vauxhall Gardens 64

London, The Wallace Collection 162

London, Wellington Barracks 209

Longstowe Hall, Cambridgeshire 134, 191

Loudham Hall, Woodbridge, Suffolk 191

Lough Cutra Castle, Gort, County Galway, Ireland 164

Madingley Hall, Cambridge 166, 197

Madresfield Gardens, Malvern, Worcestershire 193

Manchester, Old Trafford 202
Milton Park, (Northants) Cambridgeshire 105, 116
Moulton, Newmarket, Suffolk 188, 197
Munstead Wood, Godalming, Surrey 207

Newhaven, Sussex 121
Newmarket, Suffolk 212
Newmarket, The Kremlin 138
Newmarket, Exning House 116
Newton Hall, Cambridgeshire 193
Northampton, 'The Priory', Billing Road 107

Odsey Grange, Ashwell, Hertfordshire 151
Offord Cluny, (Hunts) Cambridgeshire 21
Old Hurst, (Hunts) Cambridgeshire 21
Old Warden Park, Biggleswade, Bedfordshire 148, 179
Oundle, Northamptonshire 15, 149, 180
Overstrand, The Pleasaunce, Norfolk 113, 116, 149, 194, 196
Oxford, Christ Church 36
Oxford, Civil Service Luncheon Club, Oxfordshire 213

Pampisford Hall, Cambridgeshire 151
Papworth Hall, Cambridge Tuberculosis Colony, Cambridgeshire 135
Papworth Industries, Papworth Everard, Cambridgeshire 211
Paxton Park, (Hunts) Cambridgeshire 151
Peckham, South London 1, 2
Peterborough, Cambridgeshire 212
Peterborough, Westwood Park, Cambridgeshire 191
Pidley-cum-Fenton, (Hunts) Cambridgeshire 44
The Pleasaunce, Overstrand, Norfolk 196
Port Lympne, Kent 149
Portholm, Godmanchester, (Hunts) Cambridgeshire 11
Preston, War Pensions Committee, Lancashire 131

Quy Hall, Cambridgeshire 151
Railway Convalescent Home, Par, Cornwall 191
Ramsey, (Hunts) Cambridgeshire 10, 89–91, 117, 135, 211
Ramsey Abbey, (Hunts) Cambridgeshire 135, 136
Ramsey Abbey School, (Hunts) Cambridgeshire 213
Ramsey, Boat Inn, (Hunts), Cambridgeshire 89
Ramsey, Bury Road, (Hunts) Cambridgeshire 139
Ramsey St Mary's School, (Hunts) Cambridgeshire 202
Raunds, Distribution Co-operative Society, Wellingborough, Northamptonshire 154
Rainham Hall, Norfolk 31
Rockingham Castle, Northamptonshire 149, 193
Royston, Herfordfshire 59

Saffron Walden, Essex 77
Sandy, Bedfordshire 39, 40
Sawtry, (Hunts) Cambridgeshire 21, 128
Sayes Court, Deptford, Kent 46
Scarborough, Yorkshire 30
Shrublands Park, Suffolk 150
Shortgrove Park, Newport, Essex 139, 170
Shugborough, Staffordshire 31
Shuttleworth Collection, Bedfordshire 149
Six Mile Bottom, The Hall, Cambridgeshire 194
Sissinghurst Castle, Kent 138
Skegness, Lincolnshire 129
Somerset House, London 63
Somersham, (Hunts) Cambridgeshire 33
Southill Park, Bedfordshire 193
Spaldwick, (Hunts) Cambridgershire 21, 212
St Ives, (Hunts) Cambridgeshire 21
St Ives, Boy's Council School, (Hunts) Cambridgeshire 204
St Ives, Lattenbury Hill (Hunts) Cambridgeshire 147
St Neots, (Hunts) Cambridgeshire 21, 97, 114

St Neots, 16 & 18 Cambridge Street, (Hunts) Cambridgeshire 56, 81, 106, 215, 220
St Neots, Cross Hall (Hunts) Cambridgeshire 41
Stamford, Lincolnshire 65
Stamford, Uffington House, Lincolnshire 150
Stebbington (Hunts) Cambridgeshire 21
Stetchworth Park, Cambridgeshire 151
Stilton Church of England School, (Hunts) Cambridgeshire 202
Stow, (Hunts) Cambridgeshire 21
Stowe, Buckinghamshire 30, 46, 47
Stradsett Hall, King's Lynn, Norfolk 150
Studley Royal, Yorkshire 23, 31
Syon House, Middlesex 37

Taplow Court, Berkshire 150
Temsford, Bedfordshire 13
Thetford, Norfolk 118
Thorndon Hall, Essex 2
Thornhaugh Hall, Wansford, (Hunts) Cambridgeshire 118
Thriplow, Cambridgeshire 213
Tollington Park School, Huntingdon 204
Tomskoi, Siberia 5
Torquay, Parks Department, Devon 207
Trentham, Staffordshire 31
Trewin Water, Welwyn, Hertfordshire 150
Tring Park, Hertfordshire 179, 194

Upton, Church of England School, (Hunts) Cambridgeshire 202
Upwood, Royal Air Force Station, Cambridgeshire 204

Wakefield Hunting Lodge, Potterspury, Northamptonshire 47
Walter Priory, York 170
Waltham Abbey, Hertfordshire 150
Warboys, (Hunts) Cambridgeshire 214
Waresley Park, (Hunts) Cambridgeshire 151
Warwick Castle, Warwickshire 31
Watford, The Grove, Hertfordshire 150

INDEX – PLACES/PLANTS   247

Wennington, (Hunts) Cambridgeshire 21, 43
Wentworth Castle, Yorkshire 31
Wentworth Woodhouse, Yorkshire 105
West Malling, Kent 206
Westwood Park, (Northants) Cambridgeshire 191
Wimpole Hall, Cambridgeshire 5, 20, 27–29, 31, 32, 42, 116, 118, 120, 152, 169, 211

Winick, (Hunts) Cambridgeshire 21
Woburn Abbey, Bedfordshire 113, 118, 194
Woburn, Park Farm Office, Bedford 113, 140
Wollaton House, Nottinghamshire 31
Wolterton Hall, Norfolk 31
Woodbury Hall, Everton, Bedfordshire 40, 166

Woodwalton, (Hunts) Cambridgeshire 44
Wrest Park, Bedfordshire 27, 29, 30
Wyton, 31st R.A.F. Squadron, (Hunts) Cambridgeshire 117
Wyton, R.A.F. Station, (Hunts) Cambridgeshire 204
Yarmouth, Norfolk 31
Yatton, Somerset 96

Plants

Abies 100, 135, 191
Abies alba 36
Abies balsamea 35
Abies nordmanniana 163
Abico Colorado 190
Abutilon 4, 68
Abutilon dodonei 3
Abutilon x milleri 4
Abutilon theophrastrus 4
Acacia 69, 73, 78, 93, 120
Acacia armata (Acacia paradoxa) 70
Acacia grandis 69
Acacia longifolia (Sidney Golden Wattle) 61
Acacia longifolia magnifica 61
Acah thorn (Acacia pseudoacacia) 38
Acanthopanax picinifolia (A. ricinifolius = Kalopanax septemlobus) 163
Acathus (Robinia pseudacacia) 36
Acer 166, 193–195, 198
Acer dasycarpum (A.saccharinum) 190
Acer negundo 193
Acer palmatum 194
Acer pseudoplatanus 150
Acer rubrum 35, 36
Achimenes (Hot Water Plant) 62
Aconitum wilsonii (A. carmichaelii Wilsonii Group) 161
Actinidia kolomitka 195
Actinidia rubricaulis 195
Aesculus indica 195
Ageratum 91
Alder 164

Almond 10, 34, 120, 210
Alpines 60, 72, 102, 111
Alstroemeria 161
Althaea 206
Althea Coeleste 206
Althea frutax (Hibiscus syriacus) 18, 34, 36, 38
Althea rubis 206
Althea lutea 4
Alyssum 68, 69, 203
Amaranthus (Love-lies-bleeding) 63
Amaygdalus Pollardii (Prunus x amygdalopersica 'Pollardii) 206
American Arborvitae 99
American Convolvulus 3, 5
American Cowslip 54
American Foxglove with purple flower 3, 4
American Apples 96
American Elm 55
American Plants 62, 62
Amorpha fruticosa (False Indigo) 36, 100
Ampelopsis sempervirens (possibly Cissus striata) 163
Ampelopsis Veitchii (A. tricuspidata 'Veitchii') 101, 150, 207
Anemones 59, 62, 65
Anemone japonica 'Alba' 161
Anemone japonica rosea 161
Antirrhinum 72, 203, 211
Apels (Apples) 10, 25, 39, 48
Aples (Apples) 17
Apples 74, 77, 78, 96, 97, 99, 103, 107, 117, 118, 133, 135, 138, 151, 166, 167, 180

Apple 'Allington Pippin' 122, 146
Apple 'Baldwin' 96
Apple 'Ben's Red' 122
Apple 'Beaumann's Reinette' 103
Apple 'Beauty of Bath' 103
Apple 'Blenheim Orange' 121, 122
Apple 'Bismark' 103
Apple 'Bramley Seedling' 103
Apple 'Brampton Seedling' 103
Apple 'Cambridge Pippin' 103
Apple 'Court of Wick' 97
Apple 'Cox's Orange Pippin' 121, 122
Apple 'Emneth Early' 103
Apple 'Golden Noble' 122
Apple 'Golden Pippin' 96
Apple 'Hector Macdonald' 122
Apple 'Histon Favorite' 99, 103
Apple 'Huntingdon Codlin' 97, 99, 103
Apple 'James Grieve' 206
Apple 'Lady Sandwich' 99, 103
Apple 'Lady Sudeley' 122
Apple 'Lane's Prince Albert' 122
Apple 'Langley Pippin' 122
Apple 'Lord Burleigh' 103
Apple 'Lord Grosvenor' 122
Apple 'Lord Stradbrooke' 122
Apple 'Mr Gladstone' 122
Apple 'Murfitt's Seedling' 97, 99, 103
Apple 'Newtown Pippin' 96
Apple 'Northern Spy' 96
Apple 'Radford Beauty' 99
Apple 'Red Victoria' 122

Apple 'Ribston Pippin' 121, 122
Apple 'September Beauty' 103
Apple 'Squire Fellowes' 103
Apple 'Sturmer Pippin' 122
Apple 'Woodley's Favourite' 97, 103
Apple 'Wood's Huntingdon' 96
Apple 'Worcester Permain' 122
Apple 'Wyken Pippin' 146
Aprecock (Apricot) 15, 17, 40, 48
Apricot 9, 41, 72, 92, 99, 103, 117, 150, 151
Arborvitae (Thuja occidentalis) 17, 72
Arbutes (Arbutus unedo) 15, 18, 26, 34
Artemisia 160
Ash, Common (Fraxinus excelsior) 16, 28, 29, 78, 120, 130, 135, 143, 148, 166, 192, 193, 197
Ashes (Fraxinus excelsior) 45
Asparagrass (Asparagus) 9, 42, 87
Asparagus argenteuil 9
Asparagus 'Giant' 102
Asparagus 'Perkins' Early Giant 138, 196
Aster 75
Aster subcaeruleus (Aster tongolensis) 161
Astilbe davidii (Aster chinensis var davidii) 161
Atriplex halimus 35
Aubretia 111
Aucuba 79, 192
Araucaria 100
Araucaria araucana (Monkey Puzzle Tree) 67
Arbutes (arbutus) 15
Auricula 54
Austrian Pines 150, 190
Azara 197
Azara microphylla 163, 195
Azaleadendrons 162
Azaleas 61, 63, 69, 72, 73, 88, 100, 149
Azalea mollis /Azalea molle 162

Baccharis haliminfolia 35
Balm of Giled Firs (Abies balsamea) 35
Balsam Poplars 75, 99

Balsam Trees (Populus candicans) 35, 38
Bamboo 100
Barbre (Berberis vulgaris) 38
Barbar Ivies Hispan 3, 4
Bat Willows 164
Beans 43, 128
Bean 'Canadian Wonder' 202
Bean 'Perkins' Prizewinner' 202
Bean 'Brooklands Giant Runner' 153
Bean 'Flageolet' 128
Beanes 9
Beans, Haricot 128
Bedding Geraniums/Pelargoniums:-
" 'Black Douglas' 110
" 'Henry Jacoby' 110
" 'Huntingdonian' 105
" 'Lass O'Gowrie' 110
" 'Masterpiece' 110
" 'Mr Henry Cox' 110
" 'Mrs Pollock' 110
" 'Mrs Robert Cannell' 110
" 'Paul Crampel' 110
" 'Queen of the Belgians' 110
" 'Sir John Holder' 110
" 'Snow Queen' 110
" 'Sophia Dumaresque' 110
" 'West Brighton Gem' 110
Bedding Plants 61, 87, 90, 92
Beech 29, 78, 99, 135, 139, 144, 167
Beet 'Covent Garden' 202
Beet 'Crimson Globe' 204
Beet 'Green Leaf' 153
Beet 'Long' 153
Beet 'Model Globe' 153
Beet 'Nutting's Dark Red' 153
Begonias 91, 92, 95
Berberis 5, 38, 67, 87, 151, 160, 154, 161, 167, 178, 192, 194, 197
Berberis aggregata 149
Berberis aquifolium (Mahonia aquifolium) 99, 164
Berberis darwinii 150, 164, 206
Berberis dictiophuylla (Berberis dictyophylla) 206
Berberis gagnepaenii (Berberis gagnepainii) 163

Berberis hispanica 4
Berberis purpurea 206
Berberis stenophylla (Berberis x stenophylla) 206
Birch, Silver 120, 151, 163, 193
Birch, Cut-leaf 190
Bladder Senes (Coronilla arborescens) 38
Blackberry 'Parsley Leaved' 207
Black Currant 135, 167, 194, 206
Black Italian Poplars 143, 191
Blackthorn 99
Bluebells 192
Blue Soringers (Syringa vulgaris) 38
Bossiacas 69
Boston Ivy 101
Box 89, 99, 197
Box, Dwarf 103
Box edging 92
Box, Gold Tipped 162
Box hedging 151, 189, 190
Bouvardia 65
Bramble 34
Bran 90
Brassicas 63
Briars 83, 84, 88, 90
Broccoli 62, 72, 204
Broccoli 'Veitch's Self-protecting' 202
Broom 33, 35
Broom Yellow 166
Brugmansia (Datura) 69
Buddleia 163, 194, 195
Buddleia alternifolia 163, 205
Buddleia amplissima 159, 163
Buddleia 'Delight' 163
Buddleia globosa 149
Buddleia gigantica 163
Buddleia 'Distinction' 163
Buddleia magnifica (Buddlcia davidii var magnifica) 163
Buddleia perfecta 163
Buddleia 'Pink Pearl' 163
Buddleia prostrata 194
Buddleia superba 163
Buddleia variabilis rosea 163
Buddleia veitchianus 163
Bure Pear 46

INDEX – PLANTS 249

Cabag (Cabbage) 45
Cabbage 9, 22, 43, 62, 129
Cabbage 'Christmas Drumhead' 202
Cabbage 'Flower of Spring' 202
Cabbage 'Milams Early Dwarf' 204
Cactus 96
Calanthus veratifolia 61
Calcedonica (Laburnum alpinum) 24
Calceolarias 63, 68, 72, 74, 68, 82, 89, 90, 91
Calkcedonen tres (Laburnum alpinum) 40
Calycanthus carolina (Allspice) (? Calycanthus florida) 100
Calycanthus praecox 192
Camellias 72, 73, 74
Campanela (Campanula) 46
Campanula 111
Campanula persicifolia grandiflora alba (C. 'Grandiflora Alba') 161
Campanula persicifolia 'Telham Beauty' 161
Canna 105
Canterberbels (Canterbury Bells) 22
Caragana altagana 5
Caragana arborescens (Catagoy ham) 5
Caragana chamlagu (sinica) 5, 100
Caragana microphylla (Caragana altagana) 3, 5
Carnations, Picotees & Pinks 52, 54, 58–60, 63–67, 70, 80, 92, 93, 106, 111, 117
Carnation 'Allwoodii' 161
Carnation 'Captain Selah' 106
Carnation, crimson bizarres 52
Carnation 'Geisha' 106
Carnation 'King of the Scarlets' 106
Carnation, purple flakes 52
Carnation, rose flakes 52
Caenation 'Royal Record' 106
Carnation, scarlet flakes 52
Carnation 'Surprise' 106
Carnation 'Sweet Marie' 106
Carnation 'The Shah'106
Carols (Poplars) 16
Carolina Bird Chere (Prunus caroliniana) 38, 41

Carolina Gelder Roses (Viburnum trilobum) 35
Carolina Poplars (Populus angulatus) 35
Carolina Suckling (Lonicera sempervirens) 36
Carrot 8, 9, 39, 43, 86, 89, 91, 117
Carrot 'Chantenay Red' 214
Catalpa 151
Catalpa kaempferi (ovata) 100
Catalpes (Catalpa bignonoides) 36
Cauliflower 'Early London' 204
Cauliflower 'Perkins' Express' 165
Ceanothus 35, 67, 160, 194, 195, 197
Ceanothus azureus grandiflorus 163
Ceanothus americanus 35
Ceanothus dentatus 163, 166
Ceanothus floribundus 163, 166
Ceanothus 'Gloire de Versailles' 162
Ceanothus 'Indigo' 150
Ceanothus rigidus 166
Ceanothuus thyrsiflorus 163
Ceanothus veitchii (Ceanothus x veitchianus) 166
Cedar 135, 138
Cedars, red 68
Ceder of Libnes (Cedrus libani) 33
Cedrus 100
Cedrus atlantica 163
Cedrus atlantica glauca (Cedrus atlantica Glauca Group) 192
Cedrus deodora 180
Cedrus libanii 140, 163
Celery 65, 66, 74, 75
Centaurea 87, 88
Cerasus oveeni 162
Ceratostigma 149
Chelone barbarta (Penstemon barbartus) 161
Cheres (Cherry) 10, 15, 17, 18, 33, 34, 36, 38, 41, 48, 99, 117
Cherry 62, 99, 103, 151
Cherry double 151, 194
Cherry, Dwarf 192
Cherry, Morello 24, 25, 180, 210
Chestnuts 28, 29, 40, 46, 83, 139, 151

Chichester Elm 54, 55
Chimonanthus 73, 160
Choisya 160
Chowzemas 71
Christmas trees 83, 114, 117, 135, 151
Chrysanthemums 73, 110, 117, 151
Cinerarias 66, 69
Cinneraria maritime (Senecio cineraria) 91
Cinneraria maritime candissima 91
Cistus 3, 150
Cistus ladanifer 5
Cistus laurifolius 163
Clematis 101, 110, 119, 139, 150, 151, 166, 178, 195, 197
Clematis 'Beauty of Worcester' 101, 102
Clematis 'Duchess of Edinburgh' 138, 165
Clematis 'Fairy Queen' 165
Clematis 'Gypsy Queen' 101, 165,
Clematis 'Jackmanii' 101, 138
Clematis 'Jackmanii Superba' 101, 102, 165, 192
Clematis 'Lady Betty Balfour' 119
Clematis 'Lady Northcliffe' 110
Clematis 'La France' 138
Clematis 'Lasurstern' 110
Clematis 'Lord Neville' 110
Clematis 'Madame Edouard Andre' 165
Clematis 'Madame Grange' 101
Clematis montana var. rubens 110
Clematis 'Mrs G Jackman' 138
Clematis 'Mrs Quilter' 110
Clematis 'Papa Christen' 100, 110
Clematis 'The President' 101
Clematis 'Ville de Lyon' 165
Clematis vitalba 210, 207
Clematis stocks 211
Cobaea scandens 91
Cocksagre 41
Codlin (Apple) 10
Coleus 90
Colletia spinosa (Anchor Plant) 68
Conifers 77, 78, 107, 111
Coreopsis grandiflora 161
Corylopsis pauciflora 162

Corylus purpurea (Corylus maxima 'Purpurea') 164
Cornela (Cornus mas) 33
Cornus 135
Cornus flaviramanea (Cornus sericea 'Flaviramea') 163
Cornus sanguinea 163
Cotoneaster 161, 195
Cotoneaster acutifolius 163
Cotoneaster ampplanta 163
Cotoneaster frigidus 161, 196
Cotoneaster harroviana 163
Cotoneaster henryi (C. henryanus) 163
Cotoneaster horizontalis 150
Cotoneaster perkinsii 205, 206
Cotoneaster rugosa henryi (C. henryanus) 163
Cotoneaster salicifolia rugosa 163
Crab stocks 59, 83, 86, 160
Crataegus 195
Crataegus carnerii 163
Crataegus gibbsii 163
Crataegus oxyacantha (Quickthorn) (C. laevigata) 12
Crataegus oxyacantha punica (C. laevigata 'Punicea') 163
Crataegus pyracantha crenuklata yunnanensis (Pyracantha crenulata) 190
Crataegus 'Paul's Scarlet' 195
Greass (Cress) 9
Cress & Mus (Mustard and Cress) 8, 9, 43
Crocus, Yellow 162
Cryptomeria 100, 164
Cryptomeria japonica 164
Cucumber 31, 32, 39, 59, 62, 66, 68, 69, 72–77
Culeflower (Cauliflower) 9
Culy flower (Cauliflower) 9, 22, 43
Cupressus 62, 72, 77, 100, 150, 192
Cupressus lawsoniana (Chamaecyparis lawsoniana) 166
Cupressus lawsoniana 'Stewartii' 163
Cupressus macrocarpa 62, 164, 191
Cupressus macrocarpa 'Lutea' 164
Currants 24, 25, 99, 149, 151, 191

Currant 'Boskoop Giant' 160
Currant 'Seabrook Black' 151
Currant 'September Black' 160
Cyclamen 60, 88, 89
Cydonia 207
Cydonia japonica (Chaenomeles japonica) 195
Cydonia marleii (maulei) (Chaenomeles japonica) 150
Cydonia 'Simone' 194
Cypros (Cypress sempervirens) 36, 77
Cytisus 68, 93, 167
Cytisus capitatus (Chamaecytisus sp) 2

Daffodils 117, 191
Dahlias 52, 59, 61, 62, 64–66, 68, 71, 73–75, 77, 88, 93, 105
Damsens (Damsons) 48, 117
Daphne 91, 163
Datura 69
Delphiniums 161, 166
Delphinium grandiflora majus 54
Deutzia 163
Deutzia crenata magnifica 206
Dillywinnias 69, 70
Doble Black Wall (Double Black Wallflower) 24
Dodecatheon meadia 54
Dodecatheon meadia gigantica 54
Dodecaton meadia var. elegans 54
Dogwood Red 150
Douglas Fir 134, 135
Douglas Fir, Colorado variety 190
Dracophyllum gracile 63
Duble Cachflyes (Silene armeria) 466
Duble flower bramble (Rubuis fruticosus fl pl) 34
Duble Sweat Briars (Rosa x eglanteria) 46
Duble yealo roses (Rosa hemisphaerica) 36, 46
Duck hundrd leaved (Rosa centifolia var) 24, 33, 36, 46
Duch hundred roses (Rosa gallica var) 34
Duck Lettuce 41
Duck Turnip 46
Duk Cheres 15
Dwarf Almonds 35

Dwarf Chere 38

Echinops ritro 161
Echium 'Wildgott' 147
Elder 92
Elm 14, 15, 24, 27–29, 40–42, 45, 47, 48, 71, 92, 99, 104, 118, 135, 148
Elm, Broad leaved 16, 45
Elm, Cornish 120, 163, 166, 194, 197, 198, 208
Elm, English 42, 100, 120, 190
Elm, Golden 194
Elm, Huntingdon 90–93, 98–100, 109
Elm, large 28, 29
Elm, Narrow-leaved English 100
Elm, small 28, 29, 42
Elm, Weeping 162
Elm, Wych 163
Elm 'Van Houteu' (Ulmus 'Van Houttei') 194
Endive 76
Epacris 63, 69, 72, 74, 75
Epiphyllum 71
Ericas 72, 82, 87, 88, 91–93
Erica ventricosa magnifica 63
Erica 'Wilmoreana' 88, 89, 92
Erigeron 'Amos Perry' 161
Eriostemon 69
Escallonia 195, 197
Escallonia 'Donard Seedling' 163
Escallonia 'Edinburgh' 163
Eucryphia 166
Eucryphia pinnitifolia 206
Eugenia ugni (Chilean Guava) 69, 100
Eupatorium odoratissima 88
Eupatorium odoratum 88
Euonimus (Euonymus latifolius) 35
Euonymus 68, 194
Euonymus alatus 150
Euonymus coccineus 206
Euonymus europaeus 192
Euonymus latifolius 195
Euonymus yedoensis (E. hamiltonianus ssp. sieboldianus) 206
Evergreen shrubs 26, 56, 67, 68, 84
Evergreen Oaks 67

INDEX – PLANTS

Ever Green Sucklings (Lonicera x americana) 16, 35–37
Exocorda albertii macrantha (E. albertii = E. korolkowu, E.macrantha =E. x macrantha) 194

Fagus 151
Felarays (Phillyreas) 16
Ferns 69, 75, 76, 83, 88, 96
Fig 10, 15, 103, 151, 160
Fig 'White Marseillles' 160
Fig 'Ringo de Mel' 160
Fig 'St John' 160
Filberts 79, 151
Fir 14, 26, 35, 38, 40, 42, 100, 164, 166, 197
Flageolet Beans 128
Fly Sucklings (Lonicera xylosteum) 33
Forest Trees 83, 111, 125, 128
Forsythia 163, 191
Forsythia spectabilis (Forsythia x intermedia 'Spectabilis') 162, 163, 195, 206
Foxglove from virginey 3, 4
Fruit trees 9, 39, 45, 56, 69, 99, 111, 116, 117, 121, 125, 135, 137–139, 149, 151, 192–194, 211
Fuchsias 70, 72–74, 82, 83, 105

Gardenias 70, 87
Garlic 213
Garrya 161
Garrya elliptica 192, 195, 207
Gelder Roses (Viburnum opulus) 10, 15
Geranium 61, 65, 67, 69, 70, 72–76, 82, 86, 88–91, 105
Geranium 'Huntingdonian' 105
Geranium 'Paul Cramper' 203
Geradia flava 4
Ghent Azaleas 166
Gilder Rose (Viburnum opulus) 42
Globe Artichoke 102, 194, 211
Globe Amaranthus 63
Gloxinias 74, 92
Gomphrena globosa 63
Gooseberry 24, 25, 39, 92, 93, 99, 135, 151, 191, 194
Gorse 99

Goss Lettuce 41
Gouve Froonchuda
Grapes 10, 25, 58, 60, 78, 83, 86, 87, 99, 103
Greengag (Greengage) 15
Green hole (Ilex aquifolium) 38
Green Lorel (Prunus lauracerasus) 34
Greens 8
Griselinia littoralis 100
Grunsel Tree (Baccharis halimifolia) 35
Gum cistus 3, 5
Gymnocladus canadensis (dioicus) (Kentucky Coffee Tree) 100

Halesia carolina (Snowdrop Tree) 100
Hamamelis 150
Hamamelis mollis 162
Hazel 83, 99, 143, 197
Heaths 60, 65, 70, 73–75
Helenium hoopsii 161
Helleborus 124
Heliotrope (Cherry Pie) 67, 70, 72, 73, 111
Heliotropium peruviana (Heliotropium arborescens) 67
Herbaceous plants 70, 102, 111, 167, 194
Herbs 102
Heuchera 161
Hibbertia 69
Hibiscus 150
Hibiscus syriacus 36
Hippophae rhamnoides 34
Holly 15, 76, 100, 138, 150, 151, 161, 163
Hollyhocks 22, 67, 69, 74, 75, 91
Honeysuckle 17, 38
Honeysuckle, Dutch 'Late Red' 160
Horse Chestnuts 138, 190, 192, 193, 195
Horse Chestnuts, White 194
Horse Radish 22
Hova celsi 72
Hoya 73
Huntingdon Elm 54, 55, 92
Hyacinth 6, 120, 124, 213

Hydrangeas 71
Hydrangea hortensis Mouselline (H. macrophylla 'Mousmee') 162
Hydrangea paniculata 'Grandiflora' 162
Hyperacan frutax (Spiraea hypericifolia) 34, 36–38
Hypericum 161
Hypericum patulum Henryii (H. pseudohenryi) 163

Iberis 111
Ilex 149
Ilex 'Golden Queen' 161
Ilex 'Silver Queen' 162
Incarvillea delavayii 161
Indgo (Amorpha fruticosa) 36, 41
Ind Goa (Amorpha fruticosa) 36
Ipomoea coccinea 5
Ipomoea hederifolia (I. hederacea) 5
Irish Ivy 88
Irish Yew 150
Irish Yew, Golden 164
Ivy 82–84, 88, 89

Jacobvinia pauciflora 88
Japanese Lilies 88
Japanese Maples 193
Jasminum 24, 25, 151, 197
Jasminum nudiflorum 68, 70, 195
Jasminum officinale 195
Jasminum x stephanense 195
Jesemines (Jasmine) 24
Juniper 62, 72, 192
Juniperus communis suecica 35
Juniperus conastii 163

Kale 'Tall Green Curled' 204
Kalmia 194
Kalmia myrtifolia (K. latiloba f. myrtifolia) 63
Kalmium 63
Kentish Cob Nuts 192
Kerria japonica 197
Kidne bens (Kidney Beans) 43
Kidney Beans 60
Kidno Beans (Kidney Beans) 9
Kohl Rabi 99, 109

Laburnnems (Laburnum anagyroides) 38

Laburnum 16, 37, 38, 93, 138, 190
Lachenalia 69
Lalicks (Syringa vulgaris) 37
Lalock (Lilac) 38, 42
Larch 28, 47, 99, 111, 134, 135, 138, 140, 141, 143, 149, 151, 193, 197
Larch, Japanese 134
Larch, Native 118, 134, 140
Large Pashon Flower (Passiflora caerulea) 45
Large Silver Spruce Firs (Abies alba) 36
Larix kurilensis (Larix gmelinii var. japonica) 140
Laurel 76, 83, 84, 135, 149, 197
Laurel caucasica 149, 150
Laurel rotundifolia 150
Laurus noibilis 35
Laurustinus 16, 150, 192
Lavender, Common 151, 164
Lavandula nana 150, 167
Lavandula 'Twickel Purple' 207
Lechemanias 68, 69
Leek 82
Lettuce 8, 16, 43, 45, 76
Lettuce 'Cos' 40, 43, 45
Lettuce 'Perkins' Pompadour' 202
Libonia floribunda 88
Ligustrum 89
Lilac 38, 87, 92, 139, 161, 206
Lilium candidum 121
Lilium martagon sibiricum 2
Lily 117
Lily of the Valley 6
Lime 27–29, 41, 52–54, 83, 92, 100, 151, 160, 163, 166, 190, 191, 193, 196, 197
Lime, Red-twigged 138, 191, 194
Linum sibiricum (Linum perenne) 4
Liptospermum (Leptospermum) 91
Liriodendron 166
Liquidamber styraciflua 163
Lobelia 89, 203
Lobelia speciosa 73
Loganberry 134, 150, 206
Lonicera 150, 160, 161, 195
Lonicera x Americana 34, 36, 7
Lonicera fragrantissima 149

Lonicera maackii 149, 163
Lonicera nitida 149, 159, 161, 167, 192, 193
Lonicera sempervirens 36
Lonicera syringantha 206
Lorel (Laurel) 38, 42, 45
Lorel Green (Prunus laurocerasus) 37
Lorel lynes (Viburnum tinus) 26, 37, 46
Lorestrys 16
Luckers Brums (Genista, Broom from Lucca) 33, 35
Lycestera 194
Lycopods 65

Magnolia 135, 166
Magnolia acuminata (Cucumber Tree) 100
Magnolia conspicua alba superba (Magnolia denudata) 163
Magnolia grandiflora 166
Magnolia grandiflora 'Exoniensis'('Exmouth') 101
Magnolia lennii (Magnolia x soulangeana 'Lennei') 163
Magnolia stellata 206
Mahonia 83
Maize 90
Malva Arborata 3, 4
Malus floribunda 151
Manetti Stock 82, 87
Mangle 61
Mangle 'Goldern Tankard' 211
Marne Radish 61
Marrow 77
Marrow 'Bush White' 203
Marrow peas 43
Maurandia 91
Medinilla magnifica 61
Melons 66, 72
Mertles (Myrtles) 15
Mezarens (Daphne mezereum) 34
Mezerans whit (Daphne mezereum alba) 33
Monthle Roses (Rosa x damascena var) 24, 34, 41, 46
Morello Cheres 24, 25, 33
Morning Glory 5
Moss Provence Rose (Rosa x centifolia) 15, 16, 18, 24, 34, 36, 41

Mountain Ash 28, 29, 120, 135, 190
Mulberries 78
Mulberes (Mulberry) 10, 16
Musk Roose (Rosa moschata) 41
Myrica cerifera (Wax Mrytle) 100
Myrobella 99, 135
Myrtle 15, 68, 192
Myrtle Leafed Box 67
Myrtus 195

Narcissus 94, 95, 120, 124, 213
Nectarine 41, 86–89, 91, 92, 99, 103, 138, 151, 166, 180, 194
Nectron, Nectr (Nectarine) 15, 17, 36, 40, 45, 48
Nepeta 166
Norway Maplc 163, 166
Norway Spruce (Picea abies) 36
Nut 'Merveille de Boluryller' (Corylus maxima 'Halle'sche Riesennuss) 190
Nut Trees 13

Oak 14, 29, 78, 134, 139, 151, 162, 193
Oak, English 99, 139, 166
Oak, Holm 130
Oenothera 91
Oleaster (Elaeagnus angustifolia) 35
Oleria 149
Onion 8, 9, 22, 24, 36, 43, 46, 93, 117, 213
Onion 'Ailsa Craig' 202
Onion 'Giant Eittan' 214
Onion 'Strasburg' 43
Orange 31
Orchids 65, 70, 96
Osiers 93
Osmanthus 149, 150, 206
Osmanthus armatus 162
Osmanthus ilicifolius (Osmanthus heterophyllus) 206

Paeony 105, 111, 166
Paeony, Tree 135
Palms 117
Pampas Grass 67
Pansy 74
Papaver 'Mahony' 161
Papaver 'Mrs Perry' 161
Pars (Pears) 10, 16, 39, 41, 47, 48

INDEX – PLANTS

Parsle seed 9
Parsley 43, 45, 46
Parsley 'Moss Curled' 202
Parsnep (Parsnip) 22, 23, 43
Pashon flower (Passiflora caerulea) 33, 41, 45
Passiflora 193
Passiflora caerulea 33, 101, 192
Parthenocissus tricuspidata 'Veitchii' 101
Pearseley, Parsle (Parsley) 8
Peaches 9, 10, 17, 35, 48, 60, 62, 74, 76, 81, 86, 87, 89, 91–93, 99, 117, 151, 166, 180, 194
Peach 'Hale's Early' 207
Pea 33, 40, 43, 79, 92, 128, 209
Pea, 'Harrison's Glory' 128
Pea, 'Marrow' 43
Pea, 'Perkins' Little Marvel' 202
Pea, 'The Gladstone' 153
Pea, 'Thomas Laxton' 154
Pease 9
Pears, Pars 17, 39, 40, 45, 48, 74, 82, 83, 89, 90, 99, 103, 107, 117, 150, 151, 192, 193
Pear 'Bergamot d'Esparen' 122
Pear 'Beurré d'Amanlis' 122
Pear 'Beurré de Capiament' 122
Pear 'Beurré Easter' 122
Pear 'Beurré Rance' 122
Pear 'Beurré Superfin' 122
Pear 'Charles Ernest' 122
Pear 'Clapp's Favourite' 122
Pear 'Doyenne Boussoch' 122
Pear 'Doyenne du Comice' 122
Pear 'Doyenne d'Ete' 122
Pear 'Duchesse d'Angouleme' 122
Pear 'Durendean' 122
Pear 'Gleu Morceau'122
Pear 'Hessle' 122
Pear 'Jargonelle' 122
Pear 'Josephine de Malines' 122
Pear 'Le Lactier' 122
Pear 'Marguarite Marillat' 122
Pear 'Marie Louise' 122, 206
Pear 'Pitmaston Duchess' 122
Pear 'Swan's Egg' 46, 103
Pear 'Williams' Bon Chretien' 122
Pear cordons 194
Peches (Peaches) 10, 35, 36, 39, 41, 48, 60, 62, 103

Pelargoniums 82, 83, 88, 89, 105
Penstemons 75, 105
Pereskia aculeate 71
Perovskia 160, 197
Persian Lilac 150
Persica rosea 150
Persion Jesemes (Syringa x persica) 35
Petunias 62, 65, 66, 72
Phelera (Phillyrea latifolia) 26, 35, 36, 42
Philadelphus 38, 192, 194
Philadelphus brachybotrys 206
Philadelphus 'Favourite' 206
Philadelphus grandiflorus (Philadelphus inodorus var grandiflorus) 163
Philadelphus tartaricus roseus 206
Philadelphus 'Virginal' 205
Phlomis 150
Phlomis fruiticosa 34
Phlox 68, 166
Picea 100
Picea abies 36, 100
Picotees 52, 80
Picotee 'Purple (heavy edged) 52
Picotee 'Purple (light edged) 52
Picotee 'Red' (heavy edged) 52
Picotee 'Red' (light edged) 52
Picotee 'Wood's Princess Alice' 52
Picotee 'Yellow' 52
Pineapple 60
Pinks 6, 58, 74
Pink 'Mrs Simpkins' 116
Pinus 100
Pinus bungeana 151
Pinus sylvestris 36
Plane 28, 47, 79, 92
Ploms (Plums) 10
Plums 10, 15, 17, 33, 39, 40, 41, 48, 82, 83, 99, 103, 107, 117, 134, 135, 150, 151, 160, 167, 192
Plum stock 86
Plum 'Czar' 122
Plum 'Monarch' 122
Plum 'Red Magnum Bonum' 151
Plum 'Rivers Early Prolific' 121, 122
Plum 'Victoria' 180

Polyanthus 60
Polyanthus 'Novelty' 145
Polygonum baldschuanicum (Fallopia baldschuanica) 207
Portugal Laurel 17, 99
Poplar 28, 29, 45, 86, 99, 100, 197
Poplar, Lombady 193
Poplar, Italian 191, 193
Poplar, Silver 134
Populus angulata 33
Populus candicans 34
Populus nigra 194
Popy 3
Portugal Lorel (Prunus lusitanica) 15, 34, 151
Potato 22, 25, 36, 43, 45, 46, 66, 70, 73, 78, 87, 92, 116, 117, 135
Potato 'Arran Chief' 117
Potato 'Arran Pilot' 213
Potato 'Beauty of Hebron' 117
Potato 'British Queen' 117
Potato 'Duke of York CL 2102' 203
Potato Dunbar Standard 'White Ware' 211
Potato 'Duke of York' 117, 203
Potato 'Early Puritan' 117
Potato 'Eclipse'117
Potato 'Epicure' 117, 204
Potato 'Evergood' 117,
Potato 'Golden Wonder' 117
Potato 'Great Scott' 117
Potato 'Jerusalem White' 117
Potato 'King Edward' 211
Potato 'King Edward VII' 117
Potato 'Langworthy' 117
Potato 'Locham' 117
Potato 'Magnificent' 117
Potato 'Mary Queen' 117
Potato 'Midlothian Early' 117
Potato 'Myatt's Ashleaf' 117
Potato 'Ninetyfold' 117
Potato 'Perkin's Early Bird' 117
Potato 'Perkin's Snowdrop' 117
Potato 'Ringleader' 117
Potato 'Schoolmaster' 117
Potato 'Sharpe's Express CL 117, 146, 203
Potato 'Sharpe's Victor' 117
Potato 'Sir J. Llewellyn' 117

Potato 'Sutton Flour Ball' 117
Potato 'The Factor' 117
Potato 'Up to Date' 117
Potato 'White Ware' 211
Primula 69
Primula wollastonii 157
Privet 70, 99, 149, 151, 166, 191, 193, 197
Privet, Golden 193
Privet, Oval Leaf 149, 166, 192, 208
Provence Rose (Rosa x centifolia) 24
Prune, Shropshire 150
Prunus 150
Prunus incisa 206
Prunus myroboleana (Prunus cerasifera Myrobalan Group) 163
Prunus myroboleana 'Mume Pink' 206
Prunus 'Pissardii' (Prunus cerasifera 'Pissardii') 100
Prunus spinosa 163
Pursland trees (Portulacaria afra) 33, 38
Pyracantha 163, 195, 207
Pyrecanter (Pyracantha coccinea) 34, 41, 42
Pyrethrums 138
Pyrethrum 'G. Feather' 91
Pyrus 150, 192, 198
Pyrus japonica (Chaenomeles japonica) 192, 206
Pyrus malus aldenhamensis (Malus x purpurea 'Aldenhamensis') 151, 163
Pyrus malus atropurpurea 163
Pyrus malus atrosanguinea 163
Pyrus malus floribunda (? Malus floribunda) 163
Pyrus malus neidzwerzkyana (Malus pumila 'Niedwzetzkyana') 163
Pyrus malus parkmanii (Malus halliana 'Parkmanii') 163
Pyrus malus purpurea (Malus x purpurea) 163
Pyrus malus sargentiana (Malus sargentii) 163
Pyrus malus scheideckeri (Malus x scheideckeri) 163
Pyrus malus spectabilis (Malus spectabilis) 163

Pyrus malus veitchii (Malus yunnanensis var. veitchii) 163
Quercus coccinea 'Splendens' 163
Quicks (Crataegus monogyna) 12, 13, 14, 41, 42, 48, 62, 71, 99, 111, 117, 137, 140, 143, 149, 151, 166, 167, 191, 211
Quince 48, 103
Quince, Portugal 192
Radish 40, 43, 45, 46, 61, 71, 74, 76, 89–92
Radish 'French Breakfast' 202, 204
Radish 'Olive-shaped Scarlet' 166
Ramnoides (Hippophae rhamnoides) 35
Ranunculus 62, 75, 91
Raspberry 59, 69, 135, 193
Raspberry 'Hornet' 135
Raspberry 'Huntingdon Yellow' 151
Raspberry 'Lloyd George' 180
Raspberry 'Queen Alexander' 123
Raspberry 'Superlative' 135
Readish (Radish) 8
Red Clover 213
Red Currant 151
Red Dogwood 150
Retinospora 100
Rheum palmatum 2
Rhododendron 166
Rhododendron 'Brayanum' 63
Rhododendron 'Broughtonii' 63
Rhododendron 'Currieanum' 63
Rhododendron 'Desdemona' 63
Rhododendron 'Doncaster' 162
Rhododendron 'Hayworth' 63
Rhododendron 'John Walter' 162
Rhododendron 'Lady Alice Fitzwilliam' 105
Rhododendron 'Lady Grey Egerton' 162
Rhododendron 'Maculatum Grandiflorum'
Rhododendron 'Madame Carvallo' 162
Rhododendron 'Nero' 63
Rhododendron 'Nigrum' 63
Rhododendron 'Onslowoanum' 63
Rhododendron 'Pink Pearl' 162

Rhododendron ponticum 164
Rhododendron 'Viscount Powerscourt' 162
Rhododendron 'Mrs William Agnew' 162
Rhubarb 102
Rhubarb 'Early Albert' 135, 193
Ribes atrosanguineum (Ribes sanguineum 'Atrorubens') 163, 206
Ribes grossularia (Ribes uva-crispa) 163
Ribes sanguineum 163
Ribes sanguineum 'Splendens' 190
Robinia hispida (Rose Acacia) 100
Robinia pseudacacia 36
Rocket 24, 41
Romonorad (Hipphophae rhamnoides) 41
Romneya coulteri 162
Rose 'Albéric Barbier' 178
Rose 'Albertine' 21, 164
Rose 'American Pillar' 210
Rose 'Amy Robsart' 185
Rose 'Angele Pernet' 164, 171, 178, 179, 182, 198, 204
Rose 'Anne of Geierstein' 185
Rose 'Anne Poulsen' 210
Rose 'Annie Maria Jacobs' 111
Rose 'Aspirant Marcel Rouyer' 172
Rose 'Baby Betty' 182
Rosa banksiae 102
Rose 'Banquet d'Or' 120
Rose 'Beauty of Waltham' 169
Rose 'Belle de Legus' 63
Rose 'Benedictine Seguin' 172
Rose 'Betty' 174
Rose 'Betty Uprichard' 164, 179, 180, 182
Rose 'Blanc Double de Coubert' 185
Rose 'British Queen' 178
Rose 'Captaine George Desirier' 171
Rose 'Cardinal Paluzzi' 63
Rose 'Madame Caroline Testout' 123, 179, 180
Rose 'Catherine Seyton' 185
Rose 'Cécile Brünner' 185
Rosa x centifolia 168
Rosa x centifolia muscosa 36

INDEX – PLANTS

Rose 'Charles Darwin' (Rosa Auspeet) ('Charles Darwin') 169
Rose 'Charles Wood' 187
Rose 'Cheerful' 179
Rose 'Christine' 179
Rose 'Cripriani' 63
Rose 'Columbia' 176, 177
Rose 'Comtesse d'Orleans' 63
Rose 'Constance' 178
Rose 'Conrad Ferdinand Meyer' 185
Rose 'Countess of Shaftesbury' 111
Rose 'Crimson Rambler' 185
Rose 'Dad Sterling' 111
Rosa x damascena 168
Rose 'Dickson's Perfection' 204
Rose 'Dorothy Page Roberts' 174
Rose 'Dorothy Perkins 178, 187, 210
Rose 'Duchess of Atholl' 182
Rose 'Easlea's Golden Wonder' 210
Rose 'Eda Meyer' 120
Rose 'Edith Nellie Perkins' 198
Rose 'Edward Mawley' 111
Rose 'E.G.Hill' 182
Rose 'Eileen Poulsen' 209
Rose 'Elegance' 210
Rose 'Elizabeth of York' 198
Rose 'Ellen Poulsen' 180
Rose 'Else Poulsen' 184, 191, 193, 210
Rose 'Emma Wright' 198
Rose 'Etoile de Hollande' 164, 180, 182, 198, 204, 210
Rose 'Excelsa' 210
Rose 'Fabrier' (? Rosa 'Colonel Fabvier') 185
Rose 'Fellemberg' 185
Rose 'Flamingo' 198
Rose 'Flora McIvor' 185
Rose 'Frau Karl Druschki' 121, 180
Rosa gallica 33, 36, 168
Rose 'Gardenia' 185
Rose 'General McArthur' 163, 175, 176, 204, 210
Rose 'George Basset' 172
Rose 'George Dickson' 179, 180
Rose 'Gloire de Dijon' 185

Rose 'Gloire de Moscow' 63
Rose 'Gloria Mundi' 182
Rose 'Golden Emblem' 179
Rose 'Golden Salmon' 183
Rosa gracilis 187
Rose 'Green-Mantle' 185
Rose 'Gruss an Teplitz' 185
Rose 'Henrietta' 179
Rose 'Hollandia' 179
Rose 'Home Sweet Home' (Rose 'Home Sweet Home' = 'Mailoeur') 186, 187, 208, 210
Rose 'Hermosa' 185
Rose 'Horace Vernet' 174
Rose 'Hugh Dickson' 120, 121, 123, 175, 176
Rose 'Independence Day' 163
Rose 'Irish Elegance' 180
Rose 'Jean G.N.Forestier' 172
Rose 'Jeanie Deans' 185
Rose 'Julia Mannering' 185
Rose 'Julien Potin' 183
Rose 'Karen Poulsen' 191, 197, 210
Rose 'King of Kings' 179
Rose 'Kirsten Poulsen' 180, 184, 193, 210
Rose 'Lady Battersea' 174, 175, 176
Rose 'Lady Forteviot' 183
Rose 'Lady Hillingdon' 123, 173, 180
Rose 'Lady Inchiquia' 179
Rose 'Lady Penzance' 185
Rose 'Lady Pirrie' 173, 179
Rose 'Lady Price' 178
Rose 'Lady Sylvia' 198, 204
Rose 'La France' 185
Rose 'La Tosca' 179
Rose 'Léonie Lamesch' 185, 192
Rose 'Le Progres' 123
Rose 'Leslie Holland' 111
Rose 'Liberty' 120
Rose 'Little Dorrit' 183
Rose 'Los Angeles' 146, 179
Rose 'Lucy Betram' 185
Rose 'Lyon' 120
Rose 'M.A.Baxter' 183
Rose 'Mabel Morse' 164, 183
Rose 'Madame Abel Chatenay' 120, 121, 171, 172, 173, 185

Rose 'Madame Butterfly' 179, 180, 183, 198, 210
Rose 'Madame Eugène Résal' 185
Rose 'Madame E. Herriot' 180
Rose 'Madame Payne' 63
Rose 'Madame Sancy de Parabere' 187
Rose 'Madame Segond Weber' 171, 173
Rose 'Marcel Rouyer' 178
Rose 'Marcier Stanhope' 164
Rose 'Maréchal Niel' 185
Rose 'Marquise de Sinety' 121
Rose 'Mde Rosary' 120
Rose 'Meg Merilees' 185
Rose 'Miss Ingram' 187
Rose 'Mistress Farmer' 172
Rosa moyesii 180, 190, 192
Rose 'Mrs John Laing' 120
Rose 'Mr W.C.Miller' 123
Rose 'Mrs Alfred Tait' 174, 175, 176
Rose 'Mrs Beatty' 183
Rose 'Mrs Bertrand Walker' 178
Rose 'Mrs R.A.Barraclough' 183
Rose 'Mrs Harold Brocklebank' 174
Rose 'Mrs Henry Morse' 164, 180
Rose 'Mrs Henry Winnett' 176
Rose 'Mrs Sam McGredy' 210
Rose 'Mrs G. A. Van Rossen' 183, 193, 210
Rose 'Nellie Perkins' 187
Rose 'Nurse Cavell' 210
Rose 'Ophelia' 178, 179
Rose 'Ophelia Supreme' 176
Rose 'Orange Perfection' 183
Rose 'Orange Triumph' 209
Rose 'Orleans' 179, 183
Rose 'Papa Lambert' 120
Rose 'Paul's Carmine Pillar' 169
Rose 'Paul's Scarlet Climber' 169
Rose 'Perle d'Or' 192
Rose 'Prince de Bulgarie' 120
Rose 'Poulsen's Yellow' 210
Rose 'Queen Mab' 185
Rose 'Rayon d'Or' 111, 120
Rose 'Red Letter Day' 179
Rose 'Reine Marie Henriette' 185
Rose 'Rembrandt' 175

Rose 'Rêve d'Or' 185
Rose 'Richmond' 121
Rosa rubiginosa 163
Rosa rugosa 'Alba' 192
Rose 'Severine' 172, 176, 177
Rose 'Shot Silk' 164, 183, 198
Rose 'Sir Claudius Pernel' 179
Rose 'Sorbet' 180
Rose 'Souvenir de Claudius Pernet' 171, 172
Rose 'Souvenir de Georges Pernet' 164
Rose 'Souvenir de George Beckwith' 172
Rose 'Souvenir des Braves' 63
Rose 'Starlight' 187
Rose 'Sunburst' 111, 179
Rose 'Talisman' 183, 204
Rose 'Theodora Madame Milterrinoz' 63
Rose 'Tom Wood' 187
Rose 'Ulrich Brünner' 179
Rose 'Una' 178
Rose 'Van Nas' (?Rose 'Van Nes') 210
Rose 'Ville de Paris' 204
Rose 'Victor Hugo' 180
Rose 'Weddingen' 174, 175, 176
Rose 'William Allen Richardson' 185
Rose 'William Kordes' 164, 187
Rose 'William Rader' 179
Rose 'Zenobia' 169
Rose 'Zéphirine Drouhin' 174
Roses: see also Appendix 1, 2 & 3
RoseSallere (Cellery) 8
Rosemary 163, 192
Rosemary 'Miss Jessopp's Upright' 163
Rubus Canadensis 149
Rubus deliciosus 150, 162
Rudbeckia purpurea (Echinacea purpurea) 161
Rhynchospermum jasminoides (Trachelospermum jasminoides) 205
Runner Bean 'Brooklands Giant' 153
Ruscus 161

Sacamars 38
Sage 193

Salix alba var. caerulea 150
Salix babylonica 191
Salix vitellena britzensis (Salix subs. vitellina 'Britzensis') 164
Sallere (Cellery) 8
Salvia Bavaria 111
Savoy 'Drumhead' 202, 204
Savoy 'Tom Thumb' 202
Saxifrage 111
Scampston Elm 55
Scarlet Flower Maple (Acer rubrum) 35, 36
Scarlet Okes (Quercus coccinea) 35
Scarlet Willow 150
Schizanthus x wisetonensis
Schoch Spruce Firs (Pinus sylvestris) 36
Scock Roose (Rosa spinosissima now Rosa pimpinellifolia) 41
Scorpin Seenes (Coronilla emerus) 34, 34
Scotch Firs (Pinus sylvestris) 36, 134, 143, 145, 191
Scotch Pine 135, 138
Sea Kale 102, 117
Sea Kale Beet 196
Seakale 'Solid Ivory' 117
Senecio cineraria 35
Senecio singularis 2
Shallot 213
Shrub Sage (Phlomis fruticosa) 34
Siberian Garagana (Siberian pea tree) 5
Siberian flax 3, 4
Silver Birch 191–193, 196
Silver Fir 78, 140
Silver Poplar 120, 135
Silver Spruce Firs 26, 36
Siringes (Philadelphus coronarius) 37
Sitka Spruce 135, 165
Snowberry 99, 197
Soft Fruit 39, 138, 139, 193, 194
Solanum jasminoides 195, 205
Somphotobums 71
Sophronitis 71
Sorbus 193
Sorbus aria 192
Soringas (Philadelphus coronarius) 38

Soringers (Syringa vulgaris) 37
Sophora japonica 'Pendula' 101
Spanish Broom 16, 35, 93
Spanish Brums (Spartium germanicum) 37, 38
Spanish Chestnuts 16, 78, 99, 138, 197
Spartium junceum 160, 180
Spiraea 163
Spinag (Spinach) 8, 36
Spiraea 160, 194
Spiraea aruncus var Kneifii (Aruncus dioicus 'Kneiffii') 161
Spiraea hypericifolia 35
Spiraea palmatum 161
Sprout 'Harrison's XXX' 203
Spruce 78, 134, 135, 191
Spruce firs 16, 26, 45, 143, 150
Spruce, Native 134, 140
Staphylea trifolia 5
Statice latifolia (Limonium latifolium) 161
Stephanandra tanakae 206
Stocks 211
Stove plants 70
Stranvaesia undulata 161, 163, 195
Stranvesia undulata fructo luteo 195
Strawberries 60, 66, 71, 99, 104, 124, 156
Strawberry 'Admiral Dundas' 104
Strawberry 'A. F. Barron' 104
Strawberry 'All Round' (Atherton) 104
Strawberry 'Black Prince' 104
Strawberry 'British Queen' 104
Strawberry 'Commander' (Laxton's) 104
Strawberry 'Dr Hogg' 104
Strawberry 'Elton Pine' 104
Strawberry 'Girons Late Prolific' 139
Strawberry 'Jas Veitch Handsome' 104
Strawberry 'John Ruskin 1890' 104
Strawberry 'Keen's Seedling' 104
Strawberry 'King George' 151
Strawberry 'King of the Earlies' 104

INDEX – PLANTS

Strawberry 'Laxton' 139
Strawberry 'Myatt's Eleanor' 104
Strawberry 'Noble' (Laxton's) 104
Strawberry 'President' 104
Strawberry 'Royal Sovereign Improved' 207
Strawberry 'Royal Sovereign Elvaston Improved' 207
Strawberry 'Sir Charles Napier' 104
Strawberry 'Sir Joseph Paxton' 104
Strawberry 'The Earl' 139
Strawberry 'The King' 151
Strawberry 'The Queen' 151
Strawberry 'V. Hericoat de Thury' 104
Strawberry 'Waterloo' 104, 139, 150
Stripd holes (Variegated Hollies) 16, 34, 38
Stripd Monthl Roses (Rosa x damascena) 24, 37
Stripd munde Roses (Rosa gallica mundi) 37
Stripd Sacamars (Acer pseudoplatanus 'Variegatum') 38
Suckling (Honeysuckle) 42
Sucklings (Lonicera periclymenum) 38, 46
Sumacs 78
Swede 59
Sweedish Juniper (Juniperus communis Suecica Group) 35
Sweet Bays (Laurus nobilis) 35
Sweet Briar 24, 26, 42, 193
Sweet mangram 43
Sweet Peas 70, 74
Swet Musk Roses (Rosa moschata) 37
Sweet William 22
Sycamore 100, 138, 166, 190, 193
Symphoricarpus 163
Symphoricarpos conglomerates 163
Symphoricarpos henryii (Symphoricarpos occidentalis var. henryi) 163
Symphoricarpos laevigatus (Symphoricarpos albus var. laevigatus) 163
Symphoricarpos occidentalis 163

Symphoricarpos parviflorus (Symphoricarpos pauciflorus – S. albus) 163
Symphoricarpos racemosus (Symphoricarpos albus) 163
Syringa 194
Syringa reflexa 206
Syringa 'Wilsonii' 206

Tamarisk 149
Tamerins (Tamarix gallica) 33
Tatose (Potatoes) 39
Taxodium 100
Taxodium distichum 164
Taxus 100
Taxus baccata 'Elegantissima' 100
Taxus semper aurea (Taxus baccata 'Semperaurea') 163
Tee Pursland (Portulacaria afra) 41
Thalictrum 111
Thalictrum dipterocarpum 161
Thorn 162
Thorn Double Crimson 190
Three thornd acates (Gleditsia triacanthos) 38
Thrift 103
Thuja 72, 100
Thuja chilensis 68
Thuja lobelli 135, 151
Thujopsis 100
Thyme 193
Tillandsia zebrine 61
Tobacco 73
Tomato 77, 213
Torenia fournieri (Wishbone Flower) 75
Tradescantia zebrine 61
Tricolor Geraniums 86, 87, 89, 90, 93
Tritoma 'Lord Roberts' (Kniphofia 'Lord Roberts') 161
Trollius 'Orange Globe' 161
Trollius 'T. Smith' 161
Tropaeoleums 69
True Pheleras (Phillyrea latifolia) 35
Tulips 59, 68, 75, 117, 120, 124, 162, 213
Tulip 'Clara Butt' 123
Tulip 'Golden Spire' 1221
Tulip 'Pride of Haarlem' 123
Tulip Trees (Liriodendron tulipifera) 34

Turke Aprecock 15
Turnep (Turnip) 8, 60, 74

Ulmus campestris 166
Ulmus campestris alba 55
Ulmus campestris acutifolia Masters 55
Ulmus campestris cornubiensis (Cornish) (Wheatleys) (Ulmus glabra 'Cornubiensis') 103
Ulmus campestris folius auriis 104
Ulmus campestris folius aureus crispa 101
Ulmus campestris folius variegates 103
Ulmus campestris Hertfordshire Elm 104
Ulmus campestris Huntingdon Elm 104
Ulmus campestris Narrow-leaved English Elm 104
Ulmus 'Cornish' 101
Ulmus crispa (Ulmus glabra 'Crispa') 101
Ulmus dampierii Wredei aura (Ulmus 'Dampieri Aurea') 101, 104
Ulmus elegantissima pendula 104
Ulmus 'Gigantic' 101, 104
Ulmus Hertfordshire 101, 103
Ulmus medio variegatus 101, 104
Ulmus montana (Scotch. True Wych) (Ulmus glabra) 104
Ulmus 'Paradox' 101
Ulmus montana crispa 104
Ulmus montana pendula (Ulmus glabra 'Pendula') 101, 104
Ulmus montana fastigiata (Ulmus glabra 'Exoniensis') 104
Ulmus montana gigantica 104
Ulmus montana vegata (Ulmus x vegeta) 55
Ulmus 'Purple-leaved' 101, 104
Ulmus suberosa pendula (Weeping ex Girton Coll. 1887) (Ulmus carpinifolia 'Propendem') 101, 104
Ulmus variegated 101
Ulmus vegeta 55
Ulmus viminalis variegata (Ulmus procera 'Viminalis Marginata') 104
Ulmus 'Weeping Camperdown' (ex Cobbett 1891) 104

Ulmus Weeping Standards 101
Veregated holes (Ilex aquifolium) 41
Vegetable Marrow 'Bush White' 203
Vegetable Seed 202
Velvet Roses (Rosa gallica) 24, 34
Venes Rag Wort (Senecio cineraria) 35
Verigated Elder (Sambucus nigra) 33
Verbascum 'Pink Domingo' 205
Verbenas 62, 67–73, 76, 86, 89, 92, 105
Verbena Lemon Scented 111
Verbena White 92
Veronica 91
Veronica salicifolia (Hebe salicifolia) 162
Veronica traversii 164
Viburnum x burkwoodii 205
Viburnum carlesii 162, 192
Viburnum lantana 163
Viburnum rhytidophyllum 163, 195
Viburnum trilobum 35
Viburnum utile 163

Vinca 164
Violets 67
Vines 24, 72–75, 78
Virginey Pistachia Nut 3, 5
Virgine Ston crop Trees (Atriplex halimus) 35
Vitis 'Appleby Towers' 165
Vitis coignetiae 195
Vitis 'Foster's Seedling' 165
Vitis 'Lady Downe's Seedling' 165
Vitis 'Madresfield Court' 165
Vitis 'Muscat of Alexandra' 165, 194
Vitis 'Muscat Hamburg' 165
Vitis vinifolia 'Purpurea' 195
Vyburnums (Viburnum lantana) 38

Walnut 78, 103, 129, 190
Wallnut (Walnut) 10, 24, 25
Weigela 167, 192, 194
Weigela 'Conquest' 163
Weigeia 'Profusion' 206
Wellingtonia 100
Wellingtonia gigantica (Sequoiadendron giganteum) 163, 164

Welsh Onion 60
Whit Meserens (Daphne mezereum f. alba) 33
Whit Poplars 28, 29
White scented pea 3
White Spire frutax (Hibiscus syriacus) 38
Whitethorn 99, 135
Willow 92, 192
Willow, Cricket Bat 191
Willows, Scarlet 150
Willow, Weeping 189
Winter aconites 162
Wisteria 66, 149, 150
Wisteria sinensis 150
Wych Elms 163

Yew 150, 166, 191, 193
Yew, English 132, 150, 194
Yew, Golden 149, 151
Yucca recurvifolia 163

Zonal Geraniums 91
Zonal Pelargoniums 90

Plant Nurseries

J. C.Allgrove, The Nursery, Middle Green, Langley, Slough, Berkshire 134, 145

Amos Perry, Hardy Plant Firm, Enfield, Middlesex 149

Mr Ash's Nursery, Twickenham, Middlesex 48

Austria & Kalan, Glasgow 182

Austin & McAslan Ltd, Mitchell Street, Glasgow, Scotland 196, 210

Avon Valley Green Houses, Falmouth, Nova Scotia, Camada 209

Bakers, Codsall, Wolverhampton 160

Barnham Nurseries Ltd, Barnham, Sufolk 196

Beckwith & Son, Hoddesdon, Hertfordshire 191, 196

Bees, Chester 182

Black Hall Nurseries, Marston Ferry Road, Oxford 160

Blackhouse Nurseries, York 196

Bonsall Nurseries, Harrogate, Yorkshire 170

Boston Rose Farms, Lincolnshire 191

Bournville Village Trust Nursery, Birmingham 150

Brecon Road Nursery, Abergavenny, Wales 140

Brooks Nursery, Western Super Mare, Somerset 181

W. & J. Brown, Rose Nurseries, Eastfield, Peterborough, Cambridgeshire 181, 196

Bryant Bulb Co. Ltd, London NW1 206

Buckden Road Nursery, Brampton, Cambridgeshire 107

J. Bunyard & Co, Maidstone, Kent 181, 182

Burscough Nurseries, Burscough Bridge, Lancashire 208

Thomas Butcher, South Norwood, Croydon, Surrey 176

Cadwell & Sons, Knutsford, Cheshire 182

F. Cant & Sons, Colchester, Essex 181, 191, 198

B. R. Cant & Sons, Rose Nurseries, Colchester, Essex 135, 178,181, 182, 198

Carter Page & Co Ltd, 52 London Wall, London 161, 196

Cashburn & Welch, The Cambria Nurseries, Huntingdon Road, Cambridge 161

Chaplin Bros, Waltham Cross, Hertfordshire 181, 196

INDEX – PLANT NURSERIES

A. Charlton & Sons, Tunbridge Wells, Kent 196

J. Cheal & Sons Ltd 160, 193

Chilbrans Ltd, Altrincham, Cheshire 160, 196

John Chivers, Histon, Cambridgeshire 99, 151, 193

G. A.Clark's Nursery, Dover, Kent 181

Cooling & Sons 103

Thomas Crisp & Son 101

W. Crowther & Son Ltd, Horncastle, Lincolnshire 196

William Cutbush & Son Ltd 196

Cutbush & Son, Barnet Nursery, Hertfordshire 160, 167, 196

Cuthbert Ltd, Southgate, London 181

Daniels Bros Ltd, Norwich, Norfolk 181

Darling's Nursery, Hull, Yorkshire 181

Dickens & Sons, Edinburgh, Scotland 181

Dicksons Nurseries, Chester 193, 196

Alex Dickson & Sons Ltd, Newtonards, Northern Ireland 181, 188, 196, 199

Dickson Brown and Tait, Manchester 196, 211

Dickson & Robinson, Manchester 181

Dickson & Son, Chester 196

Dobbie & Son, (Co) Ltd, Edinburgh, Scotland 137, 160, 167, 170, 178, 179, 181, 183, 191, 193, 196, 199

Fisher Holmes and Co Nursery, (Handsworth Nursery) Sheffield, Yorkshire 83

Fisher & Silbray, Handsworth nr Sheffield, Yorkshire 105, 134, 196

Forest Orchard Nurseries, Melbury Heath, Falfield, Gloucestershire 160

Forest Poducts Ltd, Huntley, Gloucestershire 208

Freeburnes Ltd, Waterdown, Hamilton, Ontario, Canada 183, 184

Fuller's Seed Shop, Covent Garden, London 4

V. N. Gauntlett & Co Ltd, Japanese Nurseries, Chiddingfold, Surrey 160, 191, 196

C. Gibson & Co, Leeming Bar, Bedale, Yorkshire 179

Giddions Nursery, Hemingford, Cambridgeshire 59

A. Goatcher & Son, Washington, Sussex 196

Goldsworth 'Old Nursery', Woking, Surrey 130

T. H. L. Grange, Orleans France 101

Grey, Williamson and Gordon, 25 Church Street, London 3

Grootendorst's Nursery, Boskoop 145

Handsworth Nurseries, Sheffield 105

Harkness & Co, Hitchin, Hertfordshire 176, 182, 184, 191, 196

A. J. Heal, Victoria Nursery, Harrogate, Yorkshire 181

R. Heal & Sons Ltd, Trinity Road, Wandsworth, London 159

Henry and Samuel's Nursery, Brompton Park, London 14

Thomas Hewitt's London Nursery, London 14, 15, 21

Hilling & Co, Orange Hill Nurseries, Chobham, Surrey 160, 207

Hilliers & Son, West Hill, Winchester, Hampshire 37, 145, 160, 181, 191, 193, 196, 208

Horticultural Botanical Association Ltd, Goff's Oak, Hertfordshire 210

Hunter King, Dumfries, Scotland 178

Hurst and Co, Leadenhall Street, London 89, 90, 94

Hurst and Co, Houndsditch, London 90

T. K. Ingram, Parkstone Nurseries, Dorset 191

G. Jackman & Son, Woking, Surrey 181

Jackson and Perkins, Newport Beach, California, U.S.A.187

J. Jeffries & Son Ltd, The Royal Nurseries, Cirencester, Sussex 196

Joffrey Bros Clematis Nursery 208

W. Jones Nursery, Woodford, Essex 181

Kennedy and Lee's Nursery, Hammersmith, London 48

Kent & Brydon, Darlington, Yorkshire 170, 196

Hugh M Kershaw Ltd, The Nurseries, (Keighly), Yorkshire 160

Ketton Brothers, Luxembourg 173–176

Lakenham Nursery, Norfolk 4

Laird and Sinclair 83

Lane's Nurseries Ltd, Berkhamstead, Hertfordshire 196

Laxton Bros (Bedford) Ltd, Bedford 196, 199

Lea Hunter & King, Dumfries 181

Little & Ballantyne 83

London and Wise, London 14, 27

Lowe and Shawyer Ltd, The Nurseries, Uxbridge, Middlesex 160

McGredy & Sons, Portadown, Northern Ireland 176, 177, 185

James Maddock's Nursery, Clapham Rise, London 8

Manor Nurseries, Arbury Road, Cambridge 151

Moxon Bros, Farmers and Root Merchants, Chatteris, Cambridgeshire 213

Murrell, The Portland Nurseries, Shrewsbury, Shropshire 138, 178, 181, 182, 191, 193, 196

Charles Noble, Sunningdale Nursery, Surrey 102

R. C. Notcutt, Woodbridge, Suffolk 196

Nursery and Seed Trade Association Ltd 93, 94, 169

Nutting and Son, Southwark Street, London 94, 154

Mr Ordoyno's Nursery, Oundle, Northamptonshire 15, 16

Parman & Co, Chard, Somerset 181

William Paul and Son, Waltham Cross, Hertfordshire 169

Pearson & Sons, Lowdham, Northumberland 181

Peed & Son, Mitcham, Surrey 196

William and John Perfect, Pontefract, Yorkshire 33

Pernet-Ducher, Rose Grower, Venissieux les Lyons, France 172, 173

Pormettter Fils, France 187

Svend Poulsen, Denmark 184, 185

G. Prince, Longworth, Berkshire 182

Ramsbotham & Co, Bletchley, Buckinghamshire 196

Benjamin Reed & Co, 72 Guild Street, Aberdeen 160

Reed & Sons Ltd, Loughton, Essex 181

Messrs Rivers Nursery, Sawbridgeworth, Hertfordshire 82, 95, 149, 196

R. V. Rogers, Pickering, Yorkshire 182, 196

G. Rowell, Seedsman, Ramsey, Cambridgeshire 89, 90

Royal Nurseries, Slough, Buckinghamshire 95

Royal Nurseries, The Triangle, Maidstone, Kent 95, 159

Royal Nurseries, Waltham Cross, Hertfordshire 95

Samson Ltd, 8–10 Portland Street, Kilmarnock 160, 181

Mr Scott's Nursery, Wycombe Abbey, Berkshire 47, 48

Slocock's Nursery, Woking, Surrey 145

James Smith Nursery, Tansley, Derbyshire 140

Richard Smith, Worcester 102

Smith & Co Nursery, Worcestershire 137

Spooner & Sons, Hounslow, Middlesex 181

Springside Nursery, Scottish Co-op Society 182

Stanfield Nurseries, Wisbech, Cambridgeshire 208

Stanstead Park Nursery, London 95

Stewart and Co 83

Strandish & Noble 63

John and George Telford, York 4, 5

Toogood & Sons, Southampton, Hampshire 181

W. Treseder Ltd, The Nursery, Truro, Cornwall 160

Trumpington Road Nursery, Cambridge 151

Turners Nursery, Slough, Berkshire 62

R. Veitch & Son, Exeter, Devon 95, 138, 170, 182, 193

Vilmorin–Andrieux & Co, Paris, France 126, 145

Victoria and Paradise Nurseries, Upper Holloway Road, London 65

Waterer's Knapp Hill Nursery, Surrey 63, 64

Waterer & Sons, Twyford, Berkshire 63, 64

Waterdown, Ontario, Canada 183

Mr Watson's House, Garden and Orchard, Priory Lane, Huntingdon 6

Mr G. West, The Nurseries, Datchet, Buckinghamshire 160

Westfield Nurseries, Eaton, Norwich, Norfolk 146

Wezelberg & Son, Near Leiden, Holland 166

Wheatcroft Bros Ltd, Ruddingford, Northamptonshire 199

S. A. Whittome Ltd, Ramsey, Cambridgeshire 211

James Wood's Nursery, Huntingdon 21

James Wood & Son, Nurserymen, Huntingdon 52

John Wood, Hartford Lane Nursery, Huntingdon 50, 55, 62, 68, 77, 78

John Wood & Son, Nurserymen, St Germain St, Huntingdon 50, 52–54, 56, 97, 99, 109, 111, 133

Wood & Ingram Nursery, The Old Nurseries, Huntingdon 96–99, 101, 106–108, 144, 202, 215, 218

Wood & Ingram, Shop, 2 & 3 George Street, Huntingdon 109, 115, 132, 133, 215, 222

Wood & Ingram, The Nurseries, Buckden Road, Brampton 107, 111, 144, 215, 216

Wood & Ingram, Thrapston Road Rose Nursery, Brampton 98, 99, 108, 109, 169

Wood & Ingram, Nursery, 16 & 18 Cambridge Street, St Neots, Cambridgeshire 56, 99, 111, 128, 215, 220

William Wood & Son Ltd, The Nurseries, Taplow, Berkshire 160

Messrs Youell & Co, Great Yarmouth, Norfolk 67